A BIBLIOGRAPHICAL GUIDE
to the Law of the
United Kingdom, the Channel Islands
and the Isle of Man

A Bibliographical Guide to the Law of the United Kingdom, the Channel Islands and the Isle of Man

SECOND EDITION

Editor:
A. G. Chloros
PROFESSOR OF COMPARATIVE LAW,
UNIVERSITY OF LONDON
KING'S COLLEGE

Published by the
Institute of Advanced Legal Studies
in cooperation with the
United Kingdom National Committee of Comparative Law
and under the auspices of Unesco
and of the
International Association of Legal Science

UNIVERSITY OF LONDON
INSTITUTE OF ADVANCED LEGAL STUDIES
1973

DISTRIBUTORS:

U.K.
Dillon's University Bookshop Ltd
1 Malet Street
London WC1E 7JB

North America:
Oceana Publications Inc.
Dobbs Ferry
New York 10522
(United States SBN 379 00176-4)

1st Edition 1956
2nd Edition 1973

ISBN 0 901190 14 4
L of C 72-91901

Printed in Great Britain by Eyre & Spottiswoode Ltd, Thanet Press, Margate

CONTENTS

FOREWORD

Contributed by Dr. H. Golsong
Director of Legal Affairs, Council of Europe, Strasbourg

In the preface to the first edition of this work, Professor F. H. Lawson wrote that "although it is hoped that a bibliography of this kind will be useful to English teachers of law and even to practitioners outside the field in which they are experts, it has been prepared mainly in order to introduce English law to foreign lawyers, and especially to 'civilians' . . . .". As a "civilian" myself, I can testify to the value of the Bibliography for those of us who are occasionally puzzled by the workings of a system of law so different from that with which we are accustomed.

However, the time is long since passed when a civil lawyer could complacently claim to an almost total lack of comprehension of the common law. That this is so is in part due to the work of the great comparative lawyers who have, over the years, shown us that although the language and terminology of the civil lawyer may differ greatly from those employed by the common lawyer, the similarities between the solutions to specific problems in different systems of law are often far greater than the differences.

But more important still are the ever increasing intercourse between States, whether for trade or tourist reasons, and the vast changes which have taken place in the last twenty-five years in the structures of European co-operation.

During the last fifteen years it has become essential for members of the legal profession of the member States of the European Communities to possess much more than a nodding acquaintanceship with each others' law and legal systems, and with the likelihood of the Communities being enlarged, this need, I might even say challenge, will become greater.

Another element should not, however, be overlooked. There is an increasing international tendency to harmonisation and even unification in the legal field, a tendency which is not confined to the European Communities. Within the framework of the Council of Europe, which comprises countries of a great variety of legal traditions, including that of the Common Law, the seventeen member States have already made considerable progress in the development of legal harmonisation and unification. The United Kingdom has often made most substantial contributions, thus bringing the benefit of many centuries of experience of a legal system with a more pragmatic approach than that of many other European systems.

It is, therefore, with eagerness that I look forward to the publication of the second edition of the Bibliography, in the firm belief that it will prove to be of great value to today's generation of lawyers, inside and outside the Common Law countries, not only as a working instrument but also as an example of outstanding scholarship.

H. GOLSONG

PREFACE TO THE SECOND EDITION

When the first edition of this Bibliographical Guide was published over fifteen years ago, it was acclaimed as a major contribution to the apparatus of research available to scholars and lawyers interested in the law of the United Kingdom. Perhaps in no other major legal area of the western world has a need for such a book been so obvious. The difficulties that beset anyone outside this country anxious to study our legal system are too well known to be restated here. As Lord Diplock in 1966 aptly put it, the Common Law "is a maze not a motorway". Even within the United Kingdom, the development of mechanical civilisation has made it necessary that all lawyers should become specialists. The scholar-polymath of old who could retain a broad but also a detailed view of the law is nowadays rare indeed, if not already extinct. But legal problems are apt to cut across artificial frontiers imposed by specialisation. How is the lawyer to venture into other fields without a guide? Thus, the ambition of this book was not only to serve as a selective companion to the voluminous literature which exists and which is constantly enriched through further publications, but also to provide, where appropriate, introductions to the various branches of the law. Though the book was intended for all lawyers and students, its particular character was that of an introduction for foreign lawyers, especially those with a "civil law" background. These objects were, indeed, amply realised and widely appreciated. It can be said without exaggeration that in some fields the introductory accounts contained classic expositions of the Common Law from the civilian lawyers' viewpoint. It is, nevertheless, the lot of the law book, particularly at a time of rapid social change, to become out of date and bibliographies are no exception. It is for these reasons that three years ago the United Kingdom National Committee of Comparative Law, under the chairmanship of Dr. Kurt Lipstein of Cambridge, resolved to recommend the publication of a second edition.

In preparing the second edition several decisions have had to be made for which the present editor alone has been responsible. Unlike the first edition, no editorial committee was set up to advise the editor. In this respect, it seemed obvious that the task should be one of revision only, not of a fundamental change in the character of the work. At the same time, account had to be taken of the fact that some of the original contributors were, for various reasons, no longer available. Questions of copyright dictated further changes. Also, in the interests of rationalisation, certain other alterations, which can be seen from the Table of Contents, have had to be made. Finally, while in the first edition individual contributions were modified by the editorial committee in the interests of consistency, the present editor's view has been throughout that, having entrusted a topic to an expert in the field, it would be inappropriate for him, acting on his own and without the help of a committee, to substitute his own judgment for that of his contributors. This may have resulted in some unevenness of treatment, some entries being very detailed, some rather summary. This is not necessarily a fault, for it is not always essential for the user of a guide to find in it what he can be assumed to know already. There is also, inevitably, some duplication—e.g. with regard to the reorganisation of the Courts and the legal professions. But, for a book which is not generally intended to be read from cover to cover, it is better to give as much information as possible in each section. At least the reader can be assured that for each topic he is in the hands of an expert, and that this is the kind of advice that he would have received had he had direct access to him. Nevertheless one proviso must be made. Publishing a book of reference has unfortunately become a long process, all the more so when there is no single author but a large team. This has meant that delays have been inevitable and it has not always been easy to incorporate the most up-to-date information in all cases. The bibliographical lists have been corrected and updated as far as possible to December 1971, but, for technical reasons, only minor alterations to the narrative sections could be made later than 1970, and virtually none later than the summer of 1971. In one instance, Labour Law, no account could be taken of the Industrial Relations Act 1971, which has brought about radical changes in labour relations.

Possibly the pure rationalist will find fault that no overall policy of relevance has been pursued. For instance, a new chapter has been added on the law of the Common Market, which may not fit in very well with the law of the United Kingdom. Nevertheless, a Common lawyer need not offer any excuses for being guided by practical considerations and by the experience of those lawyers, both British and foreign, likely to consult this book.

It is one of the editor's more pleasant tasks to acknowledge the help he has received both from his contributors and from others. As far as the contributors are concerned, I must here acknowledge their assistance in some detail:

Sir William Arnold (Guernsey); Professor H. K. Bevan (Persons and Family Law and Names); Dr. A. J. Boyle (Legal Education); Professor L. Neville Brown (The Legal Profession); Professor E. J. Cohn (The Common Market); Professor W. R. Cornish (Industrial Property); J. C. Freeman (Crime); Professor L. C. B. Gower (Partnership & Company Law); Professor R. H. Graveson (Private International Law); Professor A. G. Guest (Torts); Dr. J. M. Holden (Negotiable Instruments & Banking); Professor A. M. Honoré (General Law of Contract, Agency, Bailment); Professor E. R. H. Ivamy (Maritime Law); Master I. H. Jacob (Civil Litigation); G. D. Kinley (The Armed Forces; The Isle of Man); Professor A. K. R. Kiralfy (The Organisation of the Courts); Mrs. V. L. Korah (Monopolies & Restrictive Practices); Professor F. H. Lawson (Bibliographies and General Accounts; The Sources of English Law; The Arrangement of English Law—General; Civil Law—General Introduction, Obligations—General; Public Law—General, and Public Services); L. Lazar (Taxation); Professor Lord Lloyd (Jurisprudence); Professor R. H. Maudsley (Unjust Enrichment); the Wor. and Rev. E. Garth Moore (Canon Law or Ecclesiastical Law); Dr. R. W. Rideout (Labour Law); Professor C. M. Schmitthoff (Commercial Law—General, Sale of Goods, Transport & Insurance, Commercial Securities & Insolvency); Professor L. A. Sheridan (Equity; Trusts); Professor T. B. Smith (Scots Law edited by Dr. G. Campbell H. Paton); Professor S. A. de Smith (The Commonwealth); Professor J. A. C. Thomas (Roman Law); J. W. A. Thornely (Security); F. H. E. Townshend-Rose (Mines & Minerals); Professor Sir Francis A. Vallat (Public International Law); R. Vibert (Jersey); Professor H. W. R. Wade (Property, Succession); J. C. W. Wylie (Northern Ireland); D.E.C. Yale (The History of English Law).

If without the contributors this book could not have appeared in print, there are others whose contribution is less apparent but no less important. And first I must acknowledge the help of the Institute of Advanced Legal Studies of the University of London. However, since Institutes are impersonal, I must express my deep appreciation and thanks to its Librarian, Mr. W. A. Steiner. From the first moment of my appointment as editor and throughout the period leading to publication, he has carried a substantial part of the burden involved. He has not only freely given me his wise counsel and support, he has also been actively engaged in all stages of the preparation of the typescript and has lightened my task enormously. I am also greatly indebted to the staff of the Institute for their work in updating the bibliographical details, preparing the author index, typing the final copy for the printer and seeing the publication through the press.

This publication was also supported by two generous grants, one from the British Academy and the other from the International Association of Legal Science, which is affiliated to UNESCO. I should like to thank both these Institutions.

It is appropriate to thank Dr. J. F. Kish for undertaking to prepare the subject index of this book.

Last but not least I must thank my own secretary, Mrs. Kay Messervy-Whiting. Throughout the period of revision she has been responsible for all the correspondence involved, the burden of producing revised texts from lists of changes and the task of keeping track of successive stages of revision. All this she has done, as always, with unfailing courtesy and charm.

A. G. CHLOROS

PREFACE TO THE FIRST EDITION

This bibliography, which has been prepared under contract with Unesco under the auspices of the United Kingdom National Committee of Comparative Law, is selective and elementary. It is also tendentious, in the sense that the compilers have felt it their duty to classify books and articles, not only in accordance with their more elementary or more advanced character, but also according to merit.

Although it is hoped that a bibliography of this kind will be useful to English teachers of law and even to practitioners outside the fields in which they are experts, it has been prepared mainly in order to introduce English law to foreign lawyers, and especially to "civilians", that is to say, lawyers brought up under continental law or the law of other countries, such as those of Latin America, which owe their general structure and many of their principles to Roman law. For such a purpose it was thought that mere lists of legal literature would be almost useless, for the real difficulty a foreign lawyer is likely to encounter is in finding in which list to look. In the last resort what would be necessary would be such a general account of English law as would enable him to find his bearings wherever he might be; but that could not be attempted here. The compromise adopted has been a prefix to each list, where necessary, a short introduction drawing the foreign lawyer's attention to peculiarities of English legal arrangement which are likely to cause him trouble. In other words, an attempt has been made to give him some elementary assistance in recognizing the main features of a legal grammar unlike his own. Sometimes the introduction is short and fragmentary; sometimes it discusses at some length the general layout of the law; sometimes it even describes legal doctrine. Since the bibliography is intended as a practical aid to study and not as a work of art, the treatment is not uniform and not even symmetrical.

The bibliography covers not only English law but also the law of other countries in the British Isles which belong to the Commonwealth of Nations, that is to say, Northern Ireland, Scotland, Jersey, Guernsey, and the Isle of Man. The term England is used as an abbreviation for England and Wales; and indeed the law of Wales is exactly the same as that of England, apart from a very few exceptions in public law relating for instance to the Church in Wales, the Welsh language and liquor licensing. The common law and equity of Northern Ireland are in principle the same as those of England and much of the statute law in the two countries is similar or even identical. On the other hand the laws of Scotland, Jersey, Guernsey and the Isle of Man, though very much influenced by the law of England in modern times, have independent origins and must not be considered variants of English law. As Scots law is less generally known than it should be, and as the other three laws are hardly known at all outside their respective jurisdictions, it has been thought not out of place to characterize them in greater detail than English law.

The task of editing the bibliography was assigned to a committee composed of Professors C. J. Hamson, O. Kahn-Freund and F. H. Lawson, Dr. K. Lipstein and Mr. K. Howard Drake, but the introductions and book-lists were supplied from a much larger circle. As they have since been much modified in the interests of consistency, it has been thought better not to prefix to the several sections the names of their authors, but to acknowledge their help here in detail:

W. H. Arnold (Guernsey); Captain A. P. Atwill, R.N. (Naval Law); Dr. D. W.

Bowett (Public International Law); Lord Chorley (Maritime Law); Professor D. J. Ll. Davies (Legal Education); Lt.-Col. G. I. D. Draper (Military Law); Dr. A. Farnsworth (Taxation); E. Garth Moore (Ecclesiastical Law); Professor L. C. B. Gower (Partnership and Company Law); Professor R. H. Graveson (Private International Law); Dr. M. Grünhut (Criminology); J. E. Hall Williams (Criminal Law and Procedure); Dr. H. A. Hammelmann (Organization of the Courts, Civil Procedure and Evidence); Professor C. J. Hamson (Tort); Dr. J. M. Holden (Maritime Law, Negotiable Instruments and Banking); A. M. Honoré (Contract and Bailment); Professor O. Kahn-Freund (Labour Law); S. J. Kneale (Isle of Man); Professor F. H. Lawson (Bibliographies and General Accounts; Sources of English Law; Arrangement of English Law—General; Civil Law—General Introduction; Obligations—General; Public Law; and Air Force Law); R. H. Maudsley (Unjust Enrichment); Professor J. L. Montrose (Northern Ireland); Dr. L. Neville Brown (The Legal Profession); G. H. Newsom (Limitations of Actions); M. J. Prichard (The History of English Law); Professor R. Powell (Agency); Dr. C. M. Schmitthoff (Sale of Goods; Transport and Insurance; Commercial Law—General; Commercial Securities and Insolvency); Dr. L. A. Sheridan (Equity and Trusts); S. A. de Smith (The Commonwealth); Professor T. B. Smith (Scots Law); Dr. S. J. Stoljar (Monopolies); J. A. C. Thomas (Roman Law and Canon Law); T. C. Thomas (Security); G. W. Tompkin (Industrial Property); J. Turner (Mines and Minerals); R. Vibert (Jersey); H. W. R. Wade (Property generally and Succession); and Dr. G. L. Williams (Jurisprudence).

The final stages of editing have been done mainly by Professor Lawson and Mr. Drake, who wish to acknowledge the help they have received from the staff of the Institute of Advanced Legal Studies, especially Miss A. Poynton. Any usefulness which the work may have for continental lawyers is due to an exceptional degree to the watchfulness of Professor Kahn-Freund.

It only remains to thank the International Committee of Comparative Law (now the International Association of Legal Science) for stimulating the production of this Guide, and Unesco for a very helpful subvention.

June 1956. F. H. LAWSON

NOTES

1. GENERAL

a. No reference to the place of publication is given when this is London.
b. When a serial publication has been published by more than one publisher, the latest publisher only is shown.
c. Capital letters are used in the text for the names of the authors of works listed in the accompanying bibliographies.

2. ABBREVIATIONS

a. The names of certain publishers have been abbreviated as follows throughout the bibliographical lists:

B	Butterworth & Co. Ltd.
CUP	Cambridge University Press
HMSO	Her Majesty's Stationery Office
OUP	Oxford University Press
S	Stevens & Sons
SLS	Solicitors' Law Stationery Society Ltd.
SM	Sweet & Maxwell Ltd.

b. The standard form of citation for Command Papers has been used, as follows:

First series,	1833–1868/69	[1] – [4222]
Second series,	1870–1899	C.1 – C.9550
Third series,	1900–1918	Cd. 1 – Cd. 9239
Fourth series,	1919–1956	Cmd. 1 – Cmd. 9889
Fifth series,	1956–	Cmnd. 1 – (current)

3. NAMES OF GOVERNMENT DEPARTMENTS REFERRED TO IN THE BIBLIOGRAPHICAL LISTS

Changes of name, composition and function of government departments frequently cause difficulties of bibliographical identification. The following list is offered as a guide to references within the bibliographical lists, and is not intended to be comprehensive.

The current form of name is given in italics.

DEPARTMENT OF EMPLOYMENT

1917–1938	Ministry of Labour
1938–1959	Ministry of Labour and National Service
1959–1968	Ministry of Labour
1968–1970	Department of Employment and Productivity
1970–	*Department of Employment*

DEPARTMENT OF HEALTH AND SOCIAL SECURITY

1917–1953	Ministry of Pensions, *merged with* Ministry of National Insurance (1945–1953) *to form*
1953–1966	Ministry of Pensions and National Insurance
1966–1968	Ministry of Social Security, *merged with* Ministry of Health (1919–1968) *to form*
1968–	*Department of Health and Social Security*

DEPARTMENT OF TRADE AND INDUSTRY

Pre 1970 Board of Trade
1970– *Department of Trade and Industry*

FOREIGN AND COMMONWEALTH OFFICE

1966 Colonial Office *merged with* Commonwealth Relations Office *to form*
1966–1968 Commonwealth Office, *which merged with* Foreign Office in 1968 *to form*
1968– *Foreign and Commonwealth Office*

MINISTRY OF DEFENCE

1947–1964 Ministry of Defence
1964– The Air Ministry, War Office and Admiralty became part of the Ministry of Defence, entitled:
Ministry of Defence. Air Force Department
Ministry of Defence. Army Department
Ministry of Defence. Navy Department

I. BIBLIOGRAPHIES AND GENERAL ACCOUNTS

1. GENERAL BIBLIOGRAPHIES

Messrs SWEET & MAXWELL published between 1955 and 1964 the second edition of a *Legal bibliography of the British Commonwealth of Nations* in seven volumes of which the first, second, fourth and fifth cover English, Irish, Scottish and Roman Law books. Their *Where to look for your law* is more summary but valuable; it substantially includes only books in print. Apart from these bibliographies, reference may be made to the latest catalogues issued by law publishers.

The American *Index to legal periodicals* also covers English periodicals.

HOLDSWORTH and WINFIELD are valuable. LEVY-ULLMANN is of much the same type but written for French students of comparative law. DAVID is a more modern book and contains bibliographies.

PRICE and BITNER contains in chapter 29 an admirable guide to the use of English source materials written from an American point of view and elsewhere gives complete lists of English reports and legal periodicals and of legal abbreviations.

Select Bibliography

BEALE, J. H., comp.
A bibliography of early English law books. Cambridge, Mass., Harvard UP, 1926. viii + 304p. (Ames Foundation publications) (*Supplement* . . . by R. B. Anderson. Cambridge, Mass., Harvard UP, 1943. xii + 50p.)

COWLEY, J. D.
A bibliography of abridgments, digests, dictionaries and indexes of English law to the year 1800. Quaritch, 1932. xcv + 196p.

DAVID, R.
Introduction à l'étude du droit privé de l'Angleterre. Paris, Sirey, 1948. 479p.

HOLDSWORTH, Sir W. S.
Sources and literature of English law. OUP, 1925. viii + 247p.

INDEX TO LEGAL PERIODICALS, vol. I– , 1908– . New York, H. W. Wilson, etc., in cooperation with the American Association of Law Libraries. (Three-yearly cumulations published after 1926)

LEVY-ULLMANN, H.
The English legal tradition: its sources and history. Macmillan, 1935. lvi + 383p.

PRICE, M. D. and BITNER, H.
Effective legal research: a practical manual of law books and their use. New York, Prentice-Hall, 1953, reprinted 1969. xiv + 633p. (3rd edition [student's edition] published by Little, Brown in 1969)

SWEET & MAXWELL, LTD
A legal bibliography of the British Commonwealth of Nations, 2nd ed. SM, 1955–64. 7 vols.

SWEET & MAXWELL, LTD

Where to look for your law, 14th ed. by C. W. Ringrose. SM, 1962. vii + 239p. (New edition in preparation)

WINFIELD, Sir P. H.

Chief sources of English legal history. Cambridge, Mass., Harvard UP, 1925. xviii + 374p.

2. GENERAL INTRODUCTIONS TO ENGLISH LAW

GLANVILLE WILLIAMS is a general introduction to the study of English law, much used by students; but as it is not only popular but learned, it is to be strongly recommended to older foreign lawyers who wish to approach English law for the first time.

GOLDSCHMIDT is excellent.

GELDART, JENKS' *Book of English law* and JAMES provide short conspectuses of English law as a whole. PHILLIPS discusses also in some detail the sources of English law. On this reference should also be made to Sir C. K. ALLEN'S classical book.

JACKSON deals mainly with the organization of the courts.

JENKS' *Digest* was originally drafted by five Oxford law teachers at the request of the Berlin Society for Comparative Jurisprudence and Political Economy on the general model of the German Civil Code. It has therefore very much the same form, content and scale as a code, though it also contains a skeleton apparatus of authorities supporting each proposition. In the current edition the General Part contained in Book I has been greatly curtailed and much of its content dispersed throughout the other books. The first two books of the first edition were translated into German with a commentary and the whole of the second edition into French. Although no more authoritative than any English legal text-book, JENKS' *Digest* is an excellent starting-point for a foreign lawyer who is accustomed to handling a civil code.

STEPHEN, though much larger than GELDART, etc., is still elementary and on a relatively small scale. It was mainly used for the solicitors' intermediate examination. It was originally based on Blackstone's famous commentaries (which still eminently repay reading), but was altered so much in subsequent editions that there is now hardly anything left of either Blackstone or Stephen. It is the only book that covers substantially the whole of English law on a systematic plan and a fairly generous scale, and is probably the best book for use by a foreign lawyer who wishes to understand the general character and structure of English law. The 19th edition, though less up to date than the current edition, is more systematic, especially in its treatment of property law.

FIFOOT is a popular account, written mainly from a historical point of view, by a master of the subject.

RUBINSTEIN is a popular book by a practising solicitor which aims at leading the layman into the law in a non-technical way and following an order which is likely to commend itself to him more than the sort of systematic order preferred by lawyers. It contains good practical advice which is not usually found in more technical books, and, though popular, is sound.

LAWSON is an attempt to analyse the most important branches of civil law on a rational and non-historical basis. It has been translated into Italian, Japanese and Spanish and might prove useful to foreign lawyers who find the logical structure of English law unfamiliar and difficult.

Select Bibliography

ALLEN, Sir C. K.
Law in the making, 7th ed. OUP, 1964. xli + 649p.
ASSOCIATION OF AMERICAN LAW SCHOOLS
Select essays in Anglo-American legal history. Boston, Little, Brown, 1907–09. 3 vols.
EVERYMAN'S OWN LAWYER, 69th ed. Technical Pr., 1962. 1024p. (Suppl.)
FIFOOT, C. H. S.
English law and its background. Bell, 1932. xvi + 279p.
GELDART, W. M.
Elements of English law, 7th ed. CUP, 1966. x + 182p.
GOLDSCHMIDT, H. W.
English law from the foreign standpoint. Pitman, 1937. xviii + 258p.
JACKSON, R. M.
Machinery of justice in England, 5th ed. CUP, 1967. xii + 494p.
JAMES, P. S.
Introduction to English law, 7th ed. B, 1969. 533p.
JENKS, E.
The book of English law, 6th revised ed. by P. B. Fairest. Murray, 1967. 384p.
JENKS, E., ed.
English civil law, 4th ed. B, 1947. 2 vols. (Previous editions entitled Digest of . . .)
KEETON, G. W. and LLOYD, D., eds.
The United Kingdom: the development of its laws and constitutions, England and Wales, Northern Ireland, the Isle of Man. S, 1955. xiv + 523p. (British Commonwealth: the development of its laws and constitutions, vol. I, part 1)
KIRALFY, A. K. R.
The English legal system, 4th ed. SM, 1967. xvii + 342p.
LAWSON, F. H.
The rational strength of English law. S, 1951. viii + 147p. (Hamlyn lectures)
PHILLIPS, O. Hood
A first book of English law, 6th ed. SM, 1970. xxxi + 346p.
RUBINSTEIN, R.
John Citizen and the law, 5th ed. Penguin, 1964. 432p.
STEPHEN, H. J.
Commentaries on the laws of England, 21st ed. Editor-in-chief: L. C. Warmington. B, 1950. 4 vols. (Suppl.)
WILLIAMS, G. L.
Learning the law, 8th ed. S, 1969. xi + 220p.

3. LEGAL ENCYCLOPAEDIAS AND DICTIONARIES

It has long been the practice to arrange general accounts of English law in alphabetical form. *The Encyclopaedia of the laws of England* is still useful, though on many points it is now obsolete. The new edition started before the last war has not since been continued.

Messrs. BUTTERWORTH publish several series which, taken together, purport to cover the whole of the law. The central and most important is *Halsbury's laws of England*, which covers the whole of case law and the more general effects of statutes and subordinate legislation. Greater detail on these topics may be found in *Halsbury's statutes of England* and *statutory instruments*. The other works in the series are the *Encyclopaedia of forms and precedents* and Atkin's *encyclopaedia of court forms in civil proceedings*. All of these have annual supplements. The articles are arranged alphabetically, but each of them is systematic and usually of pretty large compass.

MOZLEY and WHITELEY, OSBORN and *The Pocket law lexicon* are short and up-to-date dictionaries.

BOUVIER and WHARTON, which are much larger, are especially useful for understanding obsolete terms found in the older authorities. STROUD and *Words and phrases* are complete guides to the interpretation which has been put on particular words and phrases in legislation and by the courts. Much use is made in practice, especially in the Chancery Division, of the great *Oxford dictionary of the English language*.

Select Bibliography

ATKIN'S ENCYCLOPAEDIA OF COURT FORMS IN CIVIL PROCEEDINGS, 2nd ed. by Lord Evershed and other lawyers. B, 1961– . (Suppl. To be published in 41 vols. 1st edition by Lord Atkin not yet fully superseded)

BOUVIER, J.
Law dictionary and concise encyclopaedia, 8th ed. by F. Rawle. Kansas City, Vernon Law Book Co., 1914. 2 vols.

BYRNE, W. J.
A dictionary of English law. SM, 1923. xliv + 942p.

ENCYCLOPAEDIA OF FORMS AND PRECEDENTS OTHER THAN COURT FORMS, 4th ed. B, 1964– . (Suppl. 3rd edition not yet fully superseded)

ENCYCLOPAEDIA OF THE LAWS OF ENGLAND, 3rd edition. Editor-in-chief: E. A. Jelf. SM, 1938–40. 5 vols.

HALSBURY'S LAWS OF ENGLAND, 3rd ed. B, 1952–64. 43 vols. (Suppl.)

HALSBURY'S STATUTES OF ENGLAND, 3rd edition. B, 1968– . (To be completed in 41 volumes)

HALSBURY'S STATUTORY INSTRUMENTS, 2nd re-issue. B., 1951– . 24 vols. (Replacement volumes published at intervals. Also supplemented by a loose-leaf service)

JOWITT, W. A., Earl Jowitt, and WALSH, C., eds.
The dictionary of English law. SM, 1959. 2 vols.

MOZLEY, H. N. and WHITELEY, G. C.
Law dictionary, 8th ed. by J. B. Saunders. B, 1970. ix + 389p.

OSBORN, P. G.
The concise law dictionary, 5th ed. SM, 1964. vii + 393p.

OXFORD ENGLISH DICTIONARY. OUP, 1933. 12 vols. (Suppl.)

POCKET LAW LEXICON, 8th ed. by A. W. Motion. S, 1951. viii + 419p.

STROUD, F.
Judicial dictionary of words and phrases, 3rd ed. SM, 1952–53. 4 vols. (Suppl.)

WHARTON, J. J. S.
Law lexicon, 14th ed. by A. S. Oppé. S, 1938. viii + 1081p.

WORDS AND PHRASES LEGALLY DEFINED, 2nd ed. under the general editorship of J. B. Saunders. B, 1969–70. 5 vols. (Suppl.)

4. GOVERNMENT PUBLICATIONS

For an understanding of the law, and especially of its history, reference to various government publications is invaluable and indeed indispensable. In particular, reference should be made to so-called blue books and white papers, which are regularly issued in preparation for and in support of legislation. The reports of Royal Commissions, Departmental Committees, etc., including those of the important Law Revision Committee and its successor the Law Reform Committee, are the closest equivalent to *travaux préparatoires* or *Motive* known to English practice. It must, however, be clearly understood that they may not be cited in court for the purpose of interpreting legislation, though they may be cited in order to show what was the previous state of the law and its defects. CLOKIE and ROBINSON is interesting and important.

A list of Reports of Royal Commissions, Courts of Inquiry and Committees, etc., published as Command Papers and commonly cited by the name of the Chairman, 1900–1962, is given in SWEET & MAXWELL *Where to look for your Law*, pp. 170–179.

FORD is a guide to the more important parliamentary papers.

Select Bibliography

CLOKIE, H. M. and ROBINSON, J. W.
Royal commissions of inquiry: the significance of investigations in British politics. Stanford UP, 1937. viii + 242p.

FORD, P. and FORD, G.
A breviate of parliamentary papers, 1900–1954. Oxford, Blackwell, 1951–61. 3 vols. (Revised editions of volumes 1 and 2 published by Irish UP in 1969)

FORD P. and FORD G.
A guide to parliamentary papers: what they are, how to find them, how to use them, new ed. Oxford, Blackwell, 1956. xiii + 79p.

FORD P. and FORD, G.
Select list of British parliamentary papers, 1833–1899, revised ed. Shannon, Irish UP, 1969. xxii + 165p.

FORD, P. and others
Select list of British parliamentary papers, 1955–64. Shannon, Irish UP, 1970. vii + 117p.

GREAT BRITAIN. Stationery Office
Catalogue of government publications. HMSO, 1922– . (Annual. Consolidated five-yearly indexes. Monthly catalogues and daily lists also issued.)

HANSARD'S CATALOGUE AND BREVIATE OF PARLIAMENTARY PAPERS, 1696–1834; with an introduction by P. Ford and G. Ford. Dublin, Irish UP, 1968. xv + viii + 220p. (Facsimile reprint of 1st edition of 1836)

SWEET & MAXWELL, LTD
Where to look for your law, 14th ed. by C. W. Ringrose. SM, 1962. vii + 239p. (New edition in preparation)

5. LEGAL PERIODICALS

Those which appear weekly are, as it were, legal newspapers, giving topical information, short articles and reviews and summary accounts of cases. Though on the whole ephemeral, they may sometimes be referred to later with profit. For *Current law*, see p. 15 below.

Law reviews of a general kind and of more permanent interest are few. The most famous is the *Law quarterly review*, which covers subjects of every kind. It emphasizes the doctrinal and historical as well as the practical aspects of the law. Its notes on recent cases are influential, and its reviews authoritative. The *Modern Law Review*, edited in London, though likewise academic in a good sense, lives up to its name. It lays more stress on legislation and pays much attention to public law. The *Cambridge law journal* has the same general character as the *Law quarterly review*. The *Journal of the Society of Public Teachers of Law* gives, more than any other periodical, information and opportunity for discussion on legal education. Its articles include reports of addresses on various topics delivered at annual meetings of the Society. The book reviews are good. The *International and comparative law quarterly*, the successor of the *Journal of comparative legislation and international law*, the *International law quarterly* and the *Transactions of the Grotius Society*, is the organ of the British Institute of International and Comparative Law. It covers a wide range of subjects.

Current legal problems is an annual publication containing special lectures on miscellaneous topics delivered at University College, London. It differs from an ordinary law journal only in having no notes or book reviews.

Other, more specialized, periodicals will be found listed under particular topics, e.g., the *Journal of criminal law* under Criminal Law.

It should be remembered that English law figures largely in the periodical literature of other common law countries, e.g., the United States, Canada and Australia; and more occasionally in continental periodicals such as *Rabels Zeitschrift*, *Clunet*, etc.

Select Bibliography

CAMBRIDGE LAW JOURNAL, vol. 1– , 1921– . CUP.

CURRENT LAW CONSOLIDATION, vol. 1, 1947–51. SM. (A cumulation of *Current Law year book*)

CURRENT LAW YEAR BOOK, 1947– . SM. (Published in monthly parts as *Current Law*)

CURRENT LEGAL PROBLEMS, vol. 1– , 1948– . S.

INDEX TO LEGAL PERIODICALS, vol. 1– , 1908– . New York, H. W. Wilson, etc., in cooperation with the American Association of Law Libraries. (Three-yearly cumulations published after 1926)

INTERNATIONAL AND COMPARATIVE LAW QUARTERLY, vol. 1– , 1952– . British Institute of International and Comparative Law, etc.

INTERNATIONAL LAW QUARTERLY, vols. 1–4, 1947–51. S.

JOURNAL DU DROIT INTERNATIONAL, vol. 1– , 1874– . Paris, Editions Techniques. (1874–1945, entitled *Journal du droit international privé*. Known as *Clunet* after the name of the founder, Edouard Clunet)

JOURNAL OF BUSINESS LAW, 1957– . S.

JOURNAL OF COMPARATIVE LEGISLATION AND INTERNATIONAL LAW, 1896–1951. Society of Comparative Legislation, etc. (1896–July 1917, entitled *Journal of the Society of Comparative Legislation*)

JOURNAL OF THE SOCIETY OF PUBLIC TEACHERS OF LAW, 1924– . B. (1938–47, not published)

LAW QUARTERLY REVIEW, vol. 1– , 1885– . S.

LAW TIMES, vols. 1–236, 1843–1965. B.

MODERN LAW REVIEW, vol. 1– , 1937– . S.

NEW LAW JOURNAL, vol. 1– , 1866– . B. (1866–1965, entitled *Law journal*)

RABELS ZEITSCHRIFT FÜR AUSLÄNDISCHES UND INTERNATIONALES PRIVATRECHT, vol. 1– , 1927– . Berlin, de Gruyter. (1943–48, not published. 1927–60, entitled *Zeitschrift für ausländisches und internationales Privatrecht*)

SOLICITORS' JOURNAL, vol. 1– , 1857– . SLS.

TRANSACTIONS OF THE GROTIUS SOCIETY, vols. 1–44, 1915–59. British Institute of International and Comparative Law, etc. (Index to whole series published in 1969 by Oceana and Wildy)

II. THE SOURCES OF ENGLISH LAW

1. GENERAL

The formal sources of English law are:

1. *Legislation.* This includes both Acts of Parliament (Statutes) and subordinate, or delegated, legislation such as regulations, orders, rules, by-laws, etc., made by the Queen in Council, government departments, committees of judges and other lawyers, local authorities, etc. Practically all subordinate legislation operating in peace time within the United Kingdom must be made in virtue of powers conferred by Act of Parliament. All subordinate legislation must give way to any inconsistent Act of Parliament. There may on any subject be degrees of subordinate legislation, some instruments operating directly under Acts of Parliament and others under other subordinate legislation. Acts of subordinate legislation (other than by-laws) operating directly under an Act of Parliament are known as Statutory Instruments.

It must be clearly understood that Acts of Parliament are the highest law. Although the United Kingdom has a political constitution which enjoys great stability, there is no legal constitution superior to Acts of Parliament and hence, although the judges can interpret Acts of Parliament, they cannot treat them as invalid on the ground that they are unconstitutional. In other words there is "no judicial review" of statutes, in the sense in which that term is used in the United States.

2. *Judge-made law.* This covers the principles which can be inferred from the decisions of courts, known as the "common law", in the wider sense, as opposed to legislation or statute law. In the narrower sense "common law" is opposed to "equity", which is also a body of judge-made principles, but of different historical origin. Under this head must also be brought the practice of administrative tribunals, which, however, like the decisions of inferior courts, cannot always be ascertained. Like the decisions of the lower courts, those of most administrative tribunals are subject to review by the higher courts. All this judge-made law corresponds to *jurisprudence* in the French sense of the term.

3. *Text-books* written by legal authors. This source corresponds roughly to *doctrine*, in the French sense, though the part it plays in English law is very different.

4. *Custom.* This is very unimportant nowadays except for mercantile and industrial custom. It is treated by the courts as fact and must be proved as such.

An English lawyer who is confronted with an unfamiliar problem goes first to a text-book or to an article in one of those legal encyclopaedias which are really collections of text-books in disguise. Similarly a student starts his study of a subject by reading a text-book, usually of a more elementary kind. But neither accepts a statement of law in a text-book as authoritative. It affords no certain indication of the way a judge will decide a case, because a judge is always free to disagree with it if he comes to the conclusion that it is unsound. Moreover, except in those relatively rare cases which cannot come before a court, English lawyers always test the validity of a legal proposition either by taking it before a judge or by trying to predict the view which a judge would take of it were it submitted to him. A few older books, such as GLANVILLE, BRACTON, COKE and Sir MICHAEL FOSTER, are an exception to this general principle. They are themselves authority, though they must give way to statute or case-law. But almost everything they contain is now either obsolete or covered by judicial decisions. The position of BLACKSTONE, who is not so remote in time, is more doubtful. Probably a judge need not follow him if he thinks he is wrong.

The old theory that the works of a living author may not be cited in court is still sometimes heard on the lips of conservative-minded judges, but very rarely, and then with a suggestion that the correct procedure is to adopt what they write as part of counsel's argument. Any passage may now be cited that counsel thinks helps his argument, subject to disapproval if the judge thinks it does not state the law correctly. Some books acquire by their own merits or the reputation of their authors—some very rapidly—a considerable amount of persuasive authority; that is to say, a judge will be disinclined to disagree with them unless they are clearly wrong. Of course they are only independent authorities where they go beyond merely stating the effect of decisions or statutes and attempt, by generalisation or analogy or criticism or otherwise, to state new principle. Some famous authors like Pollock have done this fairly extensively. Although a more systematic approach towards the law is gaining ground, the majority of the books used by practitioners are only used as indexes to the real authorities, statutes or cases. In other words, there is very little in English law corresponding to Continental *doctrine*, and, such as it is, it is nearly always suspect to the practising lawyer or judge, as representing what the author thinks ought to be the law rather than what it is. Nevertheless text-books on English law are extremely numerous and quite indispensable except to the expert in his own narrow field. Almost the whole of this bibliography will be taken up by works of this kind. An increasing use is being made of articles and notes in legal periodicals, but as yet not so much as in the United States.

The continental lawyer will be startled by this attitude of the English legal profession and courts towards *doctrine*. It must be borne in mind that English law has been and is being developed by the Bar, that is to say, by that branch of the legal profession which is to a large extent engaged in litigation, that the judges are all drawn from the Bar and in a sense remain members of the Bar even when they have ascended the Bench, and that the Bench and Bar, through the Inns of Court, the guilds in which the Bar is organized, control the training of those practitioners from whose ranks the judges are recruited. The academic teaching of the law is a comparatively recent phenomenom and is only gradually gaining in importance.

Whatever the problem he wishes to solve the English lawyer will try to find a case exactly covering it, for, subject to the rules governing the hierarchy of precedents the decision in that case determines authoritatively the decision in the case before him. But he may have to put up with something else. At this point the question arises, what are the relations between judge-made law and statute?

Some parts of English law are unaffected by statute. Sometimes they are very extensive; thus there is very little statute law in the law of tort. The law is then based entirely on the decisions in former cases and is known as judge-made law. It is all a question of finding the right case and then making certain that the decision was not reversed on appeal and has not since been overruled either expressly or by implication. But it may well be that the whole of the law on a particular subject, e.g., divorce law or the law of national insurance, is based ultimately on statute. Can the practitioner then safely place his own interpretation on the statute and call on a judge to accept it? No, he will still look for a judicial decision interpreting the statute and will consider that authoritative even though in his eyes it runs clean counter to what the statute itself says. He may think that the decision would be overruled by a higher court and may be willing to act upon his opinion against that of the lower court; but the position will be in no way different from what it would have been had the decision been based on pure judge-made law.

These are the two extreme, and the commonest, cases. But the point may be one where there was originally judge-made law and then a statute. Here too the lawyer will look for a decision interpreting the statute, for although the statute may have modified the judge-made law, it is itself apt to become a foundation for more judge-made law of an interpretative kind. In a sense the judge always has the last word, for although the legislature may continually reverse his interpretations, on each occasion he may have to interpret the reversing statute, though at any stage the task may become almost automatic.

It cannot be too strongly emphasized that an English lawyer will always look for a judicial decision and will feel happiest if he finds one directly in point that he can trust. If he cannot find one, and there is no statute, he will try to reason from principle, inferring the principle from the general run of the judge-made law on the subject. Even where he has to interpret a statutory provision which has not yet been interpreted, he will apply judge-made rules of statutory interpretation. He will not extend a statutory provision by analogy, though he may do so to a principle of judge-made law. In a sense therefore, although there is no doubt that a statute can alter any rule or principle of judge-made law, the latter enjoys a sort of latent superiority which is, incidentally, further expressed by the rule that a statute must be interpreted so as to interfere as little as possible with the common law. However this rule is less rigorously followed now than formerly, in certain parts of the law, such as those governing the welfare state.

Select Bibliography

BLACKSTONE, Sir W.

Commentaries on the laws of England. Oxford, Clarendon Pr., 1765–69. 4 vols. (For details of various editions see HOLDSWORTH, *History of English law*, vol. 12, p. 712)

BRACTON, H. de

De legibus et consuetudinibus Angliae, ed. by G. E. Woodbine; translated with revisions and notes by S. E. Thorne. Cambridge, Mass., Belknap Pr. of the Harvard UP, in association with the Selden Society, 1968– . (To be completed in 5 volumes)

COKE, Sir E.

Institutes of the laws of England. In 4 parts. 1628–44. (Various publishers and many subsequent editions)

FOSTER, Sir M.

A report . . . to which are added discourses upon a few branches of the Crown law, 3rd ed. . . . containing new cases. E. and R. Brooke, 1792. xxxvi + 441p. (For full details *see* Chapter 10, Section 1)

GLANVILLE, R. de

Tractatus de legibus et consuetudinibus regni Angliae qui Glanvilla vocatur, ed. with introduction, notes and translation by G. D. G. Hall. Nelson, in association with the Selden Society, 1965. lxx + 213p. (Nelson's medieval texts)

2. STATUTES AND STATUTORY INSTRUMENTS

All legislative documents, including bills in Parliament, Acts of Parliament and statutory instruments (i.e. acts of subordinate legislation), are printed by the Queen's Printer and can be obtained immediately from Her Majesty's Stationery Office (H.M.S.O.). All the statutes so printed for each year are bound up in one or more volumes and are then published both by H.M.S.O. and as part of the Law Reports for the year by the Incorporated Council of Law Reporting. The statutory instruments for the year are similarly bound up and published by H.M.S.O. Wherever possible, lawyers prefer to use annotated editions of both statutes and statutory instruments, since they refer to cases in which such enactments have been interpreted. *Halsbury's statutes of England* and *Halsbury's statutory instruments* are annotated editions arranged according to subject-matter with the same headings as *Halsbury's laws of England.* Each series is brought up to date by an annual supplement. *Current laws statutes annotated* is a similar series. Many text-books are really commentaries on statutes or groups of statutes on related topics. There are also special series of annotated statutes on such topics as income tax.

All the public general statutes still in force in the United Kingdom at the end of 1948 (with the exception of those which can be repealed by the Parliament of Northern Ireland), together with the Church Assembly Measures, are reprinted in chronological order in the *Statutes revised.* This third edition is the first one which speaks as a whole from one date. It is brought up to date annually by non-cumulative supplements containing lists of alterations made during the current year. There is a similar revised collection of Statutory Instruments and their predecessors, which were known as Statutory Rules and Orders.

The *Chronological table* and the *Index to the statutes* [*in force*] are publications which serve as a complete guide to the Statute Book. A similar table to the Statutory Instruments is published annually, and an index every two years.

ILBERT contains a most interesting account of the way in which the Statute Book has been gradually purged of obsolete material and large masses of scattered material brought together by consolidation. Both processes have gone much farther since he wrote, and a separate group of draftsmen now devote their time exclusively to the work of consolidation. It is worth mentioning that English lawyers distinguish consolidation, which covers merely statutes, from codification, which restates the whole of the law on a topic, whether statute, common law or equity. Thus the law of partnership has been codified in the Partnership Act, 1890, which deals with what corresponds to the *Société en nom collectif* or the *Offene Handelsgesellschaft.* On the other hand, the Companies Act, 1948, which deals with associations corresponding to *Sociétés anonymes* or *Aktiengesellschaften* and *Sociétés à responsabilité limitée* or *Gesellschaften mit beschränkter Haftung*, is only a consolidating statute, for much company law is still uncodified common law or equity.

Besides public general statutes, Parliament passes many so-called private, or local or personal statutes. These are promoted by local authorities or public utilities, or even by private persons for the purpose of altering, for instance, family settlements. They are published separately and are sometimes hard to get. A list of such statutes passed during each year, together with an index, is printed annually. There are also indexes of past private Acts. The foreign lawyer will hardly ever need to consult them, but it is necessary to know of their existence, for they have been of immense importance in the development of local government and of public and public utility services, and they still serve to differentiate the law on local lines. Their importance has, however, greatly diminished with the growth of subordinate legislation.

Select Bibliography

Text books

HUGHES, C.
The British statute book. Hutchinson, 1937. 168p.
ILBERT, Sir C. P.
Legislative methods and forms. OUP, 1901. xxxi + 372p.
ILBERT, Sir C. P.
The mechanics of law making. New York, Columbia UP, 1914. viii + 209p.

Of the three books noted above HUGHES is the most up to date work, although ILBERT, *Mechanics* . . . is a popular account contained in a series of lectures in America.

Encyclopaedia

HALSBURY'S LAWS OF ENGLAND, 3rd ed. B, 1952–64. 43 vols. (Suppl.)

Legislation

CURRENT LAW STATUTES ANNOTATED, 1947– . SM.
GREAT BRITAIN
Chronological table of the statutes . . . to the end of . . . HMSO. (Annual)
GREAT BRITAIN
Index to government orders in force on 31st December . . . HMSO. (Biennial. 1891–1950, entitled *Index to the statutory rules and orders in force;* 1951–60, entitled *Guide to government orders*)
GREAT BRITAIN
Index to local and personal acts, 1801–1947. HMSO, 1949. vii + 1140p. (Annual suppl. and supplementary index, 1948–66)
GREAT BRITAIN
Index to the statutes . . . in force on 31st December . . . HMSO. (Annual)
GREAT BRITAIN
Local and personal acts . . . tables and index. HMSO. (Annual)
GREAT BRITAIN
Public general acts and Church Assembly measures, 1926– . HMSO. (Annual. 1866–1925, entitled *Public general statutes*)
GREAT BRITAIN
The statutes: third revised edition . . . 1235–1948. HMSO, 1950. 33 vols. (Cover title: *Statutes revised*)
GREAT BRITAIN
Statutory instruments . . ., 1890– . HMSO. (Annual. 1890–1947, entitled *Statutory rules and orders*)
GREAT BRITAIN
Statutory rules and orders and statutory instruments revised to December 31st, 1948. HMSO, 1949–52. 25 vols.

GREAT BRITAIN
Table of government orders . . . covering the general instruments to 31st December . . . HMSO. (Annual. Supplemented every six months by a Noter-up)

HALSBURY'S STATUTES OF ENGLAND, 3rd ed. B, 1968– . (To be completed in 41 volumes)

HALSBURY'S STATUTORY INSTRUMENTS, 2nd re-issue. B, 1951– . 24 vols. (Replacement volumes published at intervals. Also supplemented by a loose-leaf service)

3. LAW REPORTS

There are now current only three series of general law reports, the *Law reports*, the *Weekly law reports*, and the *All England law reports*. The two former are published by the Incorporated Council of Law Reporting, which comprises representatives of both branches of the legal profession. The *Weekly law reports* are in two parts, one containing cases which are not likely to be of permanent interest and so are not reprinted later, the other containing cases which will be reprinted, as revised at leisure by the reporters and the judges, in the *Law reports*. The *All England law reports* also are brought out very rapidly after cases have been decided. *The Times* newspaper prints summary reports daily of cases of general interest. Since they are made by barristers, they can be cited in court, but this would happen only if the case was not reported elsewhere. There are other series of curtailed reports, and there are several series of reports dealing with limited subjects such as tax law, patent law, social insurance law. Older series may still have to be consulted.

Before 1865, when the Incorporated Council of Law Reporting started to publish the *Law reports*, almost all the reports, except the *Law journal* and *Law times reports*, were known by the names of the reporters. The majority of these "nominate" reports were reprinted in full in the series known as the *English reports*, which also contains some slight annotations. The *Revised reports* covers the same ground from 1785, and while it is not quite so complete, it also reprints a few cases from other reporters. A foreign lawyer would hardly ever need to go outside the *English reports*.

Lists of the various Reports may be found in SWEET & MAXWELL'S *Guide* and *Where to look for your law*, in PRICE and BITNER, and prefixed to any volume of *Halsbury's laws of England*. A famous historical work is WALLACE.

Select Bibliography

Text books and guides

FOX, Sir J. C.
A Handbook of English law reports from the last quarter of the eighteenth century to the year 1865 . . .; Part 1: House of Lords, Privy Council and Chancery reports. B, 1913. viii + 107p. (No more parts published)

MORAN, C. G.
The Heralds of the law. S, 1948. vi + 114p.

PRICE, M. O. and BITNER, H.
Effective legal research: a practical manual of law books and their use. New York, Prentice Hall, 1953, reprinted 1969. xiv + 633p. (3rd edition [student's edition] published by Little, Brown in 1969)

SWEET & MAXWELL, LTD
Guide to the law reports and statutes, 4th ed. SM, 1962. 143p.
SWEET & MAXWELL, LTD
Where to look for your law, 14th ed. by C. W. Ringrose. SM, 1962. viii + 239p. (New edition in preparation)
VEEDER, V. V.
"The English reports, 1292–1865", in *Harvard law review*, 15 (1901): pp. 1–25 and 109–117. (Reprinted in part in *Select essays in Anglo-American legal history*, vol. 2. Issued by the Association of American Law Schools. (Boston, Little, Brown, 1908))
WALLACE, J. W.
The Reporters, 4th ed. Boston, Soule and Bugbee, 1882. vi + 654p.

Law reports

ALL ENGLAND LAW REPORTS, 1936– . B. (*Consolidated index*, 1936–65, 2 vols., and annual cumulative index, 1966–)
ALL ENGLAND LAW REPORTS REPRINT, 1558–1935. B, 1957– . 37 vols.
ENGLISH REPORTS, 1220–1865. Edinburgh, Green, 1900–32. 178 vols. (Vols 170–76, *Nisi Prius*, cover the period 1688–1867)
LAW JOURNAL REPORTS, vols 1–9, 1823–31. New series, vols. 1–118, 1839–1949. Law Journal. (From 1950– incorporated in the *All England law reports*, q.v.)
THE LAW REPORTS, 1866– . Incorporated Council of Law Reporting. (Now published in 4 series: *Appeal Cases, Chancery Division, Queen's Bench Division, Probate Division*. The Council publishes a *Consolidated index*, 1951– , supplemented by a *Cumulative index*)
LAW TIMES REPORTS, old series, 1843–60. 34 vols. New series, vols. 1–177, 1859–1947. Law Times. (From 1948—incorporated in the *All England law reports*, q.v.)
LLOYD'S LAW REPORTS, 1919– . Lloyd's. (1919–1952, entitled *Lloyd's list law reports*)
REVISED REPORTS, 1785–1866. SM, 1891. 149 vols. (*Index-digest*, 2 vols., and *Table of cases* also published)
THE TIMES LAW REPORTS, 1884–1952. The Times Publishing Co. 71 vols.
WEEKLY LAW REPORTS, 1953– . Incorporated Council of Law Reporting

4. DIGESTS OF CASE-LAW

Digests of case-law aim at covering all reported cases according to a subject arrangement. The entries describe the cases as succinctly as possible and extract the legal principles which can be inferred from them. They give a ready means of ascertaining the case-law on a topic, but do not enable anyone to dispense with the reports of the cases themselves.

The *Law reports digest of cases* contains a reference to every case reported in the *Law reports* and other contemporaneous reports from 1865 onwards together with a list of statutes judicially considered during the same period. *Mews' digest of English case law* contains the reported decisions of the superior courts and a selection of the Scottish and Irish courts to the end of 1924, and is kept up to date by supplements. The *English and Empire digest* is a complete digest of every English case reported from early times and is arranged alphabetically by subject in 56 volumes. Other jurisdictions such as Scotland, Ireland and the Dominions are arranged separately by footnotes on each page. It is kept up to date by continuation volumes and supplements. *Current law* professes, with a very fair approach to success, to give monthly "*all* the law from *every* source". The *Current law year book* sums up annually all that has appeared in the monthly numbers. *Current law consolidation*, 1947–51, sums up all the law for the five years in question. All three publications are digests, but not merely of case-law. They also show all references to other cases which have been made during their respective periods.

Select Bibliography

CURRENT LAW, no. 1– , Jan. 1947– . SM.

CURRENT LAW CITATOR, 1947– . SM.

CURRENT LAW CONSOLIDATION, vol. 1, 1947–51. SM. (A cumulation of *Current law year book*)

CURRENT LAW YEAR BOOK, 1947– . SM. (Published in monthly parts as *Current law*)

ENGLISH AND EMPIRE DIGEST, 2nd ed. B, 1950–1970. 56 vols. (Kept up to date by cumulative supplements and continuation volumes)

INCORPORATED COUNCIL OF LAW REPORTING
The law reports . . . digest of cases, 1865–1951. The Council. 13 vols. (1951, entitled *The law reports . . . complete current digest*)

MEWS, J.
Digest of English case law . . . to the end of 1924, 2nd ed. SM, 1925–28. (Kept up to date by supplements containing cases reported 1925–51, 14 vols)

1 # III. THE HISTORY OF ENGLISH LAW

There are several modern works covering all branches of the history of English Law, but the range of works covering particular aspects of that history is so vast in quantity and various in quality that a bibliography of this nature can only include works on a highly selective basis. The balance of the modern literature, especially for medieval legal history, is upon the side of institutional studies. Works of historical jurisprudence directed to doctrinal and substantive development are fewer in number. The works selected below have been chosen, nevertheless, with a view to the interests of those studying English legal history upon matters of legal development rather than institutional development. Many important works dealing with the history of government and of the administration of law are excluded, but a summary of much such modern work, of interest to lawyers, is to be found in the introductory essay by CHRIMES to the 7th edition of Holdsworth's *History of English law* Vol. I (1956), pp. 1–77. Moreover, the selection has excluded works such as Bracton's *De legibus* and Blackstone's *Commentaries*, on the ground that though such works often contain much valuable historical exposition, both by the original authors and later editors, yet now these texts are more properly to be regarded as themselves among the sources of legal history. Otherwise even a select bibliography of primary material of such nature would require hundreds of entries.

BIBLIOGRAPHICAL ACCOUNTS OF PRIMARY SOURCES

The principal original sources and other works can be discovered most readily through Winfield's *Chief sources of English legal history* and Sweet and Maxwell's *Legal bibliography*. Winfield discusses the original sources; Sweet and Maxwell's *Bibliography* gives details of almost every law book published in England before 1800 and most of those published between 1800 and the present day. Volume I covers the period down to 1800 and is arranged according to subject-matter; it contains not merely books published before 1800 but also later works dealing with subjects prior to 1800. Volume II, 1801–1954, is arranged under authors, but does contain a subject-matter index.

Select Bibliography

BLAND, D. S.
A bibliography of the Inns of Court and Chancery. Selden Society, 1965. xi + 75p. (Selden Society supplementary series, vol. 3)

CHENEY, C. R. ed.
Handbook of dates for students of English history. Royal Historical Society, 1945, repr. 1955. xvii + 164p. (Chapter on legal chronology by Plucknett)

GREAT BRITAIN. Stationery Office.
British national archives. HMSO, 1969. 76p. (Sectional list no. 24) (Lists all publications of British Public Record Offices)

GREAT BRITAIN. Stationery Office.

Guide to the contents of the Public Record Office. HMSO, 1963–69. 3 vols. (Vol. I: Legal records, etc; vol. II: State papers and departmental records; vol. III: Documents transferred 1960–1966)

KIRALFY, A. K. R. and JONES, G. H.

Guide to the publications of the Selden Society, vols 1–79. Quaritch, 1960. iv + 168p. (Summaries of both introductions to, and contents of, the annual publications of the Society)

MILSOM, S. F. C.

"Select bibliography and notes", in *The history of English law, vide infra,* by Sir F. Pollock and F. W. Maitland, 2nd ed., reissued with a new introduction . . . (CUP, 1968), pp. lxxv–xci. (Includes section on original sources for medieval legal history, supplementing Maitland's "List of texts used", pp. xix–xxii)

MULLINS, E. L. C.

Texts and calendars: an analytical guide to serial publications. Royal Historical Society, 1958. xi + 674p. (Royal Historical Society guides and handbooks, no. 7)

SWEET & MAXWELL, LTD

A legal bibliography of the British Commonwealth of Nations, 2nd ed. SM, 1955–64. 7 vols.

A touchstone for the older nominate reporters is:

WALLACE, J. W.

The reporters, 4th ed. Boston, Soule & Bugbee, 1882. vi + 654p.

WINFIELD, Sir P. H.

The chief sources of English legal history. Cambridge, Mass., Harvard UP, 1925. xviii + 374p.

General works

a. detailed works

ALLEN, Sir C. K.

Law in the making, 7th ed. OUP, 1964. xli + 649p.

DICEY, A. V.

Lectures on the relation between law and public opinion in England during the nineteenth century, 2nd ed.; with a preface by E. C. S. Wade. Macmillan, 1962. xciv+506p.

The most comprehensive account of English legal history is:

HOLDSWORTH, Sir W. S.

A history of English law. Methuen, 1903–66, reprinted 1966. 16 vols. (Various editions. Tables and index to vols. I–IX by E. Potton, Methuen, 1932)

HOLMES, O. W.

The Common law, new ed. by M. D. Howe. Macmillan, 1968. xxviii + 337p.

MILSOM, S. F. C.

Historical foundations of the Common law. B, 1969. xvi + 466p. (Notes at pp. 375–429 contain much bibliographical information)

The last mentioned work is mainly an exploratory and explanatory study of the jurisprudential and conceptual developments of the Common law in the context of process and pleading.

Despite its title, a wide-ranging and extremely valuable work is:

PLUCKNETT, T. F. T.
A concise history of the Common law, 5th ed. B, 1956. xxvi + 746 + 56p.

POLLOCK, F. and MAITLAND, F. W.
The history of English law before the time of Edward I, 2nd ed., with introduction and select bibliography, by S. F. C. Milsom. CUP, 1968. cviii + 688p.

The new introduction to this work, pp. xxiii-lxxiii, is principally an interpretative account of basic legal ideas of the early Common law, and the bibliography, pp. lxxv–xci, comprehensively surveys the literature, including periodical articles, published since the second edition.

REEVES, J.
History of the English law from the time of the Saxons to the end of the reign of Elizabeth, new ed. by W. F. Finlason, 1869. 3 vols.

STENTON, D. M.
English justice between the Norman conquest and the Great Charter, 1066–1215. Allen & Unwin, 1965. ix + 238p.

STREET, T. A.
The foundations of legal liability. Northport, N.Y., Thompson, 1906. 3 vols.

b. less detailed

BAKER, J. H.
An introduction to English legal history. B, 1971. xxi-330p.

FIFOOT, C. H. S.
English law and its background. Bell, 1932. xvi + 279p.

HARDING, A.
A social history of English law. Penguin, 1966. 503p.

JENKS, E.
A short history of English law, 6th ed. Methuen, 1949. xxxvi + 442p.

KEETON, G. W.
The Norman conquest and the Common law. Benn, 1966. 238p.

MAITLAND, F. W.
The forms of action at Common law. CUP, 1936. xii + 92p.

POTTER, H.
An historical introduction to English law and its institutions, 4th ed. by A. K. R. Kiralfy. SM, 1958. xxxii + 675p.

SMITH, J. H.
Cases and materials on the development of legal institutions. St. Paul, Minn., West, 1965. xxviii + 757p.

VEALL, D.
The popular movement of law reform, 1640–1660. OUP, 1970. xxvi + 259p. (Bibliography, pp. 241-251.)

WINDEYER, W. J. V.
Lectures on legal history, 2nd revised ed. Sydney, Law Book Co., 1959. xxiv + 335p.

Collected papers

AMES, J. B.
Lectures on legal history and miscellaneous legal essays. Cambridge, Mass., Harvard UP, 1913. viii + 553p.

ASSOCIATION OF AMERICAN LAW SCHOOLS.
Select essays in Anglo-American legal history. Boston, Little, Brown, 1907–09. 3 vols.

HOLDSWORTH, Sir W. S.
Essays in law and history, edited by A. L. Goodhart and H. G. Hanbury. OUP, 1946. xv + 302p.

MAITLAND, F. W.
Collected papers, edited by H. A. L. Fisher. CUP, 1911. 3 vols.

WINFIELD, Sir P. H.
Select legal essays. SM, 1952. xv + 292p.

Special works

a. Land law

BEAN, J. M. W.
The decline of English feudalism, 1215–1540. Manchester UP, 1968. xii + 335p.

HOLDSWORTH, Sir W. S.
An historical introduction to the land law. OUP, 1927. xxiv + 339p.

KERRIDGE, E.
Agrarian problems in the sixteenth century and after. Allen & Unwin, 1969. 216p. (Historical problems: studies and documents, 6)

MAITLAND, F. W.
Domesday Book and beyond: three essays on the early history of England; with an introduction by E. Miller. Collins, 1960. 605p. (Reissue of CUP edition, 1897)

PLUCKNETT, T. F. T.
Legislation of Edward I. OUP, 1949. xv + 168p. (Ford lectures, Oxford, 1947)

SIMPSON, A. W. B.
An introduction to the history of the land law. OUP, 1961. xx + 276p.

b. Equity

JONES, G. H.
History of the law of charity, 1532–1827. CUP, 1969. xxiii + 270p. (Cambridge studies in English legal history)

JONES, W. J.
The Elizabethan Court of Chancery. OUP, 1967. xvii + 528p.

KERLY, D. M.
An historical sketch of the equitable jurisdiction of the Court of Chancery. CUP, 1890. xiv + 303p.

MAITLAND, F. W.
Equity, 2nd ed. revised by John Brunyate. CUP, 1936, reprinted 1969. xxiv + 342p.

SPENCE, G.
The equitable jurisdiction of the Court of Chancery. Stevens & Norton, 1846–49. 2 vols.

TURNER, R. W.
The equity of redemption. CUP, 1931. lxxi + 198p. (Cambridge studies in English legal history)

YALE, D. E. C.
Lord Nottingham's manual of Chancery practice and prolegomena of chancery and equity. CUP, 1965. xv + 385p.

c. Contract and tort

BARBOUR, W. T.
The history of contract in early English equity. OUP, 1914. 237p. (Oxford studies in social and legal history, vol. IV)

FIFOOT, C. H. S.
History and sources of the Common law: tort and contract. S, 1949. xvii + 446p.

FLETCHER, E. G. M.
The carrier's liability. S, 1932. xvi + 281p.

HOLDEN, J. M.
The history of negotiable instruments in English law. Athlone Pr., 1955. xxxix + 350p. (University of London legal series, no. 3)

JACKSON, R. M.
The history of quasi-contract in English law. CUP, 1936. xxxi + 134p. (Cambridge studies in English legal history)

KIRALFY, A. K. R.
The action on the case. SM, 1951. xxxi + 247p.

d. Criminal law

BELLAMY, J. G.
The law of treason in England in the later Middle Ages. CUP, 1970. xviii + 266p. (Cambridge studies in English legal history)

HUNNISETT, R. F.
The medieval coroner. CUP, 1961. xiii + 217p. (Cambridge studies in English legal history)

HURNARD, N. D.
The king's pardon for homicide before A.D. 1307. CUP, 1969. xiv + 394p.

KAYE, J. M.
Placita corone. Quaritch, 1966. xxxix + 42p. (Selden Society supplementary series, vol. 4)

PIKE, L. O.
A history of crime in England. Smith, Elder, 1873–76. 2 vols.

PLUCKNETT, T. F. T.
Edward I and criminal law. CUP, 1960. vii + 104p.

PUGH, R. B.
Imprisonment in medieval England. CUP, 1968. xvi + 420p. (Cambridge studies in English legal history)

RADZINOWICZ, L.
A history of the English criminal law and its administration from 1750. S, 1948–68. 4 vols.

STEPHEN, J. F.
A history of the criminal law of England. Macmillan, 1883. 3 vols.

e. Procedure and pleading

BOOTE, R.
An historical treatise of an action or suit at law, 7th ed. by G. T. White, 1839. 2 vols.

SUTTON, R.
Personal actions at common law. B, 1929. xv + 219p.

THAYER, J. B.
A preliminary treatise on evidence at the common law. Boston, Little, Brown, 1898. xxxvi + 636p.

f. Biographical and professional

ATLAY, J. B.
The Victorian chancellors. Smith, Elder, 1906–08. 2 vols.

BIRKS, M.
Gentlemen of the law. S, 1960. xi + 304p.
CAMPBELL, J., baron Campbell.
Lives of the chief justices of England, 3rd ed. Murray, 1874. 4 vols.
CAMPBELL, J., baron Campbell.
Lives of the lord chancellors, 5th ed. Murray, 1868. 10 vols.
COHEN, H. J.
A history of the English bar and attornatus to 1450. SM, 1929, reprinted 1967. x + 622p.
THE DICTIONARY OF NATIONAL BIOGRAPHY, FROM THE EARLIEST TIMES TO 1900, edited by Leslie Stephen and others. OUP, 1921-22, repr. 1967-68. 22 vols. (Originally published by Smith, Elder, 1885-1901, in 66 vols. Supplements covering 1900-1960 in 6 vols, each with cumulative index)
EDWARDS, J. L. J.
The law officers of the Crown. SM, 1964. xvii + 425p.
FIFOOT, C. H. S.
Lord Mansfield. OUP, 1936. vi + 262p.
Better than his account of the judges in twelve volumes is:
FOSS, E.
Biographia juridica: a biographical dictionary of the judges of England, 1066-1870. Murray, 1870. xv + 792p.
HEUSTON, R. F. V.
Lives of the lord chancellors, 1885-1940. OUP, 1964. xxiii + 632p.
KEETON, G. W.
Lord Chancellor Jeffreys and the Stuart cause. Macdonald, 1965. xviii, 19-553p.
ROBSON, R.
The attorney in eighteenth century England. CUP, 1959. xii + 182p. (Cambridge studies in English legal history)

IV. THE ARRANGEMENT OF ENGLISH LAW

1. GENERAL

English law has no authoritative arrangement such as in many countries is determined by a more or less complete codification. Thus all complete statements of the law are to a great extent alphabetical. Moreover, although the existence of several branches of the law is perfectly well recognized, the limits of each of them may depend on the opinion of each author dealing with them. If an author thinks he will make his book better or more useful by including or excluding some topic, he is at liberty to do so. Some subjects have little or no literature outside the great encyclopaedias. Indeed, a textbook normally contains either the topics regularly included in the examination curriculum of a particular subject or the material which a specialist in such a subject would expect it to contain.

To a great extent, of course, the subjects which demand a certain independence of treatment are the same as those well-known to Continental law, such as contracts, sale, company law, shipping, income tax, death duties. But there is no clear connection between them. At least no such connection appears in legal literature. This will probably surprise much more those Continental lawyers who are civilists or commercialists than those who are public lawyers. Indeed English law as a whole seems as formless as Continental public law.

Thus the arrangement adopted in this work is not authoritative. It represents merely that which the compilers regard as most suitable for its purpose, namely that of introducing foreign, and in particular Continental, lawyers to English law.

As in most countries, the most important breaks in the unity of law occur because the courts or other bodies administering the law are arranged in different hierarchies. It is accordingly very important to know where in England the breaks are.

The most important point to be noted by a Continental lawyer trying to understand the arrangement of subject-matter in English legal literature is that, since the celebrated Court of Star Chamber was abolished in 1641, there has never been any distinction between public and private law jurisdictions or in principle between public and private law themselves. There are no administrative courts exercising a general jurisdiction with regard to claims arising between the citizen and the state, but separate administrative tribunals for numerous different purposes have been created by a large number of statutes. Only some of these are however administrative courts in the Continental sense, i.e., tribunals adjudicating on claims based on the existing public law. Many, perhaps most, of them, are in fact administrative authorities acting in judicial form, i.e., authorities which through their own administrative acts create rights and duties but do so on the basis of proceedings resembling those of a court, and in some instances ordinary courts themselves act as administrative authorities in judicial form (e.g., in the law of liquor licences). Where administrative courts in the Continental sense adjudicate on existing claims or liabilities, an appeal from their decisions sometimes lies to the ordinary courts (e.g., in the law of income tax) but not always (not normally, e.g., in the law of social insurance). But whether this is the case or not, the ultimate control of the legality of administrative acts rests with the ordinary courts, and this is one of the main reasons why there is no recognized distinction between public and private law and why no independent literature in administrative law has been developed until recently: the remedies which correspond most closely to the French *recours pour excès de pouvoir*, known as "prohibition" and "certiorari", are remedies in the ordinary courts of law. Thus, although administrative tribunals are outside the hierarchy of the ordinary courts, the superior courts regard them as subject to their control and they consider the substantive law administered by administrative tribunals as part of the general law which is within the knowledge of the ordinary courts. They also control the ecclesiastical courts inasmuch as they prevent them from exceeding their jurisdiction, but they do not pretend to understand the substantive ecclesiastical law which they administer within their jurisdiction. It should be added that each House of Parliament exercises an independent jurisdiction in matters of parliamentary privilege.

On the other hand, the Continental lawyer will find the familiar distinction between civil and criminal courts (which are largely separate) and, correspondingly, between civil and criminal substantive law. It should be added, however, that the higher criminal courts and the higher civil courts are mainly staffed by the same judges and that the lowest courts, viz., the courts of summary jurisdiction, and the highest court, viz., the House of Lords, are both civil and criminal courts. The Continental lawyer will also find that civil procedure is much closer in type to criminal procedure than on the Continent and, consequently, an important part of the literature on procedure, especially the law of evidence, is largely common to both. The line between civil and criminal substantive law is not always drawn precisely at the same places as abroad, but essentially the distinction is that to which the Continental lawyer is accustomed.

Within the field of private law the Continental lawyer will look in vain for the distinction between civil and commercial law. It is true that in the Middle Ages the Law Merchant, a more or less international body of mercantile custom, was administered in separate courts and that later, when it began to be administered in the ordinary common law courts, it was treated as a fact to be found in each case by juries of merchants, but since the middle of the eighteenth century, commercial or mercantile law has been administered by these courts as law, i.e., it was merged in the common law and the earlier distinction between commercial and civil law has entirely disappeared in modern English Law. Thus there does not exist anything that could properly be called "*droit commercial*" or "*Handelsrecht*", i.e. (very few exceptions apart) there is no body of legal principles applicable to merchants as a class, and no difference, e.g., between mercantile and ordinary sales, partnerships, guarantees, etc., while the law of negotiable instruments and the law of bankruptcy apply to merchants and non-merchants alike. (There remain important vestiges of differences, chiefly concerning the bona fide acquisition of ownership from a non-owner.) Where English lawyers speak about "commercial law" or "mercantile law" they do so either (a) for procedural purposes because in the High Court a slightly different procedure applies to cases entered in the "commercial list", although the judge who decides these cases administers the same substantive law as any other judge, or (b) for pedagogic purposes because in some universities "mercantile" or "commercial" law is a teaching and examination subject, meaning those parts of the general law which are thought to be mainly of interest to business men. In fact the courses (and books) on commercial law include largely what is comprised under this heading on the Continent. It should be added that the former Court of Admiralty administered a separate body of admiralty law (covering certain aspects of maritime law) closely connected with the civil, i.e., the mediaeval Roman law. Admiralty law is now administered by the same civil courts as the common law, but it maintains a certain doctrinal independence, largely because the separate bar which formerly practised it has survived as such. This is a body of doctrines applying to collisions at sea, salvage, and kindred matters.

The Continental lawyer will find one distinction which does not correspond to anything to which he is accustomed, that between common law and equity, the nearest equivalent to which, within his own field of knowledge, is that between *jus civile* and *jus honorarium* in ancient Rome. Like the latter it can only be understood as referring to two different phases of historic growth. Whether a given topic belongs to the common law or to equity has little to do with the place of the particular subject within a systematically arranged body of legal principles, but much with the period in which the legal institution or principle in question originated. Formerly the distinction was of much greater importance because there were two different sets of courts administering the common law and equity, the latter being known as the Court of Chancery. These courts have been amalgamated for almost a century, but the old distinction survives in that between the "Queen's Bench Division" and the "Chancery Division" of the High Court, and hence in a certain doctrinal independence of the substantive rules, closely connected with the practice of barristers to specialize in the practice before either of these divisions.

These distinctions or absences of distinction are not always faithfully reflected in the literature of the law, though they are apt to leave traces where least expected. Thus there are separate books on commercial (or mercantile) law, but they often include an introduction describing the general law of contract, which would on the Continent be considered part of civil law. Again government is ordinarily so different in kind from private intercourse that public law subjects, such as public health and public assistance, are dealt with in different books from private law subjects, such as contract, but the responsibility of public authorities, whether arising from contract or otherwise, is for the most part treated as the same as that of private persons. On the other hand, the line between common law and equity tends to disappear, albeit slowly. There are still books which profess to deal with equity as a separate part of the law, but most books deal with separate subjects such as property or contract, and take both common law and equity in their stride.

It is as well to add a note about difficulties of terminology, which recall, though they are not the same as, those of Roman law. The term *common law* is often used to mark off English law, and all those laws, such as Canadian, Australian and American law, which are substantially derived from it, from the so-called *civil law*, which is largely of Roman origin. In this sense Irish law is a common law system, whereas Scots law is not.

Secondly, *common law* is distinguished from statute law, as being, not the product of legislation, but a body of rules and principles which can be inferred from the past decisions of courts of law.

Thirdly, it is distinguished from *equity*, as being the law made originally by the judges of the three courts of common law, together with the principles since developed in line with it, whereas equity is the corresponding product of the court of Chancery. Sometimes *common law* is made to include that part of statute law which amends common law rules or principles, as opposed to equity and the statutory modifications of equity.

Sometimes *common law* is even used to designate the parts of civil law which are of common law origin with the exception of the law of real (i.e., landed) property. It is in this sense that it was used in a few books which professed to treat of the common law, and when one speaks of a barrister as being a good common lawyer, one says nothing about his prowess in the realm of real property law.

Thus the meaning of *common law* (and indeed of *equity*) must, like that of *ius civile*, be determined according to the context in which it is used. Sometimes it excludes equity and statute law, sometimes equity but not statute law, sometimes statute law but not equity. Sometimes it is used in contradistinction to the civil law, sometimes to statute law, sometimes to equity. It never includes the civil law, canon law or ecclesiastical law. It is never used in contradistinction to other common law systems such as Irish or American law.

2. EQUITY

English equity differs from corresponding notions in other legal systems in that it never claimed to modify the rules of common law. Before 1876, equity was administered in a court (the Court of Chancery) separate from those in which common law disputes were tried. The Court of Chancery sought to achieve fair dealing between parties by taking the common law position as given, and issuing directions to the parties as to the manner of exercise, or prohibiting the exercise, of their acknowledged common law rights. Disobedience to such a direction was punishable, usually by imprisonment, as contempt of the Court of Chancery. If neither party resorted to the Court of Chancery, the common law would operate in full vigour even though the case might be one in which the rule of equity would (had it been invoked) have achieved a different result.

Unlike the common law, equity never set out to give an answer to every question: equity intervened only when the common law would lead to a decision conceived by the Court of Chancery to be contrary to conscience. This happened generally in the law of property, and always on the civil side.

In its early days, equity was a broad general notion—an approximation to a use of natural law in deciding litigation. During the seventeenth century it became common to refer to precedents, and reports of cases in the Court of Chancery began to be published. By the nineteenth century, equity was just as much subject to the doctrine of precedent as was the common law, and that remains true today. While the equitable solution to a given problem may generally be more satisfactory than that of the common law, this is not invariably so; equity is sometimes arbitrary and technical. The tendency now is to leave to the legislature the task of improving the law (including equity). Parliament, however, was not very active in this direction before the establishment of the Law Commission in 1965, and in some quarters, since the middle of this century, there has been a call for a new equity. But even the existing equity is still capable of development (as is the common law). For example, during recent years there have been considerable developments in the equitable rules relating to (i) occupation of houses by persons with no common law proprietary interest; and (ii) gratuitous agreements to vary contracts. On the other hand, the equitable right accorded by lower courts in the early 1950s to a deserted wife, to go on living in a house belonging to the husband as long as the marriage lasted, was severely curtailed by a House of Lords decision in 1965. This matter is now subject to special legislation.

Since 1875, common law and equity have been administered by the same judges. Cases are looked at from both points of view at the same time, and finally disposed of in one court. The statutes which brought about this result also provided that, in the event of a conflict between the rules of common law and equity with regard to any matter, the rules of equity were to prevail. There are reasons, however, why it is still necessary to know whether a rule is one of common law or of equity. Common law remedies are granted as of right, while equitable remedies are discretionary. This means that even where a case susceptible of equitable relief has been made out, the judge will decline to award that relief if satisfied that justice will be done by leaving the parties to the rules of the common law. Thus, an injunction (an equitable order that a wrongful act shall not be done) will not be issued to restrain a breach of contract if damages (the only common law remedy) for the breach will put the injured party in as satisfactory a position. It also means that where such a case for relief has been made out, the judge may refuse relief on the ground that the person seeking it has acted unconscionably in the transaction. The judge may, alternatively, grant relief on terms (where that would be equitable) that something be done in favour of the defendant by the successful plaintiff, such as restitution of gains when a contract is rescinded for mistake.

Another reason for continuing to distinguish between rules of common law and rules of equity is the doctrine of purchase for value without notice. If A has a common law estate in land, and B has an equitable interest in the same land (e.g. A holds on trust for B), and A transfers for value the common law estate to C, who neither knows nor negligently ignores the existence of B's right, then B has no right against C. Had B's right been based on the common law it would have been superior to C's right even though C had acted in good faith. (In respect of some types of property these rules have been superseded by a system of registration of dealings, priorities of successive dealings being determined by the order of registration.)

Equity jurisdiction can be roughly divided among four main heads—(1) Additional remedies where there is a common law cause of action, e.g., injunction, specific performance of contracts, ordering accounts, appointing receivers. (2) Rescission or modification of obligations which would be fully valid at common law, e.g., for fraud (of which equity took a much wider view than the common law), innocent misrepresentation, or mistake. (3) Equitable obligations regulating the exercise of common law rights ("fiduciary duties"). The chief creation of equity under this head is the trust. (4) Detailed rules of various kinds avoiding the arbitrariness of common law technicalities in dealings with property. The modern mortgage is an important example: equity, since the seventeenth century, has allowed a much more extensive right of redemption than that accorded to the mortgagor by the common law.

Select Bibliography

General books on equity (some including trusts)

ASHBURNER, W.

Principles of equity, 2nd ed. by D. Browne. B, 1933. xlix + 520 + 30p.

CLARK, G. L. ed.

Equity. Indianapolis, Bobbs-Merrill, 1954. 2 vols. (Vol. 1: Cases, Vol. 2: Text)

HANBURY, H. G.

Modern equity, 9th ed. by R. H. Maudsley. S, 1969. xcvi + 738p.

KEETON, G. W. and SHERIDAN, L. A.

Equity. Pitman, 1969. lxxx + 585p.

MAITLAND, F. W.

Equity, 2nd ed. by J. W. Brunyate. CUP, 1936, reprinted 1969. xxiv + 342p. (This volume is composed of the text of a course of lectures)

NEWMAN, R. A.
Equity and the law: a comparative study. New York, Oceana, 1961. 280p.

PETTIT, P. H.
Equity and the law of trusts. B, 1966. cxx + 491p.

POTTER, H.
An introduction to the history of equity and its courts. SM, 1931. v + 109p.

SNELL, E. H. T.
Principles of equity, 26th ed. by R. E. Megarry and P. V. Baker. SM, 1966. clxvii + 768p.

TILEY, J.
A casebook on equity and succession. SM, 1968. xxii + 432p. (Includes commentary)

YALE, D. E. C., ed.
Lord Nottingham's Chancery cases. Quaritch, for the Selden Society, 1957-61. 2 vols (Publications of the Selden Society, vols 73 and 79)

Assignment of choses in action

MARSHALL, O. R.
The assignment of choses in action. Pitman, 1950. xxiv + 216p.

Fraud

ARENSON, J. T.
The doctrine of undue influence in Anglo-American law. Leiden, Groen en Zoon, 1953. vi + 77p.

KERR, W. W.
Kerr on the law of fraud and mistake, 7th ed. by D. L. McDonnell and J. G. Monroe. SM, 1952. liv + 738p.

SHERIDAN, L. A.
Fraud in equity: a study in English and Irish law. Pitman, 1957. xliii + 235p.

Powers of appointment

FARWELL, Sir G.
A concise treatise on powers, 3rd ed. by C. J. W. Farwell and F. K. Archer. S, 1916. lxxx + 767p.

Remedies

FRY, E.
A treatise on the specific performance of contracts, 6th ed. by G. R. Northcote. S, 1921. l + 741 + 108p.

KERR, W. W.
Kerr on the law and practice as to receivers, 13th ed. by R. Walton. SM, 1963. lvi + 386p.

KERR, W. W.
A treatise on the law and practice of injunctions, 6th ed. by J. M. Paterson. SM, 1927. lxiv + 743p.

V. THE ADMINISTRATION OF JUSTICE

1. THE ORGANIZATION OF THE COURTS

The English courts of law are customary in origin, administering justice in the name of the ruling monarch, in whose name all judges are appointed. In the course of time the courts have been the subject of legislation, such as the Supreme Court of Judicature and Administration of Justice Acts and the Courts Act, and several statutes on the criminal courts such as the Criminal Justice Acts of 1948 and 1967 and the Criminal Appeal Act 1968. However, none of these laws is comprehensive and reference to textbooks for a more systematic treatment is necessary

In principle there are separate hierarchies of civil and criminal courts, following different procedures, but this separation does not always extend to the judges themselves. Thus the same High Court judge may try both civil and criminal cases on circuit (see below). Some domestic disputes are tried by criminal magistrates, under the Matrimonial Proceedings (Magistrates' Courts) Act 1960. On the other hand most family law matters are civil and have been dealt with by the High Court (see below), and some divorce jurisdiction is exercised by the local (civil) county courts under the Matrimonial Causes Act 1967.

The administration of civil justice has tended to remain centralized in the High Court in London and, although a system of civil courts in provincial cities is to be created, judges are at present sent out from time to time into the provinces to try civil cases on circuit. A system of county courts was set up in the last century and there are now 90 county court judges, several of them sitting in several court houses. Their upper limit of jurisdiction is £750 in most cases. The High Court consisted of three separate divisions, the Queen's Bench trying debt and civil injury cases, the Chancery, trying various property disputes, and until 1971 the Probate, Divorce and Admiralty Division, trying miscellaneous matters originating in canon and Civil law rather than traditional English law. This last Division has been replaced by a Family Division, so far as its domestic jurisdiction is concerned; its other business being assigned to the other two Divisions of the High Court.

The most serious crimes (tried formally, on indictment) were tried by High Court judges at Assizes several times a year. Offences next in order of gravity were tried at Quarter Sessions, held four or eight times a year, sitting with a legally trained chairman and lay magistrates. The whole hierarchy of criminal courts has been re-planned and a Crown Court is being set up which will try serious crimes and which will operate in different parts of the country. Minor offences are tried less formally by lay magistrates, advised on legal matters by a professional lawyer acting as their clerk. The appointment and removal of lay magistrates is regulated by the Justices of the Peace Acts 1949 and 1968. In many cases an accused person may elect to be tried at a higher court instead.

Trial by jury is limited in civil cases to a few types of claim, including libel. It is invariable in criminal trials in the Crown Courts but is not used in magistrates' courts. The jury is not used in appeal courts.

Trial judges in England are invariably appointed from members of the practising Bar. Judges of appeal courts are normally promoted from the High Court Bench but occasionally directly appointed from the Bar.

Appeals from judgments in the High Court and the Crown Courts go to the Court of Appeal. In 1966 this court, set up as a civil court of appeal in 1875, merged with the former Court of Criminal Appeal, originally established in 1907. This system of appeals will be effected by the setting up of the Crown Court which has already been verified. A Divisional Court of the Queen's Bench Division hears appeals on points of law from Magistrates' courts.

Final appeal lies to the House of Lords, at one time the same as the House of Parliament of that name, but now a court of professional judges regulated by the Appellate Jurisdiction Acts of 1876 and 1947. It has heard civil appeals from early times but criminal appeals in indictable cases only since 1907 and criminal appeals from magistrates' courts only since the Administration of Justice Act 1960. A direct appeal from the High Court, by-passing the Court of Appeal, has been possible since 1 January 1970, in appropriate cases.

For the sake of efficiency, business managers are now being appointed in the High Court to deal with routine administration.

Select Bibliography

ABEL-SMITH, B. and STEVENS, R.

Lawyers and the courts: a sociological study of the English legal system 1750-1965. Heinemann, 1967. xiv + 501p.

ARCHER, P.

The Queen's courts, 2nd ed. Penguin Books, 1963. x + 293p.

GRAVESON, R. H., ed.

Law: an outline for the intending student. Routledge & Kegan Paul, 1967. vi + 207p.

HANBURY, H. G.

English courts of law, 4th ed. OUP, 1967. vii + 152p.

JACKSON, R. M.

The machinery of justice in England, 5th ed. CUP, 1967. xii + 494p.

KIRALFY, A. K. R.

The English legal system, 4th ed. SM, 1967. xvii + 342p.

WALKER, R. J. and WALKER, M. G.

The English legal system, 2nd ed. B, 1970. xxix + 520p.

ZANDER, M., ed.

What's wrong with the law? BBC, 1970. ix + 126p. (Revised version of nine talks given on the BBC third programme)

2. THE LEGAL PROFESSION

The legal profession in England is divided into two distinct branches, barristers and solicitors.

This dichotomy, which is not endemic in a common law system, is attributable to the distinction made at an early date in English legal history between the attorney, who appeared in court merely as the representative of the litigant, and the advocate, who pleaded and put his case before the court. The distinction is perpetuated today by the rule that no person may be both barrister and solicitor at the same time, although a member of one branch may quit it in order to proceed to the other and such interchange is not infrequent.

Before proceeding to outline how the two branches differ essentially in organization and functions, one may indicate certain features which they have in common.

Both barristers and solicitors constitute professions in that they impose strict qualifications for admission to their ranks and are protected from usurpation of their functions or exploitation of their titles by the unadmitted. Admission is open to adult persons of either sex and is unrestricted in point of number. British nationality is required for a solicitor, but not for a barrister. Both sides of the profession include many who do not practise as barristers or solicitors but hold posts, not necessarily legal, in central and local government services, the universities, and private business.

In legal precedence, solicitors rank second to barristers; in this note, however, they may be more conveniently treated first. Unlike the higher branch of the profession, solicitors are officers of the Supreme Court and, as such, subjected to strict statutory control regarding their admission, remuneration, conduct, book-keeping and accounts. Breaches of professional conduct and ethics come before a Disciplinary Committee nominated by the Master of the Rolls, who is the president of the Court of Appeal. The general control and welfare of solicitors is in the hands of the Law Society, which is a body incorporated by charter and composed exclusively of solicitors, although membership is not obligatory. By statute the Law Society is also charged with the administration of the legal aid and advice scheme under which the services of barristers and solicitors may be obtained free or on a contributory basis, according to one's means. In addition to, and independent of, the Law Society, whose headquarters are in London, there are a number of provincial law societies, some of greater antiquity, who look after the interests of solicitors in their particular locality.

Against this professional background, the individual solicitor may practise in various capacities. He may be employed at a salary either by another solicitor or by a local authority, government department, or commercial enterprise; he may be a partner in a firm of solicitors; or he may practise on his own account having either purchased an established practice or started a new venture of his own—for there is no limit on the number of practices.

The work of a solicitor is very varied. The distinction from the barrister is most marked in litigation. In the superior courts (with minor exceptions) the barrister alone has a right of audience, that is, a right to plead for a client who desires legal representation before the court, while the solicitor has no more than a right to practise, that is, to carry through the procedural steps in the action. The role of the solicitor is here close to that of the early attorney; it is also one of liaison between the lay client and the barrister. Thus, in a civil action, it is the solicitor to whom the client will first go for advice: the solicitor will gather the evidence and prepare the case for submission to a barrister of his own choosing whom he will ask to advise on the prospects of successful litigation. The solicitor will report "counsel's opinion" to his client and, if the client so instructs, take the necessary procedural steps to commence the action and bring it on for hearing. At this stage, counsel's part is confined to the "settling of the pleadings", that is, the drafting of the documents required to be exchanged between the litigants prior to the hearing in order to narrow the points at issue between them; should counsel desire a conference with the client it must take place in the presence of the solicitor. The filing of papers in the office or registry of the court and the correspondence with the opposing litigant or his solicitors are carried out by the solicitor. At the actual hearing, counsel will conduct the case and plead for the lay client.

In certain inferior courts the solicitor, too, has a right of audience and so may himself plead as his client's advocate, although even in these courts he or his client will often prefer to entrust the advocacy to a barrister. Nevertheless, most of the advocacy in petty sessional and county courts is done by solicitors, a fact which blurs the sharpness of the distinction between the two branches of the profession.

It is not only in litigation that the solicitor acts as the link between the barrister and the lay client. In general, in both contentious and non-contentious matters, it is contrary to the rules of the Bar for its members to receive instructions except through the medium of a solicitor. The strictness of the rule requiring the solicitor's intervention is emphasized by the narrowness of the exceptions.

Besides his role as intermediary between barrister and client, the solicitor has a virtual monopoly of conveyancing, that is, the preparation of documents (usually under seal) for the transfer or mortgaging of landed property and sometimes also of movable property; though in complicated cases barristers are consulted and sometimes act as draftsmen. The administration of estates is also his exclusive preserve, and, with conveyancing, often forms the most lucrative side of his practice. He is also active in the drafting of wills, the formation of companies, and the administering of trusts, and clients frequently appoint him trustee of their property or executor of their wills. Moreover, there is hardly any aspect of human affairs upon which his advice will not sometimes be sought, be it the investment of a fortune or the barking of a neighbour's dog.

The documents which a solicitor prepares, even where their preparation is by law his monopoly, do not have any special evidential value simply by virtue of his participation.[1] As in the civil law countries, this quality of authenticity can only be conferred by the seal and signature of a notary public. Most notaries public in England are also practising solicitors: the few who are not constitute the only exception to the twofold division of the English legal profession, but this exception is not of great importance, as English law makes little use of notarial instruments except in matters of bills of exchange and maritime law and where documents are intended for transmission abroad. A solicitor may also hold the distinct office of Commissioner for Oaths, before whom affidavits and declarations are made for various evidential purposes.

Barristers, it will now be realized, operate in a more restricted field. Their most publicized function is that of advocates in the superior courts, where they enjoy an exclusive right of audience for those litigants (the vast majority) who do not elect to conduct their own case. They also plead in the inferior courts, in which their right of audience is shared by solicitors. In either class of court they will have received their instructions from a solicitor, who will also carry out the various procedural steps in consultation, where necessary, with the barrister who is "briefed".

Many barristers take little or no part in litigation. Some amass a minute knowledge of some particular branch of the law upon which solicitors draw for the guidance of their clients and themselves. Others devote themselves to the technicalities of drafting and assist solicitors to effectuate the most complicated wishes of their clients. To borrow medical terms, barristers are the specialists of the law, solicitors its general practitioners—though this is not invariably true.

Barristers, wherever they practise,[2] must belong to one of the four Inns of Court.[3] These are ancient unincorporated societies situated in London and enjoying the management of their own affairs free from any state control but subject to a shadowy supervisory power vested in the judges. Each Inn is autonomous under the government of its Benchers, but the regulations relating to admission and call

---

[1]In French terminology they are *actes sous seings privés*, not *actes authentiques*.

[2]Some practise exclusively in London; others attach themselves to provincial circuits, where they belong to the Circuit Bar Mess and become subject to its Circuit Rules. About one quarter of the practising Bar have their chambers in provincial towns.

[3]Lincoln's Inn, Inner Temple, Middle Temple, Gray's Inn.

to the Bar are now common to all four and administered by a joint body, the Senate of the Inns of Court. The Senate enforces a strict but non-statutory code of professional discipline and etiquette. In addition, the General Council of the Bar, elected by the profession as a whole, watches over the general interests of the Bar, especially in the matter of remuneration.

The Bar is a liberal profession in that its members must be ready to give their services without charge. Their services being in theory gratuitous, they are not allowed to sue for their fees, which are not contractually owed but in the nature of *honoraria*. However, they can insist on their payment in advance. As against this, a barrister cannot be sued for the negligent discharge of his duties in the conduct of litigation. A solicitor, on the other hand, can both sue for his fees and be sued for negligence. Nor can barristers practise in partnership or be employed by each other; they may, however, group themselves in chambers and share the use of a common secretariat and clerk.

There are two grades of barrister, Queen's Counsel, who are the leading members of the profession, and Juniors. Elaborate rules govern the relations between the two grades in order to ensure a fair distribution of work. High Court Judges are usually recruited from Queen's Counsel, and elevation to "the Bench" is regarded as the consummation of a barrister's career.[4]

---

[4]This principle of promotion from Bar to Bench is a most striking feature of the administration of justice in England. Solicitors are only eligible for a limited range of judicial appointments.

Select Bibliography

General

The first five books are simple reading for beginners:

HANBURY, H. G.
English courts of law, 4th ed. OUP, 1967. vii + 152p. (Chapter 10)

HARVEY, C. P.
The advocate's devil. S, 1958. xi + 166p.

JACKSON, R. M.
The machinery of justice in England, 5th ed. CUP, 1967. xii + 494p.

RADCLIFFE, G. R. Y. and CROSS, A. G. N., Baron Cross of Chelsea
The English legal system, 5th ed. by Lord Cross of Chelsea and G. D. G. Hall. B, 1971. x + 472p. (Chapter 21)

STEPHEN, H. J.
Commentaries on the laws of England, 21st ed. Editor-in-chief: L. C. Warmington. B, 1950. 4 vols. (Suppl.) (Vol. 3: book 1, pt. 4)

WILLIAMS, G. L.
Learning the law, 8th ed. S, 1969. ix + 220p.

Further reading

ABEL-SMITH, B. and STEVENS, R.
Lawyers and the courts: a sociological study of the English legal system 1750-1965. Heinemann, 1967. xiv + 501p.

ALLEN, F. J.
The law as a vocation. Cambridge, Mass., Harvard UP, 1924. viii + 83p.

CARR-SAUNDERS, Sir A. M. and WILSON, P. A.
The professions. OUP, 1933. viii + 536p. (2nd impression, Cass, 1964)

CLAY, J. L. and others
The young lawyer. B, 1955. vii + 167 + 8p.

DU CANN, C. G. L.
The legal profession: barristers and solicitors. Ross, 1945. 64p.

EMERY, G. F.
Relations between barristers and solicitors and the public or lawyers and their clients, 3rd ed. Pitman, 1930. 131p.

GOWER, L. C. B.
"The organisation and remuneration of the English and French legal professions", in *A comparison of English and French law and legal procedure,* being a series of papers discussed at the Anglo-French legal conference held in London, June 1947 (The Law Society, 1947), pp. 43-59

HALSBURY'S LAWS OF ENGLAND, 3rd ed. B, 1952-64. 43 vols. (Suppl.) (Vol. 3: Barristers; vol. 28: Notaries; vol. 36: Solicitors)

LUND, Sir T. G.
The practice and etiquette of the Bar affecting solicitors. The Law Society, 1953. 30p.

MEGARRY, R. E.
Lawyer and litigant in England. S, 1962. x + 205p. (Hamlyn lectures, no. 14)

SWEET & MAXWELL, LTD
Guide to a career in the law, 7th ed. SM, 1971. vii + 85p.

ZANDER, M.
Lawyers and the public interest. Weidenfeld & Nicolson, 1968. xi + 342p.

Solicitors

ABRAHAMS, G.
The legal mind: an approach to the dynamics of advocacy. H.F.L., 1954. xii + 252p.

BIRKS, M.
Gentlemen of the law. S, 1960. xi + 304p.

CHRISTIAN, E. B. V.
Solicitors: an outline of their history. S, 1925. 166p.

CORDERY, A.
Law relating to solicitors, 6th ed. by G. J. Graham-Green. B, 1968. cxxxvii + 769p. (Suppl.)

EDDY, J. P.
Professional negligence. S, 1955. xii + 146p.

FRANQUEVILLE, A. C. F., comte de
"Les avoués en Angleterre", in *Séances et travaux de l'Académie des Sciences Morales et Politiques (Institut de France),* nouvelle série, 33 (1890), premier semestre, (cxxxiii[e] de la collection): pp. 390-418

HERBERT, D.
The law as to solicitors: based on the Solicitors' Act, 1932. Eyre and Spottiswoode, 1932. xxii + 322p.

LAW SOCIETY'S DIGEST. The Law Society, 1954. xl + 639p. (Suppl.) (Vol. 1: Conveyancing practice and costs)

THE LAW SOCIETY
Records of the Society of Gentlemen Practisers in the courts of law and equity called The Law Society. The Law Society, 1897. cxiii + 360p.

LOCK, H. O.
Advice to a young solicitor. S, 1946. vi + 71p.

LUND, Sir T. G.

The Solicitors' Act, 1941. B, 1943. xiii + 136 + 15p.

ROBSON, R.

The attorney in eighteenth century England. CUP, 1959. xii + 182p. (Cambridge studies in English legal history)

SUPREME COURT PRACTICE. SM, S and B. 2 vols. (Published triennially, but with half-yearly cumulative supplements)

Notaries

BROOKE, R.

Treatise on the office and practice of a notary of England with a collection of precedents, 6th ed. by J. Charlesworth. S, 1939. xv + 464p.

Barristers

BLAND, D. S.

A bibliography of the Inns of Court and Chancery. Selden Society, 1965. xi + 75p. (Selden Society supplementary series, vol. 3)

BOULTON, W. W.

A guide to conduct and etiquette at the Bar of England and Wales, 5th ed. B, 1971. viii + 107p.

COHEN, H. J.

A history of the English Bar and attornatus to 1450. SM, 1929, reprinted 1967. x + 622p.

DAWSON, J. P.

"The growth and decline of English case law", in *The oracles of the law* (Ann Arbor, Univ. of Michigan Law School, 1968), pp. 1-99

DU CANN, R.

The art of the advocate. Penguin Books, 1964. 183p.

FRANQUEVILLE, A. C. F., comte de

"Le barreau anglais", in *Séances et travaux de l'Académie des Sciences Morales et Politiques (Institut de France)*, nouvelle série, 32 (1889), deuxième semestre, (cxxxii^e de la collection): pp. 529-72 and 728-64

MARCHANT, J. R. V.

An essay on the legal position of counsel in England. Clowes, 1905. xiii + 179p.

MORRIS, Sir H. S.

The barrister. Bles, 1930. 192p.

WROTTESLEY, Sir F. J.

Letters to a young barrister. SM, 1930. iii + 115p.

3. LEGAL EDUCATION: ENGLAND AND WALES

The pattern of legal education in England and Wales has been formed by two factors of central importance. These are the past exclusion of English law from the ancient universities and the division of the legal profession into two branches, each with its own professional organization. English law did not become part of the regular academic curriculum until the late nineteenth century. Even today the universities have no part in the professional training of solicitors and barristers. Responsibility not only for regulating conditions of admission but also for teaching and examining rests with the Law Society (solicitors) and the Council of Legal Education (barristers). The work of instruction for professional examinations is carried out in two law schools under the control of these two bodies.

Law as an academic discipline

Academic degree courses in law are provided in the great majority of universities in England and Wales. In most universities law is studied (for three years) as an honours degree course in isolation from other subjects. In some universities legal studies are combined with other relevant disciplines. There has been a remarkable growth since 1945 in the size and number of law faculties and departments. The regulations of the Law Society and the Council of Legal Education now give considerable advantages to law graduates, and a law degree has come to be accepted as the first stage in legal education. Academic lawyers have their own professional organization, the Society of Public Teachers of Law. Membership is largely confined to university teachers. The Society, among its other activities, publishes a *Journal* which devotes rather more space to the problems of legal education than do other law journals. Postgraduate study and research in law has flourished in a special way in Oxford, Cambridge and London Universities. The Institute of Advanced Legal Studies was established in 1945 by London University to provide advanced library facilities and other research services for legal scholars in the United Kingdom and from elsewhere.

Academic law teaching is also conducted in a large number of technical colleges and colleges of commerce for students preparing for the external degree in law of London University, or for the degree of the Council of National Academic Awards. The Association of Law Teachers was formed in 1965 primarily to serve the interests of law teachers outside the universities. It publishes a *Journal*, the *Law Teacher*, and a bi-monthly *Bulletin*.

Professional education and training: Barristers

By tradition the legal education of bar students was one of the main functions of the four Inns of Court. The intending barrister must still join one of these Inns and must "keep term" by dining in the Hall of his Inn for a period of three years before he may be "called to the bar" by that Inn. A graduate may be called to the bar after "keeping term" for two years and complete his third year after call. Today, however, the rest of his legal education is controlled on behalf of the Inns by the Council of Legal Education. The teaching side of the Council's work is carried out in the Inns of Court School of Law.

The Council is currently (in the period 1969-1972) introducing a new system of courses of instruction and examination syllabuses. These are designed to modernize and raise the standards of legal education for barristers. This new scheme makes a sharp distinction between the educational stage (Part I) and the training stage (Part II). Part I includes most of the basic subjects covered in university law courses. Consequently, a law degree in which these subjects are covered gains exemption from the Part I examinations. For non-graduates new requirements of admission to an Inn have been introduced which are equivalent to university entrance standards. The Part II courses and examinations will concentrate upon teaching professional techniques. This will be accompanied by practical exercises in advocacy and work in chambers. These exercises will be compulsory for those intending to practise in England and Wales, and are intended to be a preparation for pupillage. A period of at least six months as pupil of an experienced barrister in chambers is still required before starting ordinary practice at the English Bar. Attendance at the lectures and tutorials provided by the Inns of Court School of Law is not compulsory for Part I but, after 1970, it will be compulsory to attend the Part II courses for those intending to practise in England and Wales.

Professional education and training: Solicitors

The Law Society requires intending solicitors to pass Part I of its qualifying examination in the basic legal subjects, but law graduates are exempted. Practical training takes the form of articles of apprenticeship to an experienced solicitor. For the non-graduate this must be for a term of five years, but graduates need only serve in articles for two years. Law graduates have the further privilege of being entitled, if they wish, to take Part II of this Qualifying Examination before entering on articles. The Part II syllabus consists of the more specialized and practical subjects. Courses of instruction for the Law Society's examinations are given by the Society's College of Law in London and Guildford (and elsewhere by certain recognized institutions). Attendance at the courses leading to the Part I examinations is compulsory for those entering articles without a university degree.

Problems of legal education

There has been a growing awareness of the need to reform the structure and methods of both academic and professional legal education. There has been considerable criticism of the system of articles and of pupillage in giving effective practical training. There has also been criticism of the qualities tested by the professional examinations. In the universities there is a growing demand from staff as well as students to reform the examination system and to include relevant arts and social science courses in the law degree syllabus. It is also widely argued that legal education should be better integrated, both as between the two branches of the profession and as between university education and professional training. The whole question of legal education has been recently considered by the Lord Chancellor's Committee on Legal Education under the Chairmanship of Mr Justice Ormrod, but the report has appeared too late for its criticisms and recommendations to be considered in this account.

Further information

Further information about regulations governing admission as a solicitor or barrister, and about the courses in preparation for professional examinations, can be obtained from the following:

The Council of Legal Education, Gray's Inn Place, London, WC1R 5DU
The Law Society, 113 Chancery Lane, London, WC2A 1PL
The Secretary, The College of Law, Braboeuf Manor, Guildford, Surrey

Select Bibliography

History

HOLDSWORTH, Sir W. S.
History of English law. Methuen, 1903-66, reprinted 1966. 16 vols. (Various editions) (Vol. 6: chapter 8, p. 431)

PLUCKNETT, T. F. T.
A concise history of the Common law, 5th ed. B, 1956. xxvi + 746 + 56p. (Part II: chapter 12)

General

ABEL-SMITH, B. and STEVENS, R.
Lawyers and the courts: a sociological study of the English legal system 1750-1965. Heinemann, 1967. xiv + 501p. (Chapters 7 and 13)

GARDINER, G. A. and MARTIN, A.
Law reform now. Gollanz, 1963. x + 302p. (Chapter XI)

GOWER, L. C. B.
"English legal training: a critical survey", in *Modern law review*, 13 (1950): pp. 137-205

HAMSON, C. J.
"The teaching of law: reflections prompted by the UNESCO enquiry 1950-52", in *Journal of the Society of Public Teachers of Law*, 2 (1952/54): pp. 19-30

JOURNAL OF THE SOCIETY OF PUBLIC TEACHERS OF LAW, 1924– . B. (1938–47, not published)

KAHN-FREUND, O.
"Reflections on legal education", in *Modern law review*, 29 (1966): pp. 121-36

LAW TEACHER, vol. 1- , 1967- . SM. (1967-70, entitled *Journal of the Association of Law Teachers*)

TWINING, W.
"Pericles and the plumber: prolegomena to a working theory for lawyer education", in *Law quarterly review*, 83 (1967): pp. 396-426

WILSON, J. F.
"A survey of legal education in the United Kingdom", in *Journal of the Society of Public Teachers of Law*, 9 (1966/67): pp. 1-144

ZANDER, M.
Lawyers and the public interest. Weidenfeld & Nicolson, 1968. xi + 342p. (Chapter 2)

Academic legal education

GREAT BRITAIN. Committee on Legal Education (Chairman: Mr. Justice Ormrod)
Report. HMSO, 1971. 249p. (Cmnd 4595)

HEALEY, F. G. and others
"Programmed instruction, teaching machines, and their possible uses in teaching law", in *Journal of the Society of Public Teachers of Law*, 8 (1964/65): pp. 275-83

MAHER, F. K. H.
"The teaching of first year law students", in *Journal of the Society of Public Teachers of Law*, 10 (1968/69): pp. 195-210

SOCIETY OF PUBLIC TEACHERS OF LAW
"Memorandum . . . to the Committee on Legal Education", in *Journal of the Society of Public Teachers of Law*, 10 (1968/69): pp. 157-68. (Also included in GREAT BRITAIN. Committee on Legal Education. *Report*, pp. 224-31. *See supra*)

TAYLOR, A. and others
"Law and the social sciences"; [a symposium comprising five papers], in *Journal of the Society of Public Teachers of Law*, 9 (1966/67): pp. 328-70

WILSON, G. P.
"The concept of a law degree: getting on with the job", in *Journal of the Society of Public Teachers of Law*, 10 (1968/69): pp. 114-18

Professional legal education

ELLIOTT, D. W.
"An enquiry into the training of graduate articled clerks", in *Journal of the Society of Public Teachers of Law*, 7 (1962/63): pp. 199-203

GREAT BRITAIN. Committee on Legal Education for Students from Africa (Chairman: Lord Denning)
Report. HMSO, 1961. 31p. (Cmnd 1255)

MEGARRY, R. E.

"Law as taught and law as practised", in *Journal of the Society of Public Teachers of Law*, 9 (1966/67): pp. 176-89

4. LEGAL EDUCATION: SCOTLAND

In Scotland, although there is also a divided legal profession, legal education is more closely integrated. University law courses provide complete exemption from professional examinations. Most practitioners hold a law degree and no professional law schools exist.

Law is taught in the Universities of Glasgow, Aberdeen, Edinburgh, Dundee and Strathclyde. The law student may read either for an ordinary LL.B. in a course of three years' duration or for an honours LL.B. in four years. Both degrees can contain some courses in arts and social science subjects, but the honours degree allows more concentration on advanced legal subjects. The universities also provide postgraduate courses in those subjects, required for admission to the profession, which have not been taken by the student in his degree course.

Advocates

Admission to the Bar is controlled by the Faculty of Advocates. A law graduate must serve a period of 21 months in a solicitors' office and thereafter a nine months period of pupillage (commonly known as devilling). An entrant who does not hold a law degree is required to sit the professional examinations.

Solicitors

The Law Society requires a period of apprenticeship of two years in the case of a law graduate followed by a post qualifying year in which the candidate is an admitted solicitor but cannot practise as a principal. A person who holds degrees in arts and law is not required to serve a post qualifying year. A non-graduate must serve an apprenticeship of five years and pass the Law Society's professional examinations.

Problems of legal education

As in England, the system of legal education is undergoing critical review. The Law Society of Scotland is considering a closer regulation of the practical training given during the apprenticeship. The universities are contemplating an extension of a degree course to four years in all cases so that more arts and social science courses can be included in the curriculum.

Further information

Further information about regulations of admission to the legal profession can be obtained from the following:

The Clerk of Faculty, Advocates Library, Parliament House, Edinburgh EH1 1RJ.

The Law Society of Scotland, Law Society's Hall, 26/27 Drumsheugh Gardens, Edinburgh EH3 7YR.

Select Bibliography

SMITH, T. B.

Scotland: the development of its laws and constitution, revised ed. S, 1962. xx + 980p. (The British Commonwealth: the development of its laws and constitutions, vol. 11) (pp. 108-15)

WALKER, D. M.

"Legal studies in the Scottish universities", in *Juridical review*, 1957: pp. 21-41 and 151-79

WILSON, J. F.

"A survey of legal education in the United Kingdom", in *Journal of the Society of Public Teachers of Law*, 9 (1966/67): pp. 1-144. (Section E: Legal education in Scotland)

VI. CIVIL LITIGATION

1. CIVIL PROCEDURE

The outstanding feature of the English system of civil procedure is the process of the trial of an action. This takes place by the unfolding of the oral evidence of the witnesses called by the parties, and it is given in the form of answers to oral questions put by way of examination and of cross-examination by the opposite party before a single Judge sitting in open court. (The trial of civil cases by a Judge sitting with a jury is now extremely rare.) What Sir Maurice Amos called the "Day in Court" becomes the climax of the action, and compels the strict concentration on the oral hearing which is held in one continuous unbroken sequence, if necessary day by day, from the start to the finish, when generally the Judge will immediately deliver an extempore oral judgment. The English system is thus dominated by the principles of orality, immediacy and finality, and conversely it provides minimal scope for adducing written evidence at the trial or for the trial to be part heard and adjourned from time to time.

The corollary of the system of oral trials is the sharp demarcation between the stages of pre-trial and trial, which constitutes another characteristic feature of the English system. The object of the pre-trial procedure is precisely to enable or require the parties to prepare their cases for trial as fully as they may, so as to eliminate all procedural problems from the trial itself. The pre-trial stage thus encompasses the entire range of the procedural processes before judgment is given, other than the actual hearing of the oral evidence of the witnesses and the oral arguments on the case. It covers all the procedural steps concerning the commencement of proceedings; the joinder of parties and of causes of action; the formulation of the claims and defences of the parties in the form of *Pleadings*, which play a predominant role in English procedure; the *Discovery* or disclosure and production of all relevant documents, which goes considerably further than the production of documents in most continental countries; the exchange or possible exchange of experts' and particularly medical reports; the administering of *Interrogatories* (questions) to obtain evidence from the opposite party; the examination or inspection of any property or thing which is the subject-matter of the action or the taking of samples or the carrying out of any observations or experiments; and a whole series of provisional or interlocutory remedies designed to preserve the *status quo*, of which the more important instances are the *Interim Injunction* and the preservation and detention of the subject-matter of the action.

The crucial focal point of the pre-trial stage is the *Summons for Directions*, which is intended to provide a robust occasion for "stock-taking" under the guidance or direction of the Master of the Supreme Court, for the purpose of ensuring that all preliminary matters have been or will be completed before the trial.

The preparation for trial is the responsibility of the parties, and not the Court. It is the parties themselves who must take all the steps and measures necessary for this purpose, including any steps to ensure that the opposite party complies with his obligations under the Rules or the Orders of the Court. The English Court has no machinery (except to some extent in the Chancery Division of the High Court) for the preparation of a "*dossier*" on the case for submission to or use by the trial court, nor has it any investigating powers of its own nor any machinery for conducting a separate or independent investigation into the dispute between the parties. The role of the English court, at the pre-trial stage no less than at the trial stage itself, is entirely passive, so that it intervenes only to ensure that the proceedings are being conducted fairly between the parties, and it does not of its own motion take any steps in the proceedings, e.g. call a witness or appoint a court expert. It is the responsibility of the parties to call what witnesses they want and in what order and this extends to expert witnesses as well. The English court acts as a kind of umpire in deciding the disputes between the parties and thus operates what is called "the Adversary System" of civil procedure.

The English system provides a wide variety of procedures for the disposal of civil cases without a trial and indeed, as the *Civil Judicial Statistics* show, the great majority of such proceedings are so disposed of. Apart from the settlement or compromise of actions, these procedures include the *Default Procedure*, under which a party who is in default in complying with the Rules of Court or an Order of the Court may have judgment entered against him without further Order or reference to the Court; *Summary Judgment*, under which the plaintiff may obtain a judgment without a trial on satisfying the Court that the defendant has no defence nor even any issue or question worthy of trial; *Summary Disposal*, under which the Court has power under the Rules or its inherent jurisdiction to strike out claims or defences which are hopeless and clearly not maintainable; *Dismissal for Want of Prosecution*, which the Court has power to order where the plaintiff has been guilty of prolonged delay which has occasioned prejudice to the defendant.

The range of remedies which the English Courts can award is wide and flexible, and reflects the predominant influence which remedies exert in the English system of procedure. The remedies may be provisional or final, legal or equitable, discretionary or as of right, and may be awarded to the plaintiff or the defendant as the circumstances of the case may warrant.

On the other hand, the methods of execution upon goods and the other modes of the enforcement of Judgments and Orders are extremely complicated and complex and present a somewhat archaic, if not also chaotic state of the law. A recent Report on the Enforcement of Judgment Debts may, if implemented, produce order and simplicity in what at present constitutes a rather difficult and complex branch of procedural law.

The Appellate system operates on the principle that the judgment at First Instance is correct and the burden is on the party attacking it to satisfy the Appellate Court that it is wrong. On this basis, the parties are generally not allowed to introduce new or fresh evidence on appeal except within well-settled principles nor is the appellant allowed to raise any point or question which he has not raised in the Court below. In this way, the English system achieves a high degree of finality in the decisions at First Instance, while at the same time reducing the volume of appeals, especially on questions of fact.

2. COSTS

In England, the problem of costs is of paramount importance in civil procedure, not only as a factor in the relationship between the client and his lawyer, but as between the opposing parties in litigation. It has been said that costs is a pervasive factor which casts its dark shadow over the whole field of civil litigation. The governing rule, which is called the indemnity rule, is that "costs follow the event", which means that in general the unsuccessful party is required to pay the costs of the successful party. Moreover, in the High Court at any rate, it is not possible to predict at the beginning of an action what the costs will be at the end, with the result that the longer the action proceeds, the more the costs become a stake in the action itself. Costs may be awarded at all stages of an action, and there are several bases for the award of costs, e.g. party and party (which is the indemnity rule), costs on the common fund basis, costs as between solicitor and own client and so forth. There is however a Taxing Office, which can determine what is the proper amount which the party who has obtained a particular award for costs can recover under his Order.

3. LEGAL AID*

The costs factor in civil proceedings operated to discourage many possible litigants from resorting to the Courts, not only because they could not afford to pay their own lawyers, but still more because, if unsuccessful, they would become liable to pay the costs of the opposite party, which they could afford even less. It came to be recognized that the result was a denial of justice to many otherwise well-deserving people. Accordingly, the legal aid system was introduced in 1949 (Legal Aid and Advice Act 1949) to mitigate this harshness, and this scheme has since worked remarkably successfully. Its basic features are that the applicant for legal aid must come within the prescribed limits as to the amount of his disposable income (which now must not exceed £750 a year) and disposable capital (which now must not exceed £500) and he must also satisfy the Legal Aid Committee that he has a reasonable claim or defence. Once he is granted a legal aid certificate to conduct the instant litigation, he will no longer be liable to pay any money for costs beyond the amount of his contribution, if any, either to his own lawyers or to the lawyers of the opposite party unless the Court expressly otherwise orders. The Legal Aid Act 1964 has enabled the Court, in certain circumstances, to award costs out of the Legal Aid Fund to successful unassisted parties.

The procedures described above apply in the High Court but also in a modified form in the County Courts, which in fact carry by far the greater load of civil cases in England, and with their proposed increased jurisdiction they will become of even greater importance in the future. The procedures in the High Court and the Court of Appeal are governed very largely by the Rules of the Supreme Court 1965 as amended, and in the County Courts by the County Court Rules 1936 as amended. There is no Code of Civil Procedure in England. For any adequate study of English civil procedure, the relevant materials must be gathered from several works.

4. LIMITATION OF ACTIONS

One particular aspect of civil procedure ought perhaps to be singled out for separate mention, and that is the *Limitation of Actions*, which in England forms part of the procedural law, and not of substantive law. In general the time limit imposed by the relevant statutes is not upon rights but upon actions, and this perhaps exemplifies in an especial degree the procedural methods of thought prevailing in English law and the habit of thinking in terms of procedural remedies rather than in terms of substantive rights.

The operation of the English system of limitation is thus in general to bar the remedy by action, but *not* to extinguish the right, which remains available to be used as a defence or even as a counteraction or as the basis for exercising any lien or other lawful remedy. In the case, however, of land the system operates to extinguish the title of the true owner as against the person in adverse possession who acquires the negative right not to be disturbed. Of course, limitation should be

*For Legal aid in criminal matters see infra, Ch. X, section 1 (c)

distinguished from Prescription, the process by which positive rights may be acquired, but this is confined within a very narrow compass in English law and is governed by a different body of rules and statutes from those relating to the limitation of action.

The main *corpus* of law relating to the limitation of actions is now embodied in the Limitation of Actions Act 1939 which, in relation to personal injury actions, has been amended by the Law Reform (Limitation of Actions) Act 1954 and the Limitation Act 1963. There is in fact, however, a multitude of statutes providing different periods of limitation for different classes of actions and proceedings which it will be here impossible to enumerate.

5. EVIDENCE

In English jurisprudence, the law of evidence forms part of the substantive law, and *not* of procedural law. For this reason, this branch of the law has become highly developed. It is certainly a distinctive feature of the common law system. Moreover, it goes very much further than the sections in the Continental Codes of Procedure devoted to the question of proof, for it contains many provisions which in the Continental Codes are found elsewhere.

As with many aspects of procedural law, the development of the English law of evidence has undoubtedly been profoundly influenced by the system of jury trials. The doctrine of Jeremy Bentham that evidence should be received from any and every source and none excluded was the very opposite of the way in which the law proceeded. On the contrary, the law of evidence became a highly technical and elaborate branch of the law, with an immense proliferation of exceptions and restrictions on the admissibility of evidence, which originally were applicable both in criminal and civil trials, but without any really coherent body of principles. For this reason the foreign lawyer will find the English law of evidence puzzling and perplexing, not least because it contains a whole body of law for which his own Code has little parallel provision. Among the more unusual aspects are the extraordinary ramifications of the so-called "Hearsay Rule", designed to exclude secondary evidence on the basis that proof can only be made by the best evidence which the nature of the case will admit.

In civil cases, however, in recent times, there has been a considerable amelioration in the rules relating to the admissibility of evidence, and a movement away from the almost casuistic restrictions governing the Hearsay Rule. In this respect the Civil Evidence Act 1968 has made great strides forward, and points the way to a more relaxed system of admitting evidence which possesses any positive value. There are movements to extend the boundaries of the Civil Procedure Act 1968 to criminal proceedings as well.

The developed system of the English law of evidence is reflected in many works of considerable scholarship and authority.

Select Bibliography

General

ABEL-SMITH, B. and STEVENS, R.
In search of justice. Allen Lane, 1968. 384p.

ABEL-SMITH, B. and STEVENS, R.
Lawyers and the courts: a sociological study of the English legal system 1750-1965. Heinemann, 1967. xiv + 501p.

AMOS, Sir M. S.
"A day in court at home and abroad", in *Cambridge law journal*, 2 (1924/26): pp. 340-49

GREAT BRITAIN. Lord Chancellor's Department
Civil judicial statistics, 1949- . HMSO (Published annually)

HALSBURY'S LAWS OF ENGLAND, 3rd ed. B, 1952-64. 43 vols. (Suppl.) (Vol. 1: Action; vol. 3: Barristers; vol. 8: Contempt of court; vol. 9: County courts; Courts; vol. 11: Damages; vol. 12: Discovery, inspection and interrogatories; vol. 16: Execution; vol. 22: Judgments and orders; vol. 23: Juries; vol. 30: Pleading; Practice and procedure; vol. 36: Solicitors)

HOLDSWORTH, Sir W. S.
A history of English law. Methuen, 1903-66, reprinted 1966. 16 vols. (Various editions) (Vol. 1: chapters I, III, V & VIII; vol. 3: chapter VI; vol. 9: chapter VII; vol. 14: section "The courts", pp. 180-204; vol. 15: section "Common law procedure and pleading", pp. 104-38)

JACOB, I. H.
"Civil procedure including courts and evidence", in *Annual survey of Commonwealth law*, 1965- . B. (Annual article)

JACOB, I. H.
"The English system of civil proceedings", in *Common Market law review*, 1 (1963/64): pp. 294-317

JACOB, I. H.
"The present importance of pleadings", in *Current legal problems*, 13 (1960): pp. 171-91

JACOB, I. H. and WHEATCROFT, G. S. A.
"Courts and methods of administering justice", in *Record of the third Commonwealth and Empire Law Conference, Sydney—Australia, 25th August—1st September 1965* (SM, 1966), pp. 305-23

JACKSON, R. M.
The machinery of justice in England, 5th ed. CUP, 1967. xii + 494p.

KIRALFY, A. K. R.
The English legal system, 4th ed. SM, 1967. xxvii + 342p.

ODGERS, W. B.
Principles of pleading and practice in civil actions in the High Court of Justice, 20th ed. by G. F. Harwood. S, 1971. xlii + 555p.

ODGERS, W. B. and others
A century of law reform; twelve lectures on the changes in the law of England during the nineteenth century. Macmillan, 1901. ix + 431p. (Chapters VI and VII)

POLLOCK, Sir F. and MAITLAND, F. W.
The history of English law before the time of Edward I, vol. 2, 2nd ed., 1898, reissued with a new introduction by S. F. C. Milsom, CUP, 1968. xv + 691p. (Chapter IX: Procedure)

RADCLIFFE, G. R. Y. and CROSS, A. G. N., Lord Cross of Chelsea
The English legal system, 5th ed. by Lord Cross of Chelsea and G. D. G. Hall. B, 1971. x + 472p.

SUTTON, R.
Personal actions at common law. B, 1929. xv + 219p.

VICK, R. W. and SHOOLBRED, C. F.
The administration of civil justice in England and Wales. Oxford, Pergamon Pr., 1968. xxi + 279p.

WALKER, R. J. and WALKER, M. G.
The English legal system, 2nd ed. B, 1970. xxxii + 536p.
ZAGDAY, M. I.
"Bentham on civil procedure", in *Jeremy Bentham and the law*, edited by G. W. Keeton and G. Schwarzenberger (S, 1948), pp. 68-78
ZANDER, M.
Lawyers and the public interest: a study of restrictive practices. Weidenfeld & Nicolson, 1968. xi + 342p.

Supreme Court

BALL, R. E.
"The Chancery Master", in *Law quarterly review*, 77 (1961): pp. 331-57
DANIELL, E. R.
Chancery practice, 8th ed. by S. E. Williams and F. Guthrie-Smith. S, 1914. 2 vols.
DIAMOND, A. S.
"The Queen's Bench Master", in *Law quarterly review*, 76 (1960): pp. 504-20
GREAT BRITAIN. Committee on Supreme Court Practice and Procedure (Chairman: Sir Raymond Evershed)
First interim report. HMSO, 1949. 59p. (Cmd 7764)
Second interim report. HMSO, 1951. 68p. (Cmd 8176)
Third interim report. HMSO, 1952. 24p. (Cmd 8617)
Final report. HMSO, 1953. 380p. (Cmd 8878)
GREAT BRITAIN. Supreme Court of Judicature
The rules of the Supreme Court (revision) 1965. HMSO, 1965. 458p. (S.I. 1965 no. 1776)
HEWARD, E.
Guide to Chancery practice, 3rd ed. B, 1966. xxiv + 152p.
HUMPHREYS, T. S.
Notes on District Registry (High Court of Justice) practice and procedure, 18th ed. by H. C. Collins. Oyez Publications, 1971. viii + 208p.
JACOB, I. H. and NEAVE, J. S.
"The rules of the Supreme Court (revision), 1962: report of lectures on changes in procedure", in *Legal executive*, 1 (1963): pp. 261-78
JACOB, I. H. and HAWKINS, W. F. S.
The rules of the Supreme Court (revision) 1965. Institute of Legal Executives, 1966. 22p. (Revised transcript of lectures)
REDMAN, W. H.
A.B.C. guide to the practice of the Supreme Court: 1964, 38th ed. SM, 1963. vi + 209p.
STURGE, L. F.
Basic rules of the Supreme Court, 3rd ed. B, 1966. xx + [14] + 281p.
SUPREME COURT PRACTICE. SM, S and B. 2 vols (Published triennially, but with half-yearly cumulative supplements)

County Courts

COUNTY COURT PRACTICE. B, SM and S. (Published annually)
GREAT BRITAIN. Royal Commission on Assizes and Quarter Sessions (Chairman: Lord Beeching)
Report. HMSO, 1969. 184p. (Cmnd 4153)

GREGORY, R. C. L.
County Court manual, 4th ed. HMSO, 1962. 141p.

Special topics

BOWER, G. S.
The doctrine of res judicata, 2nd ed. by Sir A. K. Turner. B, 1969. lix + 455p.

CORNISH, W. R.
The jury, revised ed. Penguin, 1971. 328p.

DEVLIN, P. A., Baron Devlin
Trial by jury, 3rd impression with addendum. S, 1966. viii + 216p. (Hamlyn lectures, 1956)

DIAMOND, A. S.
"The summons for directions", in *Law quarterly review*, 75 (1959): pp. 43-52

GALE, C. J.
Easements, 13th ed. by M. Bowles. SM, 1959. li + 426p.

GREAT BRITAIN. Committee on Personal Injuries Litigation (Chairman: Sir C. R. N. Winn)
Report. HMSO, 1968. 234p. (Cmnd 3691)

ZAMIR, I.
The declaratory judgment. S, 1962. xxii + 337p.

Costs

GOWER, L. C. B.
"The cost of litigation: reflections on the Evershed Report", in *Modern law review*, 17 (1954): pp. 1-23

GREAT BRITAIN. Committee on the Enforcement of Judgment Debts (Chairman: Mr. Justice Payne)
Report. HMSO, 1969. 456p. (Cmnd 3909)

GREAT BRITAIN. National Board for Prices and Incomes
Report no. 54: *Remuneration of solicitors*. HMSO, 1968. 66p. (Cmnd 3529)

Limitation of actions

GREAT BRITAIN. Committee on Limitation of Actions in Cases of Personal Injury (Chairman: Sir Edmund Davies)
Report. HMSO, 1962. 19p. (Cmnd 1829)

FRANKS, M. J. A.
Limitation of actions. SM, 1959. lix + 323p.

PRESTON, C. H. S. and NEWSOM, G. H.
Limitation of actions, 3rd ed. by G. H. Newsom and L. Abel-Smith. SLS, 1953. lii + 371p. (Suppl.)

WOOLF, A. D.
The time barrier in personal injury claims. B, 1969. viii + 88p.

Evidence

BEST, W. M.
The principles of evidence and practice as to proofs in courts of common law, 12th ed. by S. L. Phipson. SM, 1922. xxxiii + 673p.

BOWER, G. S. and TURNER, Sir A. K.
The law relating to estoppel by representation, 2nd ed. by Sir A. K. Turner. B, 1966. lvi + 380p.

COCKLE, E.
Cases and statutes on evidence, 11th ed. by G. D. Nokes. SM, 1970. xxvii + 590p.

COWEN, Z. and CARTER, P. B.
Essays on the law of evidence. Oxford, Clarendon Pr., 1956. xix + 278p.

CROSS, A. R. N.
Evidence, 3rd ed. B, 1967. xcvi + 565p. (Suppl.)

CROSS, A. R. N. and WILKINS, N.
An outline of the law of evidence, 3rd ed. B, 1971. xxxix + 269p.

GREAT BRITAIN. Law Reform Committee
13th report: *Hearsay evidence in civil proceedings*. HMSO, 1966, 26p. (Cmnd 2964)
15th report: *The rule in Hollington v. Hewthorn*. HMSO, 1967. 23p. (Cmnd 3391)

NOKES, G. D.
An introduction to evidence, 4th ed. SM, 1967. xlvi + 535p.

PHIPSON, S. L.
Manual of the law of evidence, 9th ed. by D. W. Elliott. SM, 1966. xxxii + 308p.

PHIPSON, S. L.
Phipson on evidence, 11th ed. by J. H. Buzzard and others. SM, 1970. cxcii + 991p. (Suppl.)

ROSCOE, H.
Digest of the law of evidence on the trial of civil actions, 20th ed. by J. S. Henderson. S, 1934. 2 vols.

STEPHEN, J. F.
A digest of the law of evidence, 12th ed. by Sir H. L. Stephen and L. F. Sturge. Macmillan, 1946, reprinted with additions 1948. lvi + 273p.

TAYLOR, J. P.
A treatise on the law of evidence, 12th ed. by R. P. Croom-Johnson and G. F. L. Bridgman. SM, 1931. 2 vols.

WILLS, W.
The law of evidence in civil and criminal cases, 3rd ed. by J. D. Finlaison S, 1938. lxxxiv + 551p.

VII. CIVIL LAW

1. GENERAL INTRODUCTION

Continental lawyers will find the pattern of English civil law peculiarly confusing, for it hardly conforms at all to the pattern of Roman law, which is perpetuated for the most part in western laws of non-English origin. The following peculiarities may be selected for treatment here.

1. It is in civil law that the distinction between common law and equity is most important, for equity has nothing to do with criminal law and equitable remedies play only a subordinate role in administrative law. On the other hand, the co-existence of common law and equity must be expected in every part of civil law, most of all in the law of property; and it also causes difficulties to foreign lawyers in some parts of commercial law, especially company law. Formerly the distinction between common law and equity was the root distinction in civil law. Nowadays academic lawyers at least think more naturally in terms of differing subject-matter, of property, contract, torts, etc. There are still books which professedly deal with equity as such, but most books now deal with such topics as real property or contract, and include all the relevant principles of both common law and equity.

2. There is no single book dealing with the whole of civil law that is comparable to Colin et Capitant, *Cours élémentaire de Droit civil français*, or Enneccerus-Kipp-Wolff, *Lehrbuch des bürgerlichen Rechts*. JENKS'S *Digest of English Civil Law* is too much like a code and the relevant portions of STEPHEN'S *Commentaries on the Laws of England* are too short and too elementary. One consequence of this lack is that certain topics which do not fall within such familiar heads as real property, contract and tort are not doctrinally treated at all; and it is impossible to find an up-to-date book which contains within it the whole of what a civilian would regard as the law of property. Thus in the first place it is unusual to find the law of movables described in the same book as the law of immovables, and secondly the books on the law of immovables have nothing to do with the defence of property or possession by action or otherwise, but are designed as introductions to conveyancing, i.e., the creation and transfer of rights in land; the actions come under the head of tort.

3. No great store is set on the distinction between real and personal rights; it is indeed not carried through with any consistency or precision. Thus the trust, one of the most characteristic institutions of English law, whilst engendering what is in the strictest sense an obligation, plays an indispensable part in the law of property and is usually dealt with in books on property. The Sale of Goods Act, 1893, codifies both the contractual and property aspects of sales.

4. The word "property" is somewhat equivocal; it signifies a specific type of *jus in re*, corresponding to *dominium*, *propriété*, *Eigentum*, but it also signifies any valuable asset and the title to such asset, *patrimoine*, *Vermögen*. In the second sense it is possible to speak about property in a patent or a contractual right as part of the property of the creditor. It follows that, e.g. the assignment of contractual rights can be and is treated as part of the law of property. On the other hand, in some contexts, property may mean ownership in a tangible thing. The word is also

used popularly, very much in the same way as *biens*, to denote the thing owned, or indeed generally things capable of being owned.

5. There are no "real" remedies in modern English law, i.e., no *rei vindicatio* or *actio negatoria*. Proprietary rights are defended by what at first sight appear to be "delictual" remedies alone, such as actions for trespass, nuisance, ejectment, detinue, or conversion. It follows that the law of tort contains much that a Continental lawyer would expect to find in the law of property.

6. The law of succession is inextricably confused with the law of property and is always included in books on property law. One result of this is that the law of property is enriched by certain notions, such as real subrogation, which in many Continental systems are almost confined to the law of succession, or perhaps also to the law of matrimonial regimes. There is, however, also a large body of literature on "administration of estates" and on "wills", and since the "law of succession" as such is a teaching and examination subject in some universities there are some students' text-books under this heading.

7. Leases create real rights and so belong to the law of property. This is not to say that there is not a personal relation between landlord and tenant, but on the whole we think of it as subordinate to the tenant's right in the land.

8. There is no coherent law of unjust enrichment, the remedies for which, incomplete as they are, must be looked for in scattered portions of the law of contract, torts and equitable remedies.

9. Family law, also called the law of domestic relations, has never achieved real unity. One reason for this is that the law of marriage and divorce is mainly derived from ecclesiastical law, though greatly modified by modern statutes, and is still the subject of proceedings in a separate division of the High Court of Justice, now called the Family Division and in the courts of summary jurisdiction. The mutual obligations of members of the family, especially as regards maintenance, are to a minor extent rooted in the common law and in ecclesiastical law. Their principal historical origin is in the poor law, now the law of national assistance, and it rests almost entirely on modern statutes. The law of parents and children and of guardianship has been very profoundly influenced by equity, but today its most important principles have been formulated in legislation which is closely connected with that on adoption, juvenile welfare and juvenile delinquency. The common law of guardianship, in so far as it deals with property rights, has been almost entirely superseded by the use of the trust, a product of equity. The common law of married women's property has been entirely superseded by modern statutes, while marriage settlements, which always operate by way of trust, are regarded as belonging to property.

10. There is no doctrine governing acts in the law (*actes juridiques*, *Rechtsgeschäfte*). Not only is the concept unknown to the practice of the law, but it is not used by academic lawyers except to some slight extent in books on general jurisprudence.

11. There is no general law of associations. There is a coherent doctrine of corporations, which applies over the vast field of company law (and incidentally of municipal corporations and other local authorities), but there are also many other associations, such as trade unions, clubs, and religious bodies other than the established Church of England. These are sometimes governed by detailed Acts of Parliament, but they all rest ultimately on consent, and fundamental problems relating to them may have to be worked out by applying the law of contract or trusts. Foundations and other institutions of an impersonal character are almost always treated as charitable trusts. In many cases associations founded for educational,

charitable, and similar purposes and not desiring to distribute profits are carried on in the form of a "company limited by guarantee", which is a special type of company under the Companies Act.

These and other peculiarities make it necessary to advise Continental lawyers, as soon as they find themselves in difficulties with English civil law, to gain at least a superficial acquaintance with the whole of the law. Otherwise they may think something is missing which is to be found in another, unexpected part of the law, and, above all, they may not be able to make effective use of the indexes of English law books. More detailed hints on the peculiarities of English classification are given under the more specific heads of private law. A good starting-point is afforded by the books listed under the head of "*General Introductions to English Law*" (Chapter I, section 2).

Select Bibliography

JENKS, E.

English civil law, 4th ed. by P. H. Winfield and others. B, 1947. 2 vols.

STEPHEN, H. J.

Commentaries on the laws of England, 21st ed. Editor-in-chief L. C. Warmington. B, 1950. 4 vols. (Suppl. to 1956)

2. OBLIGATIONS

(a) *General*

The law of obligations is never treated as a single and separate branch of English law. Indeed, the word "obligation", in the technical language of the law, was, and still is, occasionally used to designate a *bond*, i.e. a document under seal by which a person acknowledges that he is bound to pay another person a specified sum of money. Moreover, English law does not make a clear distinction between real and personal rights, and so the institution of the trust, which one may expect to find operating in every part of English law, straddles, as it were, any line that is sought to be made between real and personal rights. However, it is convenient to group together the general law of contract, agency, bailment, tort, trusts and unjust enrichment.

(b) *The General Law of Contract*

The list of books on the general principles of the English law of contract is to a considerable extent self-explanatory. A person wishing to obtain a general view of the subject first may profitably begin with one of the works listed in the section on "General Introductions to English Law", or, for a Continental approach to the subject, with the *Traité de droit Comparé*, by Arminjon, Nolde and Wolff, Vol. III, pp. 97-152. Of the regular students' text-books it is most advisable to begin with TREITEL, read in conjunction with CHESHIRE AND FIFOOT, whose approach is less orthodox. POLLOCK and SALMOND AND WILLIAMS offer a more advanced treatment of certain aspects of the subject.

Contracts in English law are either contracts under seal (specialties) or simple contracts. Contracts under seal are distinguished in the first place by their abstract character. A promise made under seal is binding in virtue of the seal, and in conception at least, is independent of the cause or consideration for which it is made.

Hence the law relating to donations *inter vivos* and settlements of property, so far as it is contractual, is dealt with under this heading, whilst promises made in return for some counter-prestation fall under simple contracts.

Promises under seal may be binding without the consent of the creditor, unlike promises by way of simple contract, and hence the subject of binding pollicitations in English law falls under this heading too. In addition, a document under seal may have the effect of transferring property or interests in property without physical delivery and in this too it differs from simple contract, except a contract for the sale of goods and certain other exceptional commercial arrangements. It follows that the contractual aspects of dispositions of property by way of settlement, trust, mortgage, dowry, etc., also fall under this heading.

As regards simple contracts the matter likely to give most difficulty is the twofold derivation of the law of contract from common law and equity. Although theoretically the two systems have now been fused for the greater part of a century there is still a tendency for common law and equitable institutions to be treated separately, at least for purposes of exposition. This is to some extent inevitable, since the only remedy given by the common law for breach of contract was damages, whilst equity gave in addition relief by way of specific performance or execution *in specie*, injunctions, rescission or annulment, rectification and indemnity. If, to take an example, one wishes to consider the effect of mistake or error on a contract, one must consider separately the possibility of mistake at common law, which would render the supposed contract a nullity, and mistake in equity, which would give rise to an action for rescission.

In general, it may be said that the equitable jurisdiction in the rescission of contracts is extremely wide; it covers not merely mistake, violence or duress and fraud, but also false statements made innocently which induce the person to whom they are made to contract, such statements being called misrepresentations. It also covers abuse of confidence by a party who is in a position to influence another (undue influence). There is, too, a general provision by which, when one party has committed a fundamental breach of contract, the other has the option of rescinding the contract by virtue, as it were, of an implied *lex commissoria*.

In general, the law of contract is characterized by its flexibility and its regard for the intentions of the contracting parties, while imperative provisions of the law are reduced to a minimum. Very little discussion is to be found of the relative importance of freedom of contract on the one hand, and the interests of society as a whole on the other, except in connection with contracts in restraint of trade, and even there, the courts have concentrated on avoiding unfair bargains arising from the personal positions of the parties, rather than on questions of general policy, which have been left to the appreciation of the legislature.

A very great importance therefore attaches to the interpretation of contracts, and many of the most important doctrines of English law have been developed under the rubric of implied terms of conditions, that is, provisions which it is supposed that the parties as reasonable persons would have made in order to give efficacy to the contract had they addressed themselves to the events that have happened. Thus, the topic of mistake is often dealt with in English law on the basis of what the parties would supposedly have provided had they known of the mistake. *Lésion*, as it occurs in Continental systems, will be found either to fall under the equitable jurisdiction mentioned above, or under this doctrine.

English rules of evidence have considerably influenced the interpretation of contracts and the two topics of interpretation and evidence are therefore grouped together in the list which follows.

Select Bibliography

Introductory work

ATIYAH, P. S.
An introduction to the law of contract, 2nd ed. OUP, 1971. x + 290p.

Textbooks

ANSON, Sir W. R.
Law of contract, 23rd ed. by A. G. Guest. OUP, 1969. xlv + 655p.

CARTER, A. T.
Elements of the law of contract, 7th ed. SM, 1931. xvi + 290p.

CHESHIRE, G. C. and FIFOOT, C. H. S.
The law of contract, 8th ed. B, 1972. lxxx + 657 + [30]p.

ODGERS, Sir C. E.
Introduction to the law of contracts. SM, 1948. xxviii + 400p.

POLLOCK, Sir F.
Principles of contract, 13th ed. by Sir P. H. Winfield. S, 1950. xliii + 610p.

SALMOND, Sir J. W. and WILLIAMS, J.
Principles of the law of contracts, 2nd ed. SM, 1945. xxxvi + 640p.

SUTTON, R. and SHANNON, N. P.
Contracts, 6th ed. by K. W. Wedderburn. B, 1963. cxx + 546 + 25p. (Proposition and explanation)

TREITEL, G. H.
The law of contract, 3rd ed. S, 1970. liii + 884p.

WILSON, J. F.
Principles of the law of contract. SM, 1957. xxxvi + 530p.

Practitioners' works and works of reference

CHITTY, J.
Chitty on contracts, 23rd ed. by A. G. Guest and others. SM, 1968. 2 vols. (Suppl.)

LEAKE, S. M.
Principles of the law of contracts, 8th ed. by R. R. A. Walker. S, 1931. ccxciv + 1088p.

Selections of decided cases

CHESHIRE, G. C. and FIFOOT, C. H. S.
Cases on the law of contract, 5th ed. B, 1969. xxvi + 510p.

COCKLE, E. and HIBBERT, W. N.
Leading cases in common law, 3rd ed. by H. J. S. Jenkins. SM, 1945. 2 vols.

KENNY, C. S.
A selection of cases illustrative of the law of contract. Based on the collection of G. B. Finch. CUP, 1922. xi + 511p.

MILES, Sir J. C. and BRIERLY, J. L.
Cases illustrating general principles of the law of contract, 2nd ed. OUP, 1937. xv + 474p.

SHIRLEY, W. S.
A selection of leading cases in the common law, 11th ed. by H. B. Thompson. S, 1931. lxxiv + 720p.

SIM, R. S. and POWELL-SMITH, V.
Casebook on contract. B, 1968. xxiv + 271p.

Digest of cases

SMITH, J. W.
A selection of leading cases in various branches of the law, 13th ed. by T. W. Chitty and others. SM, 1929. 2 vols. (Vol. 1: pp. 120, 148, 331, 350, 358, 373, 406; vol. 2: pp. 1, 57, 529, 601)

Consideration

GREAT BRITAIN. Law Revision Committee
6th interim report: *Statute of frauds and the doctrine of consideration.* HMSO, 1937. 36p. (Cmd 5449)

Mistake, misrepresentation, undue influence

BOWER, G. S.
The law of actionable misrepresentation, 2nd ed. B, 1927. xliii + 454 + 76p.
GREAT BRITAIN. Law Reform Committee
10th report: *Innocent misrepresentation.* HMSO, 1962. 15p. (Cmnd 1782)
KERR, W. W.
Kerr on the law of fraud and mistake, 7th ed. by D. L. McDonnell and J. G. Monroe. SM, 1952. liv + 738p.
STOLJAR, S. J.
Mistake and misrepresentation. SM, 1968. xvi + 160p.

Remedies

FRY, Sir E.
A treatise on the specific performance of contracts, 6th ed. by G. R. Northcote. S, 1921. l + 741 + 108p.
GAHAN, F.
The law of damages. SM, 1936. lxxx + 242p. (Article 5)
KERR, W. W.
A treatise on the law and practice of injunctions, 6th ed. by J. M. Paterson. SM, 1927. lxiv + 743p. (Chapter X)
MAYNE, Sir J. D. and MCGREGOR, H.
Damages, 12th ed. SM, 1961. lxxiii + 932p. (Suppl.)

Third parties

FINLAY, A. M.
Contracts for the benefit of third persons. SM, 1939. xi + 150p.
MARSHALL, O. R.
The assignment of choses in action. Pitman, 1950. xxiv + 216p. (Bibliography, pp. xxi-xxiv)

Discharge

COOTE, B.
Exception clauses. SM, 1964. xxii + 163p.

GREAT BRITAIN. Law Revision Committee
7th interim report: *The rule in Chandler v. Webster.* HMSO, 1939. 11p. (Cmd 6009)

MCELROY, R. G.
Impossibility of performance, ed. by G. L. Williams. CUP, 1941. xl + 255p.

MCNAIR, A. D., Baron McNair and WATTS, A. D.
The legal effects of war, 4th ed. CUP, 1966. li + 469p. (Chapters 4 and 5)

ROGERS, P. H. T.
The effect of war on contract: a companion volume to Chitty on contracts. SM, 1940. vii + 171p.

TROTTER, W. F.
The law of contract during and after war, 4th ed. B, 1940. xli + 727p.

WEBBER, G. J.
The effect of war on contracts, 2nd ed. SLS, 1946. lxviii + 754 + 48p.

WILLIAMS, G. L.
The Law Reform (Frustrated Contracts) Act, 1943. S, 1944. viii + 92p.

Interpretation and evidence

BEAL, E.
Cardinal rules of legal interpretation, 3rd ed. by A. E. Randall. S, 1924. lxxxiv + 725p. (Parts III and IV)

BURROWS, Sir R.
Interpretation of documents, 2nd ed. B, 1946. lxix + 121 + [9] p.

ODGERS, Sir C. E.
Construction of deeds and statutes, 5th ed. by G. Dworkin. SM, 1967. xlv + 488p.

Estoppel

BOWER, G. S. and TURNER, Sir A. K.
The law relating to estoppel by representation, 2nd ed. by Sir A. K. Turner. B, 1966. lvi + 380p.

EWART, J. S.
An exposition of the principles of estoppel by misrepresentation. Toronto, Carswell, 1900. xlvii + 548p.

Plurality of parties

WILLIAMS, G. L.
Joint obligations. B, 1949. 179p.

Government contracts—*see* Constitutional law

Moneylenders

MESTON, D., Baron Meston
The law relating to moneylenders, 5th ed. Oyez, 1968. xxxix + 402p.

THORP, L. T. and WATSON, A. A.
The law of moneylending. Wilson, 1928. xv + 133p.

Foreign point of view

ARMINJON, P. and others

Traité de droit comparé. Paris, Librairie générale de droit et de jurisprudence, 1950-51. 3 vols. (Vol. 3: pp. 97-152)

MITCHELL, J. D. B.

The contracts of public authorities: a comparative study. Bell, for London School of Economics, 1954. xxxii + 256p.

RHEINSTEIN, M.

Die Struktur des verträglichen Schuldverhältnisses im anglo-amerikanischen Recht. Berlin, de Gruyter, 1932. 256p. (Beiträge zum ausländischen und internationalen Privatrecht, Heft 5)

WET, J. C. de, and YEATS, J. P.

Die Suid-Afrikaanse kontraktereg en handelsreg, 3rd ed. Durban, B, 1964. lxix + 621p. (On South African law, but discusses English institutions)

(c) *Agency*

1. Certain features of the Anglo-American law of agency should be noted:

(a) The relation between the principal and the agent is usually, but not invariably, contractual.

(b) An undisclosed principal may sue and be sued on a contract made by an agent with a third party, provided that the agent has authority to make the contract.

(c) Many cases are concerned with the extent of a principal's liability for an agent's unauthorized acts.

2. The content of a book on the law of agency varies with the definition of an agent. In the United States and Canada servants are treated as one group of agents (other agents being called independent contractors), and as a result the law of master and servant is brought under the classification of the law of agency. In England the tendency has been to draw a distinction between agents and servants, with a resulting distinction in bibliographical classification. In the law of tort, however, there is an increasing tendency to bring under one head liability for both agents and servants.

3. In England, it is more common than in the United States and Canada to treat agency as an extension of the limits of operation of a contract rather than as a separate legal institution. Consequently an elementary account of the law of agency is often included in books on the law of contract.

Select Bibliography

A detailed analytical treatment of the subject, with many references to the Anglo-American literature, can be found in:

POWELL, R.

The law of agency, 2nd ed. Pitman, 1961. liv + 467p.

The standard practitioners' book is:

BOWSTEAD, W.

Bowstead on agency, 13th ed. by F. M. B. Reynolds and B. J. Davenport. SM, 1968. cxiii + 484p.

This book contains a number of statements of principles, followed by notes and abundant illustrations from the cases. The present editors have introduced some discussions of the principles set out.

Useful introductory works are:

FRIDMAN, G. H. L.

The law of agency, 3rd ed. B, 1971. lvii + 334p.

HANBURY, H. G.

The principles of agency, 2nd ed. S, 1960. xix + 235p.

STOLJAR, S. J.

The law of agency: its history and present principles. SM, 1961. xli + 341p.

A comparable American introduction is:

MECHEM, F. R.

Outlines of the law of agency, 4th ed. by P. Mechem. Chicago, Callaghan, 1952. 444p.

The principal American classics are:

AMERICAN LAW INSTITUTE

Restatement of the law of agency, second. St. Paul, Minn., The Institute, 1958. 3 vols.

MECHEM, F. R.

A treatise on the law of agency, 2nd ed. Chicago, Callaghan, 1914. 2 vols.

STORY, J.

Commentaries on the law of agency, 9th ed. by C. P. Greenough. Boston, Little, Brown, 1882. xlvii + 674p.

(d) *Bailment*

Bailments form a special and perhaps unique branch of English law. The general conception is that of a delivery of possession of a movable thing upon the terms that it is to be redelivered or otherwise dealt with on the instructions of the person delivering (bailor), or in accordance with the agreement between the parties. It includes such transactions as hire, loan of goods, pledge, deposit, carriage of goods and repair of goods, and may be either gratuitous or for reward; it therefore cuts across the law of contract, for while bailments are often contracts, they need not be, and includes matters which are usually dealt with under the headings of personal property or torts.

Select Bibliography

BEAL, E.

The law of bailments. B, 1900. lx + 774p.

JONES, Sir W.

An essay on the law of bailments, 4th ed. with notes . . . and an essay on the law of coach proprietors and carriers, by W. Theobald. Sweet, 1833. xii + 123 + lxii p.

PATON, G. W.

Bailment in the common law. S, 1952. xl + 454p.

(e) *Torts*

There are a number of points in which the English law of torts differs markedly from delictual liability in civil law systems. In the first place, there are no general provisions which confer a right of action such as Article 1382 of the French Code Civil. Rather, the law of torts consists of a number of separate delicts, which are characterised by the nature of the interest which the particular tort is designed to protect and by the manner or instrumentality by which the injury is inflicted. Some of these torts require that the wrongdoer should have acted intentionally; in others, negligence will suffice; while others still are torts of strict liability. Secondly, it must be appreciated that the law of torts covers an immense field, much wider than that comprehended by delict in the civil law. Tort is historically the basis of much of the common law. Actions in tort will be found in such diverse fields as the protection of industrial and intellectual property, unfair trade competition, labour relations, injuries to servitudes, the liability of bankers in relation to bills of exchange, and the liability of public authorities and government officials. Thirdly, the distinction between tort and contract is not so rigidly maintained as in many civil law systems, and in particular the English concept of "bailment"—the transfer of possession of personal property by one person to another for a limited purpose—may give rise to liability in tort, even if there is a contract, e.g. for the carriage of goods.

Standard Text-Books

A useful and stimulating introduction to the English law of torts can be found in FLEMING, *An introduction to the law of torts,* which may be followed by a perusal of a major work *The law of torts* by the same author. Students in universities mainly rely on the text-books by SALMOND or WINFIELD, and the statements of principle contained in these works are frequently cited by the judges. In recent years, students' text-books by STREET and JAMES have also gained popularity. For the practitioner, the most detailed general treatise is that of CLERK AND LINDSELL. But the practitioner will no doubt also refer to the relevant title in *Halsbury's laws of England* and to a specialist work on the particular tort with which he is concerned. Probably the most widely used book in practice is one on damages in personal and fatal injury actions by KEMP. It is not possible to give a complete list of all the monographs on individual torts, but the select bibliography set out below refers to the most important of these.

Select Bibliography

Introductory

FLEMING, J. G.
An introduction to the law of torts. OUP, 1967. vi + 230p.

General text books

CLERK, J. F. and LINDSELL, W. H. B.
Clerk and Lindsell on torts, 13th ed. by A. L. Armitage and others. SM, 1969. ccvii + 1258p. (Suppl.)

FLEMING, J. G.
The law of torts, 4th ed. Sydney, Law Book Co. of Australasia, 1971. lii + 669p.

JAMES, P. S.
General principles of the law of torts, 3rd ed. B, 1969. cxviii + 471p.

SALMOND, Sir J. W.
Salmond on the law of torts, 15th ed. by R. F. V. Heuston. SM, 1969. cxii + 840p.
STREET, H.
The law of torts, 4th ed. B, 1968. lxxxvii + 534p.
WINFIELD, Sir P. H.
Winfield and Jolowicz on tort, 9th ed. by J. A. Jolowicz with T. E. Lewis and D. M. Harris. SM, 1971. xlvii + 692p.

Particular topics

ATIYAH, P. S.
Vicarious liability in the law of torts. B, 1967. lxi + 452p.
CHARLESWORTH, J.
The law of negligence, 5th ed. by R. A. Percy. SM, 1971. cii + 802p.
FRIDMAN, G. H. L.
The modern law of employment. S, 1963. clxii + 1065p. (Suppl.)
GATLEY, J. C. C.
Libel and slander, 6th ed. by R. L. McEwen and P. S. C. Lewis. SM, 1967. cxxiii + 768p.
KEMP, D. A. MCI. and others
The quantum of damages. Vol. 1: Personal injury claims, 3rd ed. SM, 1967. (Suppl.) Vol. 2: Fatal injury claims, 2nd ed. SM, 1962. (Suppl.)
MARSDEN, R. G.
The law of collisions at sea, 11th ed. by K. C. McGuffie. S, 1961. lxxxvi + 975p. (Suppl.) (British shipping laws, vol. 4)
MAYNE, J. D. and MCGREGOR, H.
Damages, 12th ed. SM, 1961. lxxiii + 932p. (Suppl.)
MUNKMAN, J. H.
Employer's liability at common law, 7th ed. B, 1971. lxxxi + 637p.
NORTH, P. M.
Occupiers' liability. B, 1971. xxxviii + 238p.
VAINES, J. Crossley
Personal property, 4th ed. B, 1967. lxix + 566p.
WILLIAMS, G. L.
Joint torts and contributory negligence: a study of concurrent fault in Great Britain, Ireland and the common-law Dominions. S, 1951. l + 558p.

General and historical

ATIYAH, P. S.
Accidents, compensation and the law. Weidenfeld & Nicolson, 1970. 633p.
ELLIOTT, D. W. and STREET, H.
Road accidents. Allen Lane, 1968. 295p.
FIFOOT, C. H. S.
History and sources of the common law: tort and contract. S, 1949. xvii + 446p.
HART, H. L. A. and HONORÉ, A. M.
Causation in the law. OUP, 1959. xxxii + 454p.
MAITLAND, F. W.
The forms of action at common law, ed. by A. H. Chaytor and W. J. Whittaker. CUP, 1936. xii + 92p.

MILLNER, M. A.
Negligence in modern law. B, 1967. xxxviii + 7 + 248p.
WINFIELD, Sir P. H.
The province of the law of tort. CUP, 1931. xii + 254p.
WINFIELD, Sir P. H.
Select legal essays. SM, 1952. xv + 292p.

Case-books

WEIR, T.
A casebook on tort, 2nd ed. SM, 1970. xxiv + 553p.
WRIGHT, C. A.
Cases on the law of torts, 4th ed. B, 1967. xxiii + 1213p.

(f) *Trusts*

The trust is a device by which the ownership of property is vested in a person (called a "trustee") subject to an obligation to deal with it for the benefit of persons (called "beneficiaries") or for the furtherance of purposes, often of a charitable nature. A beneficiary owns an equitable interest. What it amounts to is that the trustee owns the property for the purpose of administering it, while the beneficiary owns it for the purpose of enjoying it. For example, from the point of view of a purchaser of the trust property the trustee is the owner, while from the point of view of levying income tax the beneficiary is the owner. Any disposable property may be held on trust. Generally a trustee is the owner of a common law title to it. However an equitable interest under a trust may itself be held on trust.

The trustee is subject to very heavy duties of honesty and efficiency, and of impartiality among the beneficiaries. The rigour of these duties, breach of which normally renders the trustee liable to replace any loss, coupled with the absence of remuneration unless authorized by the creator of the trust or by the court, makes fewer and fewer individuals willing to undertake trusteeship. Accordingly a great amount of trust work is done by companies which act as professional trustees, bargaining for payment when accepting the obligation; these are frequently banks or subsidiaries of banks. There is also a Public Trustee, who is in effect a government department and who, though he can refuse to undertake the duties of a trustee, cannot do so merely because he regards the trust property as too small to merit the trouble of administering it.

Trusts may be classified as express, resulting (or implied), constructive, and statutory.

An express trust is one which is intentionally created by act of the parties. Employed for various purposes at different times, its main uses nowadays are as follows: (1) On marriage or death, as a means of making provisions extending well into the future for several people. Property can be vested in trustees, who have full powers of management, while a succession of limited equitable interests can be given, e.g., to wife, children and other relations. Modern developments in taxation (especially estate duty and capital gains tax) are making such settlements rarer. (2) To secure the benefit of property to someone (e.g., an infant or lunatic) who is not competent to manage it. (3) Particularly on death, to ensure a sale at the most favourable moment and distribution of the proceeds. (4) To set up a fund to achieve a purpose, e.g., for the improvement of hospital facilities in London (charitable), or for maintaining the donor's dog (not charitable). A charitable trust, i.e., one for the public benefit, receives preferential treatment, such as tax exemption. (5) To keep beneficial interests off the title. By the device of a trust, the dividing up of the enjoyment of property—particularly land, dealing with which used to be very complicated—amongst many people can be carried out without making the property difficult to deal with. A purchaser can buy from the trustee without worrying about who is entitled to beneficial interests. The trustee then holds the purchase-money on trusts similar to those previously affecting the property he sold. In other words, in effect the trust attaches to the value of the land and not to the individual piece of land. Two or more of these five purposes often coincide. (6) To provide for simple co-operative investment by small investors (the unit trust), by-passing the stock exchange and avoiding the disadvantages of the rule that a company incorporated under the Companies Acts cannot buy its own shares.

Unincorporated associations, including friendly societies, trade unions and many clubs, have the form of trusts, so that the law of trusts partly fills the gap left by the lack of a general regulation of non-profit-making associations. In the case of registered trade unions, management in the form of a trust is prescribed by statute.

Resulting trusts are those implied by equity where the parties did not expressly create a trust, but where the intention of the parties to a transaction is that property shall not be enjoyed, or not enjoyed exclusively, by the person in whom it is vested, e.g., where two people advance the purchase-money in buying land but it is conveyed to only one of them.

Constructive trusts are those implied by equity independently of the intention of the parties where property becomes vested in a person under circumstances in which it would be inequitable for him to keep it, e.g., where a purchaser buys trust property knowing that the sale to him is a breach of the trust, the purchaser holds on a constructive trust for the beneficiaries of the broken express trust. Thus the constructive trust is one of the devices through which English law gives partial effect to the principle of unjust enrichment. In other words, the difference between a resulting and a constructive trust is that in the former the law gives effect to what it presumes to be the intention of the parties, in the latter to what it holds to be the duty of a party irrespective of intention.

Statutes sometimes state that in certain circumstances, independently of the intention of the parties, there shall be a trust. For example, a statutory trust for the distribution of property arises on intestacy.

The courts have, by statute, wide supervisory powers over trusts, and also claim an inherent jurisdiction in certain cases to which their statutory powers do not extend. They can make orders enlarging the administrative powers of the trustees in emergencies unforeseen by the creator of the trust, and can authorize, on behalf of future beneficiaries or beneficiaries not sui juris, a variation of the beneficial interests. Cheap and speedy applications for directions can be made to the court in cases concerning administration or interpretation of trusts, and the process started by what is known as an "originating summons",* which is used for this purpose, provides, in a way, a parallel to a *jurisdictio voluntaria*. The supervisory functions of the Chancery Division of the High Court over administration of trust property of all kinds, including property of infants under guardianship, and, in many cases, of deceased's estates correspond to those exercised by continental courts over the *gestion* of guardians, executors, etc.

---

*See supra Chapter VI section 1, "Civil Procedure".

Select Bibliography

General books on trusts

(Many of the general books on equity devote much space to the trust)

BOGERT, G. G. and BOGERT, G. T.
The law of trusts and trustees, 2nd ed. St. Paul, Minn., West, 1965. 15 vols. (Suppl.)

DE WULF, C.
The trust and corresponding institutions in the civil law. Brussels, Bruylant, 1965. 201p. (Centre interuniversitaire de droit comparé. Collection, no. 10)

HARTMANN, W.
Der Trust im englischen Recht. Zürich, Juris-Verlag, 1956. 102p.

KEETON, G. W.
The law of trusts, 9th ed. Pitman, 1968. lxi + 522p. (Copies obtainable with an *Irish supplement* by L. A. Sheridan, xiv + 50p.)

KEETON, G. W.
Modern developments in the law of trusts. Belfast, Northern Ireland Legal Quarterly, 1971. xxv + 342p.

LEPAULLE, P. G.
Traité théorique et pratique des trusts en droit interne, en droit fiscal et en droit international. Paris, Rousseau, 1932. vii + 463p.

LEWIN, T.
Lewin on trusts, 16th ed. by W. J. Mowbray. SM, 1964. cl + 883p.

NATHAN, J. A. and MARSHALL, O. R.
A casebook on trusts, 5th ed. by O. R. Marshall. S, 1967. xxx + 509p. (Includes commentary)

NEWMAN, R. A.
Newman on trusts, 2nd ed. Brooklyn, N.Y., Foundation Pr., 1955. xiii + 600p.

PARKER, D. B. and MELLOWS, A. R.
The modern law of trusts, 2nd ed. SM, 1970. xxx + 446p.

SCOTT, A. W.
The law of trusts, 3rd ed. Boston, Little, Brown, 1967. 6 vols. (Suppl.)

UNDERHILL, A.
Law relating to trusts and trustees, 11th ed. by C. M. White and M. M. Wells. B, 1959. clvii + 617 + 67p. (Suppl.)

Charitable trusts

CROWTHER, C. E.
Religious trusts. Oxford, Ronald, 1954. xxiii + 143p.

KEETON, G. W. and SHERIDAN, L. A.
The modern law of charities, 2nd ed. Belfast, Northern Ireland Legal Quarterly, 1971. lviii + 404p.

SHERIDAN, L. A. and DELANY, V. T. H.
The cy-près doctrine. SM, 1959. xxxvi + 166p. (Suppl.)

TUDOR, O. D.
Tudor on charities, 6th ed. by D. H. McMullen, S. G. Maurice and D. B. Parker. SM. 1967. lxx + 755p.

Implied, resulting and constructive trusts

VINTER, E.

A treatise on the history and law of fiduciary relationship and resulting trusts, 3rd ed. Cambridge, Heffer, 1955. xxv + 391p.

WATERS, D. W. M.

The constructive trust. Athlone Pr., 1964. xxiii + 353p. (University of London legal series, no. 8)

(g) *Unjust Enrichment*

Unjust enrichment is not an accepted head of study in English law. In fact it has been stated in the House of Lords by Lord Porter that he was "content for the purposes of this case (*Reading* v. *Attorney General*, [1951] A.C. 507) to accept the view that (the law of unjust enrichment) forms no part of the law of England". Most of the ground that is covered in other systems of law by the doctrine of unjust enrichment is covered in English law by actions in quasi-contract and tort, and by suits in equity. The results obtained from these actions are comparable with those of Continental systems; but there is no exact correspondence. English law is in many ways less ready to allow a plaintiff to recover; and where recovery is allowed it is allowed under any one of many actions at law or in equity, and not under any general principle.

Quasi-contractual actions for money judgments lie at common law in certain limited circumstances. The availability of an action depends at the present day on rules established by prior decisions. There are certain accepted heads of liability, of which the following may be given as the most common examples:

(i) The action for money had and received by the defendant to the plaintiff's use.
(ii) The action for money paid by the plaintiff to the defendant's use.
(iii) The action for money paid under a mistake of fact.
(iv) The action for money paid under duress.
(v) The action for money paid on a consideration that has wholly failed.
(vi) Claims on a *quantum meruit*.

No attempt here is made to give a complete list. There is much overlapping between the various actions, and there is dispute on the question whether certain actions are or are not quasi-contractual.

In the days of the forms of action, quasi-contractual actions had their origin in the writ *indebitatus assumpsit*, and this connection with *assumpsit*, the writ on which modern contract law is based, has led to an association between contract and quasi-contract; and to the theory that, since in quasi-contractual actions there is no express agreement, one must be implied. Recovery is said only to be possible when a contract to pay can be implied on behalf of the defendant. This doctrine was introduced in the nineteenth century and reached the peak of its popularity in *Sinclair* v. *Brougham*, [1914] A.C. 398. The earlier cases had based quasi-contractual liability on the justice of the plaintiff's claim (*Moses* v. *Macferlan* [1760] 2 Burr. 1005). Academic and judicial opinion at the present day is divided on this matter, but the tendency of recent years has been to abandon the theory of the implied contract. Such a theory imposed an unnecessary restriction in that it insisted that recovery must be denied, however much desired, if it were for some reason impossible (e.g. on grounds of infancy, *ultra vires*, etc.) to imply a contract; and yet the implication of a contract provided no principle on which to decide whether in certain circumstances an action lay. Supporters of the theory argued that it was historically inevitable owing to its connection with *assumpsit*, and, since *Sinclair* v. *Brougham*, have argued that the authority of that case decides once and for all that such is the basis of quasi-contractual liability.

Actions in tort will lie in some cases in circumstances in which an action in quasi-contract will also lie; the actions of duress and fraud may be given as examples. In circumstances in which an action in tort and in quasi-contract will lie, the plaintiff has his choice. If he sues in quasi-contract, he is said to "waive the tort".

In addition to the personal actions at common law, claims in equity are allowed. These may be either personal or proprietary (sometimes called actions *in personam* and actions *in rem*). Speaking generally, a personal action is allowed to recover from a fiduciary money obtained in breach of a fiduciary relationship and is also available to an unpaid or underpaid legatee or intestate successor to recover money from persons, not being bona fide purchasers for value, to whom it has been wrongly paid (see *Re Diplock* [1947] Ch. 716; [1951] A.C. 251). A proprietary action is one by which property may be recovered by the owner from a fiduciary or from a third party, other than a bona fide purchaser, to whom the fiduciary has given or paid it, provided the property is still recognizable as that of the plaintiff. This is a limitation not placed on the personal actions. Money can be followed in this way, and is recognizable in a fund as that of the plaintiff provided that it can be shown that the fund has never, since the payment, sunk below the sum by which it was increased by the receipt of the plaintiff's money. If it has, then part at least of the plaintiff's money must have been paid away; but the defendant is assumed to pay away his own money first. Where there are more claimants than one, each with a right to follow their own money into a fund, their claims abate proportionately. It was thought at one time that this right to follow or to trace property was a right available in equity only between fiduciaries (*Re Hallett* [1880], 13 Ch. D.696); it is now established that it is available against third parties who are not in a fiduciary relationship to the plaintiff provided the property has passed through the hands of a person in a fiduciary relationship to him (*Re Diplock, supra*).

It will be seen that the English law on this subject is not a logical consistent whole. Emphasis at present is to try to collect together the individual actions and permit a more thorough development in a manner in which the doctrine of unjust enrichment would play a substantial part; such development has taken place in most American jurisdictions. Academic opinion is becoming more strongly in favour of such development, and this view is not without support among the judges. However, it is not possible at present to forecast the results of this modern development.

Select Bibliography

History and background

AMES, J. B.

"The history of assumpsit", in *Lectures on legal history and miscellaneous legal essays* (Cambridge, Mass., Harvard UP, 1913), lectures XII–XV, pp. 122–71.

AMES, J. B.

"The history of assumpsit II—Implied Assumpsit", in *Harvard law review*, 2 (1888): pp. 53-69.

JACKSON, R. M.

The history of quasi-contract in English law. CUP, 1936. xxxi + 134p.

English books

GOFF, R. L. A. and JONES, G. H.
The law of restitution. SM, 1966. lxxix + 508 + 32p.

HANBURY, H. G.
Modern equity, 9th ed. by R. H. Maudsley. S, 1969. xcvi + 738p. (Suppl.) (Chapter 22: section 5)

MAUDSLEY, R. H. and BURN, E. H.
Trusts and trustees: cases and materials. B, 1972. li + 672p.

NATHAN, J. A. and MARSHALL, O. R.
A casebook on trusts, 5th ed. by O. R. Marshall. S, 1967. xxx + 509p. (Chapter 8: pp. 267-325)

STOLJAR, S. J.
The law of quasi-contract. Sydney, Law Book Co. of Australasia, 1964. xxviii + 223p.

WATERS, D. W. M.
The constructive trust. Athlone Pr., 1964. xxiii + 343 + 10p. (University of London legal series, no. 8)

WILLIAMS, G. L.
The Law Reform (Frustrated Contracts) Act, 1943. S, 1944. viii + 92p.

WINFIELD, Sir P. H.
The law of quasi-contracts. SM, 1952. xiv + 140p.

WINFIELD, Sir P. H.
The province of the law of tort. CUP, 1931. xii + 254p. (Chapter 7)

Articles

ALLEN, Sir C. K.
"Fraud, quasi-contract and false pretences", in *Law quarterly review*, 54 (1938): pp. 201-16. (pp. 217-19, Postscript by A. L. Goodhart)

DENNING, Sir A. T.
"The recovery of money", in *Law quarterly review*, 65 (1949): pp. 37-50.

FRIEDMANN, W.
"The principle of unjust enrichment in English law", in *Canadian Bar review*, 16 (1938): pp. 243-72 & 365-86.

GOFF, R. L. A.
"Reform of the law of restitution", in *Modern law review*, 24 (1961): pp. 85-100.

GUTTERIDGE, H. C. and DAVID, R. J. A.
"The doctrine of unjustified enrichment", in *Cambridge law journal*, 5 (1933/35): pp. 204-29.

HOLDSWORTH, Sir W. S.
"Unjustifiable enrichment", in *Law quarterly review*, 55 (1939): pp. 37-53.

JONES, G. H.
"Change of circumstances in quasi-contract", in *Law quarterly review*, 73 (1957): pp. 48-64.

JONES, G. H.
"Unjust enrichment and the fiduciary's duty of loyalty", in *Law quarterly review*, 84 (1968): pp. 472-502.

MCCONVILLE, D. A.
"Tracing and the rule in Clayton's case", in *Law quarterly review*, 79 (1963): pp. 388-409.

MAUDSLEY, R. H.
"Proprietary remedies for the recovery of money", in *Law quarterly review*, 75 (1959): pp. 234-52.
ROULSTON, R. P.
"A plea for restitution", in *Tasmanian University law review*, 1 (1958): pp. 80-97.
SCOTT, A. W.
"The right to follow money wrongfully mingled with other money", in *Harvard law review*, 27 (1913): pp. 125-38.
SCOTT, A. W.
"Constructive trusts", in *Law quarterly review*, 71 (1955): pp. 39-50.
SCOTT, G. K.
"Restitution from an innocent transferee who is not a purchaser for value", in *Harvard law review*, 62 (1949): pp. 1002-20.
SEALY, L. S.
"Fiduciary relationships", in *Cambridge law journal*, 1962: pp. 69-81.
SEALY, L. S.
"Some principles of fiduciary obligation", in *Cambridge law journal*, 1963: pp. 119-40.
SEAVEY, W. A. and SCOTT, A. W.
"Restitution", in *Law quarterly review*, 54 (1938): pp. 29-45.
TREITEL, G. H.
"The Infants Relief Act, 1874", in *Law quarterly review*, 73 (1957): pp. 194-211
ATIYAH, P. S.
"The Infants Relief Act, 1874—a reply", with "A short rebutter" by G. H. Treitel, in *Law quarterly review*, 74 (1958): pp. 97-104 and 104-107.
WINFIELD, Sir P. H.
"Mistake of law", in *Law quarterly review*, 59 (1943): pp. 327-42.
WINFIELD, Sir P. H.
"Quasi-contract arising from compulsion", in *Law quarterly review*, 60 (1944): pp. 341-55.
WRIGHT, R. A., Baron Wright
"Sinclair v. Brougham", in *Legal essays and addresses* (CUP, 1939), pp. 1-33. (Reprinted from *Cambridge law journal*, 6 (1936/38): pp. 305-26)
WRIGHT, R. A., Baron Wright
"United Australia Ltd. v. Barclays Bank Ltd.", in *Law quarterly review*, 57 (1941): pp. 184-202.

American books

AMERICAN LAW INSTITUTE
Restatement of the law of restitution. St. Paul, Minn., the Institute, 1937. xxv + 1033p.
DAWSON, J. P.
Unjust enrichment: a comparative analysis. Boston, Little, Brown, 1951. viii + 201p.
KEENER, W. A.
A treatise on the law of quasi-contracts. New York, Baker, Voorhis, 1893. xxxii + 470p.
PALMER, G. E.
Mistake and unjust enrichment. Columbus, Ohio State UP, 1963. 114p.

SCOTT, A. W.
The law of trusts, 3rd ed. Boston, Little, Brown, 1967. 6 vols. (Suppl.) (Chapter 13)

WOODWARD, F. C.
The law of quasi-contracts. Boston, Little, Brown, 1913. lxi + 498p.

Casebooks

DAWSON, J. P. and PALMER, G. E.
Cases on restitution. New York, Bobbs-Merrill, 1958. 1044p.

WADE, J. W.
Cases and materials on restitution, 2nd ed. Brooklyn, N.Y., Foundation Pr., 1966. 866p.

3. PROPERTY

(a) *General*

The law of property is the part of English law which is most likely to cause difficulty to the foreign lawyer. In the first place, it is customarily regarded as comprising about half of civil law, and includes, not only property law in the narrower sense, but also the law of settlements, including marriage settlements (and, thus a considerable portion of the land relating to *Régime matrimonial* or *Güterstand*), and the law of succession. On the other hand, it is not regarded as including the actions for the protection of property and possession (or, indeed, the law of possession itself), which are regarded as part of the law of torts; and the trust, which plays an immensely important part in property law, is treated as a separate institution.

There are few books giving an account of the law of property as a whole. One which does so, however, is LAWSON. HARGREAVES' account in Volume I of the 21st edition of STEPHEN is also valuable.

English law divides things, not into movables and immovables (except for purposes of private international law), but into real and personal property. Real property descended on death to the heir by primogeniture, whereas personal property (or *chattels*) vested in the personal representative (executor or administrator) on behalf of the deceased's relations. The former comprised all immovables, with the exception of leaseholds, but with the addition of a few movables of trifling importance. The latter comprised almost all other property (including *choses in action*) with the addition of leaseholds. Leaseholds were treated as personal property because they were originally regarded as mere contracts standing outside the feudal system of tenures. Originally they could not, like other immovable property, be recovered *in specie*, but later they were for this purpose assimilated to immovables and accordingly they came to be called *chattels real*, *chattels* because they descended as personalty on intestacy, *real* because in most other respects they were assimilated to real property. Now that there is the same scheme of succession to both real and personal property, there is no point in distinguishing between real property and chattels real; and, indeed, for a long time previously it had been customary to deal with the latter in books on real property.

The most logical arrangement of the law of property would be to divide it into interests peculiar to land, interests peculiar to pure personalty, and equitable interests common to land and to pure personalty; for much of the English law of property has to do, not with land or movables treated as physical objects, but with funds (*patrimoines*, *Vermögen*) which may change their physical content from time to time. Such funds are the objects over which the equitable interests of the third class can subsist. But in actual fact these interests are almost always dealt with in books on real property, for the law relating to them was originally developed in relation to real property and extended only later to personalty; and these books reflect the ordinary course of legal education, in which personal property tends to be treated as an appendix to real property or to be dealt with incidentally in courses on sale of goods and other topics of commercial law or to be omitted altogether. The arrangement of those books which treat land law as the core of the law of property is followed here, the whole of property law, except such as relates only to movables, being dealt with under the head of real property. Trusts, which are both property and obligation, are dealt with separately.

Select Bibliography

LAWSON, F. H.

Introduction to the law of property. OUP, 1958. xii + 200p.

STEPHEN, H. J.

Commentaries on the laws of England, 21st ed. Editor-in-chief: L. C. Warmington. B, 1950. 4 vols. (Suppl.) (Vol. 1: Law of property, edited by A. D. Hargreaves).

STRAHAN, J. A.

A general view of the law of property, 7th ed. S, 1926. lxii + 483p.

(b) *Possession*

Possession plays a very important part in English law, but is rarely dealt with in a general or coherent fashion. Indeed, there is only one complete treatise on possession, POLLOCK AND WRIGHT, which appeared as long ago as 1888. Discussions of possession must be looked for in books on the law of torts, for trespass is an interference with possession, in criminal law, for larceny was originally, and is still in most cases, a criminal invasion of possession, and in the law relating to real property and limitation of actions, for adverse possession for the required period operates to bar an action for the recovery of land. Historically account must be taken of the distinction between seisin (*saisine*, *Gewere*) and possession, the former relating to freehold, but not leasehold land. Today it is only possession that matters.

There is a strong tendency to include possession in jurisprudence both for literary and for examination purposes. Accordingly reference should be made to the general books on jurisprudence.

Select Bibliography

AMES, J. B.

"The disseisin of chattels", in *Lectures on legal history and miscellaneous legal essays* (Cambridge, Mass., Harvard UP, 1913), pp. 172-91.

GOODHART, A. L.

Essays in jurisprudence and the common law. CUP, 1931. xiii + 295p. (Chapter 6)

HOLDSWORTH, Sir W. S.
An historical introduction to the land law. OUP, 1927. xxiv + 339p.
HOLMES, O. W.
The common law, new ed. by M. D. Howe. Macmillan, 1968. xxviii + 337p.
LIGHTWOOD, J. M.
A treatise on possession of land, with a chapter on the Real Property Limitation Acts, 1833 and 1874. S, 1894. xvi + 342p.
MAITLAND, F. W.
Collected papers, edited by H. A. L. Fisher. CUP, 1911. 3 vols. (Vol. 1: pp. 329-84; 407-57)
MEGARRY, R. E. and WADE, H. W. R.
The law of real property, 3rd ed. S, 1966. xcvi + 1138 + 37p. (Chapter 16)
POLLOCK, Sir F. and WRIGHT, Sir R. S.
An essay on possession in the common law. OUP, 1888. xvi + 244p.

(c) *Law of Land*

The English law of land, technically known as real property, is a subject separate from all others; it is taught and studied by itself without reference even to the law of personal property (movables, bills of exchange, etc.). It has always been regarded as a difficult subject both for students and for practitioners. Under the feudal system it became specialized and complicated at a very early stage of English legal history, and it has developed on its own lines ever since. There was little statutory reform before the nineteenth century; and although the subject is today governed by elaborate legislation, it still stands upon its old foundations. The legislation is not a code, and is unintelligible to persons not trained in the older rules of common law and equity.

Important changes were made by a group of Acts passed in 1925. Textbooks published before that date are therefore primarily of historical interest. Many works used by practitioners before 1925 are still in use in revised editions. But for a general introduction to the subject it is essential to use a book which was first written after 1925.

Within the scope of this subject are included all transactions relating to land, for example leases, conveyancing (contracts for the sale or lease of land and the rights of vendor and purchaser and also the technique of creating and transferring proprietary rights in land) mortgages (securities), easements (servitudes), and the law of succession in so far as it has special rules for land. Leases are still classed technically with personal property rather than with real property; but this is a matter of nomenclature only, and leases are usually dealt with in books on real property for obvious reasons of convenience.

The law relating to future interests, which includes the rule against perpetuities (the rule designed to prevent the tying-up of property by forbidding the creation of unduly remote rights to take effect in future), is of great importance in real property and the textbooks therefore treat it in detail, although the rule against perpetuities applies equally to other forms of property than land. The law of trusts is another subject which embraces all forms of property but which is so essential to the mechanism of the land law that some of its more fundamental rules are usually explained in general textbooks. The same is true of the law of wills and intestacy (succession). The law of limitation of actions has a special place in real property because it makes possible a prescriptive title to land, and the special rules about this are explained in general textbooks.

Social legislation governing the tenure and use of land is abundant, but is selectively treated in books on land law. The Settled Land Acts, which since 1882 have conferred special powers upon owners of limited interests such as tenants for life, still remain part of the subject as it is taught and studied. But general works on land law usually give only summary accounts of the twentieth-century legislation on rent restriction (security of tenure and control of rents of leasehold property) and on planning (control of the use of land). These last two topics are undoubtedly an important part of the land law in a general sense, but they require separate treatment.

A part of the subject which has greatly grown in importance is the statutory system of registration of title to land, which is now in force in most urban areas and in many counties.

The general works most used by students are CHESHIRE, MEGARRY and MEGARRY AND WADE. These give an account of the subject suitable for university and professional examinations. They are also referred to by practitioners on points of general principle.

The shortest works on the subject are HARGREAVES and LAWSON. These are elementary surveys for beginners which explain the historical development of the subject, stripped of most of its complications. They can be recommended as simplified introductions but not as textbooks.

The most extensive general text-book is MEGARRY AND WADE, which is used both by students and practitioners. Practitioners also use a multitude of books on special topics, and no attempt has been made to produce a unified work which will expound the law in full detail in all its departments. But the appropriate titles of *Halsbury's Laws of England* supply this want to some extent. WOLSTENHOLME AND CHERRY is a book much used for reference. It is not an exposition, but an edition of the legislation of 1925 with numerous annotations; the present edition is nearly forty years out of date, and is useful only to the profession. A less bulky edition of these Acts with annotations is HOOD AND CHALLIS; this is also out of date, but is of some use to students. Practitioners may also still refer to pre-1926 textbooks such as CHALLIS or WILLIAMS; but these are classic works on the older law which are no longer of general authority.

In the following list of books an asterisk (*) indicates books written primarily for students. A double asterisk (**) indicates books particularly recommended to students who come to the subject for the first time.

Select Bibliography

General works

**CHESHIRE, G. C.
The modern law of real property, 11th ed. by E. H. Burn. B, 1972. lix + 961 + 58p.

HALSBURY'S LAWS OF ENGLAND, 3rd ed. B, 1952-64. 43 vols. (Suppl.) (vol. 8: Copyhold; vol. 10: Compulsory acquisition; vol. 12: Easements; vol. 23: Land charges, Land registration and Landlord and tenant; vol. 24: Limitation of actions; vol. 27: Mortgage; vol. 29: Perpetuities; vol. 32: Real property and Rent charges; vol. 34: Sale of land; vol. 37: Town and country planning; vol. 39: Wills)

*HARGREAVES, A. D.
An introduction to the principles of land law, 4th ed. by G. A. Grove and J. F. Garner. SM, 1963. xv + 204p.

*LAWSON, F. H.
Introduction to the law of property. OUP, 1958. xii + 200p.
*MAUDSLEY, R. H. and BURN, E. H.
Land law: cases and materials, 2nd ed. B, 1970. lxi + 719p.
**MEGARRY, Sir R. E.
A manual of the law of real property, 4th ed. by P. V. Baker. S, 1969. li + 652p.
**MEGARRY, R. E. and WADE, H. W. R.
The law of real property, 3rd ed. S, 1966. xcvi + 1138 + 37p.
*RADCLIFFE, G. R. Y.
Real property law, 2nd ed. OUP, 1938. xxxii + 396p.
*RIVINGTON, H. G.
Law of property in land, 5th ed. by E. S. Green and R. A. Donell. Law Notes Lending Library, 1959. xxvii + 547p.
*TOPHAM, A. F.
Real property, 11th ed. by V. Powell-Smith. B, 1969. xxiv + 325p.

Conveyancing (sale of land)

**BURNETT, J. F. R.
Elements of conveyancing, 8th ed. SM, 1952. xxxi + 508p.
CURTIS, Sir G. H. and RUOFF, T. B. F.
The law and practice of registered conveyancing, 2nd ed. S, 1965. lxxvii + 1246p.
EMMET, L. E.
Notes on perusing titles and on practical conveyancing, 15th ed. by J. G. Smith and J. T. Farrand. SLS, 1967. ccxxiv + 1409p. (Suppl.)
GEORGE, E. F.
The sale of land. SM, 1952. lxiii + 576p.
*GIBSON, A.
Conveyancing, 20th ed. by R. H. Kersley. Law Notes Lending Library, 1970. cxxxiv + 898p.
*HOLLAND, J. A. and LEWIS, J. R.
Principles of registered land conveyancing. B, 1967. xiii + 239p.
RUOFF, T. B. F.
Concise land registration practice, 2nd ed. SM, 1967. xix + 309p.
WILLIAMS, T. C.
The law of vendor and purchaser, 4th ed. by T. C. Williams and J. M. Lightwood. SM, 1936. 2 vols.
WILLIAMS, W. J.
The law and practice relating to the contract for sale of land and the title to land, 3rd ed. B, 1966. clxviii + 791p. (Suppl.)

History

CHALLIS, H. W.
Law of real property chiefly in relation to conveyancing, 3rd ed. by C. Sweet. B, 1911, reprinted 1963. xlv + 524p. (Irish supplement by L. A. Sheridan B, 1956. x + 33p.)
HOLDSWORTH, Sir W. S.
An historical introduction to the land law. OUP, 1927. xxiv + 339p.

*SIMPSON, A. W. B.

An introduction to the history of the land law. OUP, 1961. xx + 276p.

WILLIAMS, J.

Principles of the law of real property, 24th ed. by R. A. Eastwood. SM, 1926. lvi + 906p.

Easements (servitudes) and restrictive covenants

ELPHINSTONE, Sir L. H.

Covenants affecting land. SLS, 1946. xxxii + 210p. (Suppl.)

GALE, C. J.

Easements, 13th ed. by M. Bowles. SM, 1959. li + 426p.

PRESTON, C. H. S. and NEWSOM, G. H.

Restrictive covenants affecting freehold land, 5th ed. SM, 1971. xxxviii + 328p.

Mortgages (securities)

COOTE, R. H.

A treatise on the law of mortgages, 9th ed. by R. L. Ramsbotham. S, 1927. 2 vols.

FISHER, W. R. and LIGHTWOOD, J. M.

The law of mortgages, 8th ed. by E. L. G. Tyler. B, 1969. cxxxvi + 697p. (Suppl.) (See also 7th ed. B, 1931. ccxii + 820 + 106p.)

*WALDOCK, C. H. M.

The law of mortgages, 2nd ed. S, 1950. xxix + 451p.

Landlord and tenant (leases)

BLUNDELL, L. A. and WELLINGS, V. G.

The complete guide to the Rent Acts. SM, 1958. li + 514p.

FOA, E.

General law of landlord and tenant, 8th ed. by H. Heathcote-Williams and others. Ipswich, Thames Bank, 1957. clxi + 902 + 158p.

MEGARRY, Sir R. E.

The Rent Acts, 10th ed. S, 1967. 3 vols. (Vol. 3 is a permanent supplement)

WOODFALL, W.

Law of landlord and tenant, 27th ed. by L. A. Blundell and V. G. Wellings. SM, 1968. 2 vols. (Suppl.)

Planning (control of use of land)

BLUNDELL, L. A. and DOBRY, G.

Town and country planning. SM, 1963. xliii + 791p.

ENCYCLOPEDIA OF THE LAW OF TOWN & COUNTRY PLANNING, edited by D. Heap. SM, 1959– . 3 vols. (loose-leaf)

HEAP, D.

Outline of planning law, 5th ed. SM, 1969. xliii + 126 + 299p.

ROBERTS, Sir J. R. H.

The law of town and country planning, 2nd ed. by G. Seward. Knight, 1963. 2 vols.

*TELLING, A. E.
Planning law and procedure, 3rd ed. B, 1970. xxvi + 325p.

Statutes (commentaries)

HOOD, H. J. and CHALLIS, H. W.
The property, settled land, trustee and administration Acts, 8th ed. by J. H. Boraston. S, 1938. cxxxii + 980p.

WOLSTENHOLME, E. P. and CHERRY, Sir B. L.
Conveyancing statutes, 13th ed. by J. T. Farrand. Oyez 1972– . 2 vols. (Vols. 3–6 in preparation)

Miscellaneous

FARWELL, Sir G.
A concise treatise on powers (i.e. powers of appointment), 3rd ed. by C. J. W. Farwell and F. K. Archer. S, 1916. lxxx + 767p.

GRAY, J. C.
The rule against perpetuities, 4th ed. by R. Gray. Boston, Little, Brown, 1942. xcv + 895p. (This American work deals also with English law and is authoritative in England)

MORRIS, J. H. C. and LEACH, W. B.
The rule against perpetuities, 2nd ed. S, 1962. li + 352p. (Suppl.)

(d) *Personal (or Movable) Property*

Personal property comprises those things that in the older law did not descend to the heir-at-law on intestacy but vested in the personal representative, i.e. the executor or administrator. As such it included all movable property and also leaseholds, though, as has been explained above, the latter are now usually dealt with as part of real property. Thus for practical purposes personal property corresponds to movables. However, it has a rather wider scope than in many other laws since it includes industrial property such as patents, trade marks and designs and copyright, and in addition personal rights acquired by the promisee in a contract. Personal property is divided into choses in possession and choses in action. The former, which are tangible objects, can be acquired by taking possession of them, the latter can be enforced only by bringing an action. Thus a ship, a horse or a book is a chose in possession, whereas a debt, a patent, a trade mark, or copyright is only a chose in action.

All these various types of property are, of course, dealt with in separate works. However, there are a few general books on personal property, even though the subject is not very coherent; they usually contain much material which is often found in books on other parts of the law. Thus although bailment is a proper subject for a book on personal property, much of the law regarding it is also found in books on contract and on torts. The actions for the recovery of personal property are also found in books on the law of torts. Since the contract for the sale of goods passes property in specific goods the law of sale of goods is regularly described in books on personal property and so also is the law of negotiable instruments, because a negotiable instrument gives birth to choses in action. Other transactions such as carriage of goods, which are more usually regarded as belonging to commercial law, and even bankruptcy, are likewise part of the law of personal property. Indeed, a student who has taken normal courses in real property, contract, torts, criminal law and commercial law has already covered a great deal of the material usually included in books on personal property.

Since books on the special parts of personal property are listed elsewhere, only the general books on the subject are given here.

Select Bibliography

GOODEVE, L. A.

The modern law of personal property, 9th ed. by R. H. Kersley. SM, 1949. lxv + 699p.

VAINES, J. Crossley

Personal property, 4th ed. B, 1967. lxix + 536 + 30p.

WILLIAMS, J.

Principles of the law of personal property, 18th ed. by T. C. Williams and W. J. Byrne. SM, 1926. lxxxviii + 831p.

4. SECURITY

The methods of providing security for the payment of a debt by a debtor to his creditor, or for the performance of some other obligation, may be divided into five categories; the fifth of which (Hire Purchase) is a sufficiently specialized variation of the second (Proprietary Security) to justify separate treatment:

(a) *Personal Security*

A third party may guarantee the performance of the debtor's obligation to the creditor. A contract of guarantee or suretyship is a contract by which a person undertakes to answer for the debt or liability of another person either personally or with his own property. The liability of the guarantor or surety is collateral to that of the principal debtor and accrues on the latter's default. Unless otherwise provided by contract or custom, the creditor may then proceed against the guarantor or surety without first being required to sue the principal debtor. A person can be a guarantor or surety without rendering himself personally liable by pledging property of his own to the creditor. Contracts of guarantee or suretyship are to be distinguished from contracts of indemnity, which create an independent and primary liability in the indemnor, since the Statute of Frauds, 1677, section 4, renders the former, but not the latter, unenforceable by action unless they are made or noted in writing.

Select Bibliography

Students' books

CHITTY, J.

Mercantile contracts, edited by B. Chedlow. SM, 1955. lx + 673p. (pp. 530-64)

HOLDEN, J. M.
Securities for bankers' advances, 5th ed. Pitman, 1971. xxxviii + 427p. (The law and practice of banking, vol. 2) (pp. 203-61)

SNELL, E. H. T.
Principles of equity, 26th ed. by R. E. Megarry and P. V. Baker. SM, 1966. clxvii + 768p. (pp. 495-509)

Reference books

CHITTY, J.
Chitty on contracts, 23rd ed. by A. G. Guest and others. SM, 1968. 2 vols. (Vol. 2: pp. 769-804)

HALSBURY'S LAWS OF ENGLAND, 3rd ed. B, 1952–64. 43 vols. (Suppl.) (Vol. 18: Guarantee and indemnity, pp. 409-540)

ROWLATT, Sir S. A. T.
The law of principal and surety, 3rd ed. by A. A. Mocatta. SM, 1936. liii + 356p.

(b) *Proprietary Security*

The creditor may require the debtor to transfer to him by way of security some proprietary right (legal or equitable) in property belonging to, or to be acquired by, the debtor. The debtor normally retains possession of the property concerned. This is generally referred to as a mortgage and is the form of security usually adopted in the case of freehold land (real property) and leasehold land (chattels real), but it is also available in the case of chattels personal, whether tangible (choses in possession) or intangible (choses in action). A mortgage of a tangible chattel may be effected orally but almost invariably it is effected by some document, which is then a bill of sale. A bill of sale is an instrument by which a personal chattel capable of transfer by delivery is mortgaged by the owner (the grantor) to another person (the grantee) in such a manner that some proprietary right in the chattel is, or is agreed to be, transferred to the grantee whilst the chattel itself remains in the possession or apparent possession of the grantor. Mortgage bills of sale are governed chiefly by the Bills of Sale Acts, 1878 and 1882, which provide that, where such transactions are effected in writing, they must comply with certain formalities, e.g. they must be in a statutory form, attested and registered in a public register; otherwise they are invalid to various extents. The transfer by way of security of ships, however, even where not completely built, is not within the scope of the Bills of Sale Acts. A mortgage of a chose in action is usually effected by an assignment of the chose by way of security followed by re-assignment on performance of the obligation secured.

Select Bibliography

Mortgages

a. Students' books

CHESHIRE, G. C.
The modern law of real property, 11th ed. by E. H. Burn. B, 1972. lix + 961 + 58p. (pp. 620–99)

GIBSON, A.
Conveyancing, 20th ed. by R. H. Kersley. Law Notes Lending Library, 1970. cxxxiv + 898p. (pp. 291-357)

HANBURY, H. G.
Modern equity, 9th ed. by R. H. Maudsley. S, 1969. xcvi + 738p. (Suppl.) (pp. 529-96)

MEGARRY, Sir R. E.
A manual of the law of real property, 4th ed. by P. V. Baker. S, 1969. li + 652p. (pp. 460-514)

MEGARRY, R. E. and WADE, H. W. R.
The law of real property, 3rd ed. S, 1966. xcvi + 1138 + 37p. (pp. 879-980)

RUDDEN, B. and MOSELEY, H.
An outline of the law of mortgages. Estates Gazette, 1967. xx + 240p. (Successor to G. D. Nokes' *Outline of the law of mortgages and receiverships*, 3rd ed., 1951)

SNELL, E. H. T.
Principles of equity, 26th ed. by R. E. Megarry and P. V. Baker. SM, 1966. clxvii + 768p. (pp. 413-78)

WALDOCK, C. H. M.
The law of mortgages, 2nd ed. S, 1950. xxix + 451p.

b. Practitioners' books

CONSTANT, B.
The law relating to the mortgage of ships. Syren & Shipping, 1920. xviii + 182p.

COOTE, R. H.
A treatise on the law of mortgages, 9th ed. by R. L. Ramsbotham. S, 1927. 2 vols.

FISHER, W. R. and LIGHTWOOD, J. M.
The law of mortgage, 8th ed. by E. L. G. Tyler, B, 1969. cxxxvi + 697p. (Suppl.) (See also 7th ed. B, 1931. ccxii + 820 + 106p)

HALSBURY'S LAWS OF ENGLAND, 3rd ed. B, 1952-64. 43 vols. (Suppl.) (Vol. 27: Mortgage, pp. 149-449)

Bills of sale

a. Students' books

GIBSON, A.
Conveyancing, 20th ed. by R. H. Kersley. Law Notes Lending Library, 1970. cxxxiv + 898p. (pp. 359-87)

GOODEVE, L. A.
The modern law of personal property, 9th ed. by R. H. Kersley, SM, 1949. lxv + 699p. (pp. 151-69)

VAINES, J. Crossley
Personal property, 4th ed. B, 1967. lxix + 536 + 30p. (pp. 345-72)

WALDOCK, Sir C. H. M.
The law of mortgages, 2nd ed. S, 1950. xxix + 451p. (pp. 75-126)

WILLIAMS, J.
Principles of the law of personal property, 18th ed. by T. C. Williams and W. J. Byrne. SM, 1926. lxxxviii + 831p. (pp. 97-102; 707-23)

b. Reference books

BALL, W. V.

Bankruptcy, deeds of arrangement and bills of sale, 5th ed. by W. V. Ball and D. Geddes. Pitman, 1934. li + 405 + 26p.

HALSBURY'S LAWS OF ENGLAND, 3rd ed. B, 1952-64. 43 vols. (Suppl.) (Vol. 3: Bills of sale, pp. 255-327)

Assignment

a. Students' books

ANSON, Sir W. R.

Law of contract, 23rd ed. by A. G. Guest. OUP, 1969. xlv + 655p. (pp. 401-18)

CHESHIRE, G. C. and FIFOOT, C. H. S.

The law of contract, 8th ed. B, 1972. lxxx + 657 + [30]p.

GOODEVE, L. A.

The modern law of personal property, 9th ed. by R. H. Kersley. SM, 1949. lxv + 699p. (pp. 200-25)

MARSHALL, O. R.

The assignment of choses in action. Pitman, 1950. xxiv + 216p. (Bibliography, pp. xxi-xxiv)

SNELL, E. H. T.

Principles of equity, 26th ed. by R. E. Megarry and P. V. Baker. (pp. 71-94)

VAINES, J. Crossley

Personal property, 4th ed. B, 1967. lxix + 536 + 30p. (pp. 248-64)

b. Reference book

HALSBURY'S LAWS OF ENGLAND, 3rd ed. B, 1952-64. 43 vols. (Suppl.) (Vol. 4: Choses in action, pp. 477-520)

(c) *Possessory Security*

The creditor may require the debtor to deliver to him possession of some chattel by way of security, the debtor retaining his proprietary right in the chattel. This form of security is not available in respect of land and is confined to tangible personal property (choses in possession) and negotiable instruments. The commonest example is a pledge or pawn, which is a form of bailment. Pledges taken by professional pawnbrokers are governed by the Pawnbrokers Acts, 1872 and 1960. A creditor may also acquire security by means of a possessory lien, which is the right to retain possession of the chattel of another person until a debt owed by that person is paid. Such a possessory lien may be either (i) *particular*, entitling the creditor to retain the chattel until he is paid some charge or claim connected with that chattel (e.g., for skill, labour and materials expended in repairing it), or (ii) *general*, entitling the creditor to retain possession of the chattel until his debtor pays the general balance of accounts between the parties whether connected with that chattel or with other similar dealings between them (e.g., the lien of a factor against his principal's goods or of a solicitor against his client's documents or other chattels). A possessory lien usually arises out of some form of bailment. Unlike a pledge, a possessory lien confers only a bare right of retention with no power to sell the chattel in satisfaction of the creditor's claim, unless such a power of sale is conferred expressly by contract or statute.

Select Bibliography

Students' books

GOODEVE, L. A.
The modern law of personal property, 9th ed. by R. H. Kersley. SM, 1949. lxv + 699p. (pp. 43-72)

HOLDEN, J. M.
Securities for bankers' advances, 5th ed. Pitman, 1971. xxxviii + 427p. (The law and practice of banking, vol. 2) (pp. 279-98)

PATON, Sir G. W.
Bailment in the common law. S, 1952. xl + 454p.

SNELL, E. H. T.
Principles of equity, 26th ed. by R. E. Megarry and P. V. Baker. SM, 1966. clxvii + 768p. (pp. 479-94)

VAINES, J. Crossley
Personal property, 4th ed. B, 1967. lxix + 536 + 30p. (pp. 123-35; 411-14)

Reference books

ATTENBOROUGH, C. L.
Law of pawnbroking, 3rd ed. by C. L. Attenborough and A. Safford. Jackson & Co. and S, 1925. xii + 227p.

BEAL, E.
The law of bailments. B, 1900. lx + 774p.

CORDERY, A.
Law relating to solicitors, 6th ed. by G. J. Graham-Green assisted by D. S. Gordon, B, 1968. cxxxvii + 769p. (Suppl.) (pp. 416–453)

FISHER, W. R. and LIGHTWOOD, J. M.
The law of mortgage, 7th ed. B, 1931. ccxii + 820 + 106p. (pp. 106-11; 275-306)

GOODE, R. M.
Hire purchase law and practice, 2nd ed. B, 1970. lxxii + 1302p. (pp. 688-709)

HALL, L. E.
Possessory liens in English law. SM, 1917. x + 101p.

JONES, Sir W.
An essay on the law of bailments, 4th ed, with notes . . . and an essay on the law of coach proprietors and carriers, by W. Theobald. Sweet, 1833. xii + 123 + lxii p.

WARREN, E. H.
The rights of margin customers against wrongdoing stockbrokers and some other problems in the modern law of pledge. Norwood, Mass., Plimpton Pr., 1941. xiv + 464p.

(d) *Charges and Non-possessory Liens*

The creditor may be content that his debtor should expressly appropriate specific property to satisfy the debt without actually transferring to the creditor either any proprietary interest in, or the possession of, any of his property. In such a case the debtor is said to charge, or to create a charge on, the specified property. Charges on land, if effected by instruments under seal, are by statute virtually equated with mortgages (see (b) above). Where a tangible personal chattel is charged by means of a written document giving the creditor a licence to seize the chattel, that document is a bill of sale (see (b) above). Where such a security arises not by contract but by operation of Equity, it is known as a non-possessory (equitable) lien, the commonest example being the non-possessory equitable lien of a vendor of land, who, having conveyed both ownership and possession of the land to the purchaser, has not been paid the full purchase price. The law also recognizes a maritime lien, which is not necessarily dependent on possession and which may be asserted by proceedings *in rem* against a ship, its cargo and freight, in respect of claims for damage caused by collisions, for bottomry bonds or respondentia, for seamen's wages and for such services as salvage. Such charges and non-possessory liens are, in effect, rights to the preferential satisfaction of a debt or claim out of a particular asset and so are akin to *privilèges*. They are usually enforced by an order of the court for sale of the asset in satisfaction of the debt or claim.

Select Bibliography

Students' books

CHORLEY, R. S. T., Baron Chorley and GILES, O. C.
Shipping law, 6th ed. Pitman, 1970. xxv + 405p. (pp. 35-45)

HOLDEN, J. M.
Securities for bankers' advances, 5th ed. Pitman, 1971. xxxviii + 427p. (The law and practice of banking, vol. 2) (pp. 299-303)

Reference books

FISHER, W. R. and LIGHTWOOD, J. M.
The law of mortgage, 7th ed. by J. M. Lightwood. B, 1931. ccxii + 820 + 106p. (pp. 112-17; 231-74)

PRICE, G.
The law of maritime liens. SM, 1940. xxiii + 264p. (Bibliography, pp. ix-xii)

(e) *Hire-Purchase*

Hire-purchase involves a highly specialized form of proprietary security((b) above). By a hire-purchase agreement the owner of goods delivers possession of them to another person who agrees to hire them at an agreed periodic rental with the option of purchasing them (usually at a nominal price after paying an agreed number of rental instalments) or of returning them and terminating the hiring. Security for performance of the hirer's obligations is provided by the owner's retention of ownership, which enables him to re-possess the goods on the hirer's default, and by the hirer's inability, as a mere bailee, to transfer ownership in the goods even to a bona fide purchaser for value (except as regards motor vehicles, as provided in the Hire-Purchase Act, 1964, Part III). Hire-purchase agreements differ from (i) "credit sale" agreements, by which both possession and ownership of the goods sold pass at once to the buyer, who may freely dispose of them and whose only obligation is a personal liability to pay the price by instalments, and (ii) "conditional-sale" agreements, by which the parties are bound to sell and buy but ownership of the goods is to pass only on the fulfilment of certain conditions (usually the payment of all instalments of the price), although the buyer may be able to deprive the seller of his ownership by transferring the goods for value to a bona fide purchaser. The Hire-Purchase Act, 1965, however, applies to all hire-purchase, credit sale and conditional-sale agreements where the hirer or buyer is not a corporate body and where the hire-purchase price or the total purchase price does not exceed (currently) £2,000. Within those limits it equates conditional sale agreements with hire-purchase agreements (so depriving the conditional buyer of his ability to transfer ownership to a bona fide purchaser), imposes stringent formalities and gives very considerable protection to hire-purchasers: e.g., against swift re-possession of the goods by an owner on the hirer's default and against provisions for excessive claims by the owner for depreciation or loss of profit on premature termination of the contract.

Hire-purchase is most commonly used as a method of acquiring goods on credit with payment of the price by instalments. It is also increasingly used, however, as a means of borrowing money on the security of chattels. A person who wishes to raise money may sell some chattel (usually a motor vehicle) to a finance company which will then at once let the chattel back to the seller on hire-purchase. The documents effecting such a transaction are likely to be held invalid under the Bills of Sale Acts, 1878 and 1882 (see (b) above), unless they truly indicate a genuine sale and re-letting on hire-purchase rather than a disguised mortgage.

Select Bibliography

Students' books

DIAMOND, A. L.

Introduction to hire-purchase law, 2nd ed. B, 1971. xxv + 169p.

VAINES, J. Crossley

Personal property, 4th ed. B, 1967. lxix + 563 + 30p. (pp. 399-414)

Reference books

CHITTY, J.

Chitty on contracts, 23rd ed. by A. G. Guest and others. SM, 1968. 2 vols. (Suppl.) (Vol. 2, pp. 410-76)

GOODE, R. M.

Hire purchase law and practice, 2nd ed. B, 1970. lxxii + 1302p.

GOODE, R. M. and ZIEGEL, J. S.

Hire-purchase and conditional sale: a comparative survey of Commonwealth and American Law. British Institute of International and Comparative Law, 1966. xliii + 289p. (Special publications, No. 8; Commonwealth law series, No. 4)

GREAT BRITAIN. Committee on Consumer Credit (Chairman: Lord Crowther)

Consumer credit: report of the Committee. HMSO, 1971. 2 vols. (Cmnd 4596)

GUEST, A. G.

The law of hire-purchase, with practice, precedents and pleadings by J. C. Tylor. SM, 1966. lix + 678p.

MACLEOD, J. K.

Sale and hire purchase. B, 1971. lvi + 449p.

5. PERSONS AND FAMILY LAW (INCLUDING THE LAW OF NAMES)

The law of persons has failed to carve out for itself a separate niche in English legal literature. BLACKSTONE treated it as a distinct category by devoting the first book of his *Commentaries on the Laws of England* to the "Rights of Persons", which contained, besides what is now called constitutional law, an account of the law of persons and of family law. This arrangement was consistent with Roman law traditions and also reflected the influence of the then prevailing theories of natural law. For these reasons a similar category of law has found its special place in the European codes. Not so in English law, without a code and only marginally affected by Roman law. Moreover, much of the law concerned with persons is drawn from several distinct bodies of law, chiefly common law and equity, and imperfectly fused by statute; for example, the law of names consists of the rules concerning the equitable remedy of injunction and some statute law.

The result has been a disparate treatment of the subject. Certain topics which in other systems are regarded as falling within the law of persons are in England dealt with elsewhere. Thus, nationality is treated within the context of constitutional law, domicile under conflict of laws (but also, for practical reasons, under divorce) loss of civil rights under criminal law, absentees under procedure and evidence and under divorce.

At one time these factors which have militated against a comprehensive exposition of the law of persons operated particularly with regard to that part of it dealing with the family, but the last decade or so has seen a remarkable change in this respect. The readiness of lawyers to interpret the family unit in a large sense and to see it in its wider social context, the mass of post war legislation affecting it and the increasing demands for its reform, and, perhaps most significantly, the acceptance of family law as a course of study at almost all the university Schools of Law have all had a coalescing effect and have led to general treatises on the subject. These changes have in turn led to a shift of emphasis in the treatment of some classes of persons. This is particularly so of minors. Although they are for some purposes still treated under other branches of law, they now fall primarily within the ambit of family law.

Select Bibliography

General works

BLACKSTONE, Sir W.
Commentaries on the laws of England. Oxford, Clarendon Pr., 1765-69. 4 vols. (For details of various editions see HOLDSWORTH, *History of English law*, vol. 12, p. 712)

COODE, C. A.
The law of the individual according to age and sex. SM, 1968. xxxviii + 259p.

Family law

a. General

BROMLEY, P. M.
Family law, 4th ed. B, 1971. lxxxii + 561p.

GRAVESON, R. H. and CRANE, F. R., eds
A century of family law, 1857-1957. SM, 1957. xviii + 459p.

HALL, J. C.
Sources of family law. CUP, 1966. xxiii + 514p. (Suppl.)

JACKSON, J.
The formation and annulment of marriage, 2nd ed. B, 1969. xlvi + 468p.

JOHNSON, E. L.
Family law, 2nd ed. SM, 1965. xlii + 357p.

PUXON, M.
Family law, 2nd ed. Penguin, 1971. 319p. (1st edition entitled *The family and the law*)

TURNER-SAMUELS, M.
The law of married women. Ipswich, Thames Bank, 1957. lv + 480p.

WEBB, P. R. H. and BEVAN, H. K.
Source book of family law. B, 1964. lii + 673p.

b. Matrimonial proceedings

ANTHONY, E. and BERRYMAN, J. D.
Legal guide to domestic proceedings. B, 1968. 151p.

GREAT BRITAIN. Royal Commission on Marriage and Divorce (Chairman: Lord Morton)
Report. HMSO, 1956. ix + 405p. (Cmd 9678)

HUMPHREYS, T. S.
Notes on matrimonial causes proceeding in county courts and district registries, 9th ed. by H. C. Collins. Oyez, 1968. viii + 177p.

MCGREGOR, O. R.
Divorce in England. Heinemann, 1957. xi + 220p.

PASSINGHAM, B.
The Divorce Reform Act, 1969. B, 1970. xii + 60p.

PUGH, L. M.
Matrimonial proceedings before magistrates, 2nd ed. B, 1966. xxxii + 406p.

RAYDEN, W.
Law and practice in divorce and family matters, 11th ed. Editor-in-chief: J. Jackson. B, 1971. cclii + 3240 + 151p. (Suppl.)

ROSEN, L.
Matrimonial offences, 2nd ed. Oyez, 1965. xlv + 361p.

TOLSTOY, D.
Divorce and matrimonial causes, including proceedings in magistrates' courts, 7th ed. by D. Tolstoy and C. Kenworthy. SM, 1971. lxvii + 627p.

WILKINSON, G. S.
Summary matrimonial and guardianship orders, 3rd ed. Oyez, 1967. 228p.

c. Children

GREAT BRITAIN. Care of Children Committee (Chairman: Dame Myra Curtis)
Training in child care. HMSO, 1946. 2 vols. (Cmd 6760; 6922) (Interim and final reports of the Committee)

GREAT BRITAIN. Committee on Children and Young Persons (Chairman: Lord Ingleby)
Report. HMSO, 1960. 179p. (Cmnd 1191)

GREAT BRITAIN. Committee on the Age of Majority (Chairman: Mr Justice Latey)
Report. HMSO, 1967. 207p. (Cmnd 3342)

GREAT BRITAIN. Committee on Local Authority and Allied Personal Social Services (Chairman: F. Seebohm)
Report. HMSO, 1968. 370p. (Cmnd 3703)

GREAT BRITAIN. Home Office
Children in trouble. HMSO, 1968. 24p. (Cmnd 3601)

HALL, Sir W. Clarke and MORRISON, A. C. L.
Law relating to children and young persons, 7th ed. by L. G. Banwell and J. R. Nicol. B, 1967. xlv + 878 + 54p. (Suppl.)

JAMES, T. E.
Child law. SM, 1962. xxxv + 202p.

JOSLING, J. F.
Adoption of children, 6th ed. Oyez, 1965. 166p.

LEEDING, A. E.
Child care manual, 2nd ed. B, 1971. xii + 167p.

PUXON, M.
Legitimacy and legitimation. Oyez, 1965. 64p.

TIMMS, N.
Casework in the child care service, 2nd ed. B, 1969. x + 180p.

WILKINSON, G. S.
Affiliation law and practice, 3rd ed. by J. F. Josling. Oyez, 1971. 191p.

Mental health

HEYWOOD, N. A. and MASSEY, A. S.
Court of protection practice, 9th ed. by D. G. Hunt and others. S, 1971. xl + 524p.

Associations

HALLIS, F.
Corporate personality: a study in jurisprudence. OUP, 1930. lxiii + 257p.

LLOYD, D.
The law relating to unincorporated associations. SM, 1938. xvi + 248p. (Yorke Prize essay, 1937)
See also Company law, Commercial law, Industrial law.

Law of names

JOSLING, J. F.
Change of name, 8th ed. Oyez, 1964, reprinted 1967. 53p.

JOSLING, J. F.
Registration of business names, 3rd ed. SLS, 1955. 41p.

6. SUCCESSION

The law of succession has not usually been studied apart from the law of property as a whole, but there is now a tendency to treat it as a separate subject. There have long been separate books, mainly for practitioners, dealing with wills and other branches of the law of succession.

Certain peculiarities of the English law of succession should be noted.

1. The whole estate of a deceased person now vests in his personal representative (executor or administrator), who takes no beneficial interest as such but gets in debts due to the deceased, pays his debts *intra vires hereditatis*, and distributes the net estate among legatees and devisees. There is no longer an heir. What remains of the estate after payment of debts and satisfaction of specific legacies or devises is handed over to residuary legatees or devisees or (in the case of total or

partial intestacy) to those entitled to take the residue. The powers of a Continental "heir" are vested in the personal representative, his beneficial rights in the residuary legatee or devisee or the next of kin.

2. There is no legitim or reserve; but certain relatives of the deceased may apply to the court for a discretionary allowance from the estate if they are not sufficiently provided for. This right is available not only in cases of testate but also of intestate succession or a combination of the two.

3. Since the rules of the law of wills are much more complex than those of intestate succession, there are no longer any separate treatises on the latter.

4. On an intestacy the surviving spouse has a first claim to £8,750 if there are issue, and to £30,000 if there are no issue but certain other near relatives of the deceased. This takes care of a large number of small or medium-sized estates, and is a rule which should be understood in connection with the principle of separation of matrimonial property and, to some extent, counteracting its effect.

5. The interpretation of wills has given rise to an immense number of technical rules of construction, all binding on the courts. Accordingly some of the books on wills are greatly inflated.

6. No line can be drawn between settlements, including marriage settlements, and succession; much that would appear in matrimonial regimes in other laws appears in England in the law of succession.

7. From a practical point of view the law of succession has been deeply influenced by the law of death duties, and in view of the dominating influence of the latter on the development especially of the law of wills, the principles governing the law of death duties are often discussed in books on succession. For books expressly dealing with death duties see the section on Taxation.

Select Bibliography

BAILEY, S. J.

The law of wills, 6th ed. Pitman, 1967. ix + 356p.

HAWKINS, F. V. and RYDER, E. C.

The construction of wills. SM, 1965. lviii + 418p.

JARMAN, T.

A treatise on wills, 8th ed. by R. Jennings. SM, 1951. 3 vols.

KER, B. S.

Wills, probate and administration. SM, 1959. xxiv + 294p.

MUSTOE, N. E.

Executors and administrators, 5th ed. B, 1952. xliv + 299p.

PARRY, Sir D. H.

The law of succession, 5th ed. SM, 1966. xxxvi + 369p.

THEOBALD, Sir H. S.

Theobald on wills, 13th ed. by S. Cretney and G. Dworkin. S, 1971. cxcv + 798p.

WILLIAMS, Sir E. V. and MORTIMER, H. C.

Executors, administrators and probate, being the 15th ed. of *Williams on executors* and the 3rd ed. of *Mortimer on probate*, by J. H. G. Sunnucks. Special editor (probate): R. L. Bayne Powell. S, 1970. clxxxviii + 1172p.

WILLIAMS, W. J.

The law relating to wills, 3rd ed. B, 1967. cccvii + 1296p. (Suppl.)

VIII. COMMERCIAL LAW

I. GENERAL

The characteristic feature of the commercial law of England is that it is not the law of a particular class of persons, such as the merchants or traders, but that it forms part of the general law of the country; it is only for reasons of convenience that commercial law is sometimes treated separately from the other branches of English law. Consequently, the boundaries of commercial law are not clearly defined in England, and textbooks on commercial law sometimes include in their ambit a review of the general law of contract and of those torts which occur frequently in business life, while some books on contract, e.g. the leading treatise of CHITTY, contain chapters dealing with special transactions normally regarded as pertaining to commercial law. The fundamental proposition that in England commercial law is merely a division of the general law of the country is best illustrated by two examples: first, every physical person may be made bankrupt, whether he is a merchant or trader or pursues another calling, profession or trade. Secondly, the general cleavage of English law into rules which have their origin in the common law and others which originate in the practice of the courts of equity, is reflected in commercial law: speaking generally, the law of commercial associations, such as partnerships and companies, is administered by the Chancery Division of the High Court, while commercial transactions and contracts are normally tried in Queen's Bench Division.

English commercial law did not always form part of the general law of the country. That development is the last stage of an evolutionary process completed in the eighteenth century. In the first period of its history, English commercial law was distinctly the law of a class, namely of cosmopolitan merchants who frequented the fairs and ports of the various European countries. In this first period which stretches from the beginnings to the time of Sir Edward Coke (1552-1632), English commercial law was the local variety of the law merchant which consisted of the international usage and practice of merchants engaged in foreign trade. The international character of the law merchant of this period may be indicated by one example: the maritime law of England was contained in the Black Book of Admiralty, a collection of documents compiled for the use of the Court of Admiralty probably in the time of Henry VI (1422-61); it was founded on the so-called Judgments of Oléron, which originated in a small commune near Bordeaux and were accepted as the general maritime law of the Atlantic ports; in the English practice as laid down in the Black Book those judgments were amended by eleven articles which were mostly of English origin. In the sixteenth century English commercial law entered into its second phase, which extends from the time of Coke to that of Lord Mansfield, who was Lord Chief Justice of England from 1756 to 1788. Coke made a determined and successful attack on the Court of Admiralty, which was the rival of the common law courts in matters of commercial jurisdiction. His view that "the law merchant is part of the laws of this realm" became, in the course of time, generally accepted, but at least in the first half of this period the lex mercatoria was still regarded as a custom applying to a special class of persons, namely to merchants engaged in foreign trade. In the second half of this period this restrictive view was gradually abandoned and the rules of commercial law began to be applied to all people engaged in commercial transactions. Characteristic of this transition is a statement of TREBY, C.J., in *Bromwich* v. *Lloyd* (1699) 2 Lut. 1582, 1585, that bills of exchange at first extended only to merchant strangers trading with English merchants, afterwards to inland bills between merchants trading with one another in England, and lastly to all persons whether traders or not. However, in most commercial proceedings it was still necessary to prove the existence of a mercantile custom if a rule of commercial law was invoked. In the third period, which begins with Lord Mansfield's term of office as Lord Chief Justice, proof was no longer required in order to establish a commercial custom. Lord Mansfield completed the integration of those customs into the common law and developed them into a body of systematic principles which provided a lasting foundation of the commercial law of England. In his time English commercial law shed the character of a class law and was completely absorbed by the general law of the country. In the nineteenth century commercial law was further rationalized and analysed by the great lawyers whose names survive in the leading treatises on the various branches of commercial law. Sir Mackenzie Chalmers drafted the Bills of Exchange Act, 1882, the Sale of Goods Act, 1893, and the Marine Insurance Act, 1906. These codes, together with that of partnership law contained mainly in the Partnership Act, 1890 and with the Companies Acts of 1948 and 1967, form the framework of modern commercial law in England; in more recent years this statutory structure has been supplemented by the Carriage of Goods by Sea Act, 1924 (founded on the Hague Rules relating to bills of lading), and the Carriage by Air Act, 1961 (based on the Warsaw Convention of 1924 and the Hague Protocol of 1955) as amended by the Carriage by Air (Supplementary Provisions) Act, 1962, which incorporated the Guadalajara Convention of 1961. Other important comprehensive statutes are the Bankruptcy Act, 1914, and the Hire-Purchase Act, 1965.

It has already been indicated that the boundaries of English commercial law are ill-defined. There exists no generally accepted division of the subject. SMITH, the last author who wrote a comprehensive treatise for practitioners on the subject, divided his work into three parts, the first dealing, under the title of *Mercantile Persons*, with the law relating to sole traders, partners, incorporated trading companies, principal and agent; the second treating *Mercantile Contracts*, namely negotiable instruments, contracts of carriage, contracts of insurance, the sale of goods and contracts of guaranties; and the third dealing with *Mercantile Remedies*, particularly in the case of bankruptcy. In this chapter, the following divisions are adopted:

2. partnership and company law;
3. the sale of goods;
4. transport and insurance;
5. maritime law;
6. negotiable instruments and banking;
7. commercial securities and insolvency;
8. industrial property;
9. mines and minerals;
10. monopolies and restrictive practices.

The literature on English commercial law is remarkable in one respect: the various branches of the subject have grown so much and have become so detailed that there does not exist an up-to-date practitioners' treatise dealing with commercial law as a whole; practitioners prefer to consult the treatises on the various branches of the subject. Students' textbooks, on the other hand, have largely maintained the old unity of commercial law, but while some, e.g. STEVENS AND BORRIE, include company law within their purview, others, like CHARLESWORTH, reserve that topic to treatment in a separate volume. These, and other features of the various works on commercial law are noted in this bibliography.

Select Bibliography

History of commercial law

ASSOCIATION OF AMERICAN LAW SCHOOLS
Select essays in Anglo-American legal history. Boston, Little, Brown, 1907-09. 3 vols. (Vol. 3)

BEWES, W. A.
The romance of the law merchant. SM, 1923. ix + 148p.

HOLDSWORTH, Sir W. S.
A history of English law. Methuen, 1903-66, reprinted 1966. 16 vols. (Vols 5 and 8)

MALYNES, G. de
Consuetudo vel lex mercatoria, or, the ancient law merchant. Islip, 1636. 333p.
This book, which is the first treatise on commercial law written in English, still makes interesting reading. The author was a business man not a lawyer.

MATHEW, Sir T.
The practice of the commercial court. B, 1902. xii + 108p.

MITCHELL, W.
An essay on the early history of the law merchant. CUP, 1904. 176p.

MOLLOY, C.
De jure maritimo et navali, or, a treatise of affairs maritime, and of commerce, 10th ed. Whieldon, 1778. 2 vols.

POLLOCK, Sir F. and others
The commercial law of Great Britain and Ireland. SM, 1913. 2 vols.

ROSCOE, E. S.
Studies in the history of the admiralty and prize courts. S, 1932. vii + 84p.

SCRUTTON, T. E.
The elements of mercantile law. Clowes, 1891. viii + 236p.

SELDEN SOCIETY
Select cases concerning the law merchant.
Vol. 1: Local courts, 1270-1638, edited by Charles Gross (Selden Society Publication no. 28)
Vol. 2: Central courts including Assizes, 1239-1633, edited by Hubert Hall (Selden Society Publication no. 46)
Vol. 3: 1251-1779, edited by Hubert Hall (Selden Society Publication no. 49)

SELDEN SOCIETY
Select pleas in the court of Admiralty.
Vol. 1: 1390-1404; 1527-1545, edited by R. G. Marsden. (Selden Society Publication no. 6)
Vol. 2: 1547-1602, edited by R. G. Marsden. (Selden Society Publication no. 11)

SMITH, J. W.
A compendium of mercantile law, 13th ed. by H. C. Gutteridge. S, 1931. ccxxvi + 888p.

Text books

BORRIE, G. J.

Commercial law, 3rd ed. B, 1970. lviii + 378p.

CHARLESWORTH, J.

Mercantile law, 12th ed. by C. M. Schmitthoff and D. A. G. Sarre. S, 1972. xlix + 485p.

This is an introductory work and does not include company law which is treated in a separate volume. (See section on company law)

DIXON, A.

An introduction to mercantile and commercial law. Heinemann, 1969. xvi + 368p.

GOODEVE, L. A.

The modern law of personal property, 9th ed. by R. H. Kersley. SM, 1949. lxv + 699p.

LIGHT, H. R.

The legal aspects of business and general principles of law, 6th ed. Pitman, 1965. xv + 368p.

LOWE, R.

Commercial law, 3rd ed. SM, 1970. xxxix + 573p.

MERRITT, N. and CLAYTON, E. G. H.

Business law. SM, 1966. xxiv + 294p.

PATON, G. W.

Bailment in common law. S, 1952. xl + 454p.

PITMAN & CO.

. . . *Commercial law*, 15th ed. by John Nevin. Pitman, 1966. xiv + 282p.

RANKING, D. F. de L'H.

Mercantile law, 12th ed. by W. W. Bigg and J. H. Thompson. H.F.L., 1966. xlii + 338p.

This work, which does not include company law, is particularly used by students of the accountancy profession.

SLATER, J. A.

Mercantile law, 15th ed. by Lord Chorley and O. C. Giles. Pitman, 1965. xliv + 484p.

This work includes the elements of company law and commercial torts. It has a valuable appendix of notes on leading cases and statutes.

SMITH, K. and KEENAN, D. J.

Essentials of mercantile law, 2nd ed. Pitman, 1969. xi + 619p.

STEVENS, T. M.

Elements of mercantile law, 15th ed. by Gordon J. Borrie. B, 1969. xlvi + 567p.

VAINES, J. Crossley

Personal property, 4th ed. B, 1967. lxix + 536 + 30p.

WILSHERE, A. N. M.

Principles of the common law, 6th ed. by A. N. M. Wilshere and B. Chedlow. SM, 1951. xlvii + 846p.

Case books

BORRIE, G. J.

Sourcebook of commercial law. B, 1967. xxix + 336p.

CHARLESWORTH, J.
Cases on mercantile law. S, 1951. xxxii + 328p.
CHORLEY, R. S. T., Baron Chorley and TUCKER, H.A.
Leading cases on mercantile law, 4th ed. B, 1962. xxxvi + 384p.
IVAMY, E. R. Hardy
Casebook on mercantile law. B, 1967. xxxiv + 370p.

Practitioners' treatises

CHITTY, J.
Chitty on contracts, 23rd ed. by A. G. Guest and others. SM, 1968. 2 vols.
MITCHELL, E.
The businessman's lawyer, 2nd ed. Business Publications, 1965. xiii + 567p.
MITCHELL, E.
The retailer's lawyer. Business Publications, 1963. xii + 285p.
SMITH, J. W.
A compendium of mercantile law, 13th ed. by H. C. Gutteridge. S, 1931. ccxxvi + 888p.

Although a great treatise, this work is now out of date, and practitioners now consult detailed treatises on specialised aspects of commercial law.

Commercial law reports and periodicals

LLOYD'S LAW REPORTS, 1919– . Lloyd's. (1919–1952, entitled *Lloyd's list law reports*)

These reports are of very great value to everyone interested in Commercial law. They are the only series of general commercial law reports still in existence.

LLOYD'S REPORTS OF PRIZE CASES, 1st series 1914-22. 10 vols. 2nd series, 1940-57. 1 vol. Lloyd's, 1915-58.

REPORTS OF BANKRUPTCY AND COMPANIES WINDING UP CASES . . . 1915-42. SM, 1916-43. 20 vols.

Cases in 1943 and later are published in the *Law reports* and *All England reports.*

REPORTS OF COMMERCIAL CASES, 1895-1941. B, 1895-1941. 46 vols.

REPORTS OF PATENT, DESIGN, TRADE MARK AND OTHER CASES . . . together with a digest of cases, 1884- . The Patent Office.

TRAFFIC CASES: being reports of cases decided by the Transport Tribunal. Vol. 22– . HMSO, 1935– . (Continuation of *Railway and canal traffic cases*, Vols. 1-21, 1855-1934)

Periodicals

JOURNAL OF BUSINESS LAW, 1957- . S.
JOURNAL OF WORLD TRADE LAW, vol. 1- . Vincent Pr., 1967- .

2. PARTNERSHIP AND COMPANY LAW

Partnerships and companies form the two principal types of commercial associations known to English law. The basic distinction between them is that partnerships are unincorporated and each partner is an agent of himself and the other partners, each of whom is in consequence liable to the full extent of his personal fortune for the partnership debts. Companies, on the other hand, are corporate entities. Hence the liability of the company is solely that of the corporate body and the members are not responsible for its debts except indirectly through calls on them in accordance with the terms of the company's constitution. This normally limits the members' liability to the nominal amount of shares for which they have subscribed, the company then being described as "limited by shares", but non-trading companies can be formed as companies limited by guarantee, the members agreeing to pay a fixed sum if needed in the liquidation of the company. Alternatively, the members' liability may be unlimited, i.e. they may, under the company's constitution, agree to guarantee the whole of the company's liabilities, but such a company is naturally uncommon.

Companies may still be formed by a special Act of Parliament or by Royal Charter, but today this rarely occurs. Overwhelmingly the common type of company is that formed under a series of statutes culminating and consolidated in the Companies Act 1948, and subsequently added to and modified by the Companies Act 1967. These, though in no sense a complete codification of company law, constitute the basic statutory framework and they apply both to England and to Scotland. In relation to the latter they are supplemented by the Companies (Floating Charges) (Scotland) Act 1961. Other statutes of vital relevance are the Prevention of Fraud (Investments) Act 1958 and the Protection of Depositors Act 1963, which, with the regulations made thereunder, supplement the Companies Acts so as to produce something approaching a legislative code of Securities Regulation.

The Companies Acts enable companies to be incorporated relatively simply and cheaply by registration with the Department of Trade and Industry. An association formed for the purposes of gain and consisting of more than 20 persons must normally either be incorporated under these Acts or under the authority of some special or general Act of Parliament (for example, co-operative and building societies can be incorporated under the Industrial and Provident Societies Acts and the Building Societies Acts respectively, and Friendly Societies can be formed as unincorporated societies under the Friendly Societies Acts). If, however, the number of members is below twenty, the parties can choose whether to adopt the form of a partnership or of a company. Since the latter confers all the advantages of corporate personality (including limited liability) with relatively little expense, the company form is gradually superseding partnership except in the professions, some of which may, as a result of a concession in the 1967 Act, have more than 20 partners. Little use is made of the limited partnership (*société en commandite*) which was only introduced into England in 1907 and which is far less convenient than a fully limited company under the Companies Acts.

The Law of Partnership was codified by the Partnership Act 1890 (modified as regards limited partnership by the Limited Partnership Act 1907).

Select Bibliography

Partnership

a. Introductory

ELMAN, P. P.

The law in relation to partners. S, 1948. vii + 84p.

b. Students' books

PENNINGTON, R. R.

Partnership and company law. B, 1962. l + 284p.

This is an introductory book covering both partnership and company law, and primarily intended for those studying for solicitors' examinations.

STRAHAN, J. A. and OLDHAM, N. H.

The law of partnership, 6th ed. by H. G. Hanbury. SM, 1944. xvi + 141p.

UNDERHILL, Sir A.

Principles of the law of partnership, 9th ed. by G. Hesketh. B, 1971. xxx + 178 + 27p.

c. Practitioners' books

LINDLEY, N., Baron Lindley

The law of partnership, 13th ed. by E. H. Scamell. SM, 1971. clii + 950p.

POLLOCK, Sir F.

Law of partnership, 15th ed. by L. C. B. Gower. S, 1952. xxxv + 272p.

This book is now much out of date, but it is of some interest as it was written by the draftsman of the Act.

Company law

There is an immense literature on company law, a subject which is studied not only by lawyers, but also by accountants, economists and the business world generally. Here it is only possible to give a selection likely to be of most use to the foreign lawyer.

a. Introductory

For a full understanding of modern English company law it is essential to appreciate how the present day company has gradually evolved from partnerships and trusts. The most scholarly treatment of the formative years will be found in two fascinating American works:

DUBOIS, A. B.

The English business company after the Bubble Act, 1720-1800. New York, The Commonwealth Fund, 1938. xxi + 522p. (Bibliography, pp. 441–72) (Publications of the Foundation for Research in Legal History, Columbia University School of Law)

HUNT, B. C.

The development of the business corporation in England, 1800-1867. Cambridge, Harvard UP, 1936. xii + 182p. (Bibliography, pp. 163–71) (Harvard economic studies, vol. 52)

Shorter summaries of the whole story are:

COOKE, C. A.

Corporation, trust and company. Manchester UP, 1950. 206p.

FORMOY, R. R.

The historical foundations of modern company law. SM, 1923. xii + 151p.

b. Students' books

CHARLESWORTH, J.

Company law, 10th ed. by T. E. Cain. S, 1972. lxiv + 555p.

GOWER, L. C. B.

The principles of modern company law, 3rd ed. S, 1969. lxxviii + 716p.

HORNBY, J. A.

An introduction to company law, 3rd ed. Hutchinson, 1969. 208p.

PENNINGTON, R. R.

Company law, 2nd ed. B, 1967. xciv + 815p.

CHARLESWORTH and HORNBY are probably the best introductory works, while GOWER is more suitable for the needs of foreign students intending to make a serious study of English company law.

c. Practitioners' books

BUCKLEY, H. B., Baron Wrenbury

Buckley on the Companies Acts, 13th ed. by J. B. Lindon. B, 1957, reprinted 1964. ccxxxii + 1230 + 165p. (Suppl.)

This is a copiously annotated edition of the companies legislation and a mine of information on points of detail.

GORE-BROWNE, Sir F.

Companies, 42nd ed. by A. J. Boyle and R. Sykes. Jordan, 1972. cxlii + 1223p.

HALSBURY'S LAWS OF ENGLAND, 3rd ed. B, 1952-64. 43 vols. (Suppl.) (Vol. 6: Companies)

PALMER, Sir F. B.

Company Law, 21st ed. by C. M. Schmitthoff and J. H. Thompson. S, 1968. cxxviii + 1556p. (Suppl.)

This book, which went through a bad period, has been enormously improved in the last two editions. The actual text is less than 900 pages, the rest consisting of appendices of legislation, regulations, etc.

PALMER, Sir F. B.

Company precedents. S, 1952-60. 3 vols. (Various editions) (Vol. 1: General forms; vol. 2: Winding up; vol. 3: Debentures)

This copiously annotated precedent book formerly exercised an immense influence on the development of the law and practice, but it is now gravely out of date.

WEINBERG, M. A.

Take-overs and mergers, 3rd ed. by M. A. Weinberg with M. V. Blank and A. L. Greystoke. SM, 1971. xxxi + 533p.

This is an invaluable monograph on the topical subject of take-overs and mergers. On these, reference should also be made to:

CITY WORKING PARTY

The City code on take-overs and mergers, 3rd revised ed. Issuing Houses Association, 1972. 47p.

This may be obtained from the Secretary, Issuing Houses Association, 20 Fenchurch Street, London EC3M 3DB. Supplementary practice notes are available from the Secretary, Panel on Take-overs and Mergers, P.O. Box 226, The Stock Exchange Building, London EC2P 2JX.

d. Official papers

It has become the practice of the Department of Trade and Industry, formerly Board of Trade, to appoint an expert committee to review the working of the Companies Act at intervals of about twenty years. The reports of these Committees leading to amending legislation are most illuminating. The latest report is that of the Jenkins Committee:

GREAT BRITAIN. Board of Trade. Company Law Committee (Chairman: Lord Jenkins)

Report. HMSO, 1962. ix + 223p. (Cmnd 1749)

The Department of Trade also publish a useful annual report on companies, which contains detailed statistics illustrating the administration of the Companies Act:

GREAT BRITAIN. Department of Trade and Industry

Companies: annual report (for the year ended December 31...). HMSO, 1891- .

Though not strictly an official publication, an essential reference source in relation to quoted companies is:

STOCK EXCHANGE

Admission of securities to quotation. Office of the Council of the Stock Exchange, 1969- . (Loose leaf) (Obtainable from the publisher)

Other organizations

References to the books on trade unions will be found in the chapter on Labour law, and to those on public corporations (a type of statutory corporation designed to operate the nationalised industries) in the section on Administrative law. As regards other types of organization distinguishable from, but to some extent analagous to, partnerships and companies, reference should be made to the following:

FORD, H. A. J.

Unincorporated non-profit associations. OUP, 1959. xxii + 151p.

HALSBURY'S LAWS OF ENGLAND, 3rd ed. B, 1952-64. 43 vols. (Suppl.) (Vol. 18: Friendly societies; vol. 21: Industrial and provident societies)

LAWTON, C. L.

Guide to the law of trustee savings banks, 3rd ed. Savings Banks Institute, 1962. 2 vols. (Suppl.)

WURTZBURG, E. A. and MILLS, J.

Building society law, 13th ed. S, 1970. xlvii + 632p. (Deals with associations formed to facilitate the purchase of houses)

3. THE SALE OF GOODS

The law relating to the sale of goods is codified in the Sale of Goods Act, 1893, which occupies a central position in this branch of law. As in the case of all codified branches of English law, the case law before the creation of the code is, after the codification, only consulted in the rare instances where a solution cannot be found by interpretation of the provisions of the code. Since 1894—the Act came into operation on January 1, 1894—a considerable and steadily expanding body of modern case law has grown up and today the provisions of the Act are complemented by the modern practice of the courts. A study of English sales law without reference to the interpretation of the provisions of the Act by the courts would not convey a complete and accurate picture of the present position; in particular, the sections of the Act dealing with the measure of damages payable by a defaulting party should be read in conjunction with recent decisions of the courts.

Four features of English sales law should be noted: first, as regards the transfer of property, English law adopts the consensual, and not the real theory: intention, and not delivery, passes property. Secondly, agreement of the parties on the price is not essential: if the parties have failed to fix the price or make arrangements for its ascertainment, a reasonable price has to be paid. Thirdly, it is a fundamental term—a condition—of the contract of sale that the seller shall transfer the property in the goods sold to the buyer; and fourthly, the tendency of English law is to restrict the right of the buyer to reject the goods and to favour his right to claim damages for breach of warranty; this tendency is particularly noticeable in the provision that among the acts which are deemed to be an acceptance of the goods, are acts "inconsistent with the ownership of the seller".

In the case of a sale by a person who has no right to sell the goods, English sales law admits a number of exceptions to the common law rule that a person cannot give a better title than he himself possesses; in these exceptional cases the title of the bona fide purchaser is protected. The same legislative tendency to protect normal transactions of commerce is noticeable in the Factors Act, 1889: some provisions of this Act are almost identical with the relevant sections of the Sale of Goods Act, 1893, and others are designed to protect persons entering into bona fide dealings with mercantile agents who dispose of goods or documents of title belonging to their principals without authority of the latter. In view of the close affinity between the principles on which the Factors Act, 1889, is founded, and those governing the part of the Sale of Goods Act, 1893, dealing with the protection of the bona fide purchaser, most English books on the general law of the sale of goods include a treatment of the provisions of the Factors Act.

Apart from books dealing with the sale of goods in general, there are works dealing with separate aspects of that branch of law, such as the law of the export trade, the law of hire-purchase, the law of auctions and the law relating to the sale of food and drugs.

Select Bibliography

a. General law

Introductory

AUSTIN, C. G.
The law of the sale of goods. Pitman, 1932. xiii + 158p.

EASTWOOD, R. A.
The contract of the sale of goods, 2nd ed. B, 1946. viii + 166 + 5p.

Text books

ATIYAH, P. S.
The sale of goods, 4th ed. Pitman, 1971. xxxii + 356p.

CHALMERS, Sir M. D.
Sale of Goods Act, 1893, 16th ed. by M. Mark. B, 1971. xciv + 350p.

FRIDMAN, G. H. L.
Sale of goods. SM, 1966. xxvii + 347p.

IVAMY, E. R. Hardy
Casebook on the sale of goods, 2nd ed. B, 1969. xx + 220p.

SCHMITTHOFF, C. M.
The sale of goods, 2nd ed. S, 1966. xxxviii + 381p.

This book attempts to review the provisions of the Act in the light of modern case law: in one of its appendices the Hire Purchase Act of 1965 is reproduced, and in another the Uniform Laws on International Sales Act, 1967.

Practitioners' treatises

BENJAMIN, J. P.

Treatise on the law of the sale of personal property, 8th ed. by D. L. Finnemore and A. E. James. SM, 1950. l + 1091p. (Suppl.)

BLACKBURN, C., Baron Blackburn

A treatise on the effect of the contract of sale, 3rd ed. by W. N. Raeburn and L. C. Thomas. S, 1910. xli + 657p.

These two books written in narrative form, treat the law of sales comprehensively. Benjamin is very expansive but has not quite shaken off the pre-code atmosphere in which it was conceived. Blackburn is now out of date, but the views of the author, where applicable, command the highest authority in the English courts.

CHITTY, J.

Chitty on contracts, 23rd ed. by A. G. Guest. SM, 1968. 2 vols.

GOODEVE, L. A.

The modern law of personal property, 9th ed. by R. H. Kersley. SM, 1949. lxv + 699p.

GREAT BRITAIN. Law Reform Committee

First Report: Statute of Frauds and Section 4 of the Sale of Goods Act, 1893. HMSO, 1953. 4p. (Cmd 8809)

HALSBURY'S LAWS OF ENGLAND, 3rd ed. B, 1952-64. 43 vols. (Suppl.) (Vol. 34 pp. 1-187 Sale of Goods.)

MITCHELL, E.

The sales executive's lawyer and businessman's guide to the law of buying and selling. Business Publications, 1966. xii + 341p.

This book is of especial value to the business man.

b. Special subjects

Export Trade Law

PURCHASE, H. G.

The law relating to documents of title to goods. SM, 1931. xxiv + 261p.

SASSOON, D. M.

C.I.F. and F.O.B. contracts. S, 1968. xxxiv + 460 + 6p. (British Shipping Laws, vol. 5)

SCHMITTHOFF, C. M.

The export trade: the law and practice of international trade, 5th ed. S, 1969. xxxii + 451p.

This book deals with the elements of export trade law as a whole. It includes in its purview, apart from the sale of goods abroad, the following topics: The Uniform Laws on International Sale of Goods; the law of agents and other representatives abroad; the finance of export (bills of exchange and documentary credits); export credit guarantees; insurance of exports; carriage of exports by sea and air; patents and trade marks abroad; arbitration and litigation; export licences; exchange control; customs regulations and relief from purchase tax.

SCHMITTHOFF, C. M.

Legal aspects of export sales, 2nd ed. Institute of Export, 1969. 76p.

A short survey of the principles of the law relating to the sale of goods abroad in the light of modern case law.

SCHMITTHOFF, C. M.

The sources of the law of international trade. S, 1964. xxvi + 292p.

(See also: Commercial credits; Carriage of goods; Insurance.)

Hire Purchase law

BROWN, H.

The practitioners' guide to hire purchase cases. SM, 1965. lxv + 271p.

DIAMOND, A. L.

Introduction to hire purchase law, 2nd ed. B, 1971. xxv + 169p.

GREAT BRITAIN. Committee on Consumer Credit (Chairman: Lord Crowther)

Consumer credit: report of the Committee. HMSO, 1971. 2 vols. (Cmnd 4596)

GUEST, A. G.

The law of hire purchase . . . with practice, precedents and pleadings by J. C. Tylor. SM, 1966. lix + 678p.

PATON, G. W.

Bailment in the common law. S, 1952. xl + 454p.

WILD, D. H.

The law of hire purchase, 2nd ed. B, 1965. xli + 341p.

Trade descriptions

EGAN, B.

Trade descriptions: the new law. LRS Publishers, 1968. 4 + 46p.

A useful introductory book for the layman.

LEAPER, W. J.

Implications for business of the new trade descriptions law. Business Books, 1968. x + 211p.

O'KEEFE, J. A.

The Trade Descriptions Act, 1968. B, 1968. xvii + 238p.

Law of auctions

BATEMAN, J.

Law of auctions, 11th ed. by D. Napley. Estates Gazette, 1954. lxxix + 593p.

Sale of food and drugs

BELL, Sir W. J. and O'KEEFE, J. A.

Sale of food and drugs, 14th ed. by J. A. O'Keefe. B, 1968. liv + 1585p. (Kept up to date with a loose leaf supplementary volume)

Uniform law on international sales

GRAVESON, R. H. and others

The Uniform Laws on International Sales Act, 1967. B, 1968. xii + 195p.

The Uniform Laws on International Sales Act is also treated in Schmitthoff's *Sale of goods,* 2nd ed. and *Export trade,* 5th ed.

4. TRANSPORT AND INSURANCE

(a) *Transport*

The natural division of the law of transport is into carriage by land, sea and air. Of these topics, carriage by sea has received the fullest treatment in English legal literature; the books dealing with that subject are listed in the section on maritime law. In Great Britain, effect is given to the Hague Rules relating to bills of lading by the Carriage of Goods by Sea Act, 1924, which, subject to certain exceptions, applies to all outward bills of lading relating to goods shipped from Great Britain. The rules of the Warsaw Convention on international air carriage are given statutory force in Great Britain, subject to certain exceptions, adaptations and modifications; with respect to international carriage by air this is done by the Carriage by Air Act, 1961, amended by the Carriage by Air (Supplementary Provisions) Act, 1962, and with respect to other carriage by air the Carriage by Air Acts (Application of Provisions) Order, 1967.

The literature dealing with the nationalization and partial de-nationalization of transport is not treated in this section.

Select Bibliography

General

POWELL-SMITH, V.

The Transport Act, 1968. B, 1969. vi + 290p.

RIDLEY, J. G.

The law of the carriage of goods by land, sea and air, 3rd ed. Shaw, 1971. xlviii + 223p.

SCHUMER, L. A.

The elements of transport, 3rd ed. B, 1967. 211p.

Carriage by air

MCNAIR, Sir A. D.

The law of the air, 3rd ed. by M. R. E. Kerr and A. H. M. Evans. S, 1964. xxxviii + 588p.

SEABROOKE, G.

Air law. Univ. of London Pr., 1964. viii + 323p.

This is an introductory book for students.

SHAWCROSS, C. N. and BEAUMONT, K. M.

Shawcross and Beaumont on air law, 3rd ed. by P. B. Keenan, A. Lester and P. Martin. B, 1966. 2 vols. (Volume 2 in 2 parts, loose leaf)

This is a comprehensive and detailed practitioners' book.

Carriage by land

BINGHAM, L.

Motor claims cases, 6th ed. by J. A. Taylor. B, 1968. liii + 821p. (Suppl.)

A digest and analysis of annotated cases and of statutory matter.

ENCYCLOPAEDIA OF ROAD TRAFFIC LAW AND PRACTICE, general editor J. Burke. SM. 3 vols. (Loose leaf publication)

An invaluable and comprehensive practitioners' book.

GIBB, A. D. and MILLNER, R.

The trial of motor car accident cases, 3rd ed. SM, 1947. vi + 345p.

KAHN-FREUND, O.

The law of carriage by inland transport, 4th ed. S, 1965. xlvii + 815p.

This is a students' book.

KITCHIN, L. D.

Road transport law, 15th ed. rewritten and revised by E. K. Wenlock. Iliffe, 1970. 7 + 231p.

This book is mainly for the layman but is of use to the lawyer in search of up-to-date information on legislation, statutory orders and practical detail.

LESLIE, A.

The law of transport by railway, 2nd ed. SM, 1928. lxx + 852p.

MCFARLANE, K.

Motorists and the law. S, 1951. vii + 119p.

A short summary written for the layman.

MAHAFFY, R. P. and DODSON, Sir G.

Road traffic acts and orders, 3rd ed. by G. Kidner. B, 1961. 2 vols.

MAXWELL, E. F. M.

The law relating to carriers' licences under the Road and Rail Traffic Act, 1933. SM, 1936. xi + 330p.

POTTER, D. C. L.

The law relating to garages and car parks. B, 1939. lxii + 384p.

ROBERTS, R. O. and GIBB, A. D.

The law of collisions on land, 5th ed. S, 1947. xlii + 479p.

TRAFFIC CASES: being reports of cases decided by the Transport Tribunal. Vol. 22- . HMSO, 1935- . (Continuation of *Railway and Canal Traffic Cases.* Vols. 1-21, 1855-1934)

This series contains reports of the decisions of the Transport Tribunal, mainly on questions of licences, under the Road and Rail Traffic Acts or the Transport Act, 1947.

WILKINSON, G. S.

Road traffic offences, 6th ed. Oyez, 1970. lxxvii + 655p.

Carriage by sea. *See under* **Maritime law**

(b) *Insurance*

Insurance is a well-developed branch of English commercial law. Apart from the law of marine insurance, which is codified in the Marine Insurance Act, 1906, the law of insurance is largely founded on the decisions of the courts. The generally accepted division of insurance law and practice is into marine and non-marine insurance. The former is again treated in the section on maritime law. National insurance and industrial insurance are not regarded by the English lawyer as being within the purview of commercial law.

Select Bibliography

General

COLINVAUX, R. P.

The law of insurance, 3rd ed. SM, 1970. lxxiv + 379p.

An excellent introduction to the subject, particularly for law students.

DINSDALE, W. A.

Elements of insurance, 4th ed. by W. A. Dinsdale and D. C. McMurdie. Pitman, 1971. xvi + 221p.

A good introduction to the basic principles of Insurance law, written particularly for the students of the Chartered Insurance Institute.

IVAMY, E. R. Hardy

General principles of insurance law, 2nd ed. B, 1970. lxxix + 596p.

MACGILLIVRAY, E. J.
MacGillivray on insurance law relating to all risks other than marine, 5th ed. by D. Browne. SM, 1961. 2 vols.
This is the leading practitioners' book on the subject.

PICARD, M. P.
Elements of insurance law, relating to all risks other than marine, 2nd ed. SM, 1939. xii + 188p.

RAYNES, H. E.
A history of British insurance, 2nd ed. Pitman, 1964. 394p.

RAYNES, H. E.
Principles of British insurance. Pitman, 1953. vii + 189p.
A useful introduction to the economic, financial and legal aspects of insurance.

Special aspects

BANFIELD, G. E.
Principles and law of accident insurance, 5th ed. Pitman, 1950. x + 171p.

DINSDALE, W. A.
Principles and practice of accident insurance, 8th ed. Buckley, 1969. xiii + 266p.
This book deals mainly with the practical aspects of insurance law.

EAGLE, M. G.
Special perils insurance. Pitman, 1963. ix + 132p.

GILBERT, G. W.
Motor insurance, 3rd ed. Pitman, 1949. xvi + 372p.

GODWIN, F.
The principles and practice of fire insurance in the United Kingdom, 7th ed. by K. C. Woods. Pitman, 1954. ix + 147p.

GOLDING, C. E.
The law and practice of reinsurance, 3rd ed. Buckley, 1954. 176p.

HONOUR, W. B.
Honour and Hickmott's principles and practice of interruption insurance, 4th ed. B, 1970. xv + 671p.

HOUSEMAN, D.
Law of life assurance, 7th ed. by E. A. Holder. B, 1970. xxiii + 280 + 25p.
This is a good general survey of the subject.

IVAMY, E. R. Hardy
Casebook on insurance law. B, 1969. xxviii + 225p.
A very useful book for students and practitioners alike.

IVAMY, E. R. Hardy
Fire and motor insurance. B, 1968. xxxv + 453p.
An excellent textbook for students.

MACKEN, A. G. and HICKMOTT, G. J. R.
The insurance of profits, 6th ed., revised and reprinted. Pitman, 1965. xi + 153p.

MADGE, P.
Professional indemnity insurance. B, 1968. xvi + 216p.

NEW, L. J.
Life assurance; from proposal to policy, 8th ed. Pitman, 1968. ix + 165p.
This is a book for students and practitioners.

RILEY, D.
Consequential loss insurances and claims, 3rd ed. SM, 1967. viii + 362p.
SHAWCROSS, C. N.
On the law of motor insurance, 2nd ed. by C. N. Shawcross and M. Lee. B, 1949. lxxxix + 752 + 92p.
SMITH, T. R. and FRANCIS, H. W.
Fire insurance theory and practice, 5th ed. Stone and Cox, 1967. 157p.
TAYLOR, H.
Fire insurance law, 2nd ed. by J. K. Jones. Pitman, 1959. xxi + 133p.
WELFORD, A. W. B.
The law relating to accident insurance, 2nd ed. B, 1932. cvi + 612 + 56p.
WELFORD, A. W. B. and OTTER-BARRY, W. W.
The law relating to fire insurance, 4th ed. by S. H. Noakes. B, 1948. civ + 544 + 55p.
WELSON, J. B.
Accident insurance claims, 2nd ed. by E. Killick. Pitman, 1963. xiii + 217p.
WELSON, J. B. and TAYLOR, H.
Insurance administration, 8th ed. by W. A. Dinsdale. Pitman, 1963. ix + 310p.
WHITMORE, E.
Employers' liability insurance. Pitman, 1962. xxiv + 231 p.

5. MARITIME LAW

"Maritime Law" is not a term which is in general use among English lawyers. There is, for example, no modern text-book which is entitled "Maritime Law". The main reason for this is one of classification. Broadly speaking, however, there are two groups or classes of subjects which may be said to comprise "Maritime Law":

(1) the group falling within the jurisdiction of the Commercial Court, e.g. contracts relating to the carriage of goods by sea and contracts of marine insurance;

(2) the group falling within the jurisdiction of the Admiralty and Prize Court, in the Queen's Bench Division of the High Court, e.g. collisions, salvage, towage, limitation of liability.

Select Bibliography

General

CHORLEY, R. S. T., Baron Chorley, and GILES, O. C.
Shipping law, 6th ed. Pitman, 1970. xxv + 405p.
MACLACHLAN, D.
A treatise on the law of merchant shipping, 7th ed. by G. St. C. Pilcher and O. L. Bateson. SM, 1932. cviii + 935p.
SINGH, N. and COLINVAUX, R. P.
Shipowners. S, 1967. xxvi + 402 + 28p. (British Shipping Laws, vol. 13)
STANTON, L. F. H.
The law and practice of sea transport. Glasgow, Brown, Son & Ferguson, 1964. xxxiii + 356p.

STEVENS, E. F.
Shipping practice, 9th ed. Pitman, 1970. x + 173p.
WRIGHT, C. and FAYLE, C. E.
A history of Lloyd's. Macmillan, 1928. xxi + 475p.

Admiralty practice

MCGUFFIE, K. C. and others
Admiralty practice. S, 1964. lxxviii + 773p. (Suppl.) (British Shipping Laws, vol. 1)

Carriage by sea

ASTLE, W. E.
Shipowners' cargo liabilities and immunities, 3rd ed. Witherby, 1967. x + 482p.
BARTLE, R. D.
Introduction to shipping law, 2nd ed. SM, 1963. xv + 241p.
CARVER, T. G.
Carriage by sea, 12th ed. by R. P. Colinvaux. S, 1971. 2 vols. (British Shipping Laws, vols 2 and 3)
IVAMY, E. R. Hardy
Casebook on carriage by sea, 2nd ed. B, 1971. xxv + 172p.
PAYNE, W.
Carriage of goods by sea, 8th ed. by E. R. Hardy Ivamy. B, 1968. xlv + 241p.
SCRUTTON, Sir T. E.
Scrutton on charterparties and bills of lading, 17th ed. by Sir W. L. McNair and others. SM, 1964. xcvi + 599p.
SELVIG, E.
Unit limitation of carriers liability: the Hague Rules. Pitman, 1961. 264p.
SUMMERSKILL, M. B.
Laytime. SM, 1966. xxvii + 282p.
TETLEY, W.
Marine cargo claims. S, 1965. xxxix + 404p.
TIBERG, H.
The law of demurrage. S, 1971. lxxx + 676p. (This is the 2nd ed. of "*The law of demurrage*", 1960, and the 2nd ed. of "*The claim of demurrage*", 1962)

Collisions at sea

MARSDEN, R. C.
The law of collisions at sea, 11th ed. by K. C. McGuffie. S, 1961. lxxxvi + 975p. (Suppl.) (British Shipping Laws, vol. 4)

General average

LOWNDES, R. and RUDOLF, G. R.
The law of general average, 9th ed. by J. F. Donaldson and others. S, 1964. xxix + 501p.
SELMER, K. S.
The survival of general average. Pitman, 1958. 312p.

International conventions

SINGH, N.
International conventions of merchant shipping. S, 1963. xv + 1327p. (British Shipping Laws, vol. 8)

Marine insurance

ARNOULD, Sir J.
The law of marine insurance and average, 15th ed. by Lord Chorley and C. T. Bailhache. S, 1961. 2 vols. (British Shipping Laws, vols 9 and 10.)

CHALMERS, Sir M. D.
Marine Insurance Act, 1906, 7th ed. by E. R. Hardy Ivamy. B, 1971. lvi + 248 + 26p.

DOVER, V.
Analysis of marine insurance clauses, 8th ed. Witherby, 1960. vii + 582p.

DOVER, V.
A handbook to marine insurance, 6th ed. Witherby, 1962. xxii + 915p.

DOVER, V. and CALVER, C. A.
The banker's guide to marine insurance of goods. Witherby, 1960. xvi + 500p.

ELDRIDGE, W. H.
Marine policies, 3rd ed. by H. Atkins. B, 1938. xlviii + 291 + 19p.

GOW, W.
Marine insurance: a handbook, 5th ed. by D. King-Page. Macmillan, 1931. xxviii + 484p.

IVAMY, E. R. Hardy
Casebook on insurance law. B, 1969. xxviii + 225p.

IVAMY, E. R. Hardy
Marine insurance. B, 1969. liv + 586p.

Merchant Shipping Acts

TEMPERLEY, R.
Merchant Shipping Acts, 6th ed. by Waldo Porges and Michael Thomas. S, 1963. cii + 872 + 82p. (British Shipping Laws, vol. 11)

Salvage

KENNEDY, W. R.
Civil salvage, 4th ed. by K. C. McGuffie. S, 1958. xl + 442p.

6. LAW OF NEGOTIABLE INSTRUMENTS AND BANKING

(a) *Law of Negotiable Instruments*

As negotiable instruments are widely used in international trade, it is not surprising that the general principles relating thereto in English law are similar to those in other systems of law. There are, however, certain features of this branch of English law which are not of general application. Thus the practice of crossing a cheque originated in England, and to this day the system is not generally recognized by the law of other countries.

Prior to the seventeenth century the law relating to negotiable instruments was administered in what may conveniently be described as "merchants' courts", where the judges were themselves usually merchants and, therefore, well versed in international trading transactions. During the seventeenth century this jurisdiction was taken over by the Common Law Courts, though special attention continued to be paid to the opinions and practices of the merchants. In 1882 an Act of Parliament was passed (the Bills of Exchange Act) which codified the law. Since then there have been several legislative amendments, and in addition the courts have been called upon to interpret many sections of the 1882 Act. Therefore it is unwise to advise on problems in this branch of English law after having studied only the codifying statute.

Select Bibliography

BYLES, Sir J. B.
Bills of exchange: the law of bills of exchange, promissory notes, bank notes and cheques, 23rd ed. by M. Megrah and F. R. Ryder. SM, 1972. lxxxviii + 471p.

CHALMERS, Sir M. D.
Chalmers on bills of exchange, 13th ed. by D. A. L. Smout. S, 1964. xlix + 420p.

Both of the books noted above are leading practitioners' books.

HOLDEN, J. M.
The history of negotiable instruments in English law. Athlone Pr., 1955. xl + 339 + 10p.

This is a very full historical account.

MEGRAH, M. H.
The Bills of Exchange Act, 1882 and negotiable instruments generally, 5th ed. Pitman, 1957. v + 181 + 16p.

RICHARDSON, D.
Guide to negotiable instruments and the Bills of Exchange Acts, 4th ed. B, 1970. ix + 187p.

Both MEGRAH and RICHARDSON are introductory books.

(b) *Banking*

Many problems of banking law are concerned with the payment and collection of cheques and other negotiable instruments, and, in relation thereto, it is useful to refer initially to the books listed in (a) above.

Banking law, however, is concerned with the general relationship between banker and customer, and there are many aspects of the subject which do not involve negotiable instruments.

Select Bibliography

CHORLEY, R. S. T., Baron Chorley and HOLDEN, J. M.
The law of banking, 5th ed. Pitman, 1967. xxviii + 316 + 14p.

CHORLEY, R. S. T., Baron Chorley and SMART, P. E.
Leading cases in the law of banking, 2nd ed. Pitman, 1966. xxx + 299 + 6p.

DAVIS, A. G.
The law relating to commercial letters of credit, 3rd ed. Pitman, 1963. xxiv + 217 + 10p.

GUTTERIDGE, H. C. and MEGRAH, M.
The law of bankers' commercial credits, 4th ed. Europa, 1968. xxiii + 241 + 20p.
HALSBURY'S LAWS OF ENGLAND, 3rd ed. B, 1952-64. 43 vols. (Suppl.) (Vol. 2 Banking)
HOLDEN, J. M.
Banker and customer. Pitman, 1970. liii + 485p. (Law and practice of banking, vol. 1)
HOLDEN, J. M.
Securities for bankers' advances, 5th ed. Pitman, 1971. xxxviii + 427p. (Law and practice of banking, vol. 2)
PAGET, Sir J.
Law of banking, 8th ed. by M. Megrah. B, 1972. lxii + 736p.

Periodicals and law reports

THE BANKER, vol. 1- , 1926- . The Banker Ltd.
THE BANKERS' MAGAZINE, vol. 1- , 1844- .(1844-89 entitled *The Bankers' magazine and Journal of the money market;* 1890–1952 entitled *The Bankers', insurance managers and agents' magazine*.)
JOURNAL OF THE INSTITUTE OF BANKERS, vol. 1- , 1879- . Institute of Bankers.
LEGAL DECISIONS AFFECTING BANKERS, vol. 1- , 1879/1900- . Institute of Bankers.

7. COMMERCIAL SECURITIES AND INSOLVENCY

For the purposes of this bibliography, it is convenient to deal with these subjects under one heading, although in modern English commercial law the tendency is to treat them separately.

(a) *Commercial securities*

This topic comprises bills of sale, liens and contracts of guarantee or suretyship. Special types of commercial securities, such as the transfer of shares or of policies of insurance by way of security, or the pledging of goods or documents of title for these purposes, or the issue of negotiable instruments, are outside the purview of this section.

A bill of sale is an instrument by which a personal chattel is mortgaged by the owner (the transferor) to another person (the transferee) in such a manner that the property in the chattel is agreed to be transferred to the transferee but the chattel itself remains in the possession of the transferor. Bills of sale are governed chiefly by two enactments, the Bills of Sale Acts, 1878 and 1882, which provide that where such arrangements are made in writing, they have to comply with certain formalities, e.g. they have to be attested, and the instruments have to be registered in a public register; otherwise they are often invalid. There are two kinds of bills of sale: absolute bills under which the property in the mortgaged chattel passes absolutely to the transferee, and bills by way of security for money; the Act of 1878 applies to the former, and both Acts apply to the latter. The transfer of ships—even where unfinished—by way of security is not within the scope of the Bills of Sale Acts.

A lien is a right of one person to retain the property of another until certain demands by the former against the latter are satisfied. Unlike a pledge, a lien does not confer on the person claiming it a right to sell the retained goods in satisfaction of the demands made by him unless the right of sale is expressly given to him by contract or statute; thus, a right of sale is given to the unpaid seller by the Sale of Goods Act, 1893, section 39, and to a bailee who has accepted goods in the course of his business for repair or other treatment, by virtue of the Disposal of Uncollected Goods Act, 1952. Liens are divided into two types: possessory liens and maritime liens. The former can only be claimed if, and as long as, the claimant has possession of the goods against which he claims the lien. Such lien may be a particular lien, i.e. a lien covering only claims arising from a particular transaction, or a general lien, i.e. a lien which by custom or contract can be exercised for the general balance owing by the owner of the goods to the claimant. A maritime lien exists on ship, cargo and freight for claims for damage caused by collisions, for bottomry bonds or respondentia, and for seamen's wages or certain other services such as towage and pilotage.

A contract of guarantee or suretyship is a contract by which a person undertakes to answer for the debt or liability of another person either personally or with his property. In modern commercial law there is hardly a difference between those two types of contract; the liability of the guarantor or surety is collateral to that of the principal debtor; the guarantor or surety is responsible when the principal debtor is in default but unless provided otherwise by contract or custom, the creditor may hold the guarantor or surety liable without first suing the principal debtor. A person can be guarantor or surety without holding himself personally liable, by pledging part of his property to the creditor. Contracts of guarantee or suretyship are distinguished from contracts of indemnity which provide for an independent and primary liability of the indemnor.

Select Bibliography

EAGLESON, J. G.

The law relating to bills of sale, contracts of sale, liens on crops and wool and stock mortgages. Melbourne, C. F. Maxwell, 1911. xxvii + 394p.

The literature on this subject is scanty, but as well as EAGLESON, the works by Sir W. Valentine BALL and Edward T. BALDWIN, which are referred to below, treat bills of sale fully.

GOODE, R. M.

Hire-purchase law and practice, 2nd ed. B, 1970. lxxii + 1302p.

GOODEVE, L. A.

Modern law of personal property, 9th ed. by R. H. Kersley. SM, 1949. lxv + 699p. (Chapter II: part 3)

PATON, G. W.

Bailment in the common law. S, 1952. xl + 454p.

PRICE, G.

The law of maritime liens. SM, 1940. xxiii + 264p.

ROWLATT, Sir S. A. T.

The law of principal and surety, 3rd ed. by A. A. Mocatta. SM, 1936. liii + 356p.

On the history of Guarantee and suretyship see the judgement of Luxmoore, J., in *Re Conley*, [1938] 2 All E.R. pp. 133–140.

(b) *Insolvency*

This topic is divided into three parts, viz. the law of bankruptcy, of deeds of arrangement and of receiverships.

1. The English Law of Bankruptcy is founded on statutes the first of which was passed in the reign of Henry VIII. The present law is contained in the Bankruptcy Act, 1914, as amended by the Bankruptcy (Amendment) Act, 1926, and the Companies Act, 1947. In English law, not only traders but all individuals, whatever their trade, calling or profession, may be made bankrupt. Companies cannot be made bankrupt; in the case of insolvency, they may be wound up voluntarily or by order of the court.

2. Deeds of arrangement are used where it is intended to administer the estate of a debtor outside the law of bankruptcy in a manner giving the creditors or their trustee control over the debtor's property. The Deeds of Arrangement Act, 1914, provides, inter alia, that certain types of deeds shall be registered in a public register, and contains machinery for procuring the creditors' assent to the deed.

3. A receiver is a person appointed by the court or by a creditor for the purpose of collecting and receiving certain property. While the institution of receivership is of general character and receivers may be appointed by the court for reasons other than the default of the debtor, receiverships are used where a debtor is in default and it is intended that an impartial person should collect his income, or income derived from particular property, or the property itself, and should make it available to the creditor. In particular, where the debtor has secured the debt by a mortgage or where the debtor is a company which has issued debentures carrying a mortgage or charge, a receiver may be appointed for the benefit of the mortgagee or debenture holder.

Most books on bankruptcy include a treatment of the law relating to deeds of arrangement, but receiverships are not normally covered by them. They are dealt with in books on equity, on mortgages and on company law.

Select Bibliography

Bankruptcy and Deeds of Arrangement

BALDWIN, E. T.

The law of bankruptcy and bills of sale, 11th ed. Stevens & Haynes, 1915. xcviii + 1422p.

This work is now obsolete.

BALL, W. V.

Bankruptcy, deeds of arrangement and bills of sale, 5th ed. by W. V. Ball and D. Geddes. Pitman, 1934. li + 405 + 26p.

A very clear and useful student's book.

CHALMERS, Sir M. D. and HOUGH, E.

The Bankruptcy Acts 1914 and 1926, and the Deeds of Arrangement Act 1914 ... with a commentary thereon by V. R. Aronson and S. J. Campling, 9th ed. Waterlow, 1938. xcii + 836p.

CRUCHLEY, I.

A handbook on bankruptcy law and practice, 2nd ed. Oyez, 1964. xl + 266p.

RINGWOOD, R.

The principles of bankruptcy, 18th ed. by H. Jacobs. SM, 1947. xliv + 272p.

SALES, C. A.

The law relating to bankruptcy, liquidations and receiverships, 5th ed. Macdonald & Evans, 1956. xliii + 446p.

THOMPSON, J. H.

The principles of bankruptcy law. HFL, 1967. xx + 139p.

An excellent book which can be strongly recommended.

WILLIAMS, Sir R. L. B. V.

Law and practice of bankruptcy, 18th ed. by M. Hunter and D. Graham. S, 1968. cxxvii + 1047p.

This leading treatise has been well brought up to date.

Receiverships

GRIFFITHS, O.

The law relating to bankruptcy, deeds of arrangement, receiverships and trusteeships, 8th ed. by P. W. D. Redmond. Macdonald & Evans, 1967. xxiv + 262p.

This is a book mainly used by students of accountancy.

KERR, W. W.

The law and practice as to receivers, 14th ed. by R. Walton. SM, 1972. lii + 385p.

An excellent legal treatise.

RANKING, D. F. de l'H. and others

The rights and duties of liquidators, trustees and receivers, 22nd ed. by H. A. R. J. Wilson and R. D. Penfold. H. F. Lynch & Co., 1955. xxxix + 461p.

This is a book used mainly by students of accountancy.

8. INDUSTRIAL PROPERTY

(a) *Patents for Inventions*

The governing statutes are the Patents Acts, 1949-1961, which should be read with the Patents Rules 1968 (S.I. 1968 No. 1389 as amended by S.I. 1968 No. 1702). The Acts and Rules are set out with annotations in the manuals of the Chartered Institute of Patent Agents and the Patent Office.

The Acts are not a complete code, though the procedure for obtaining Letters Patent has been laid down by statute and the Patent Office is a creation of statute. The British patent system dates back over three hundred years and much of the law, especially that relating to the validity and infringement of patents is only to be obtained from decided cases and from the text-books in which they are discussed. Since 1883 reports of patent cases have not generally been included in the ordinary series of law reports, and for cases since that date reference should be made to the special series, *Reports of Patent Design, Trade Mark and Other Cases*, London, Patent Office, 1884- . Another series intended to provide more rapid reports of industrial property cases, is the *Fleet Street Patent Law Reports*, London, 1963- .

The British method of dating a patent, with its system of provisional and current specifications and the system of priorities which results, is unusual and requires careful study by those familiar with systems of law not derived from the current British legislation.

Select Bibliography

General

BAXTER, J. W.
World patent law and practice. SM, 1968. xiv + 363p. (Suppl.)
A most useful compendium of law and practice in different countries, including Britain.

BOEHM, K.
The British patent system. CUP, 1967. x + 184p. (Vol. 1: Administration)

FOX, H. G.
Monopolies and patents: a study of the history and future of the patent monopoly. Toronto, University of Toronto Pr., 1947. xxv + 388p.
The most extensive historical treatment of the patent system.

GRACE, H. W.
A handbook on patents. Knight, 1971. viii + 185p.

GREAT BRITAIN. Committee to examine the Patent System and Patent Law (Chairman: M. A. L. Banks)
Report: the British patent system. HMSO, 1970. xx + 234p. (Cmnd 4407)

MEINHARDT, P.
Inventions, patents and trade marks. Gower Pr., 1971. xvii + 397p.

WHITE, T. A. B. and JACOB, R.
Patents, trade marks, copyright and industrial designs. SM, 1970. xv + 189p.
A useful short account of all the major fields of industrial property law.

Law reports

FLEET STREET PATENT LAW REPORTS, no. 1- , 1963- . Fleet Street Patent Law Reports Ltd.

REPORTS OF PATENT, DESIGN, TRADE MARK AND OTHER CASES . . . together with a digest of cases, 1884- . The Patent Office.

Manuals

THE CHARTERED INSTITUTE OF PATENT AGENTS
The Patents Acts, 1949–1961, 2nd ed. SM, 1968. ix + 377p. (Suppl.)

GREAT BRITAIN. Patent Office
Patent Office manual of office practice (patents). Patent Office, 1969– . (Loose leaf)

Text books

MELVILLE, L. W.
Precedents on industrial property and commercial choses in action. SM, 1965. xxxv + 287p.
This book gives much useful information on dealings in patents and other industrial property.

TERRELL, T.
The law of patents, 12th ed. by D. Falconer and others. SM, lxviii + 706p.

WHITE, T. A. B.
Patents for inventions and the registration of industrial designs, 3rd ed. S, 1962. lvi + 640p.
The two books noted above are the leading works of reference for legal practitioners and patent agents.

(b) *Industrial Designs*

The governing statute is the Registered Designs Act, 1949, together with the Copyright Act, 1956, section 10, as amended by the Design Copyright Act, 1968. Again decided cases are needed to elucidate certain fundamental conceptions upon which the statutes are based, and these are generally reported only in the *Reports of Patent Cases* and the *Fleet Street Patent Law Reports* (supra).

Select Bibliography

GREAT BRITAIN. Board of Trade. Departmental Committee on Industrial Designs (Chairman: K. Johnston)

Report. HMSO, 1962. 143p. (Cmnd 1808)

RUSSELL-CLARKE, A. D.

Copyright in industrial designs, 4th ed. SM, 1968. xx + 237p.

WHITE, T. A. B.

Patents for inventions and the registration of industrial designs, 3rd ed. S, 1962. lvi + 640p.

(c) *Plant Variety Rights*

This new form of industrial property was created by the Plant Varieties and Seeds Act, 1964. It confers rights similar to those of patentees of inventions on the breeders of new plant varieties, and creates a register of plant variety names coupled with exclusive rights in the name of a new breed for its breeder. The best account of the law and practice relating to applications for protection is to be found in the *Encyclopaedia of Court Forms and Precedents in Civil Proceedings*, 2nd ed., Vol. 31, pp. 278 ff.

(d) *Trade Secrets*

The broad jurisdiction of courts of equity to restrain breaches of confidence has increasing importance in the fields of industrial "know-how" and commercial secrets. The law has developed through judicial decisions, many of the authorities being reported only in the *Reports of Patent Cases* and the *Fleet Street Law Reports* (supra).

Select Bibliography

TURNER, A. E.

The law of trade secrets. SM, 1962. xxxi + 519p. (Suppl.)

A discussion of English and United States law on the subject.

(e) *Trade Marks*

Registered trade marks are dealt with under the Trade Marks Act, 1938. Reference should also be made to the Trade Mark Rules, HMSO (S.R. & O. 661 of 1938). The obscurity of certain provisions of the Act makes it essential to give careful consideration to the case-law, mostly to be found in the *Reports of Patent Cases* and the *Fleet Street Patent Law Reports* (supra) and to the leading textbook, KERLY.

No general doctrine of unfair competition has yet emerged in English law, but unregistered trade marks and other forms of deception as to the origin of goods or the ownership of a business are regulated by the law of passing off, malicious falsehood and related economic torts, which are discussed in general textbooks on the law of tort. Misuse of trade marks, registered and unregistered, together with the passing off of goods or businesses, may lead to criminal liability under the Trade Descriptions Act, 1968.

Select Bibliography

KERLY, Sir D. M.
The law of trade marks and trade names, 10th ed. by T. A. B. White and R. Jacob. SM, 1972. xciii + 807p.

O'KEEFE, J. A.
The Trade Descriptions Act, 1968. B, 1968. xvii + 238p.

(f) *Copyright*

The Copyright Act, 1956 is the closest of the industrial property statutes to a complete code, but the law is further developed in decided cases. These were regularly published in MACGILLIVRAY, E. J., *Copyright Cases*, 9 vols, London, The Publishers' Association, between 1901 and 1949. Since then cases that do not appear in the ordinary series of law reports may be found in *The Author*, London, Society of Authors, 1889- .

Select Bibliography

BOGSCH, A.
The law of copyright under the Universal Convention, 3rd revised ed. New York, R. R. Bowker & Co., 1968. xxxvi + 696p.

CARTER-RUCK, P. F. and SKONE JAMES, E. P.
Copyright: modern law and practice, ed. by F. E. Skone James. Faber, 1965. 640p.

COPINGER, W. A. and SKONE JAMES, F. E.
Copyright, 11th ed. by E. P. Skone James. SM, 1971. xlviii + 920p.

WHALE, R. F.
Copyright: evolution, theory and practice. Longman, 1971. x + 217p.

9. MINES AND MINERALS

The law as to mines and minerals falls into two main categories: (a) ownership of minerals and rights to work them, including liability for damage caused in doing so, and (b) safety, health and welfare provisions relating to the operation of mines and quarries.

There is no established legal definition of the term "minerals". Broadly, they are substances in or under land, other than the soil, that have a use or value of their own. The common law rule is that the owner of surface land also owns the underlying minerals, but the rule is subject to exceptions. Unworked gold and silver are owned by the Crown. The working of lead and tin is in some places subject to local customs. The exploitation of petroleum (which by definition includes mineral oil and natural gas) is controlled under the Petroleum (Production) Act, 1934. Uranium and similar substances are dealt with under the Atomic Energy and Radioactive Substances Acts, 1946 to 1954, and minerals in the Continental Shelf are subject to the provisions of the Continental Shelf Act, 1964. Virtually all coal is owned and worked by the National Coal Board under the provisions of the Coal Industry Nationalisation Act, 1946 and relevant provisions of the Coal Act, 1938.

In order to work minerals it is normally necessary to have a freehold or leasehold interest in them, or a licence to work them. Specimen mining leases will be found in books of conveyancing precedents: see section on Real Property. The working of minerals underground in a mine usually results in the withdrawal of support from the surface, so that subsidence damage occurs. If the minerals are worked by opencast operations (i.e. quarrying) large areas of the surface will be disturbed. It is, therefore, necessary to distinguish between the right to work minerals and the right to withdraw support or otherwise affect the surface land and buildings etc. in the course of working minerals. The right to work minerals depends upon owning them, or having been granted the right to work them by the owner. The right to withdraw support from the surface depends partly on the terms of the deed which "severs" ownership of the minerals from ownership of the surface land, and partly on statutory provisions, e.g. Part II of the 2nd Schedule to the Coal Act, 1938.

If the necessary rights cannot otherwise be acquired (e.g. by lease or licence) application may be made to the court under the Mines (Working Facilities and Support) Act, 1966 for a working facilities order. Such an order will confer a right to search for and work minerals as well as any necessary ancillary rights, relating to such matters as the withdrawal of support, wayleaves, occupation of the surface, the disposal of waste material, and so on. The rights that can be obtained depend to some extent on the kind of minerals involved: working facilities orders in respect of coal are available only to the National Coal Board. A working facilities order is useful where it is necessary to be free from legal restrictions (e.g. those imposed under old deeds) which restrict or prevent the development of minerals; or where ownership of the minerals is split up among a great many people. On the grant of a working facilities order, compensation is payable where rights are overreached. The 1966 Act also provides for the granting of orders for the support of surface land and buildings which lack a right of support. Such orders are rarely made because the payment which would normally have to be made for the minerals "sterilised" by a support order is usually prohibitive.

The National Coal Board have a virtual monopoly in the ownership and working of coal, but they license the working of small mines by others under powers contained in section 36 of the Coal Industry Nationalisation Act, 1946. Working coal by opencast operations is regulated by the Opencast Coal Act, 1958. Those operations require the authorisation of the Minister of Power (the authorisation having effect as "deemed" planning permission) and are carried out by contractors working for a Department of the National Coal Board known as the Opencast Executive.

Some surface installations, such as railways, canals, reservoirs, motorways, etc. are protected under what is known as a mining code, an example of which will be found in Part IV of the 3rd Schedule to the Water Act, 1945. Broadly, the effect of a mining code is that a statutory undertaker which acquires surface land (say for a reservoir) does not acquire at the same time the supporting minerals, thereby avoiding the expense of buying minerals that may never be worked. Any mineral operator is required to give notice to the statutory undertaker when workings approach within a prescribed distance of the protected surface installation. The statutory undertaker then has the opportunity, on payment of compensation, to "sterilise" minerals necessary to ensure support for the surface. If the statutory undertaker does not take this action, the code permits the mineral operator to work the minerals, and the extent of his liability for any subsidence damage that occurs depends primarily upon the terms of the code which applies in the particular case, but also to some extent upon the general law.

The opening of mines and quarries requires specific planning permission under the Town and Country Planning Acts, 1962 to 1968: see Chapter 7, section 3(c). In many cases existing mining operations are covered by "deemed" planning permission granted under the Town and Country Planning General Development Order, 1963 No. 709—see Classes XVIII and XIX in the 1st Schedule to the Order. This "deemed" planning may be taken away by a direction made under article 4 of the Order, and it then becomes necessary to apply for specific planning permission if the mineral workings are to continue. Conditions (e.g. limiting extraction, regulating the use of the surface for tipping, requiring site restoration etc.) can be imposed under planning control, and compensation is available only to a limited extent if planning permission is refused or granted subject to onerous conditions.

Generally, where subsidence damage occurs, liability depends upon the terms of the deed which severed ownership of the surface land from ownership of the mines, and upon the terms and conditions on which the working of the minerals has been permitted. Where subsidence damage is caused by the working of coal, the National Coal Board have extensive liability under the Coal-Mining (Subsidence) Act, 1957, all kinds of property being protected. The scheme of the Act is that the National Coal Board are liable to carry out, or pay for, works necessary to render the damaged property reasonably fit for its normal use. Their financial liability does not, however, exceed the depreciation in the value of the property caused by the subsidence damage. A claimant has a choice of proceeding under the 1957 Act or by any other means available to him (e.g. a deed of severance). The 1957 Act also imposes on the Board obligations to re-house people who are temporarily displaced because of subsidence damage, and in some circumstances they are liable for injury caused by the happening of subsidence damage. The Mineral Workings Act, 1951 provides for the restoration of land used for the working of ironstone by opencast operations.

Safety requirements to be observed in the working of mines and quarries are contained in the Mines and Quarries Acts, 1954 and 1969 and regulations and orders made under those Acts. (The 1969 Act is concerned with the stability of tips.) If a contravention occurs, the owner and the manager and under-manager of the mine or quarry concerned are liable to criminal proceedings, which could result in a fine or imprisonment. Also liable to prosecution are various officials in the management hierarchy if they have been "charged" by the owner with securing fulfilment of the statutory requirement that has been contravened. Apart from criminal proceedings, a civil action for damages can be brought by anyone injured (or by a widow or other dependant in the case of death) where a contravention has occurred or there has not been a safe system of work.

The Acts of 1954 and 1969 are mainly concerned with safety, health and welfare, but the 1954 Act also contains restrictions on the employment of females or young persons below ground, and on the number of hours they may be employed at mines. Restrictions on hours of work below ground are also contained in the Coal Mines Regulation Act, 1908. Several statutes of the 19th century are still relevant to the working of mines and quarries: they will be found in *Hal bury's Statutes of England*, referred to in the bibliography below. The Mines and Quarries Act, 1954 also contains provisions relating to the reporting and investigation of accidents and diseases. Government inspectors have wide powers in relation to enforcement of the various safety provisions.

The law of Scotland differs in some respects from that of England and Wales, but the differences are not substantial so far as concerns the law relating to minerals and mines and quarries.

Select Bibliography

Encyclopaedic works

ENGLISH AND EMPIRE DIGEST, 2nd ed. B, 1950–1970. 56 vols. (Suppl.) (Vol. 33: Mines, minerals and quarries)

HALSBURY'S LAWS OF ENGLAND, 3rd ed. B, 1952-64. 43 vols. (Suppl.) (Vol. 26: Mines, minerals and quarries)

HALSBURY'S STATUTES OF ENGLAND, 3rd ed. B, 1968- . (To be completed in 41 volumes) (Vol. 22: Mines, minerals and quarries)

HALSBURY'S STATUTORY INSTRUMENTS, 2nd re-issue. B, 1951- . 24 vols. (Vol. 14: Mines, minerals and quarries)

In using the four works mentioned above, reference to the latest cumulative supplements and annual continuation volumes will ensure that the information is substantially up to date. For quick reference to the subject *Halsbury's laws of England* is best.

General works

ENEVER, F. A.
The law of support in relation to minerals. SLS, 1947. xiv + 162p.

This is the only book available which deals exclusively with the subject indicated by the title.

GREAT BRITAIN. Department of Trade and Industry
The law relating to safety and health in mines and quarries. HMSO, 1970-72. 4 parts. (Part 1: Acts, Part 2: Mines of coal, stratified ironstone, shale and fireclay, Part 3: Miscellaneous mines, Part 4: Quarries)

These are Government publications containing the text of the Mines and Quarries Act, 1954, and of the regulations and orders. Some of the regulations as printed have since been amended, revoked and replaced by others.

MACSWINNEY, R. F.
The law of mines, quarries and minerals, 5th ed. SM, 1922. xxxiv + 421p.

This is a useful work for reference to general principles, but is now very out of date.

NATIONAL COAL BOARD
The Colliery Official's handbook to the Mines and Quarries Act, 1954. National Coal Board, 1957. 98p.

A practical handbook on the 1954 Act.

PICKERING, J. R.

The Mines and Quarries Act, 1954. B, 1957. xii + 243p.

A lawyer's book on the 1954 Act.

SINCLAIR, J.

Coal mining law. Pitman, 1958. vii + 429p.

This book deals more particularly with the Mines and Quarries Act, 1954.

TOWNSHEND-ROSE, F. H. E.

The British coal industry. Allen & Unwin, 1951. 162p.

Describes the process by which first coal, and later the collieries, were nationalised; and the set-up in the nationalised coal industry.

TOWNSHEND-ROSE, F. H. E.

Introduction to mining law. Colliery Guardian, 1958. 59p.

An elementary account of the subject consisting of articles reprinted from the *Colliery Guardian.*

10. MONOPOLIES

In the nineteenth century there were two common law doctrines that might have been developed to restrain traders from combining to restrict competition. Since the Middle Ages the common law courts had refused to enforce a contract that restrained trade unreasonably. But, in contrast to the position in some United States jurisdictions, it was held that it is in no way wrongful to make or give effect to such contracts. The inability to sue on a contract that restrains trade unreasonably may be important when the restraint is accepted by the plaintiff's customer or supplier. The suppliers of petrol in the United Kingdom paid considerable sum for their retailers' undertakings not to stock other brands, and they lost the benefit of some of this expenditure when the House of Lords decided in *Esso Petroleum* v. *Harper's Garage* [1968] A.C. 269 that many of them were void as an unreasonable restraint of trade. In the case of horizontal cartels between producers, or between suppliers at the same level of trade, the inability to sue is probably not much of a disincentive, so the doctrine of restraint of trade is a weapon of limited application. But it may be argued that since the common law courts rarely consider the market power of the covenantee, and are hardly in a position to assess it, the common law doctrine which protects the freedom of the trader, rather than competition, is anomalous, and that the statutory bodies considered below should be left to decide whether a contract restricts competition rather than whether it restrains trade.

The other common law restriction on restraints of trade was the tort of conspiracy. It is actionable to combine to injure anyone by illegal means, or out of pure spite, when no trade interest is thereby protected. But in the famous case of *Mogul S.S. Co., Ltd.* v. *McGregor, Gow & Co. and others* [1892] A.C. 25 the House of Lords limited this tort. The defendants who were the members of a shipping conference deliberately combined to ruin a shipowner who attempted to enter the tea carrying trade. The combination probably was a contract in unreasonable restraint of trade, but the House held that this only made it void, and did not make it illegal to give effect to it. Consequently the conference had not used illegal means and the protection of their legitimate trade interest in monopolising the tea carrying trade was a defence. No attempt was made to decide whether people in England who buy tea would be better served by the scheduled sailings provided by the conference or by a more competitive freight market.

The Restrictive Trade Practices Acts, 1956 and 1968 require the parties to specified classes of agreements or arrangements to furnish particulars thereof to the Registrar of Restrictive Trading Agreements. The agreements affected are those under which at least two persons accept restrictions in respect of the prices to be charged, the quantities or kinds of goods to be produced or the persons, areas, etc. to be supplied. These include most of the agreements likely to restrict competition, although there are exemptions for many sorts of vertical agreements between a customer and his supplier, or a patentee and his licensee etc. If particulars of an agreement that should be notified are not furnished in due time, the agreement is void and anyone who can prove that he has been injured by the effect given to it can sue for breach of statutory duty, though he may have difficulty in proving the existence of the agreement, or in quantifying his loss. The Registrar has no powers of search and has experienced considerable difficulty in ensuring that all registrable agreements are notified to him. He is required to refer all agreements entered on his register to the Restrictive Practices Court, though there are provisions dispensing with a reference of agreements which are not of such significance as to call for an investigation, and those which have expired before he starts proceedings. There is also a provision for the temporary exemption by the Department of Trade and Industry of rationalisation agreements of substantial importance to the national economy—but it has been used only on one occasion. Few agreements have survived a reference to the Restrictive Practices Court, which must declare them to be contrary to the public interest unless they can be justified in one or more of the ways specified in section 21(1) of the 1956 Act as amended in 1968. Under the Resale Prices Act, 1964, it has become illegal to attempt to maintain minimum or fixed resale prices for all classes of goods other than books and medicaments.

Under the Monopolies and Mergers Acts of 1948 and 1965, the Monopolies Commission was set up to decide whether the existence of market power, or the things done as a result of it or in order to preserve it may be expected to operate against the public interest. They have no power of initiation, but the Department of Trade and Industry may refer to them the supply or export of any class of goods or services when the one third test is satisfied. This is that, of the reference products supplied in the U.K., or a substantial part of it, one third is supplied or acquired by either (1) a single person or corporate group, or (2) by two or more persons who whether voluntarily or not and whether by agreement or not, so conduct their affairs as to restrict competition. Most of the early references related to the fixing of prices by trade associations, but since 1956 the agreements that are subject to registration under the Restrictive Trade Practices Act cannot give rise to a reference to the Commission. The two or more persons whose one third share of the market may be a cause for reference, have therefore been either those agreeing about the charges for services, or firms who individually make vertical contracts with their customers that have been drafted to fall within the exemptions of the 1956 Act, but it may possibly include an oligopolistic situation, where there are only a few suppliers who take each others' probable reactions into account when making market decisions, and so cannot afford to compete aggressively in price. The Department can also refer prospective or recently consummated mergers to the Commission if, as a result of the enterprises ceasing to be distinct, the one third rule will apply, or apply to a greater extent in respect of any goods or services; or where the assets taken over are valued at over £5 million in the enterprise's accounts. If the Commission concludes that any of these conditions are satisfied, whether the dominant firm conditions, the cartel conditions or the merger ones, the Department of Trade and Industry has power to make an order forbidding certain kinds of conduct, and even ordering divestiture. Its powers, however, are not limited to the remedies recommended by the Commission. In fact it has made few orders, but prefers to negotiate undertakings by the firms, since these can be modified more easily if conditions change.

In the United Kingdom there are no per se offences except the collective enforcement of resale price maintenance by blacklist. It has been thought that collaboration may be desirable in some undefined circumstances, even if competition is restricted. The Department of Trade and Industry may refer to the Commission certain mergers, or goods and services in respect of which the one third test is satisfied, but it is under no duty to do so, and large parts of the United Kingdom trade and industry have not been referred. The Commission have not been given exclusive criteria to apply when deciding whether the market power or behaviour of the firms operates or may be expected to operate against the public interest, but should take into account anything they consider relevant. They have rarely condemned the market power enjoyed by a dominant firm, though they frequently condemn aspects of that firm's behaviour, especially where it excludes new entrants. They also assume that price or charge fixing agreements operate against the public interest unless there is some unusual justification in the context of a particular class of products. Those agreements that are subject to the Restrictive Trade Practices Act are more difficult to defend, but no tribunal, whether the common law courts, the Restrictive Practices Court or the Commission necessarily condemns restrictions of trade or competition.

On December 17, 1970, the Secretary of State announced the setting up of working parties to consider the reform of both the restrictive practices and monopolies legislation.

Select Bibliography

Books

ALLEN, G. C.

Monopoly and restrictive practices. Allen & Unwin, 1968. 183p.

Professor Allen was a member of the Monopolies Commission and discusses the policy towards market power in the light of British experience.

BARKER, R. E. and DAVIES, G. R., eds

Books are different: an account of the defence of the net book agreement before the Restrictive Practices Court in 1962. Macmillan, 1966. xx + 938p.

A detailed account of one case before the Restrictive Practices Court; one of the few sources for the Court's procedure.

BROCK, C.

The control of restrictive practices from 1956: a study of the Restrictive Practices Court. McGraw-Hill, 1966. [7] + 194p.

An attempt by an economist to discover an economic model in the Court's judgments.

CRANE, H.

Sweet encounter: the confectionery resale price maintenance case. Macmillan, 1969. 216p.

DIPLOCK, W. J. K., Baron Diplock

The role of the judicial process in the regulation of competition. OUP, 1968. 27p. (Hebrew University of Jerusalem, Lionel Cohen lectures, 13th series, 1967)

The author is a former President of the Restrictive Practices Court.

GALBRAITH, J. K.

American capitalism: the concept of countervailing power, revised ed. Penguin Books, 1963, reprinted 1968. 223p. (Revised edition first published in U.S.A. in 1956 and in Great Britain by Hamish Hamilton in 1957)

An excellent introduction to the economics of this subject, but not concerned primarily with the United Kingdom.

GUÉNAULT, P. H. and JACKSON, J. M.

The control of monopoly in the United Kingdom. Longmans, 1960, reprinted 1962. ix + 197p.

Describes the composition and procedure of the Commission and analyses some of the criteria developed by it. The Commission produced few reports between 1960 and 1966, so the book is almost as up to date as ROWLEY.

HUNTER, A.

Competition and the law. Allen & Unwin, 1966. 3 + 328p.

A very readable book by an economist, which includes some U.K. law.

HUNTER, A., ed.

Monopoly and competition: selected readings. Penguin Books, 1969. 429p. (Bibliography, pp. 399-407)

A collection of readings on economics, mainly chapters from books.

KORAH, V. L.

Monopolies and restrictive practices. Penguin Books, 1968. 256p.

An elementary introduction by a lawyer to the economics and U.K. law.

LEVER, J. F.

The law of restrictive practices and resale price maintenance, new ed. SM, 1964. xvi + 167p. (Revised in CHITTY on *Contracts*, 23rd ed., SM, 1968. Vol. 2, pp. 569-670)

A concisely written analysis of the law relating to agreements restricting competition, by one of the leading practitioners.

PICKERING, J. F.

Resale price maintenance in practice. Allen & Unwin, 1966. 3 + 236p.

An investigation by an economist into the effect of forbidding the collective enforcement of resale price maintenance by blacklists, and of allowing individual manufacturers to sue those with whom they had made no contract.

ROWLEY, C. K.

The British Monopolies Commission. Allen & Unwin, 1966. 3 + 394p.

An account of the Commission's procedure and an analysis of the criteria it developed.

STEVENS, R. and YAMEY, B. S.

The Restrictive Practices Court: a study of the judicial process and economic policy. Weidenfeld & Nicolson, 1965. xxi + 260p.

An assessment by an economist and a lawyer of the Restrictive Practices Court: the criteria it has evolved, its sources of information, etc.

WILBERFORCE, R. O., Baron Wilberforce, and others

The law of restrictive trade practices and monopolies, 2nd ed. SM, 1966. xxxv + 841p. (Suppl.)

The largest book for practitioners.

YAMEY, B. S., ed.

Resale price maintenance: studies. Weidenfeld & Nicolson, 1966. vii + 303p.

An analysis of the economic effects of resale price maintenance and of its abolition or control in seven legal systems.

Official publications

While the judgments of the Restrictive Practices Court are normally reported in 1 W.L.R. and in the All E.R., the Incorporated Council of Law Reporting has produced a special series of Restrictive Practices Cases in which the main points from counsel's arguments are also summarised. By March 1972 the 3rd part of volume 7 was published.

The reports of the Monopolies Commission are now too numerous to list. They are published by HMSO, usually as House of Commons Papers, but occasionally under a Command number. Many are out of print. The Board of Trade issues annual reports under the Monopolies and Mergers Acts, also published by HMSO.

GREAT BRITAIN, Board of Trade
Mergers: a guide to Board of Trade practice. HMSO, 1969. iv + 82p.

GREAT BRITAIN. Board of Trade. Committee on Resale Price Maintenance (Chairman: G. H. Lloyd-Jacob)
Report. HMSO, 1949. vi + 122p. (Cmnd. 7696)

GREAT BRITAIN. Department of Employment. Registrar of Restrictive Trading Agreements
Restrictive trading agreements: report, 1956/59– . HMSO, 1961– . (Five reports so far published: Cmnd. 1273, 1603, 2246, 3188, 4303)

GREAT BRITAIN. Department of Trade and Industry
Competition, monopoly and restrictive practices: a select bibliography. HMSO, 1970. 132p.

Prepared by economists and rather scrappy on the law; not limited to Commonwealth experience.

ORGANIZATION FOR ECONOMIC CO-OPERATION AND DEVELOPMENT. Committee of Experts on Restrictive Business Practices
Market power and the law: a report. Paris, OECD, 1970. 206p. (Subtitle: A study of the restrictive business practice laws of OECD member countries and of the EEC and ECSC dealing with market power)

ORGANIZATION FOR ECONOMIC CO-OPERATION AND DEVELOPMENT. Committee of Experts on Restrictive Business Practices
Refusal to sell: a report. Paris, OECD, 1969. 120p.

Short works and periodical articles

a. Cartels and resale price maintenance

COMPARATIVE ASPECTS OF ANTI-TRUST LAW IN THE UNITED STATES, THE UNITED KINGDOM AND THE EUROPEAN ECONOMIC COMMUNITY: a report of a conference on June 14th, 15th and 16th, 1963. British Institute of International and Comparative Law, 1963. v + 153p. (International and Comparative Law Quarterly. Supplementary publication no. 6, 1963)

HEATH, J.
Still not enough competition? Business restrictive practices re-examined, 2nd ed. Institute of Economic Affairs, 1963. 48p. (Hobart paper, 11) (Reprinted with postscript in the collected edition of Hobart papers 8-12, entitled *Ancient or modern: essays in economic efficiency and growth,* 1964)

This contains a useful list of articles that appeared in economic periodicals.

HEYDON, J. D.
"The frontiers of the restraint of trade doctrine", in *Law quarterly review*, 85 (1969): pp. 229-51.

HOWE, M.
"The Restrictive Practices Court and the definition of the Market", in *The Manchester school of economic and social studies*, 34 (1966): pp. 41-61.

HUTTON, G., ed.
Source-book on restrictive practices in Britain, with a select bibliography by J. Hennessy. Institute of Economic Affairs, 1966. 71p. (Research monograph no. 7)

KNOX, F. and HENNESSY, J.
Restrictive practices in the building industry. Institute of Economic Affairs, 1966. v + 54p. (Research monograph no. 1)

KORAH, V. L.
"The tile case", in *The Solicitor quarterly*, 3 (1964): pp. 318-38.

LEVER, J. F.
"Bipartite arrangements and the Restrictive Trade Practices Acts, 1956 and 1968", in *Law quarterly review*, 85 (1969): pp. 177-97.

LYSAGHT, C.
"A 'just price' in the Restrictive Practices Court", in *Current legal problems*, 24 (1971): pp. 82-109.

LYSAGHT, C.
"The Restrictive Practices Court and the promotion of exports", in *Northern Ireland legal quarterly*, 21 (1970): pp. 18-32.

RICHARDSON, G. B.
"Price notification schemes", in *Oxford economic papers*, 19 (new series) (1967): pp. 359-69.

SKEOCH, L. A.
"The abolition of resale price maintenance: some notes on Canadian experience", in *Economics*, 31 (new series) (1964): pp. 260-69.

YAMEY, B. S.
Resale price maintenance and shoppers' choice, 4th ed. Institute of Economic Affairs, 1964. 58p. (Hobart paper, 1)

b. Mergers

ELLIS, T. S.
"A survey of the government control of mergers in the United Kingdom", in *Northern Ireland legal quarterly*, 22 (1971): pp. 251-300 and 459-97.

KAY, M. R.
"Conglomerate mergers", in *Journal of business law*, 1969: pp. 265-75.

KORAH, V. L.
"The control of conglomerate mergers in the United Kingdom", in *Antitrust bulletin*, 15 (1970): pp. 759-79.

KORAH, V. L.
"Legal regulation of corporate mergers in the United Kingdom", in *Texas international law journal*, 5 (1969): pp. 71-111. (1965-71, entitled *Texas international law forum*)

ROWLEY, C. K.
"Mergers and public policy in Great Britain", in *Journal of law and economics*, 11 (1968): pp. 75-132.

c. The Monopolies Commission

SUTHERLAND, A.

The Monopolies Commission in action. CUP, 1969. 96p. (University of Cambridge, Department of Applied Economics, Occasional papers no. 21)

A criticism of the Commission by an economist, with suggestions for reform.

Periodicals

OXFORD ECONOMIC PAPERS, 17 (1965)

The whole of the third number of this volume is devoted to monopolies and restrictive practices.

There are regular contributions on the United Kingdom law in:

ANNUAL SURVEY OF COMMONWEALTH LAW, 1965- . B.

JOURNAL OF BUSINESS LAW, 1957- . S.

IX. LABOUR LAW

1. GENERAL

The Labour Law of the United Kingdom is peculiar in the sense that no industrialised country in the world has relied less on law as an instrument to regulate industrial relations. Matters such as workshop safety and social insurance are, of course, extensively covered by legislation, but the general impression cf collective bargaining, trade union affairs, and even dismissal, is of judicial and legislative withdrawal. The legal bibliography has naturally suffered from this. Since the first edition of this Bibliography there has been a notable change of attitude. Labour Law is now taught in most British universities, and in other places of higher education, to degree standard, the value of law as a regulator of industrial conduct is widely discussed, the judiciary has shown itself much more willing to enter the field, and governments to introduce legislation on such subjects as Redundancy Payments. Proposals for the statutory regulation of industrial conflict have recently matured, and there is no doubting the indications of a greatly increased legal presence in industrial relations. The bibliography has not yet improved to a corresponding degree but it has made many large strides so that it is no longer necessary, as it was in the first edition of this work, to refer to elementary guides because no full discussion of the subject is available. In that edition also general works on contract and tort were cited. It is true that labour law draws on general principles of contract to constitute the contract of employment, and of tort to found both the law of compensation for industrial injury and liability for industrial conflict, but these aspects have now become noticeably related to particular industrial problems and are better considered in the specialized works which are now available.

It remains true that the subject as a whole covers a very large area and general works are important to its study. COOPER's *Industrial law* has long been the principal text book of this nature. FRIDMAN is a most comprehensive work containing a great deal of legislative material but is somewhat lacking in feeling for the background of the subject. WEDDERBURN, *The worker and the law* (A Penguin Publication) is a notable contribution to an understanding of this sociological and economic background. WEDDERBURN, *Cases and materials on labour law* is an excellent and full compilation of sources of law, as well as containing a certain amount of practice.

Because the subject covers such a wide area it tends to break up into specialized topics, a number of which are well covered. BATT deals with the contract of employment whilst MEYERS is an excellent theoretical study of the legal basis of this section. Employers' liability for injury has long been covered fully by MUNKMAN and the subdivision of this topic concerning the Factories Act by REDGRAVE. SAMUELS, *Factory law* is now considerably out of date. ATIYAH, although highly specialized, is another excellent study of the detailed aspect of vicarious liability, which has played such a significant role in the development of this liability. CITRINE has now been joined by a good sociologically based textbook—GRUNFELD—on trade union law and some of the shorter works like SAMUELS can now be used simply as introductions.

Despite this increase in legal material and, in many cases, its wide coverage of background information, the fact that the United Kingdom has had a relatively uncontrolled system of voluntary industrial relations still makes it necessary to refer extensively to non-legal works, some of which are unfortunately dated, but are still useful reading if this limitation is born in mind. It is true that there is now a rapidly developing system of labour courts but this is in its infancy. Minimum wage legislation, as such, does not exist and its parallel must be studied in non-legal material on Wages Councils. The lack of contractual enforceability of collective agreements and of any successful attempt formally to control strikes, has meant that industrial relations as a whole must largely be studied outside the law. The classics TILLYARD; SHARP; and FLANDERS AND CLEGG are all, to a greater or lesser degree, dated, as are many of the less well known works. This is particularly serious because of the rise of plant bargaining. They must be regarded as being replaced by rather less general works, of which FLANDERS, *Fawley productivity agreements* and the *Research papers* of the ROYAL COMMISSION of 1965-1968 stand out

Select Bibliography

General works

COOPER, W. M. and WOOD, J. C.
Outlines of industrial law, 5th ed. B, 1966. lxxvi + 445 + 26p.

CRONIN, J. B. and GRIME, R. P.
Labour law. B, 1970. xlviii + 500p.

FRIDMAN, G. H. L.
The modern law of employment. S, 1963. clxii + 1065p. (Suppl.)

WEDDERBURN, K. W.
Cases and materials on labour law. CUP, 1967. xxix + 784p.

WEDDERBURN, K. W.
The worker and the law, 2nd ed. Penguin Books, 1971. 587p. (Bibliography, pp. 528-49)

Specialized works

ATIYAH, P. S.
Vicarious liability in the law of torts. B, 1967. lxi + 452p.

BATT, F. R.
Law of master and servant, 5th ed. by G. J. Webber. Pitman, 1967. cix + 698p.

CITRINE, N. A.
Trade union law, 3rd ed. by M. A. Hickling. S, 1967. lxiv + 772p.

DAVIES, R.
The Offices, Shops and Railway Premises Act, 1963. Oyez, 1965. xliii + 299p.

DIX, D. Knight
Contracts of employment, 3rd ed. B, 1968. xxxii + 351p.

ENCYCLOPAEDIA OF FACTORIES, SHOPS and OFFICES: LAW AND PRACTICE, edited by P. Allsop. SM, 1962- . 2 vols. (Loose-leaf)

GRODIN, J. R.
Union government and the law: British and American experiences. Los Angeles, Univ. of California Institute of Industrial Relations, 1961. 209p.

GRUNFELD, C.
Modern trade union law. SM, 1966. xii + 517p.

GRUNFELD, C.
Trade unions and the individual in English law. Institute of Personnel Management, 1963. 60p. (Industrial relations series, no. I)

MCKOWN, R.
Comprehensive guide to factory law, 4th ed. G. Godwin, 1968. viii + 163p.

MEYERS, F.
Ownership of jobs: a comparative study. Los Angeles, Univ. of California Institute of Industrial Relations, 1964. 114p.

MUNKMAN, J. H.
Employer's liability at common law, 7th ed. B, 1971. lxxxi + 637p.

REDGRAVE, A.
Factories Acts, 21st ed. by I. Fife and E. A. Machin. B, 1966. lxiv + 15 + 1400p.

REDGRAVE, A.
Offices and shops, by I. Fife and E. A. Machin. B, 1965. lviii + 570p. (An extension of the above to cover later legislation)

RIDEOUT, R. W.
Reforming the Redundancy Payments Act. Institute of Personnel Management, 1969. 48p.

RIDEOUT, R. W.
The right to membership of a trade union. Athlone Pr., 1963. xliv + 243p. (University of London legal series, no. 5)

RIDEOUT, R. W.
Trade unions: some social and legal problems. Tavistock, 1964. 54p.

SAMUELS, H.
Factory law, 8th ed. Knight, 1969. xxxv + 825p.

WEDDERBURN, K. W. and DAVIES, P. L.
Employment grievances and disputes procedures in Britain. Los Angeles, Univ. of California Pr., 1969. xvi + 300p.

WILLIAMS, J. L.
Accidents and ill-health at work. Staples, 1960. 516p.

Other books

BAYLISS, F. J.
British wages councils. Oxford, Blackwell, 1962. x + 177p.

COLE, G. D. H.
An introduction to trade unionism. Allen & Unwin, 1953. 324p.

DJANG, T. K.
Factory inspection in Great Britain. Allen & Unwin, 1942. 255p.

FLANDERS, A.
The Fawley productivity agreements, 2nd ed. Faber, 1966. 360p.

FLANDERS, A.
Trade unions, 7th ed. Hutchinson, 1968. 212p.

FLANDERS, A. and CLEGG, H. A., eds
The system of industrial relations in Great Britain. Oxford, Blackwell, 1954, reprinted 1964. viii + 380p. (Corrected impression)

GREAT BRITAIN. Department of Employment
British labour statistics: historical abstract 1886–1968. HMSO, 1971. 436p.

GREAT BRITAIN. Department of Employment. Chief Inspector of Factories
Report, 1878- . HMSO (Published annually) (1878–1938 issued by the Home Office)

GREAT BRITAIN. Department of Employment and Productivity
In place of strife: a policy for industrial relations. HMSO, 1969. 40p. (Cmnd 3888)

GREAT BRITAIN. Ministry of Labour
Industrial relations handbook, revised ed. HMSO, 1961. vi + 234p.

GREAT BRITAIN. Registry of Friendly Societies
Report of the Chief Registrar, 1875- . HMSO (Published annually)

GREAT BRITAIN. Royal Commission on Trade Unions and Employers' Associations (Chairman: Lord Donovan)
Report. HMSO, 1968. ix + 352p. (Cmnd 3623)

GREAT BRITAIN. Royal Commission on Trade Unions and Employers' Associations (Chairman: Lord Donovan)
The role of shop stewards in British industrial relations, by W. E. J. McCarthy. HMSO, 1966. vi + 81p. (Research paper no. 1)
Disputes procedures in British industry, by A. I. Marsh. HMSO, 1966. x + 27p. (Research paper no. 2 (1))
Disputes procedures in Britain, by A. I. Marsh and W. E. J. McCarthy. HMSO, 1968. xvi + 121p. (Research paper no. 2 (2))
Industrial sociology and industrial relations, by A. Fox. HMSO, 1966. v + 34p. (Research paper no. 3)
Productivity bargaining, and *Restrictive labour practices*, by the Commission's secretariat. HMSO, 1967. vi + 67p. (Research paper no. 4 (1) and (2))
Trade union structure and government, by J. Hughes. HMSO, 1967 (part 1) and 1968 (part 2). 2 vols (Research paper no. 5 (1) and (2))
Trade union growth and recognition, by G. S. Bain. HMSO, 1967. xi + 117p. (Research paper no. 6)
Employers' associations, by V. G. Munns and W. E. J. McCarthy. HMSO, 1967. xii + 122p. (Research paper no. 7)
Three studies in collective bargaining, by J. Stieber, W. E. J. McCarthy, A. I. Marsh and J. W. Staples. HMSO, 1968. viii + 64p. (Research paper no. 8)
Overtime working in Britain, by E. G. Whybrew. HMSO, 1968. vi + 96p. (Research paper no. 9)
Shop stewards and workshop relations, by W. E. J. McCarthy and S. R. Parker. HMSO, 1968. viii + 157p. (Research paper no. 10)
Two studies in industrial relations: (1) *The position of women in industry*, by N. Seear, and (2) *Changing wage payment systems*, by R. B. McKersie. HMSO, 1968. v + 65p. (Research paper no. 11)

GUILLEBAUD, C. W.
The wages councils system in Great Britain, 2nd ed. Welwyn, Nisbet, 1962. 28p.

HEDGES, R. Y. and WINTERBOTTOM, A.
The legal history of trade unionism. Longmans, 1930. xix + 170p.

HEPPLE, B.
Race, jobs and the law in Britain, 2nd ed. Penguin Books, 1970. 343p. (Law and society) (Bibliography, pp. 309-21)

HUTCHINS, B. L. and HARRISON, A.
A history of factory legislation, 3rd ed. King, 1926. xvi + 298p.

KAHN-FREUND, O., ed.
Labour relations and the law—a comparative study. S, 1965. viii + 231p. (British Institute studies in international and comparative law, no. 2)

KAMIN, A., ed.
Western European labor and the American corporation. Washington D.C., Bureau of National Affairs, 1970. xxvii + 546p.

KNOWLES, K. G. J. C.
Strikes. Oxford, Blackwell, 1952. xiv + 330p. (Oxford University Institute of Statistics monograph no. 3)

MCCARTHY, W. E. J.
The closed shop in Britain. Oxford, Blackwell, 1964. xii + 294p.

MACKENZIE, W. W., Baron Amulree
The industrial court: practice and procedure. B, 1923. viii + 44 + 8p.

MILNE-BAILEY, W.
Trade union documents. Bell, 1929. xxvii + 552p. (Bibliography, pp. 537-540)

PELLING, H. M.
A history of British trade unionism. Macmillan, 1963. xi + 287p.

RICHARDSON, J. H.
An introduction to the study of industrial relations. Allen & Unwin, 1954. 442p.

ROBERTS, B. C., ed.
Industrial relations, revised ed. Methuen, 1968. 299p.

SELLS, D. M.
British wages boards. Washington D.C., Brookings Institution, 1939. xv + 389p.

SHARP, I. G.
Industrial conciliation and arbitration in Great Britain. Allen & Unwin, 1950. 466p.

SYMONS, J.
The general strike. Cresset, 1957. xi + 259p.

TILLYARD, Sir F.
The worker and the state, 3rd ed. Routledge, 1948. xii + 302p.

WEBB, S. J., Baron Passfield, and WEBB, B., Baroness Passfield
The history of trade unionism, revised ed. Longmans, 1920. xviii + 784p.

WEBB, S. J., Baron Passfield, and WEBB, B., Baroness Passfield
Industrial democracy. Longmans, 1920. xxxix + 899p.

Periodicals

A number of journals publish articles of interest in this field.

BRITISH JOURNAL OF INDUSTRIAL RELATIONS, vol. 1- , 1963- . London School of Economics.

INDUSTRIAL LAW REVIEW, vol. 1-14, 1946/47-1959/60. Leigh-on-Sea, Essex, Thames Bank Publishing Co., (Ceased publication)

JOURNAL OF BUSINESS LAW, 1957- . S.

MODERN LAW REVIEW, vol. 1- , 1937- . S.

2. SOCIAL INSURANCE

The law of social insurance, strictly speaking, ceased to be part of Labour Law on 5 July 1948 with the coming into force of the National Insurance Act. Thereafter it can be considered as a branch of the law of social security which includes the National Health Service, Family Allowance and Supplementary Benefits (formerly

National Assistance). Much of this law is, however, still included in courses on Labour Law.

The National Insurance (Industrial Injuries) Act replaced the Workmen's Compensation system. On the same date jurisdiction under both Acts passed to separate tribunals and the Commissioners of National Insurance. On only a few matters reserved for decision by the Minister is there a right of appeal to the ordinary courts. Workmen's Compensation decisions are now of little value since, though similar principles are applied in the new system, there are now a large number of Commissioners' decisions explaining their application.

Workmen's Compensation was normally well documented but unfortunately all aspects of Social Insurance Law are currently very poorly covered. POTTER and STANSFELD, which might have become the standard work of reference both on national insurance and industrial injuries has not reappeared for over twenty years, and is out of date. Nothing has appeared effectively to take its place. The various systems of reporting Commissioners' decisions are all more or less unsatisfactory.

The BEVERIDGE report is essential to an understanding of the system but the student of present law and practice will find considerable difficulty in following this up.

Select Bibliography

BEVERIDGE, W. H., Baron Beveridge

Social insurance and allied services. HMSO, 1942. 299p. (Cmd 6404) (Report made by the author as Chairman of the Inter-departmental committee on social insurance and allied services)

HARRIS, R. W.

National health insurance in Great Britain 1911-1946. Allen & Unwin, 1946. 224p.

POTTER, D. C. L. and STANSFELD, D. H.

National insurance, 2nd ed. B, 1949. xix + 553p.

POTTER, D. C. L. and STANSFELD, D. H.

National insurance—industrial injuries, 2nd ed. B, 1950. xix + 392p.

TILLYARD, Sir F.

Unemployment insurance in Great Britain 1911-1948. Leigh-on-Sea, Essex, Thames Bank Publishing Co., 1949. ix + 233p.

VESTER, H. and CARTWRIGHT, H. A.

Industrial injuries. SM, 1961. 2 vols.

YOUNG, A. F.

Industrial injuries insurance. Routledge, 1964. xi + 180p.

3. SOCIAL SECURITY

So far as the law is concerned social security centres on those aspects dealt with under social insurance. The largely procedural aspects of social security are covered by the practice of the Department of Health and Social Security and very little material has been published on this, although the Department itself produces some useful advisory material. The reports of decisions are in need of rationalization but the various series are set out here.

Select Bibliography

GREAT BRITAIN. Department of Health and Social Security
Index and digest of decisions given by the commissioners under the National Insurance Acts, the National Insurance (Industrial Injuries) Acts, and the Family Allowances Acts. HMSO, 1964– . 2 vols. (Loose leaf. Suppl.)

GREAT BRITAIN. Department of Health and Social Security
Reported decisions of the commissioner under the National Insurance Acts, vol. 1- , 1948/52- . HMSO (Loose decisions are issued and then periodically published in bound vols)

GREAT BRITAIN. Department of Health and Social Security
Reported decisions of the commissioner under the National Insurance (Industrial Injuries) Acts, vol. 1- , 1948/52 . HMSO. (Loose decisions are issued and then periodically published in bound vols)

X. CRIME

1. CRIMINAL LAW AND PROCEDURE

(a) *The Nature of English Criminal Law*

The criminal law of England reflects its common law origins. Indeed some of the principal offences still lack statutory definition. Thus murder, manslaughter, conspiracy (a wide offence) and rape, for example, are still not defined by Act of Parliament although legislation has intruded in some instances by prescribing punishments and penalties. The principles of *mens rea* and many of the defences such as insanity, mistake and intoxication rest on the common law. Other crimes which were originally common law offences are now provided for by statute. Theft and most other offences against property fall into this category as do bigamy and perjury and most of the offences against the person. Where Parliament has enacted penalties, unless they are fixed, they are almost invariably treated as maxima.

Besides these categories of crime in which case-law has played so important a part, legislation (by statute, or still more by subordinate measures) has intervened increasingly since the middle of the nineteenth century. Entirely new offences have been created to meet growing problems, for example, of road traffic and public health. Of 1,606,728 persons found guilty in 1969 of offences of all kinds, 58·9% were convicted of summary traffic offences. Many of these statutory offences are regarded as being of strict liability, as *mens rea* is not required.

(b) *The Classification of Offences*

The ancient classification of crimes into treasons, felonies and misdemeanours has now been altered by the Criminal Law Act, 1967, section 1, which has abolished the anachronistic distinction between felonies and misdemeanours. Section 2 provides a new division into arrestable and non-arrestable offences according, broadly, as to whether or not the offence is punishable by five or more years of imprisonment. There are special powers of arrest without warrant in the case of arrestable offences and section 4 creates a new crime of assisting those who commit these more serious crimes. The old law concerning parties to offences has thus been rationalized and brought up to date.

(c) *Procedure*

A separation of offences into indictable and summary remains and is important procedurally. All common law offences are indictable and so are all statutory ones unless statute has provided otherwise. All the more serious crimes are indictable including treason, murder, manslaughter, rape, robbery, theft, arson and forgery.

Prosecutions are notionally brought on behalf of the Crown, but the prosecutor himself (the one laying the information) may be a police officer, a private person, the Director of Public Prosecutions, or a representative of a Government department. The accused is ordinarily an individual, but may be a corporation.

A trial upon indictment takes place before an Assize Court or Court of Quarter Sessions with a jury of twelve. Summary matters are dealt with by magistrates (usually lay) without a jury and, in general, carry a maximum sentence of not more than six months' imprisonment. If an offence is to be tried on indictment the accused will first be brought before a Magistrates' Court to ascertain whether or not the evidence amounts to a prima facie case against him and only if it does will he be indicted for trial before a higher court. If no prima facie case is established he will be discharged forthwith. Depending on the facts of the instant case, it may frequently be possible for it to be dealt with summarily even though it is really indictable. Small thefts, for example, are often disposed of in this way. There is no procedural classification equivalent to the Continental system exemplified by the French *crimes*, *délits* and *contraventions*. Of the 1,606,728 persons found guilty of offences of all kinds in 1969, 98% were dealt with by magistrates' courts. Of the 304,070 within this number who were convicted of indictable crimes, approximately 88% were tried in magistrates' courts. From the magistrates' courts appeals lie at the instance of either side to the courts above.

(d) *Legal Aid**

Legal aid to finance the services of a solicitor or of solicitor and counsel for the defence of an accused person may be granted on application to the appropriate court. Magistrates' Courts must make a legal aid order whenever it appears to the court to be in the interests of justice to do so and when the accused's financial circumstances indicate that he needs assistance in paying for his defence. Unless the offence is indictable and of special difficulty the order will be for representation by a solicitor only. Similar principles apply in the higher courts but the order will cover the services of a barrister as well as a solicitor in courts in which the latter have no right of audience or when other circumstances justify this course. If legal aid is granted to an accused he may thereafter be ordered to make a contribution towards the costs of his defence and his financial position may be investigated for an appropriate assessment to be made.

(e) *Law Reform and Codification*

The organization of certain courts administering criminal justice is likely to be much modernized following the Report of the Royal Commission on Assizes and Quarter Sessions (Cmnd 4153/1969, HMSO).

The traditional processes of legislation and judicial interpretation continue to develop the criminal law. In some areas, for example road traffic offences, subordinate forms of legislation have played a major part. Great impetus has been given to the process of renovation by the Law Commissions Act, 1965. Pursuant to this legislation, the Law Commission has been created for the purpose of promoting reform of the law through Parliament. In the field of the criminal law its work has been directed not only towards immediate necessary revisions (for example in the restoration of a subjective test of *mens rea* in murder) but also towards long-term reformation of the structure of the criminal law and then to its eventual codification. In conjunction with the Criminal Law Revision Committee and other bodies it is first proceeding to examine the general principles as well as certain specific offences such as damage to property, forgery, perjury, bigamy and offences against the person. The Theft Act, 1968 which radically revises crimes against property has been a significant achievement.

---

* For legal aid in civil matters see Ch. VI section 1 (3).

When brought fully into operation, the Children and Young Persons Act, 1969, will provide that only exceptionally may children under the age of fourteen be subjected to criminal proceedings for offences other than murder. (The present age of criminal responsibility is ten years.) The statute extensively revises modes of dealing with juveniles.

(f) *Basic works of reference*

Because of the recent and extensive developments which have taken place in the criminal law, substantial portions of the older popular books are now of historical interest only. Into this category must fall C. K. KENNY, *Outlines of criminal law* (19th ed.). The most widely used practitioners' book on indictable crimes remains ARCHBOLD, *Pleading, evidence and practice in criminal cases.* This is now in its 37th ed. (1969) and it deals succinctly and authoritatively with all facets of crime and criminal procedure. STONE'S JUSTICES' MANUAL is published annually and covers the details of summary offences.

The leading text-book is probably SMITH & HOGAN, *Criminal law* (2nd ed.) 1969, which deals in a lucid way with the more academically interesting heads of the criminal law. The footnotes provide a helpful guide to further material, but the book does not aim to cover criminal procedure. HARRIS, *Criminal law* (21st ed.), 1968, is a text-book which treats perhaps a greater variety of offences than anything similar and includes more than two hundred pages on procedure. Glanville WILLIAMS, *Criminal law: the general part* (2nd ed.), is jurisprudentially elaborate as to the general principles relating to criminal law and this is planned to be followed by a second volume which will discuss specific crimes. A number of students' casebooks are available. All contain the latest leading cases and excerpts from the judgments in them. Those by ELLIOTT AND WOOD, CROSS AND JONES, TURNER AND ARMITAGE are perhaps the most popular.

Select Bibliography

General text-books—practitioners' and students' books

ARCHBOLD, J. F.
Pleading, evidence and practice in criminal cases, 37th ed. by T. R. F. Butler and M. Garsia. SM, 1969. clxxxiv + 1510p. (Suppl.)

BAKER, E. R. and WILKIE, G. H.
Criminal law, 2nd ed. by E. R. Baker. B, 1969. ix + 193p. (Suppl.) (Police promotion handbooks, no. 1)

CROSS, A. R. N. and JONES, P. A.
An introduction to criminal law, 6th ed. B, 1968. xlvii + 366 + 36p.

GARSIA, M.
Criminal law and procedure in a nutshell, 13th ed. by Celia Hampton. SM, 1968. xv + 127p.

GORE, T. and MAUNDY, C. L.
Criminal law. B, 1969. vi + 161p.

HARRIS, S. F.
Criminal law, 21st ed. by A. Hooper. SM, 1968. lvi + 839p. (Suppl.)

KENNY, C. S.
Outlines of criminal law, 19th ed. by J. W. C. Turner. CUP, 1966. lxxv + 680p.

MORIARTY, C. C. H.
Police law, 20th ed. by Sir W. J. Williams. B, 1970. xx + 726p.
RUSSELL, Sir W. O.
Crime, 12th ed. by J. W. C. Turner. S, 1964. 2 vols.
SMITH, J. C. and HOGAN, B.
Criminal law, 2nd ed. B, 1969. lxxix + 588p.
STEWART, S. W.
A modern view of the criminal law. Oxford, Pergamon Pr., 1969. xxiii + 262p.
STONE'S JUSTICES' MANUAL. B. 2 vols. (Published annually)
WILLIAMS, G. L.
Criminal law: the general part, 2nd ed. S, 1961. liv + 929p.

Specific crimes and legislation

BROWNLIE, I.
The law relating to public order. B, 1968. xli + 227p.
EDDY, J. P. and LOEWE, L. L.
The new law of gaming, including the annotated text of the Gaming Act 1968, with notes on some of the principal games. B, 1969. xvi + 322p. (Suppl.)
GREAT BRITAIN. Criminal Law Revision Committee
8th report: *Theft and related offences*. HMSO, 1966. 140p. (Cmd 2977)
GRIEW, E. J.
The Theft Act, 1968. SM, 1968. xx + 174p.
HARRIS, B.
A short guide to the Criminal Justice Act, 1967, as it affects magistrates' courts, 2nd ed. Chichester, Justice of the Peace, 1969. 34p.
MEDICAL PROTECTION SOCIETY and others
The Abortion Act, 1967: proceedings of a symposium held by the Medical Protection Society in collaboration with the Royal College of General Practitioners at the Royal College of Obstetricians and Gynaecologists, London 7th February 1969. Pitman Medical, 1969. [8] + 115p. (Includes the text of the Act)
ROYDHOUSE, E.
The Criminal Law and Criminal Justice Acts, 1967. B, 1968. xxx + 446p. (Butterworths' annotated legislation service , no. 163)
SHOOLBRED, C. F.
A guide to recent criminal legislation. Oxford, Pergamon Pr., 1968. xii + 154p.
SMITH, J. C.
The law of theft. B, 1968. xxii + 226p.

Procedure

ARCHBOLD, J. F.
Pleading, evidence and practice in criminal cases, 37th ed. by T. R. F. Butler and M. Garsia. SM, 1969. clxxxiv + 1510p. (Suppl.)
ARGUILE, R.
Criminal procedure. B, 1969. xxviii + 268p.
BAKER, E. R. and WILKIE, G. H.
Criminal evidence and procedure, 3rd ed. B, 1971. ix + 226p. (Police promotion handbooks, no. 2)
CARVELL, I. G. and GREEN, E. S.
Criminal law and procedure. SM, 1970. xxxviii + 410p.

DEVLIN, J. D.
Criminal courts and procedure, 2nd ed. B, 1967. xlv + 274p.
DEVLIN, P. A. Baron Devlin
The criminal prosecution in England. OUP, 1960. viii + 118p.
GRAHAM-GREEN, G. J.
Criminal costs and legal aid, 2nd ed. B, 1969. xxv + 309p.
NAPLEY, D.
Crime and criminal procedure. Oyez, 1963. vi + 76p.
ROSCOE, H.
Criminal evidence: the law, evidence and practice in criminal cases, 16th ed. by A. A. G. Clark and A. Garfitt. S, 1952. lxxvi + 1068p.
SHOOLBRED, C. F.
The administration of criminal justice in England and Wales. Oxford, Pergamon Pr., 1966. xxiii + 158p.
STONE'S JUSTICES' MANUAL. B. 2 vols. (Published annually)
WILLIAMS, G. L.
The proof of guilt: a study of the English criminal trial, 3rd ed. S, 1963. viii + 373p. (Hamlyn lectures, no. 7)
WILSHERE, A. M.
Criminal procedure, 4th ed. by H. A. Palmer and Henry Palmer. SM, 1961. xxxii + 338p.

Sentencing

MCCLEAN, J. D. and WOOD, J. C.
Criminal justice and the treatment of offenders. SM, 1969. xvii + 327p.
THOMAS, D. A.
Principles of sentencing: the sentencing policy of the Court of Appeal Criminal Division. Heinemann Educational Books, 1970. l + 350p. (Cambridge studies in criminology, vol. 37)

Miscellaneous aspects

BRETT, P.
An inquiry into criminal guilt. SM, 1963. xvii + 228p.
DAVIES, D. S. and others
The modern approach to criminal law. Macmillan, 1945. ix + 511p. (English studies in criminal science, vol. 4)
EDWARDS, J. L. J.
Mens rea in statutory offences. Macmillan, 1955. xiv + 297p. (English studies in criminal science, vol. 8)
FITZGERALD, P. J.
Criminal law and punishment. OUP, 1962. xi + 279p.
GREAT BRITAIN. Law Commission
Imputed criminal intent (Director of Public Prosecutions v. *Smith)* HMSO, 1967. 17p. (Law Com. no. 10)
HART, H. L. A.
The morality of the criminal law. OUP, 1965. 52p. (Lionel Cohen lectures, 1964)
HOWARD, C.
Strict responsibility. SM, 1963. xx + 220p.

LEIGH, L. H.
The criminal liability of corporations in English law. Weidenfeld & Nicholson. 1969. vii + 221p. (L.S.E. research monographs, no. 2)

WILLIAMS, G. L.
The mental element in crime. OUP, 1965. [i] + 121p. (Lionel Cohen lectures, 1965)

History and historical sources

BLACKSTONE, Sir W.
Commentaries on the laws of England. Oxford, Clarendon Pr., 1765-69. 4 vols. (For details of various editions see HOLDSWORTH, *History of English law*, vol. 12, p. 712)

COKE, Sir E.
The third part of the institutes of the laws of England: concerning high treason, and other pleas of the Crown, and criminal causes. Flesher, 1644. 243p. (Many subsequent editions)

EAST, Sir E. H.
A treatise of the pleas of the crown. London, 1803. 2 vols.

FOSTER, Sir M.
A report of some proceedings on the Commission of Oyer and Terminer and Gaol Delivery for the trial of rebels in the year 1746 in the county of Surrey, and of other Crown cases. To which are added discourses upon a few branches of the Crown law, 3rd ed. with an appendix . . . additional notes and references by . . . M. Dodson. E. & R. Brooke, 1792. xxxvi + 441p.

HALE, Sir M.
Methodical summary of the law relating to the pleas of the Crown, 7th ed. by a gentleman of the Inner Temple. B. Tovey, 1773. 1 vol. in 3.

HAWKINS, W.
A treatise of the pleas of the Crown, 7th ed. by T. Leach. London, 1795. 4 vols.

RADZINOWICZ, L.
A history of English criminal law and its administration from 1750. S, 1948-68. 4 vols.

STEPHEN, Sir J. F.
A history of the criminal law of England. Macmillan, 1883. 3 vols.

Casebooks

CROSS, A. R. N. and JONES, P. A.
Cases on criminal law, 4th ed. B, 1968. xxxiii + 365p.

ELLIOTT, D. W. and WOOD, J. C.
A casebook on criminal law, 2nd ed. SM, 1969. xxx + 418p.

TURNER, J. W. C. and ARMITAGE, A. L.
Cases on criminal law, 3rd ed. CUP, 1964. xiv + 664p.

Journals and law reports

CRIMINAL APPEAL REPORTS, 1908- . SM.

CRIMINAL LAW REVIEW, 1954- . SM. (Monthly)

JOURNAL OF CRIMINAL LAW, vol. 1- , 1937- . The Journal.

JUSTICE OF THE PEACE AND LOCAL GOVERNMENT REVIEW, vol. 1- , 1837- . Justice of the Peace, Ltd.

2. CRIMINOLOGY

The definition and scope of criminology as a separate discipline are, in England, as elsewhere, still evolving. Criminology may be taken in its widest sense to embrace not only the manifestations and aetiology of crime and antisocial behaviour, but also their control and treatment (including what might properly be dealt with separately as penology). Criminology is concerned with the incidence of crime and the functioning of the criminal law in a social context and also with the investigation of the factors found to be related to criminality. "Delinquency" is sometimes employed as a synonym for crime, but is perhaps more widely used to refer to the criminal behaviour of juveniles.

Most English universities nowadays offer some teaching in criminology, either at undergraduate or postgraduate level, but, because of its wide frame of reference, the subject appears in courses on sociology, psychology and allied fields more frequently than in law. It is, of course, an element in the training of all social workers involved with offenders and a wide range of courses is also offered by the extra-mural departments of the major universities so that those professionally involved with criminality have the opportunity to keep themselves up-to-date. But the importance of criminology to lawyers is coming increasingly to be recognized and is reflected in the syllabi of the more progressive degree courses. Well-attended conferences are organized for the judiciary and the legal profession.

In 1957 the Home Office Research Unit achieved official status as a Government instrumentality to conduct and co-ordinate research. Some of the published results of its work are listed in the bibliographical section of this note. Research is also undertaken by groups and individuals working within the universities. Despite budgetary limitations, much useful work is being done on a wide variety of aspects, including some which are new or which have been somewhat neglected hitherto, such as the criminality of women, problems of addiction and race relations. The Home Office has also a standing committee on the treatment of offenders whose function is to keep policy and methods under review and to advise the Government. In 1959 the Department of Criminal Science of the University of Cambridge became the Institute of Criminology and under the direction of Professor Sir Leon Radzinowicz it has continued to lead the universities in teaching and research. Some of its publications appear in the bibliography.

The results of research and changes in informed opinion have led to rapid developments in the treatment of offenders. In the last twenty years entirely new types of institutions have been opened, such as detention centres and attendance centres for young offenders. Capital punishment for murder and corporal punishment, even for breaches of discipline in penal institutions, have been abolished. The average daily population of all prison service establishments, however, had become 32,461 in 1968 (31,656 males, 805 females). Based on the present steep rate of increase the figure is expected to reach 40,000 early in the present decade. Several more prisons have been built including more which are "open" and special-purpose establishments for psychiatric treatment and industrial training. The Report of the Inquiry into prison escapes and security (1966) has contributed to a greatly increased need for more "secure" accommodation. Pre-release hostels now assist rehabilitation. Parole and suspended sentences (introduced under the Criminal Justice Act, 1968) are intended to help cope with the increasing numbers of persons liable to be sentenced to imprisonment. Wide-ranging reforms in the treatment of young offenders will be introduced by the Children and Young Persons Act, 1969 when it becomes fully operative.

The United Kingdom's contribution to criminology has been maintained through the various international instrumentalities and through participation in conferences at home and abroad. London was the venue for the Second United Nations Congress on Crime and the Treatment of Offenders in 1960.

A growing number of organizations is concerned with aspects of criminology. Among them are the Howard League for Penal Reform which celebrated the centenary of its parent body in 1966. Its organ is the *Howard journal.* The address of the Secretary is 125 Kennington Park Road, London S.E.11. The address of the Secretary of the British Society for Criminology is 65 Mortlake Road, Ilford, Essex. The Institute for the Study and Treatment of Delinquency is at 8 Bourdon Street, London, W.1. It publishes the *British journal of criminology* (formerly the *British journal of delinquency*). The address of the British Academy of Forensic Science is 1-3 Chancery Lane, London W.C.2 (organ: *Medicine, science and the law*). Recently the National Association for the Care and Resettlement of Offenders has been formed to co-ordinate work in its field. Its address is 125 Kennington Park Road, London, S.E.11.

In a subject developing as rapidly as criminology the compilation of a satisfactory bibliography is especially difficult. Many of the well-known older works are now out of date, but some are listed because they occupy important places in the development of the subject or retain some special interest of their own. Much is to be gained from Government publications ("blue books" and "white papers") which are available from Her Majesty's Stationery Office, P.O. Box No. 569, London, S.E.1.

A widely-used general text-book is Nigel WALKER, *Crime and punishment in Britain.* A simpler survey is contained in Howard JONES, *Crime and the penal system,* while D. J. WEST, *The young offender* covers its field neatly and with authority. Recently published is J. E. Hall WILLIAMS, *The English penal system in transition.*

The principal journals and periodicals in this field are the *British journal of criminology*, the *Howard journal*, the *Criminal law review* and *Medicine, science and the law.*

Select Bibliography

Works on crime in general, offenders and the aetiology of crime

AINSWORTH, M. D. and others

Deprivation of maternal care: a reassessment of its effects. Geneva, World Health Organization, 1962. 165p. (Bibliography, pp. 159-65) (WHO public health papers, no. 11)

ANDRY, R. G.

Delinquency and parental pathology: a study in forensic and clinical psychology, revised ed. Staples Pr., 1971. xv + 189p.

ANDRY, R. G.

The short-term prisoner: a study in forensic psychology, with a foreword by H. Mannheim. S, 1963. xxii + 162p.

BENNETT, I.

Delinquent and neurotic children. Tavistock Publications, 1960. xii + 532p.

BOSS, P.

Social policy and the young delinquent. Routledge & Kegan Paul, 1967. viii + 102p.

BOWLBY, J.
44 juvenile thieves. Baillière, 1946. 56p. (Bibliography, pp. 55-56)

BOWLBY, J.
Child care and the growth of love, 2nd ed. [A report to the W.H.O. abridged and edited by M. Fry] Penguin, 1965. 254p.

BRITISH CONGRESS ON CRIME, 1966
Frontiers of criminology: summary of the proceedings . . . edited by H. J. Klare and D. Haxby, Pergamon Pr., 1967. xii + 147p.

BURT, Sir C. L.
The young delinquent, 4th revised ed. Univ. of London Pr., 1944. xx + 662p.

CARDIFF TEACHERS' ASSOCIATION
Juvenile delinquency and the incidence of maladjustment: Cardiff survey. Cardiff, the Association, 1969. 84p.

CARR-SAUNDERS, Sir A. M. and others
Young offenders: an enquiry into juvenile delinquency. CUP, 1942. x + 168p.

CHAPMAN, D.
Sociology and the stereotype of the criminal. Tavistock Publications, 1968. xii + 260p. (Bibliography, pp. 249-55)

COHEN, A. K.
Delinquent boys: the culture of the gang. Routledge & Kegan Paul, 1956, reprinted by Collier-Macmillan, 1971. 198p.

COWIE, J. and others
Delinquency in girls. Heinemann Educational, 1968. x + 220p. (Bibliography, pp. 183-89) (Cambridge studies in criminology, vol. 23)

CROPWOOD ROUND-TABLE CONFERENCE, 1st, Cambridge, 1968
Psychopathic offenders: papers presented to the Conference, edited by D. J. West. University of Cambridge Institute of Criminology, 1968. 86p.

DOWNES, D. M.
The delinquent solution: a study in subcultural theory. Routledge & Kegan Paul, 1966. xi + 284p.

EAST, Sir W. N. and others
The adolescent criminal: a medico-sociological study of 4,000 male adolescents. Churchill, 1942. xi + 327p.

EYSENCK, H. J.
Crime and personality, revised ed. Paladin, 1970. 211p.

FORD, D. F. W.
The delinquent child and the community. Constable, 1957. xii + 204p.

FRIEDLANDER, K.
The psycho-analytical approach to juvenile delinquency. Routledge & Kegan Paul, 1947. vii + 296p.

FYVEL, T. R.
The insecure offenders. Rebellious youth in the welfare state, revised ed. Penguin in association with Chatto & Windus, 1963. 264p.

GIBBENS, T. C. N.
Trends in juvenile delinquency. Geneva, World Health Organization, 1961. 56p. (Public health papers, no. 5)

GLOVER, E. G.
The roots of crime. Imago, 1960. xiii + 422p. (Selected papers on psycho-analysis, vol. 2)

GREAT BRITAIN. Home Office
Criminal statistics, England and Wales. HMSO, 1858- . (Published annually)

GREAT BRITAIN. Home Office
Society and the criminal, by Sir W. N. East. HMSO, 1949. vii + 315p.

GREAT BRITAIN. Home Office. Commissioner of Police of the Metropolis
Report. HMSO, 1870- . (Published annually)

GREAT BRITAIN. Home Office. H.M. Chief Inspector of Constabulary
Report. HMSO, 1857- . (Published annually)

GREAT BRITAIN. Home Office. Departmental Committee on Criminal Statistics
Report. HMSO, 1967. iv + 63p. (Cmnd 3448)

GREAT BRITAIN. Home Office. Research Unit
Probationers in their social environment: a study of male probationers aged 17-20, together with an analysis of those reconvicted within 12 months, by M. Davies. HMSO, 1969. vii + 203p. (Research studies, no. 2)

GREAT BRITAIN. Home Office. Research Unit
Delinquent generations: a paper based on a communication to the British Association for the Advancement of Science . . . Glasgow, 1958, by L. T. Wilkins. HMSO, 1961. iv + 19p. (Studies in the causes of delinquency and the treatment of offenders, no. 3)

GREAT BRITAIN. Home Office. Research Unit
Persistent criminals: a study of all offenders liable to preventive detention in 1956, by W. H. Hammond and E. Chayen. HMSO, 1963. ix + 237p. (Studies in the causes of delinquency and the treatment of offenders, no. 5)

GREAT BRITAIN. Home Office. Research Unit
Types of delinquency and home background: a validation study of Hewitt and Jenkins' hypothesis, by E. Field. HMSO, 1967. vi + 21p. (Studies in the causes of delinquency and the treatment of offenders, no. 10)

GREAT BRITAIN. Home Office. Research Unit
Studies of female offenders, by N. Goodman and J. Price. HMSO, 1967. v + 78p. (Studies in the causes of delinquency and the treatment of offenders, no. 11)

GRYGIER, T. and others, eds
Criminology in transition: essays in honour of Hermann Mannheim. Tavistock Publications, 1965. xix + 308p.

HOWARD LEAGUE FOR PENAL REFORM
Changing concepts of crime and its treatment, edited by H. J. Klare. Pergamon Pr., 1966. ix + 186p.

JONES, H.
Crime and the penal system, 3rd ed. University Tutorial Pr., 1965. vii + 302p.

JONES, H.
Crime in a changing society. Penguin, 1965. 174p.

MCCLINTOCK, F. H. and AVISON, N. H.
Crime in England and Wales. Heinemann Educational, 1968. xxiii + 317p. (Cambridge studies in criminology, vol. 22)

MCDONALD, L.
Social class and delinquency. Faber, 1969. 240p. (Bibliography, pp. 225-36)

MANNHEIM, H.
Comparative criminology: a text-book. Routledge & Kegan Paul, 1965. 2 vols.

MANNHEIM, H.
Juvenile delinquency in an English Middletown. Kegan Paul, 1948. xi + 131p.

MANNHEIM, H.
Pioneers in criminology. S, 1960. xi + 402p.

MANNHEIM, H.
Social aspects of crime in England between the wars. Allen & Unwin, 1940. 382p.

MANNHEIM, H.
War and crime. Watts, 1941. ix + 208p.

MAYS, J. B.
Crime and the social structure, revised ed. Faber, 1967. 256p.

MAYS, J. B.
Growing up in the city: a study of juvenile delinquency in an urban neighbourhood, revised ed. Liverpool UP, 1964. vii + 225p. (Social research series)

MAYS, J. B.
On the threshold of delinquency. Liverpool UP, 1959. x + 243p.

MORRIS, T.
The criminal area: a study in social ecology. Routledge & Kegan Paul, 1958. xiii + 202p.

MORRIS, N.
The habitual criminal. Longmans, Green, 1951. viii + 395p. (Publications of the London School of Economics)

NEUSTATTER, W. L.
Psychological disorder and crime. Christopher Johnson, 1953. 248p.

PEARCE, J. D. W.
Juvenile delinquency: a short text-book on the medical aspects of juvenile delinquency. Cassell, 1952. x + 395p.

RADZINOWICZ, L.
Ideology and crime: a study of crime in its social and historical context. Heinemann, 1966. xii + 152p. (James S. Carpentier lectures, 1965)

RADZINOWICZ, L.
In search of criminology. Heinemann, 1961. vii + 254p.

RADZINOWICZ, L. and TURNER, J. W. C., eds
Mental abnormality and crime. Macmillan, 1944, reprinted 1949. xxiv + 316p.

ROLLIN, H. R.
The mentally abnormal offender and the law: an enquiry into the working of the relevant parts of the Mental Health Act, 1959. Oxford, Pergamon Pr., 1969. xvi + 139p.

ROLPH, C. H.
Common sense about crime and punishment. Gollancz, 1961. 175p.

SMART, F.
Neurosis and crime, edited by B. C. Brown. Duckworth, 1970. xx + 178p.

STOTT, D. H.
Delinquency and human nature. Dunfermline, Carnegie United Kingdom Trust, 1950. viii + 460p.

SYMPOSIUM ON THE MENTALLY ABNORMAL OFFENDER, London, 1967
The mentally abnormal offender, edited by A. V. S. de Reuck and R. Porter. Churchill, 1968. xii + 260p. (CIBA Foundation Symposia)

TRASLER, G. B.
The explanation of criminality. Routledge & Kegan Paul, 1962. ix + 134p.

WALKER, N.
Crime and insanity in England. Edinburgh UP, 1968. 2 vols (Vol. 1: The historical perspective)

WALKER, N.
Crime and punishment in Britain, 2nd revised ed. Edinburgh UP, 1968. xv + 373p. (Bibliography, pp. 335-52)

WEST, D. J.
The habitual prisoner. Macmillan, 1963. x + 125p. (Cambridge studies in criminology, vol. 19)

WEST, D. J.
Present conduct and future delinquency: first report of the Cambridge study in delinquent development. Heinemann Educational, 1969. xvi + 207p. (Cambridge studies in criminology, vol. 25)

WEST, D. J.
The young offender. Duckworth, 1967. 333p.

WHITLOCK, F. A.
Criminal responsibility and mental illness. B, 1963. viii + 156p.

WILLS, W. D.
Common sense about young offenders. Gollancz, 1962. 175p.

WILSON, H.
Delinquency and child neglect. Allen & Unwin, 1962. 195p. (Published for the Sir Halley Stewart Trust)

WOOTTON, B. F., Baroness Wootton of Abinger
Crime and the criminal law: reflections of a magistrate and social scientist S, 1963.

WOOTTON, B. F., Baroness Wootton of Abinger
Social science and social pathology. Allen & Unwin, 1959. 400p.

Particular forms of crime and social deviance

BRITISH SOCIAL BIOLOGY COUNCIL. Committee on Prostitution
Women of the streets: a sociological study, edited by C. H. Rolph. Secker & Warburg, 1955. xvi + 248p.

CAMBRIDGE UNIVERSITY. Faculty of Law. Department of Criminal Science
Sexual offences: a report. Macmillan, 1957. (English studies in criminal science, vol. 9)

CHESSER, E.
Why suicide? Arrow Books, 1968. 192p.

GEBHARD, P. H. and others
Sex offenders: an analysis of types. Heinemann, 1966. xxxv + 923p.

GIBBENS, T. C. N. and PRINCE, J.
Child victims of sex offences. Institute for the study and treatment of delinquency, 1963. 23p.

GIBBENS, T. C. N. and PRINCE, J.
Shoplifting. Institute for the study and treatment of delinquency, 1962. 162p.

GLOVER, E. G.
The psychopathology of prostitution, 3rd ed. Institute for the study and treatment of delinquency, 1969. 20p.

GLOVER, E. G.
The social and legal aspects of sexual abnormality. Institute for the study and treatment of delinquency, 1947. 16p. (Publications of the Institute, no. 3. Reprinted from the *Medico-legal review*, 13 (1945): pp. 133-48)

GREAT BRITAIN. Advisory Committee on Drug Dependence. Hallucinogens Subcommittee (Chairman: Baroness Wootton)
Cannabis: report. HMSO, 1968. vii + 79p. (Bibliography, pp. 57-63)

GREAT BRITAIN. Advisory Committee on Drug Dependence. Amphetamines Subcommittee (Chairman: Sir E. Wayne)

The amphetamines and lysergic acid diethylamide (LSD): Report. HMSO, 1970. vii + 51p.

GREAT BRITAIN. Home Office

Offences of drunkenness. Statistics of the number of offences . . . proved in England and Wales for the year . . . compared with the number . . . proved in previous years. HMSO, 1950- . (Published annually)

GREAT BRITAIN. Home Office. Research Unit

Murder, by E. Gibson and S. Klein. HMSO, 1961. iv + 43p. (Studies in the causes of delinquency and the treatment of offenders, no. 4)

This study is updated by the following:

GREAT BRITAIN. Home Office

Murder 1957 to 1968: a Home Office Statistical Division report on murder in England and Wales. HMSO, 1969. vi + 94p. (Home Office research studies, no. 3)

INTERNATIONAL SYMPOSIUM ON THE DRUNKENNESS OFFENCE, London, 1968

Proceedings . . . edited by T. Cook, D. Gath and C. Hensman. Oxford, Pergamon Pr., 1969. xv + 186p.

JAMES, T. E.

Prostitution and the law. Heinemann, 1951. ix + 160p.

JONES, T.

Drugs and the police. B, 1968. 80p.

LAURIE, P.

Drugs: medical, psychological and social facts, 2nd ed. Penguin, 1971. 191p.

LEECH, K. and JORDAN, B.

Drugs for young people: their use and misuse. Wallington, Religious Education Pr., 1967. vii + 135p.

MCCLINTOCK, F. H.

Crimes against the person. Manchester Statistical Society, 1963. 32p.

MCCLINTOCK, F. H. and others

Crimes of violence. Macmillan, 1963. x + 287p. (Cambridge studies in criminology, vol. 18)

MCCLINTOCK, F. H. and GIBSON, E.

Robbery in London. Macmillan, 1961. xix + 147p. (Cambridge studies in criminology, vol. 14)

NEUSTATTER, W. L.

The mind of the murderer. Christopher Johnson, 1957. viii + 232p.

SAINSBURY, P.

Suicide in London. An ecological study. Chapman & Hall, 1955. 116p. (Maudsley monographs, no. 1)

ST. JOHN-STEVAS, N. A. F.

Life, death and the law. A study of the relationship between law and Christian morals in the English and American legal systems. Eyre & Spottiswoode, 1961. 375p.

SKINNER, A. E. and CASTLE, R. L.

78 battered children: a retrospective study. National Society for the Prevention of Cruelty to Children, 1969. [5] + 21p.

STENGEL, E.

Suicide and attempted suicide. MacGibbon & Kee, 1965. 140p. (Studies in social pathology)

WEST, D. J.

Homosexuality, revised ed. Penguin, 1960. 200p.

WEST, D. J.

Murder followed by suicide. Heinemann, 1965. vii + 181p. (Cambridge studies in criminology, vol. 21)

WILSON, C. W. M., ed.

The pharmacological and epidemiological aspects of adolescent drug dependence: proceedings of the Society for the Study of Addiction, London, 1 and 2 September, 1966. Oxford, Pergamon Pr., 1968. xviii + 515p.

Punishment and the treatment of offenders

BLOM-COOPER, L. J., ed.

The hanging question: essays on the death penalty. Duckworth, for the Howard League for Penal Reform, 1969. [5] + 138p. (Bibliography, pp. 135-38)

CARLEBACH, J.

Caring for children in trouble. Routledge & Kegan Paul, 1970. viii + 198p.

CAVENAGH, W. E.

Juvenile courts, the child and the law, revised ed. Penguin, 1967. 300p.

CENTRAL AFTER-CARE ASSOCIATION

Prison and borstal after-care: report of the Council of the . . . Association. HMSO, 1960-64. (Published annually)

CROPWOOD ROUND-TABLE CONFERENCE, 2nd, Cambridge, 1968

The residential treatment of disturbed and delinquent boys: papers presented . . . edited by R. F. Sparks and R. Hood. University of Cambridge Institute of Criminology, 1968. 76p.

CROSS, A. R. N.

Paradoxes in prison sentences. OUP, 1965. 26p. (Oxford University inaugural lectures)

DUNLOP, A. B. and MCCABE, S.

Young men in detention centres. Routledge & Kegan Paul, 1965. xii + 180p.

EMERY, F. E.

Freedom and justice within walls: the Bristol prison experiment. Tavistock Publications, 1970. xvi + 119p. (Studies in social ecology and pathology)

FOX, Sir L. W.

The English prison and borstal systems. Routledge & Kegan Paul, 1952. xiii + 479p.

FRY, M.

Arms of the law. Gollancz, for the Howard League for Penal Reform, 1951. 255p.

GIBBENS, T. C. N.

Psychiatric studies of borstal lads. OUP, 1963. viii + 230p. (Maudsley monographs, no. 11)

GLOVER, E. R.

Probation and re-education, 2nd ed. revised. Routledge & Kegan Paul, 1956. xii + 292p.

GREAT BRITAIN. Central Office of Information

The treatment of offenders in Britain. HMSO, 1968. [3] + 34p. (C.O.I. reference pamphlet 35) (Bibliography, pp. 33-34)

GREAT BRITAIN. Home Office

Penal practice in a changing society: aspects of future development (England and Wales). HMSO, 1959. iv + 32p. (Cmnd 645)

GREAT BRITAIN. Home Office
The adult offender. HMSO, 1965. 12p. (Cmnd 2852)

GREAT BRITAIN. Home Office
Probation service in England and Wales, 4th ed. HMSO, 1964. 24p.

GREAT BRITAIN. Home Office
Report of the enquiry into prison escapes and security, by Admiral of the Fleet, the Earl Mountbatten of Burma. HMSO, 1966, reprinted 1967. vi + 93p. (Cmnd 3175)

GREAT BRITAIN. Home Office
Report on the work of the Prison Department. HMSO, 1963- . (Published annually. Succeeds the annual reports of the Commissioners of Prisons, 1878-1962)

GREAT BRITAIN. Home Office
The sentence of the court: a handbook for courts on the treatment of offenders, 2nd ed. HMSO, 1969. x + 76p. (Suppl.)

GREAT BRITAIN. Home Office
Statistics relating to approved schools, remand homes and attendance centres in England and Wales. HMSO, 1962- . (Published annually)

GREAT BRITAIN. Home Office. Council on the Employment of Prisoners
Report: The organisation of work for prisoners. HMSO, 1964. 15p.

GREAT BRITAIN. Home Office. Advisory Council on the Penal System
Detention centres. HMSO, 1970. vii + 56p.

GREAT BRITAIN. Home Office. Advisory Council on the Treatment of Offenders
Report: Preventive detention. HMSO, 1963. vi + 38p.

GREAT BRITAIN. Home Office. Advisory Council on the Treatment of Offenders
Report: Corporal punishment. HMSO, 1960. v + 58p.

GREAT BRITAIN. Home Office. Departmental Committee on Corporal Punishment
Report. HMSO, 1938, reprinted 1947. vi + 153p. (Cmd 5684)

GREAT BRITAIN. Home Office. Departmental Committee on Prisons
Report. HMSO, 1895. 2 vols. (C 7702 and C 7702-I)

GREAT BRITAIN. Home Office. Probation and After-care Department
Report on the work of the . . . Department, 1962-65 [and] *1966-68*. HMSO, 1966; 1969. (Cmnd 3107; 4233)

GREAT BRITAIN. Home Office. Research Unit
Prediction methods in relation to borstal training, by Dr. H. Mannheim and L. T. Wilkins. HMSO, 1955. vi + ii + 276p. (Studies in the causes of delinquency and the treatment of offenders, no. 1)

GREAT BRITAIN. Home Office. Research Unit
Probation research: a preliminary report, by S. Folkard and others. HMSO, 1966. vi + 58p. (Studies in the causes of delinquency and the treatment of offenders, no. 7)

GREAT BRITAIN. Home Office. Research Unit
Probation research: a survey of group work in the probation service, by H. Barr. HMSO, 1966. vii + 94p. (Studies in the causes of delinquency and the treatment of offenders, no. 9)

GREAT BRITAIN. Home Office. Research Unit
Trends and regional comparisons in probation (England and Wales), by H. Barr and E. O'Leary. HMSO, 1966. vii + 50p. (Studies in the causes of delinquency and the treatment of offenders, no. 8)

GREAT BRITAIN. Home Office. Research Unit
The use of the Jesness Inventory on a sample of British probationers, by M. Davies.

HMSO, 1967. iv + 20p. (Studies in the causes of delinquency and the treatment of offenders, no. 12)

GREAT BRITAIN. Home Office. Research Unit

The Jesness Inventory: application to approved school boys, by J. Mott. HMSO, 1969. iv + 26p. (Studies in the causes of delinquency and the treatment of offenders, no. 13)

GREAT BRITAIN. Home Office. Select Committee on Capital Punishment

Report, with the proceedings, evidence (1929-30 and 1930-31) appendices and index. HMSO, 1931. cxiv + 681p.

GREAT BRITAIN. Home Office. Working Party on the Organisation of the Prison Medical Service

Report. HMSO, 1964. [i] + 18p.

GREAT BRITAIN. Home Office and SCOTLAND. Home & Health Department

Probation and after-care directory, with information about social work in Scotland. HMSO. (Published annually and kept up to date by supplements)

GREAT BRITAIN. Royal Commission on Capital Punishment

Report. HMSO, 1953. x + 505p. (Cmd 8932)

GREAT BRITAIN. Royal Commission on the Penal System in England and Wales (Chairman: Lord Amory)

Minutes of evidence. HMSO, 1967. iii + 211p.

GRÜNHUT, M.

Penal reform: a comparative study. OUP, 1948. xv + 486p.

GRÜNHUT, M.

Probation and mental treatment. Tavistock Publications, 1963. vii + 56p.

HART, H. L. A.

Punishment and responsibility: essays in the philosophy of law. Oxford, Clarendon Pr., 1968. ix + 271p.

HEATH, J.

Eighteenth century penal theory. OUP, 1963. viii + 288p.

HONDERICH, T.

Punishment: the supposed justifications. Hutchinson, 1969, reprinted by Penguin Books, 1971. ix + 202p.

HOOD, R.

Borstal re-assessed. Heinemann, 1965. xii + 244p. (Cambridge studies in criminology, vol. 20)

HOOD, R.

Homeless borstal boys: a study of their after-care and after-conduct. Bell, 1966. 103p. (Occasional papers on social administration, no. 18)

HOWARD, D. L.

The English prisons: their past and their future. Methuen, 1960. xv + 174p

HOWARD, D. L.

John Howard: prison reformer. Christopher Johnson, 1958. 186p.

JARVIS, F. V.

Probation officers' manual. B, 1969. xvi + 265p. (Suppl.)

JOHNSON, W. B.

The English prison hulks, revised ed. Chichester, Phillimore, 1970. x + 205p

KING, J. F. S., ed.

The probation service, 2nd revised ed. B, 1964. xiii + 252p.

KLARE, H. J.

Anatomy of prison. Penguin, 1962. 159p.

KLARE, H. J.
Delinquency, social support and control systems. Bell, 1966. 30p. (Sperry and Hutchinson lectures, London School of Economics, 1966)

KOESTLER, A. and ROLPH, C. H.
Hanged by the neck: an exposure of capital punishment in England. Penguin, 1961. 143p.

MCCLEAN, J. D. and WOOD, J. C.
Criminal justice and the treatment of offenders. SM, 1969. xvii + 327p.

MCCLINTOCK, F. H. and others
Attendance centres. Macmillan, 1961. xiv + 152p. (Cambridge studies in criminology, vol. 13)

MACK, J. A.
Police juvenile liaison—practice and evaluation: reporting a training course for police juvenile liaison officers. Glasgow University School of Social Study, 1968. [4] + 30p.

MANNHEIM, H.
Criminal justice and social reconstruction. Kegan Paul, 1946. x + 290p. (Bibliography, pp. 272-80)

MANNHEIM, H.
The dilemma of penal reform. Allen & Unwin, 1939. 238p.

MANNHEIM, H.
Group problems in crime and punishment; and other studies in criminology and criminal law. Routledge & Kegan Paul, 1955. x + 309p.

MILLER, D.
Growth to freedom: the psychosocial treatment of delinquent youth. Tavistock Publications, 1964. xxv + 223p.

MOBERLY, Sir W.
The ethics of punishment. Faber, 1968. 386p.

MONGER, M.
Casework in probation. B, 1964. x + 242p.

MONGER, M.
The English probation hostel. National Association of Probation Officers, 1969. 48p. (Probation papers, no. 6)

MORRIS, P.
Prisoners and their families. Allen & Unwin, 1965. 327p. (P.E.P. publications)

MORRIS, T. and MORRIS, P.
Pentonville: a sociological study of an English prison. Routledge & Kegan Paul, 1963. xv + 398p.

MORRISON, R. L.
Stresses of change in probation and after-care. Institute for the Study and Treatment of Delinquency, 1969. 16p. (Dennis Carroll memorial lectures, no. 2)

PAKENHAM, F. A., Earl of Longford
The idea of punishment. Chapman, 1961. 103p.

PARSLOE, P.
The work of the probation and after-care officer. Routledge & Kegan Paul, 1967. viii + 104p.

PARTRIDGE, R.
Broadmoor. A history of criminal lunacy and its problems. Chatto & Windus, 1953. vi + 278p.

PATERSON, Sir A.
Paterson on prisons: collected papers, edited by S. K. Ruck. Muller, 1951. 192p.

PUGH, R. B.
Imprisonment in medieval England. CUP, 1968. xvi + 420p.

RADZINOWICZ, L.
A history of English criminal law and its administration from 1750. S, 1948-68. 4 vols.

RICHARDSON, H. J.
Adolescent girls in approved schools. Routledge & Kegan Paul, 1969. xii + 297p.

ROSE, A. G.
Five hundred borstal boys. Oxford, Blackwell, 1954. vi + 199p. (Oxford University Delegacy for Social Training monograph, no. 1)

ROSE, A. G.
Schools for young offenders. Tavistock Publications, for the Institute for the Study and Treatment of Delinquency, 1967. ix + 244p.

ROSE, A. G.
The struggle for penal reform. The Howard League and its predecessors. S, 1961. xii + 328p.

ST. JOHN, J.
Probation: the second chance. Vista, 1961. 280p.

SCHAFER, S.
Restitution to victims of crime. S, 1960. ix + 130p.

SCOTT, G. R.
Flagellation. Tallis Pr., 1968. 192p.

SMITH, A. D.
Women in prison: a study in penal methods. S, 1962. x + 372p.

STOCKDALE, E.
The court and the offender. Gollancz, 1967. 208p.

STRATTA, E.
The education of borstal boys: a study of their educational experiences prior to, and during, borstal training. Routledge & Kegan Paul, 1970. xii + 228p.

TOBIAS, J. J.
Crime and industrial society in the nineteenth century. Batsford, 1967. 288p. (Studies in economic and social history)

TURNER, M. L.
Safe lodging: the road to Norman House. Hutchinson, 1961. 303p.

TUTTLE, E. O.
The crusade against capital punishment in Great Britain. S, 1961. xii + 177p.

WALKER, N.
Sentencing in a rational society. Allen Lane, 1969. iii-xii + 239p. (Bibliography, pp. 226-32)

WATSON, J. A. F.
The child and the magistrate, new and revised ed. Cape, 1965. 384p.

WATSON, J. A. F.
Which is the justice? Allen & Unwin, 1969. 242p.

WEBB, S. J., Baron Passfield, and WEBB, B., Baroness Passfield
English prisons under local government. Longmans, 1922, reprinted by Cass, 1963. lxxvi + 261p.

WILKINSON, G. S.
Suspended sentences. Chichester, Justice of the Peace, 1968. [1] + 36p. (Reprinted, with revisions, from *Justice of the Peace and local government review,* July-August 1968)

WILLS, W. D.

The Hawkspur experiment: an informal account of the training of wayward adolescents, 2nd ed. Allen & Unwin, 1967. 193p.

WOLFF, M.

Prison—the penal institutions of Britain—prisons, borstals, detention centres, attendance centres, approved schools and remand homes. Eyre & Spottiswoode, 1967. 303p.

Periodicals

BRITISH JOURNAL OF CRIMINOLOGY, DELINQUENCY AND DEVIANT SOCIAL BEHAVIOUR, no. 1- , 1960- . Institute for the Study and Treatment of Delinquency. (1950-60, entitled *British journal of delinquency*)

CRIMINAL LAW REVIEW, 1954- . SM.

HOWARD JOURNAL, no. 1- , 1921- . Howard League for Penal Reform.

INTERNATIONAL JOURNAL OF OFFENDER THERAPY AND COMPARATIVE CRIMINOLOGY, vol. 1- , 1957- . Association for the Psychiatric Treatment of Offenders. (1957-61, published as *A.P.T.O. journal;* 1961-66 as *Journal of offender therapy*)

JOURNAL OF CRIMINAL SCIENCE, no. 1- , 1948- . Department of Criminal Science, Faculty of Law, University of Cambridge.

JUSTICE OF THE PEACE AND LOCAL GOVERNMENT REVIEW, no. 1- , 1837- . Justice of the Peace and Local Government Review.

THE MAGISTRATE. Bulletin of the Magistrates' Association, no. 1- , 1921- . Magistrates' Association.

MEDICINE, SCIENCE AND THE LAW. Official journal of the British Academy of Forensic Sciences, no. 1- , 1960- . SM, for the Academy.

MEDICO-LEGAL JOURNAL, vol. 1- , 1933- . Medico-Legal Society of London. (1933-46, entitled *Medico-legal and criminological review*. Succeeded the Society's *Transactions*, vols 1-26, 1904-33)

POLICE. The monthly journal of the Police Federation, no. 1- , 1968- . Police Federation.

POLICE JOURNAL, 1- , 1928- . Police Journal.

POLICE REVIEW, no. 1- , 1893- . Police Review Publishing Co. Ltd.

PRISON SERVICE JOURNAL, no. 1- , 1960- . Home Office Prison Department.

PROBATION. Journal of the National Association of Probation Officers, no. 1- , 1929- . National Association of Probation Officers.

SOCIAL WORK TODAY, vol. 1- , 1970- . British Association of Social Workers. (Incorporates *Case conference*, vols 1-16, 1954-70)

XI. PUBLIC LAW

I. GENERAL

(a) *The Background*

Public law cannot easily be detached from its background of history and political, parliamentary and administrative practice; and the English background is peculiar and difficult to understand. Very often the law bears a marked resemblance to the law in foreign countries but the practice is entirely different. Accordingly even the lawyer must be prepared to read books on Constitutional History, Politics and the Machinery of Government.

Fortunately for Constitutional History he need now have recourse to only one book, KEIR. The companion work, JOLLIFFE, is not so necessary.

The books on Constitutional Law regularly contain information on the structure and working of parliamentary and cabinet government, and on the process of administration; but it is usually scanty and rather formal, and does not give a living picture. On parliamentary and cabinet government the standard works are now JENNINGS, *Parliament* and *Cabinet Government*. They should be supplemented by MACKINTOSH. All three books deal with both law and practice. The older classical works of HEARN, BAGEHOT and LOWELL still repay study, though they deal with politics at an earlier, on the whole pre-democratic stage. The memoirs and biographies of dead statesmen often contain invaluable and indeed indispensable material on the actual working of cabinet government. A notable example is NICOLSON. AMERY is a most valuable set of lectures by an elder statesman; MORRISON largely describes the personal experience of a leading minister in the Attlee Labour government. WALKER gives a similar account of the Wilson Cabinet.

It is very difficult to obtain a satisfactory picture of the administrative system from books. In the first place, there is not one system. There are many types of authorities, of which the most prominent are (1) government departments staffed by civil servants under the control of ministers responsible to the House of Commons; (2) public corporations, operating in a semi-independent manner like ordinary business concerns but under the remote control of ministers and Parliament in matters of high policy; and (3) local authorities, which are usually councils chosen locally for limited areas by popular election. Both public corporations and local authorities have administrative staffs which are in practice permanent but are not composed of civil servants. Unlike government departments, they are not regarded as the Crown, and do not share its privileges and immunities. What is more, the process of administration varies greatly in the various classes of authority; and within each class individual authorities have their own peculiar ways of doing business. Very often their internal organization is not regulated by law, though it may affect the ordinary citizen who has to deal with them. The relations between different authorities are formally regulated by law, but this is often only a basis for practical arrangements which cannot be understood from a mere reading of the law.

A short but good general account of the system is HARRISON. Rather more descriptive are the three chapters by LAWSON in BRIERLY. There are many short books on the working of local government, of which the most accessible are perhaps MAUD and JACKSON. A classic personal description of local government in Manchester is given in SIMON. It is rather harder to find a living picture of what actually goes on in government departments. Probably the best is in CRITCHLEY especially Chapter 4, "The Day's Work". It can be usefully supplemented by a reading of DALE and MUNRO. Certain administrative tribunals are described in POLLARD.

Select Bibliography

AMERY, L. C. M. S.
Thoughts on the constitution, 2nd ed. OUP, 1953, reissued 1964. xiv + 195p.

BAGEHOT, W.
The English constitution; with an introduction by R. H. S. Crossman, and a bibliography on British central government and politics. Watts, 1964. 359p.

BIRCH, A. H.
The British system of government, 2nd ed. Allen & Unwin, 1968. 284p.

BIRCH, A. H.
Representative and responsible government. Allen & Unwin, 1964. 252p.

BRIERLY, J. L. and others
Law and government in theory and practice. Odhams, 1948. 384p.

CAMPION, G. F. M., Baron Campion, and others
British Government since 1918. Allen & Unwin, 1950. 232p.

CRITCHLEY, T. A.
The civil service today. Gollancz, 1951. 150p.

DALE, H. E.
The higher civil service of Great Britain. OUP, 1941. xiv + 232p.

DUNNILL, F.
The civil service: some human aspects. Allen & Unwin, 1956. 226p.

GINSBERG, M., ed.
Law and opinion in England in the twentieth century. S, 1959. viii + 407p.

GOUGH, J. W.
Fundamental law in English constitutional history. OUP, 1955. ix + 229p.

HARRISON, W.
The government of Britain, 6th ed. Hutchinson, 1960. 175p.

HEARN, W. E.
The government of England, 2nd ed. Longmans, 1886. xvi + 636p.

JACKSON, W. E.
Local government in England and Wales, 4th ed. reprinted with an additional preface. Penguin Books, 1969. 222p.

JENNINGS, Sir W. I.
Cabinet government, 3rd ed. CUP, 1959. x + 587p.

JENNINGS, Sir W. I.
Parliament, 2nd ed. CUP, 1957. xii + 574p.

JENNINGS, Sir W. I.
Party politics. CUP, 1960–62. 3 vols.

JOLLIFFE, J. E. A.
The constitutional history of medieval England from the English settlement to 1485, 4th ed. Black, 1961. vii + 524p.

KEIR, Sir D. L.
The constitutional history of modern Britain since 1485, 9th ed. Black, 1969. viii + 600p.

LOWELL, A. L.
The government of England. New York, Macmillan, 1920. 2 vols.
MACKENZIE, R. T.
British political parties, 2nd ed. Heinemann, 1963. xv + 694p.
MACKINTOSH, J. P.
The British Cabinet, 2nd ed. S, 1968. xv + 657p.
MAITLAND, F. W.
The constitutional history of England: a course of lectures, edited by H. A. L. Fisher. CUP, 1909. xxviii + 547p.
MORRISON, H. S., Baron Morrison of Lambeth
Government and parliament: a survey from the inside, 3rd ed. OUP, 1964. 384p.
MUNRO, C. K.
The fountains in Trafalgar Square: some reflections on the civil service. Heinemann, 1952. x + 202p.
MURRAY, C. de B.
How Scotland is governed, revised ed. Glasgow, Art and Educational Publishers, 1947. 228p.
NICOLSON, Sir H. G.
King George the fifth: his life and reign. Constable, 1952. xxiii + 570p.
POLLARD, R. S. W., ed.
Administrative tribunals at work: a symposium. S, 1950. xx + 154p. (Studies in public administration, no. 3)
REDCLIFFE-MAUD, J. M., Baron Redcliffe-Maud and FINER, S. E.
Local government in England and Wales, 2nd ed. OUP, 1953. vi + 230p.
ROYAL INSTITUTE OF PUBLIC ADMINISTRATION
The organisation of British central government, 1915–64. A survey by a study group edited by D. N. Chester, 2nd ed. by F. M. G. Willson. Allen & Unwin, 1968. 521p.
SIMON, E. D., Baron Simon
A city council from within. Longmans, 1926. xx + 246p.
STEWART, J. D.
British pressure groups. OUP, 1958. xii + 273p.
TASWELL-LANGMEAD, T. P.
English constitutional history, 10th ed. by T. F. T. Plucknett. SM, 1946. xxviii + 833p.
WALKER, P. Gordon
The Cabinet, revised ed. Heinemann Educational, 1972. 208p.
WHEARE, Sir K. C.
Government by committee. OUP, 1955. 264p.
WHEELER-BENNETT, Sir J. W.
King George VI. Macmillan, 1958. xiv + 891p.

(b) *General Introduction to the Law*

Although there is no formal written constitution, the law relating to government is almost entirely in written form; the part played by common law and equity is very small. They provide a few remedies, around which has grown a small but important body of substantive doctrine, and there are a few public officers who exist at common law and have acquired their powers from common law. Much of the law relating to the Crown is comprised in the Royal Prerogative, which is a comprehensive term used to express the powers vested in the Executive by the common law, i.e. not by statute. Although the Crown cannot legislate, it can exercise the treaty making power, the power to declare war and peace, the pardoning power and many other inherent powers. The legal basis of these powers, i.e. the Royal Prerogative, is defined as the pre-eminence which the Sovereign enjoys over and above all other persons by virtue of the common law but out of its ordinary course by right of her regal dignity, and as comprehending the special dignities, liberties, privileges, powers and royalties allowed by the common law to the Crown of England. But this formula conceals the fact which is decisive from a political point of view, that the Queen exercises the prerogative powers she enjoys on the advice of the Cabinet, the Prime Minister, or the particular minister concerned (e.g., the pardoning power on the advice of the Home Secretary) and that the Cabinet is normally responsible to Parliament for the advice it (or any of its members) tenders to the Crown. The ultimate control over the exercise of the Royal Prerogative thus rests with Parliament.

It will be seen from the foregoing that the traditional legal principle does not give a picture of political realities. The rule that the Queen exercises her Royal Prerogative on the advice of her Ministers is one of those customs or usages which regulate much of the actual working of government and which are known by the name Dicey invented for them, namely conventions, for which see DICEY, JENNINGS and MACKINTOSH. Other examples of conventions are the rule that the Queen will not withhold her Royal Assent from Bills passed by both Houses of Parliament, and the rule that the Government must either advise the Crown to dissolve Parliament or resign on being defeated in the House of Commons on a major issue. Whether these *conventions* are to be classified as principles of law or as non-legal customs overlaying the law is a terminological question depending on the definition of law one adopts. If, following Dicey, one defines law as the sum total of those rules which are capable of being enforced by courts of justice, one will, with Dicey, consider the conventions of the constitution as principles of a non-legal character. But even if one adopts this view, one cannot understand British constitutional law without taking account of them. If one considers only those principles which Dicey regarded as principles of law—which Dicey indeed did not do—one obtains not a picture but a caricature of the constitution.

A distinction is made between "central government" and "local government", the latter comprising the municipal authorities, their organization and powers. Continental lawyers are familiar with this distinction, but they must realize that it has, in Britain, a significance different from that which it has on the Continent; in peace time, there are no "all purpose" authorities forming part of the Central Government outside London. Certain Government Departments have a regional and local organization and exercise their powers through inspectors and other officers outside the capital, but there is no regional or local organization of the Central Government as a whole. Most of what, in many Continental countries, is done outside the capital by the regional and local representatives of the Central Government is, in Britain, done by local authorities as such. The dual organization of decentralized and local authorities does not, in its Continental form, exist in this country, for reasons connected with the history of England in the seventeenth century.

The constitution, powers and duties of almost all public authorities are laid down in statutes or statutory instruments, and those powers are enumerated specifically. There is no "general clause" vesting in any authority a power to protect the public and its members. It follows that there is no general concept of "police", "*pouvoir policier*", or "*Polizeigewalt*", and the functions of what are called the "police" are restricted to matters connected with the prevention and suppression of crime, keeping order, etc. The police have nothing to do with health services, building regulations or other welfare measures. The body of law governing the organization of central and local authorities is extremely detailed and complicated, though much has been done to consolidate it in large comprehensive statutes and bring it into compendious form. Many public services, especially, but not only, the nationalized industries, are administered by so-called "public corporations", i.e., independently of the central or local government authorities, but, within certain limits, subject to ministerial directives.

The literature of public law falls into two classes. The details relating to the constitution, powers and duties of public authorities are dealt with in practitioners' books, which are of the same type as, for instance, in the law of real property. They are commonly editions of the relevant statutes and statutory instruments, with the interpretations which have been put on them by the courts. This type of book calls for no further comment of a general kind. The rest of the literature needs further discussion.

No technical distinction is made between constitutional and administrative law. Indeed, the term *administrative law* was hardly used by lawyers until very recently, but it is now increasingly used as signifying a body of doctrine roughly corresponding to the general part of French administrative law, i.e., the constitution, operation, powers, duties and liabilities of public authorities, including public corporations, and the control of the legality of administrative acts. It thus includes subordinate legislation, the remedies against public authorities and the judicial control of public authorities, which (to some extent) takes the place of a general *contentieux administratif* or *Verwaltungsstreitverfahren*. The description of local authorities and of the functions they perform is separated from the general body of administrative law and discussed under the head of "local government".

For the purposes of this bibliography a distinction will be made between constitutional law, general administrative law, local government, and practitioners' books on the particular public services, whether belonging to central or to local government. But while there are books dealing exclusively with administrative law, general books on constitutional law always deal with general administrative law.

Select Bibliography

DICEY, A. V.

Introduction to the study of the constitution, 10th ed. by E. C. S. Wade. Macmillan, 1959. cxcviii + 535p.

The 8th edition, the last by Dicey himself, reprinted in 1920, is still worth reading.

JENNINGS, Sir W. I.

Cabinet government, 3rd ed. CUP, 1959. x + 587p.

MACKINTOSH, J. P.

The British Cabinet, 2nd ed. S, 1968. xv + 657p.

(c) *Constitutional Law*

A slight but excellent introduction is AMOS. The author was for many years a judge in Egypt and had received a thorough training in both English and French law. He had foreigners very much in mind when writing this book. Although disfigured by small mistakes and out of date in detail, it still retains its value as a general introduction. JENNINGS, *The British Constitution*, is more up to date and is stronger on administration.

There are three useful general textbooks. WADE AND PHILLIPS is an entirely new book, which originally appeared in 1931. It covers all the ground. HOOD PHILLIPS is a new edition of a book which had appeared successively under the titles CHALMERS, CHALMERS AND ASQUITH and CHALMERS AND HOOD PHILLIPS. It was originally rather jejune and unsatisfactory. It has now been improved out of all recognition. It is on the same general lines as WADE AND PHILLIPS, but contains more detail. ANSON, equally comprehensive and a famous book in its time, is now out of date. The title *Constitutional Law* in *Halsbury's Laws of England* contains a general introduction but thereafter deals only with the Sovereign and the Royal Family, the Royal Prerogative, the Ministry and the Government Departments, and the hereditary revenues of the Crown.

DICEY deals with three topics, the Sovereignty of Parliament, the Rule of Law, and the Conventions of the Constitution. It also contains appendices on related topics. It is best used in the 9th edition, by E. C. S. Wade, who added a long introduction and appendices on Administrative Law, and Public Meetings and Liberty of Discussion. But the Introduction with which Dicey prefaced the 8th edition, and some of the appendices omitted from the 9th edition, are still worth reading. Dicey did not attempt a complete statement of the law, and has sometimes been unfairly criticized for not doing what he did not set out to do. His book has greatly influenced the later development of the law and has created an orthodox view of the constitution which is not always supported by his text. This view has been severely and effectively criticized by the late Sir Ivor JENNINGS, particularly in *The law and the constitution*, a book of the same type as DICEY, pungent, vivid and illuminating, but covering much the same ground and therefore no more comprehensive. The little known EMDEN, *Principles of British constitutional law* is best described by its subtitle, "Being a short study of the functions and mutual relations of the executive, the legislature and the judiciary". It is largely out of date in detail but remains a valuable discussion of the Separation of Powers and related topics.

On Parliament the best short introduction is ILBERT, *Parliament*. Ilbert was for long a high parliamentary official. For the general working of Parliament the standard book is now JENNINGS, *Parliament*. For procedure, REDLICH is historical, CAMPION is introductory, and ERSKINE MAY is full and authoritative. For the relations between Parliament and the electorate the best book, largely historical, is EMDEN, *The people and the constitution.*

For cabinet government see JENNINGS, *Cabinet government*, MACKINTOSH and WALKER. They contain much information about the Government Departments and other parts of the machinery of central government. This is also described in the various volumes of the *Whitehall Series*, written by permanent heads or other high officials in government departments; they are still, though largely out of date, useful in a general way. Fifteen volumes of a new series have appeared. The law on this subject is probably best set out in the title *Constitutional Law* in *Halsbury's Laws of England.*

On the liberties of the subject there is much in DICEY and in JENNINGS, *The law and the constitution.* See also BROWNLIE, *The law relating to public order*; DENNING, *Freedom under the law*; MACDERMOTT, *Protection from power under English law*; STREET, *Freedom, the individual and the law*, and WILLIAMS, *Not in the public interest.*

On the constitutional position of the armed forces there is much valuable material in the *Manual of military law*, unfortunately in places rather out of date.

It is useful to have near at hand collections of documents. Unfortunately there is no handy collection of statutory material actually in force. It would indeed be very difficult to compile one since the total mass of statutes dealing with Public Law is immense, and it is almost impossible to detach the provisions which are of primary and general importance from those which relate to matters of detail. However, there are excellent collections of documents relating to Constitutional History. A good collection covering the whole of modern English history is STEPHENSON AND MARCHAM. In much greater detail are various collections which deal consecutively with different periods, STUBBS, LODGE AND THORNTON, TANNER, PROTHERO, GARDINER, COSTIN AND WATSON, LE MAY and HANHAM.

Largely, but not entirely, historical is EMDEN, *Selected speeches on the constitution.* Mainly modern are three case-books covering both constitutional and administrative law, KEIR AND LAWSON, HOOD PHILLIPS and WILSON, the first of which also includes many introductory essays. On the same lines is JENNINGS AND YOUNG, though it contains more statutory material and has much information on the constitutions of the various countries of the Commonwealth.

Select Bibliography

Documents

COSTIN, W. C. and WATSON, J. S.
The law and working of the constitution: documents 1660–1914, 2nd ed. Black, 1964. 2 vols.

EMDEN, C. S., ed.
Selected speeches on the constitution. OUP, 1939. 2 vols.

GARDINER, S. R.
The constitutional documents of the Puritan Revolution, 1625–1660, 3rd ed. OUP, 1906. lxiv + 476p.

GREAT BRITAIN. Committee on the Civil Service, 1966–68 (Chairman: Lord Fulton)
Vol. 1: *Report.* HMSO, 1968. 2 + 206p. (Cmnd 3638)
Vol. 2: *Report of a management consultancy group.* HMSO, 1968. 115p.
Vol. 3 (1): *Surveys and investigations: social survey of the Civil Service.* HMSO, 1969. vii + 443p.
Vol. 3 (2): *Surveys and investigations.* HMSO, 1968. viii + 465p.
Vol. 4: *Factual, statistical and explanatory papers.* HMSO, 1968. 651p.
Vol. 5 (1): *Proposals and opinions; parts 1 and 2, Government Departments and Staff Associations.* HMSO, 1968. x + 435p.
Vol. 5 (2): *Proposals and opinions; parts 3 and 4, Organisations and individuals.* HMSO, 1968. 437–1166p. (Continuous pagination with Vol. 5 (1).)

HANHAM, H. J.
The nineteenth century constitution, 1815–1914: documents and commentary. CUP, 1969. xxiv + 486p.

JENNINGS, Sir W. I.
Constitutional laws of the Commonwealth, 3rd ed. OUP, 1957. xxiv + 496p. (Vol. 1, The Monarchies.) (A second volume, planned to cover countries other than monarchies was never published. Previous edition, 1952, complete in 1 volume)

KEIR, Sir D. L. and LAWSON, F. H.
Cases in constitutional law, 5th ed. OUP, 1967. xxxv + 559p.
KEITH, A. B., ed.
Selected speeches and documents on British colonial policy, 1763–1917. OUP, 1948. 2 vols in 1.
KEITH, A. B., ed.
Speeches and documents on the British Dominions, 1918–1931. OUP, 1932. xlvii + 501p.
LE MAY, G. H. L., comp.
British government, 1914–53: select documents. Methuen, 1955. xvi + 416p.
LODGE, E. C. and THORNTON, G. A.
English constitutional documents, 1307–1485. CUP, 1935. xxv + 430p.
MADDEN, F., comp.
Imperial constitutional documents, 1765–1965: a supplement, 1st edition reprinted with additions. Blackwell, 1966. viii + 119p. (Supplement to Keith, A. B. *Selected speeches* . . . see above)
PHILLIPS, O. Hood
Leading cases in constitutional and administrative law, 3rd ed. SM, 1967. xix + 452p.
PROTHERO, G. W., ed.
Select statutes and constitutional documents illustrative of the reigns of Elizabeth and James I, 4th ed. OUP, 1913. cxxv + 490p.
STEPHENSON, C. and MARCHAM, F. G.
Sources of English constitutional history: a selection of documents from A.D. 600 to the present. Harrap, 1938. xxxiv + 906p.
STUBBS, W.
Select charters and other illustrations of English constitutional history, 9th ed. by H. W. C. Davis. OUP, 1913. xix + 528p.
TANNER, J. R.
Constitutional documents of the reign of James I, 1603–1625. CUP, 1930. xv + 389p.
TANNER, J. R.
Tudor constitutional documents, 1485–1603, 2nd ed. CUP, 1951. xxiv + 636p.

General texts

AMOS, Sir M. S.
The English constitution. Longmans, 1930. xi + 194p.
ANSON, Sir W. R.
The law and custom of the constitution.
Vol. 1: *Parliament*, 5th ed. by M. L. Gwyer. OUP, 1922. xxiv + 443p.
Vol. 2: *The Crown*, 4th ed. by A. B. Keith. OUP, 1935. 2 vols.
BROWNLIE, I.
The law relating to public order. B, 1968. xli + 227p.
CAMPION, G. F. M., Baron Campion
An introduction to the procedure of the House of Commons, 3rd ed. Macmillan, 1958. xxi + 350p.
CHESTER, D. N. and BOWRING, N.
Questions in Parliament. OUP, 1962. 335p.
DENNING, A. T., Baron Denning
Freedom under the law. S, 1949. viii + 126p. (Hamlyn lectures, 1st series)

DE SMITH, S. A.
The new Commonwealth and its constitutions. S, 1964. xvi + 312p.
DE SMITH, S. A.
The vocabulary of Commonwealth relations. Athlone Pr., 1954. 27p.
DICEY, A. V.
Introduction to the study of the constitution, 10th ed. by E. C. S. Wade. Macmillan, 1959. cxcviii + 535p.
(The 8th edition, the last by Dicey himself, reprinted in 1920, is still worth reading.)
EMDEN, C. S.
The people and the constitution, 2nd ed. OUP, 1956. ix + 339p.
EMDEN, C. S.
Principles of British constitutional law. Methuen, 1925. xix + 221p.
FAIRLIE, H.
The life of politics. Methuen, 1968. 271p.
GREAT BRITAIN. Ministry of Defence. Army Department
Manual of military law. Part 1, 11th edition. HMSO, 1965– . Part 2, 9th edition. HMSO, 1965– . Part 3, 1st edition. HMSO, 1958– . 3 vols. Loose-leaf. (Suppl.)
HALSBURY'S LAWS OF ENGLAND, 3rd ed. B, 1952–64. 43 vols. (Suppl.) (Vol. 7: Constitutional Law)
HANSON, A. H. and WISEMAN, H. V.
Parliament at work. S, 1962. xi + 358p.
HEUSTON, R. F. V.
Essays in constitutional law, 2nd ed. S, 1964. xi + 204p.
ILBERT, Sir C. P.
Parliament: its history, constitution and practice, 3rd ed. by Sir C. Carr. OUP, 1948. ix + 229p.
JENNINGS, Sir W. I.
The British constitution, 5th ed. CUP, 1966. xi + 218p.
JENNINGS, Sir W. I.
Cabinet government, 3rd ed. CUP, 1959. x + 587p.
JENNINGS, Sir W. I.
The law and the constitution, 5th ed. Univ. of London Pr., 1959. x + 354p.
JENNINGS, Sir W. I.
Parliament, 2nd ed. CUP, 1957. xii + 574p.
MACDERMOTT, J. C., Baron MacDermott
Protection from power under English law. S, 1957. viii + 196p.
MACKINTOSH, J. P.
The British Cabinet, 2nd ed. S, 1968. xv + 657p.
MARSHALL, G.
Parliamentary sovereignty and the Commonwealth. OUP, 1957. x + 277p.
MARSHALL, G. and MOODIE, G. C.
Some problems of the constitution, 4th revised ed. Hutchinson, 1967. 172p.
MAY, T. E., Baron Farnborough
Erskine May's treatise on the law, privileges, proceedings and usage of Parliament, 18th ed. by Sir B. Cocks. B, 1971. xxxv + 1108p.
MITCHELL, J. D. B.
Constitutional law, 2nd ed. Edinburgh, Green, 1968. xxxix + 364p.
PHILLIPS, O. Hood
Constitutional and administrative law, 4th ed. SM, 1967. xxxix + 865p.

PHILLIPS, O. Hood
Leading cases in constitutional and administrative law, 3rd ed. SM, 1967. xix + 452p.
REDLICH, J.
The procedure of the House of Commons: a study of its history and present form. Constable, 1908. 3 vols. (Translated from German)
RIDGES, E. W.
Constitutional law, 8th ed. by G. A. Forrest. S, 1950. xxviii + 550p.
ROBERTS-WRAY, Sir K.
Commonwealth and Colonial law. S, 1966. liv + 1008p.
ROWAT, D. C., ed.
The Ombudsman, 2nd ed. Allen & Unwin, 1968. xxiv + 7-384p.
SCHOFIELD, A. N.
Parliamentary elections, 3rd ed. Shaw & Sons, 1959. xxxix + 1021p. (Suppl.)
STEPHEN, H. J.
Commentaries on the laws of England, 21st ed. Editor in chief L. C. Warmington. B, 1950. 4 vols. (Suppl.) (Vol. 3 pp. 265–600)
STREET, H.
Freedom, the individual and the law, 3rd ed. Penguin Books, 1972. 324p.
STREET, H.
Justice in the welfare state. S, 1968. x + 130p. (Hamlyn lectures, 20th series)
WADE, E. C. S. and PHILLIPS, G. G.
Constitutional law, 8th ed. by E. C. S. Wade and A. W. Bradley. Longmans, 1970. xxxvi + 767p.
WHEARE, Sir K. C.
The constitutional structure of the Commonwealth. OUP, 1960. xiv + 201p.
WHEARE, Sir K. C.
Legislatures, 2nd ed. OUP, 1968. vii + 166p.
WHEARE, Sir K. C.
The Statute of Westminster and Dominion status, 5th ed. OUP, 1953. xvi + 347p.
WILLIAMS, D. G. T.
Keeping the peace. Hutchinson, 1967. 264p.
WILSON, G. P.
Cases and materials on constitutional and administrative law. CUP, 1966. xxv + 609p.

The Whitehall series

BIGGE, Sir L. A. Selby
The Board of Education, 2nd ed. Putnam, 1934. 329p.
FIDDES, Sir G. V.
The Dominions and Colonial Offices. Putnam, 1926. 288p.
FLOUD, Sir F. L. C.
The Ministry of Agriculture and Fisheries. Putnam, 1927. 330p.
GORDON, H. C.
The War Office. Putnam, 1935. xvi + 358p.
HEATH, Sir T. L.
The Treasury. Putnam, 1927. 238p.
MOYLAN, Sir J. F.
Scotland Yard and the Metropolitan Police, revised ed. Putnam, 1934. xvii + 398p.

MURRAY, Sir G. E. P.
The Post Office. Putnam, 1927. 229p.
NEWSHOLME, Sir A.
The Ministry of Health. Putnam, 1925. 271p.
SETON, Sir M. C. C.
The India Office. Putnam, 1926. 229p.
SMITH, Sir H. L.
The Board of Trade. Putnam, 1928. 288p.
TILLEY, Sir J. A. C. and GASELEE, Sir S.
The Foreign Office. Putnam, 1933. xiv + 335p.
TROUP, Sir C. E.
The Home Office, 2nd ed. Putnam, 1925. 267p.

The New Whitehall series

No. 1 NEWSAM, Sir F. A.
The Home Office. Allen & Unwin, 1954. 224p.
2 STRANG, W., Baron Strang and others
The Foreign Office. Allen & Unwin, 1955. 226p.
3 JEFFRIES, Sir C. J.
The Colonial Office. Allen & Unwin, 1956. 222p.
4 EMMERSON, Sir H. C.
The Ministry of Works. Allen & Unwin, 1956. 171p.
5 MILNE, Sir D.
The Scottish Office and other Scottish government departments. Allen & Unwin, 1957. viii + 232p.
6 KING, Sir G. S.
The Ministry of Pensions and National Insurance. Allen & Unwin, 1958. 162p.
7 JENKINS, Sir G.
The Ministry of Transport and Civil Aviation. Allen & Unwin, 1959. 3–232p.
8 INCE, Sir G. H.
The Ministry of Labour and National Service. Allen & Unwin, 1960. 215p.
9 MELVILLE, Sir H. W.
The Department of Scientific and Industrial Research. Allen & Unwin, 1962. 200p.
10 CROMBIE, Sir J. I. C.
Her Majesty's Customs and Excise. Allen & Unwin, 1962. 224p.
11 WINNIFRITH, Sir A. J. D.
The Ministry of Agriculture, Fisheries and Food. Allen & Unwin, 1962. 271p.
12 BRIDGES, E. E., Baron Bridges
The Treasury. Allen & Unwin, 1964. 248p.
13 JOHNSTON, Sir A.
The Inland Revenue. Allen & Unwin, 1965. 201p.
14 SHARP, Evelyn, Baroness Sharp
The Ministry of Housing and Local Government. Allen & Unwin, 1969. 253p.
15 CLARK, Sir F.
The Central Office of Information. Allen & Unwin, 1970. 184p.

(d) *Administrative law*

The literature has been greatly enriched recently. The best compendious statements of the general part are GARNER, GRIFFITH AND STREET, which gives ample bibliographical material, and WADE. Casebooks are YARDLEY, and GRIFFITH AND STREET, *Casebook on administrative law*. SCHWARTZ was written from an American point of view. Interesting lectures are *Concerning English administrative law*, by Sir C. T. CARR, the greatest contemporary authority on statutes and statutory instruments, who also wrote an earlier book on *Delegated legislation*. There are classical blue books on Subordinate Legislation and Administrative Jurisdiction, the *Report of the Committee on Ministers' Powers* and the *Report of the Committee on Administrative Tribunals and Enquiries*. Apart from the specialist *Public law*, the journal which devotes most space to Administrative Law is the *Modern law review*. For subordinate legislation see also ALLEN, *Law and orders*, a polemical book which, however, contains much useful detail. SIEGHART is largely comparative. The late Lord HEWART'S violent attack on administrative justice, *The new despotism*, is perhaps still worth reading. More recent works are ALLEN, *Administrative jurisdiction* and STREET, *Justice in the welfare state*.

Two older books, though now largely out of date in matters of detail, still repay reading. KOELLREUTTER was perhaps the pioneer work on English administrative jurisdiction, but it never received much notice in England. FREUND, in which English law appears in comparison with American law and certain Continental systems, especially German law, contains the only systematic analysis of various types of discretions. It is greatly to be desired that the work should be done again, exhaustively, for present-day English administration. GNEIST'S works, at one time very famous, are now hopelessly out of date and misleading.

In this literature the term "administrative tribunal" often occurs. For such tribunals see the classic work of ROBSON and also POLLARD. The term "administrative tribunal" as used in the entire Anglo-American literature means two entirely different things.

(i) An "administrative tribunal" *proprio sensu*, *i.e.* a tribunal outside the ordinary courts which adjudicates on existing rights and duties, *e.g.*, the National Insurance Commissioner.

(ii) An administrative authority acting in judicial form, *i.e.*, creating new rights and duties by orders made after having heard those interested and taken evidence, *e.g.*, the Minister of Housing and Local Government acting under the Public Health Acts or Housing Acts making slum clearance and similar orders.

Unfortunately the term is made to include special tribunals adjudicating entirely between citizens on private law matters such as rent tribunals. These have nothing whatever to do with administrative law.

The reason why this comprehensive term "administrative tribunal" is used for all these bodies is that, as explained below, they are, in the absence of an express statutory provision to the contrary, all subject to the control of the ordinary courts through the so-called "prerogative orders", a feature they share with the inferior courts such as courts of summary jurisdiction.

The Committee on Administrative Tribunals and Enquiries (the "Franks Committee") reported in 1957.

The part of English administrative law which corresponds to *le contentieux administratif* may be divided into two parts, governing respectively actions brought against public authorities to recover property or to enforce liability in contract or tort, and special remedies used to control the acts of public authorities by forcing them to act, preventing them from acting or quashing their acts. Although there are now many kinds of administrative tribunals which aid in the administration of such social services as national insurance or the national health service, the granting of remedies against public authorities and the judicial control of public authorities has always been done by the ordinary courts, *i.e.*, the High Court, the Court of Appeal and the House of Lords.

It has always been assumed that the substantive law governing remedies against public authorities is the ordinary private law applied between private persons, though there may be a few minor exceptions. The same has always been true of the procedure to be used against all authorities which were not included under the term the Crown and its servants, i.e., virtually all authorities engaged in the central government of the country. All of this law was set out many years ago in Gleeson ROBINSON, a book which is still substantially accurate. The Crown was not liable in tort, though its servants were, and a special procedure had to be used against the Crown. Crown immunity in tort has been abolished and the procedure practically assimilated to that between subjects by the Crown Proceedings Act, 1947, though there are certain exceptions. There are three commentaries on the Act, WILLIAMS, Bickford SMITH and BELL. STREET is comparative.

The judicial control of public authorities has always been done through special remedies, some, such as actions for declarations or injunctions, also available at private law, and others, such as the so-called prerogative orders of mandamus, prohibition and certiorari, peculiar to public law. Between them they do very much the same work as the *recours pour excès de pouvoir*. All of this is discussed in the general works on Constitutional and Administrative Law, and much can be found in the article on Crown Proceedings in *Halsbury's Laws of England* and in many articles, especially in the *Modern law review*. The leading specialist work is DE SMITH.

There is no doctrine of the *domaine public*. Crown lands are owned in the same way as private land and they are administered according to a law closely analogous to that governing land comprised in a family settlement. The only comprehensive account is in the article on Constitutional Law in *Halsbury's Laws of England*.

According to an important doctrine the limits of which are not very clearly defined, an enactment does not impose obligations on the Crown unless it is expressly stated that it does. Thus, while the Factories Act, which makes provision for the health, safety and welfare of workers employed in factories, applies, in express terms, to factories belonging to or in the occupation of the Crown, the Contracts of Employment Act does not extend to employees employed by the Crown. This doctrine does not apply to local authorities or to public corporations.

Select Bibliography

ALLEN, Sir C. K.
Administrative jurisdiction. S, 1956. xv + 101p.

ALLEN, Sir C. K.
Law and orders, 3rd ed. S, 1965. xviii + 412p.

BELL, R. M.
Crown proceedings. SM, 1948. xxxii + 251p.

CARR, Sir C. T.
Concerning English administrative law. OUP, 1941. ix + 189p.

CARR, Sir C. T.
Delegated legislation: three lectures. CUP, 1921. vi + 72p.

DE SMITH, S. A.
Judicial review of administrative action, 2nd ed. S, 1968. lii + 629p.

DICEY, A. V.
"The development of administrative law in England", in *Law quarterly review*, 31 (1915): pp. 148–53, reprinted in his *Introduction to the study of the law of the Constitution*, 10th ed. (Macmillan, 1959), pp. 492–9.

FREUND, E.
Administrative powers over persons and property: a comparative study. Univ. of Chicago Pr., 1928. xxi + 620p.

GALEOTTI, S.
The judicial control of public authorities in England and in Italy: a comparative study. S, 1954. x + 253p.

GARNER, J. F.
Administrative law, 3rd ed. B, 1970. xliv + 473p.

GNEIST, R. von
The history of the English Constitution. New York, Putnam, 1886. 2 vols.

GREAT BRITAIN. Committee on Administrative Tribunals and Enquiries (Chairman: Sir Oliver Franks)
Memoranda submitted by Government departments, vols. 1–6. HMSO, 1956.
Minutes of evidence taken before the Committee . . . with appendices and index. HMSO, 1956–7. 1185 + 187p.
Report. HMSO, 1957. v + 115p. (Cmnd 218)

GREAT BRITAIN. Committee on Ministers' Powers
Memoranda by Government departments. HMSO, 1932. 156p.
Minutes of evidence. HMSO, 1932. 324p.
Report presented by the Lord High Chancellor . . . April 1932. HMSO, 1948. vi + 138p. (Cmd 4060)

GRIFFITH, J. A. G. and STREET, H.
A casebook of administrative law. Pitman, 1964. xvi + 423p.

GRIFFITH, J. A. G. and STREET, H.
Principles of administrative law, 4th ed. Pitman, 1967. xlii + 338p.

HALSBURY'S LAWS OF ENGLAND, 3rd ed. B, 1952-64. 43 vols. (Suppl.) (Vol. 2: Crown proceedings)

HAMSON, C. J.
Executive discretion and judicial control: an aspect of the French Conseil d'État. S, 1954. x + 222p. (Hamlyn lectures, 6th series)

HART, Sir W. O.
Introduction to the law of local government and administration, 8th ed. B, 1968. lxxi + 784 + 92p.

HEWART, G., Baron Hewart
The new despotism. Benn, 1929. 307p.

ILBERT, Sir C. P.
Legislative methods and forms. OUP, 1901. xxx + 372p.

ILBERT, Sir C. P.
The mechanics of law-making. New York, Columbia UP, 1914. viii + 209p. (Carpentier lectures, 1913)

INNS OF COURT CONSERVATIVE AND UNIONIST SOCIETY
Rule of law: a study. Conservative Political Centre, 1955. 64p.

JENNINGS, Sir W. I.
Principles of local government law, 4th ed. by J. A. G. Griffith. Univ. of London Pr. xxii + 316p.

KOELLREUTTER, O.
Verwaltungsrecht und Verwaltungsrechtsprechung im modernen England: eine rechtsvergleichende Studie. Tübingen, Mohr, 1912. vii + 226p.
MARSHALL, H. H.
Natural justice. SM, 1959. xxiii + 201p.
POLLARD, R. S. W., ed.
Administrative tribunals at work: a symposium. S, 1950. xx + 154p. (Studies in public administration, no. 3)
ROBINSON, G. E.
Public authorities and legal liability. Univ. of London Pr., 1925. cx + 286p.
ROBSON, W. A.
Justice and administrative law, 3rd ed. S, 1951. xxxiii + 674p.
RUBINSTEIN, A.
Jurisdiction and illegality: a study in public law. OUP, 1965. xii + 256p.
SCHWARTZ, B.
Law and the executive in Britain. New York UP and CUP, 1949. viii + 388p.
SIEGHART, M. A.
Government by decree: a comparative study of the history of the ordinance in English and French law. S, 1950. xxix + 343p.
SMITH, J. R. Bickford
The Crown Proceedings Act, 1947. B, 1948. xii + 156p.
STREET, H.
Governmental liability. CUP, 1953. 223p. (Cambridge studies in international and comparative law, no. 4)
STREET, H.
Justice in the welfare state. S, 1968. x + 130p. (Hamlyn lectures, 20th series)
VANDYK, N. D.
Tribunals and enquiries. Oyez Publications, 1965. xxviii + 274p.
WADE, H. W. R.
Administrative law, 3rd ed. OUP, 1971. xix + 363p.
WILLIAMS, D. G. T.
Not in the public interest. Hutchinson, 1965. 224p.
WILLIAMS, G. L.
Crown proceedings. S, 1948. xviii + 157p.
WILLIS, J.
Parliamentary powers of English government departments. Cambridge, Mass., Harvard UP, 1933. vi + 214p. (Harvard studies in administrative law, vol. 4)
YARDLEY, D. C. M.
A source-book of English administrative law, 2nd ed. B, 1970. xxxviii + 453p.
ZAMIR, I.
The declaratory judgment. S, 1962. xxii + 337p.
MODERN LAW REVIEW, vol. 1– , 1937– . S, for the Modern Law Review.
PUBLIC LAW, 1956– . S.

(e) *Local Government*

The local administration of the public services is conducted only in part by local branches of the central government, such as the Post Office. Traditionally it has been carried on by what are called local authorities and this is still to a large extent true. Only local administration so carried on is called in England "local government". A third kind of administration has appeared only in recent times, namely that conducted by the great public corporations such as the B.B.C., the National Coal Board and the British Railways Board.

What may be called the general law of local government comprises the rules regulating the types and the composition of local authorities, including elections to membership in them, the ways in which they acquire powers, local government finance, including the general power of local authorities to raise and spend money, and their relations with Parliament, the central government departments and the ordinary courts of justice.

The legal literature on local government was until fairly recently enumerative and hardly readable. The non-legal and especially the historical literature was, at any rate from and after the publication of the WEBBS' great books, usually of high quality. The change in the legal books came with JENNINGS' admirable little book, which is still the best starting-point. The reader should then go on to HART, which is more detailed, but scientific and comprehensive. WRIGHT AND HOBHOUSE is in some respects more functional. The other books are almost all technical and advanced in character. They are usually large and detailed analyses of the statutory provisions of a single service; they are books written by legal practitioners or local government officers for legal practitioners or local government officers. They do, however, contain introductory chapters which give a more general picture both of the subject itself and of its relationship to other similar subjects. Readers should be warned that at the time of writing (August 1972) a bill is passing through Parliament which radically alters the types, distribution and functions of local authorities. Most of the books listed below should, until new editions appear, be read together with the new Local Government Act and the consequential legislation which will probably follow it.

Important periodical literature and specialized reports of cases are devoted to local government.

Select Bibliography

BEATTIE, D. J.
Ultra vires in its relation to local authorities. SLS, 1936. xxxix + 323p.

BROWN, R. D. S.
A guide to compulsory purchase and compensation, 5th ed. SM, 1962. xx + 139p.

CHESTER, D. N.
Central and local government. Macmillan, 1951. ix + 421p.

CORPORATION OF THE CITY OF LONDON
The Corporation of London. Its origin, constitution, powers and duties. OUP, 1950. ix + 251p.

CRIPPS, C. A., Baron Parmoor
Cripps on compulsory acquisition of land: powers, procedure and compensation, 11th ed. by H. Parrish. S, 1962. cvi + 1247p. (Suppl.)

CROSS, C. A.
Principles of local government law, 4th ed. SM, 1971. lxvi + 518p.

DOWSON, Sir O. F. and WIGHTWICK, H. W.
The law relating to local elections in England and Wales, 4th ed. by H. W. Wollaston. Knight, 1962. xxxiii + 458p.

FARADAY, P. M.
Faraday on rating, 5th ed. by Sir A. S. Comyns Carr and others. Estates Gazette and SM, 1951. xl + 499p.

GREAT BRITAIN. Committee on the Management of Local Government *Management of local government*. HMSO, 1967. 5 vols (Vol. 1: Report of the Committee; vol. 2: The local government councillor; vol. 3: The local government elector; vol. 4: Local government administration abroad; vol. 5: Local government administration in England and Wales)

GREAT BRITAIN. Royal Commission on Local Government in England, 1966-69 (Chairman: Lord Redcliffe-Maud)

Vol. I: *Report*. HMSO, 1969. xii + 376p. (Cmnd 4040)

Vol. II: *Memorandum of dissent by Mr D. Senior*. HMSO, 1969. iv + 275p. (Cmnd 4040-I)

Vol. III: *Research appendices*. HMSO, 1969. v + 247p. (Cmnd 4040-II)

Minutes of evidence. HMSO, 1967-9. 14 parts.

Written evidence. HMSO, 1968-9. 10 parts.

Research studies, nos. 1-10. HMSO, 1968-9. 10 vols.

GRIFFITH, J. A. G.

Central departments and local authorities. Allen & Unwin, for the Royal Institute of Public Administration, 1966. 574p.

HART, Sir W. O.

Introduction to the law of local government and administration, 8th ed. B, 1968. lxxi + 784p.

HEADRICK, T. E.

The town clerk in English local government. Allen & Unwin, 1962. 223p.

HOBSON, N.

Local government, 3rd ed. by P. Dow. Shaw, 1957. lxxiii + 632p.

JACKSON, R. M.

The machinery of local government, 2nd ed. Macmillan, 1965. xiv + 390p.

JEFFERY, A. J. W.

Compulsory purchase of land by local authorities. Leigh-on-Sea, Thames Bank Publishing Co., 1949. xx + 145p.

JENNINGS, Sir W. I.

Principles of local government law, 4th ed. by J. A. G. Griffith. Univ. of London Pr., 1960. xxii + 316p.

LAMB, P. C.

A guide to rating practice and procedure, 3rd ed. by G. Eyre and M. Spence. Estates Gazette, 1963. xi + 133p.

LAWRANCE, D. M.

Compulsory purchase and compensation, 4th ed. Estates Gazette, 1967. xxiii + 367p.

LAWRANCE, D. M.

Modern methods of valuation of land, houses and buildings, 5th ed. by D. M. Lawrance, W. H. Rees and W. Britton. Estates Gazette, 1962. xviii + 514p.

LOCAL GOVERNMENT FORMS AND PRECEDENTS IN ENGLAND AND WALES, ed. by A. N. Schofield and A. V. Risdon. B, 1953-57. 5 vols and index. (Suppl.)

MACMILLAN, H. P., Baron Macmillan, ed.

Local government law and administration in England and Wales. B, 1934-69 47 vols in 51. (Vols 1-14 and annual continuation vols 15-47)

MORRISON, H. S., Baron Morrison

How London is governed, revised ed. People's UP, 1949. xiv + 191p.

NICHOLLS, A. W.

Compensation for the compulsory acquisition of land. Hadleigh, Thames Bank Publishing Co., 1952. xxvii + 447p.

REDCLIFFE-MAUD, J. M., Baron Redcliffe Maud, and FINER, S. E.
Local government in England and Wales, 2nd ed. OUP, 1953. vi + 230p.

ROBSON, W. A.
The government and misgovernment of London, 2nd ed. Allen & Unwin, 1948. 518p.

RYDE, W. C.
Ryde on rating: the law and practice, 12th ed. by David Widdicombe and others. B, 1968. cxxv + 1451 + 86p. (Suppl.)

SCHOFIELD, A. N.
Byelaws of local authorities. B, 1939. lix + 366p.

SCHOFIELD, A. N.
Local government elections, 5th ed. Shaw, 1970. xvi + 585p.

WARREN, J. H.
Municipal administration, 2nd ed. Pitman, 1954, xiii + 249p.

WRIGHT, Sir R. S. and HOBHOUSE, H.
An outline of local government and local finance in England and Wales. SM, 1951. xv + 497p.

History

KEITH-LUCAS, B.
The English local government franchise: a short history. Oxford, Blackwell, 1952. 258p.

LASKI, H. J. and others
A century of municipal progress, 1835–1935. Allen & Unwin, 1935. 511p.

LIPMAN, V. D.
Local government areas, 1834–1945. Oxford, Blackwell, 1949. x + 506p.

REDLICH, J.
Local government in England, edited and translated by F. W. Hirst. Macmillan, 1903. 2 vols (Book 1: *The history of local government in England* reissued with an introduction by B. Keith-Lucas, 2nd ed., 1970)

SMELLIE, K. B.
A history of local government, 4th ed. Allen & Unwin, 1968. 176p.

SPENCER, F. H.
Municipal origins: an account of English private bill legislation relating to local government, 1740–1835. Constable, 1911. xi + 333p.

WEBB, S. J., Baron Passfield, and WEBB, B., Baroness Passfield
English local government from the revolution to the Municipal Corporations Act. Longmans, 1906-29. 8 vols.

2. PUBLIC SERVICES

(a) *Local Government Services*

Two words of warning are needed here. First, for historical reasons, topics are sometimes found dealt with under unfamiliar and sometimes quite surprising heads; thus the law of Public Health includes much of the law of streets, but does not include the National Health Service or the medical inspection of children in schools. The reader is advised to refer in the first place to HART'S *Introduction* (see p. 159) or to the consolidated index volume of *Halsbury's Laws*.

Secondly, the law relating to the organization and regulation of the police is part of local government law. For, with the exception of the Metropolitan Police, which functions only in Greater London (except for the City of London) and small parts of the adjoining counties, there is no police force under the direct control of the central government. The several police forces are provided by certain local authorities under the general supervision and inspection of the Home Office; but in their enforcement of the law they take orders from no one, not even the local authorities, though they must, in a general way, be prepared to conform to their wishes. While local authorities have full powers of appointment and dismissal in respect of their officers except for some restrictions as to some of the most senior posts, appointments and discipline of police officers are governed by special legislation. Thus the Home Office bears very little resemblance to a Ministry of the Interior. As pointed out above, the word "police" has a much narrower meaning than the corresponding terms used in many Continental legal systems. It means mainly those departments charged with the prevention and suppression of crime and the maintenance of public order.

Thirdly: there is no general body of law governing the powers of supervision vested in central authorities in relation to local authorities. In practice these powers of supervision are to some extent exercised through the system of "grants", i.e., the system whereby central authorities, under powers conferred by law, pay grants to local authorities provided the latter comply with certain standards. Local authorities are also subject to supervision through a system of auditing of accounts by independent auditors who exercise some of the functions of administrative tribunals. Reference should also be made to the new Local Government Act (see p. 161).

Select Bibliography

General

GRIFFITH, J. A. G.

Central departments and local authorities. Allen & Unwin, 1966. 574p. (Royal Institute of Public Administration publications)

Education and children

HALL, Sir W. Clarke and MORRISON, A. C. L.

Clarke Hall and Morrison's law relating to children and young persons, 7th ed. by L. G. Banwell and J. R. Nicol. B, 1967. xlv + 878 + 54p. (Suppl.)

IKIN, A. E.

The Education Act 1944, with explanatory notes. Pitman, 1944. xxviii + 396p.

TAYLOR, G. and SAUNDERS, J. B.

The new law of education, 6th ed. B, 1965. xxi + 629 + 66p.

Public health

GARNER, J. F.

The law of sewers and drains under the Public Health Acts, 4th ed. Shaw, 1969. xli + 202p.

GLEN, W. C.

Public health, 16th ed. by Sir P. R. Barry and H. A. P. Fisher. Eyre & Spottiswoode, 1953. lxiv + 745p.

KNIGHT, C., publisher

Knight's Public Health Acts and other statutes relating to housing, food and allied subjects 1875–1952. Knight, 1952. 2 vols. (Loose-leaf)

LUMLEY, W. G. and LUMLEY, E.
The Public Health Acts annotated, 12th ed. by E. Simes and C. E. Scholefield. B, 1950-59. 12 vols and index. (Suppl.)

Burial

Davies, M. R. R.
The law of burial, cremation and exhumation, 3rd ed. Shaw, 1971. lx + 244p.

FELLOWS, A. J.
The law of burial and generally of the disposal of the dead, 2nd ed. Hadden, Best, 1952. xliii + 603p.

Highways

PRATT, J. T. and MACKENZIE, W. W., Baron Amulree
Law of highways, 21st ed. by H. Parrish and Lord de Mauley. B, 1967. xcii + 1245 + 51p. (Suppl.)

Housing

ENCYCLOPAEDIA OF HOUSING LAW AND PRACTICE, ed. by C. A. Cross and A. Bramall. SM, 1958- . 2 vols. (Loose-leaf)

SCHOFIELD, A. N. and SALES, H. B.
Housing law and practice, 4th ed. Shaw, 1966- . 2 vols. (Loose-leaf)

WOODS, E. C.
Housing control in the interests of public health: an examination of the powers and procedures available to local authorities. (The author), 1955. xii + 133 leaves. (LL.M. thesis, Univ. of London, 1955)

Planning

ENCYCLOPAEDIA OF THE LAW OF COMPULSORY PURCHASE AND COMPENSATION, new ed. General editor: H. J. J. Brown. SM, 1960- . 2 vols. (Loose-leaf)

ENCYCLOPAEDIA OF THE LAW OF TOWN AND COUNTRY PLANNING. General editor: D. Heap. SM, 1959- . 3 vols. (Loose-leaf)

HEAP, D.
The new town planning procedures: how they affect you. SM, 1968. xvii + 130p.

HEAP, D.
The New Towns Act, 1946. SM, 1947. xv + 180 + 21 + 25 + 83p.

HEAP, D.
An outline of planning law, 5th ed. SM, 1969. xliii + 299p.

HILL, H. A.
Town and Country Planning Acts, 5th ed. by C. F. Fay and M. Rich. B, 1967. lvi + 1014p.

LAMB, P. C. and EVANS, M. B.
The law and practice of town and country planning. Staples Pr., 1951. xvi + 899p.

TELLING, A. E.
Planning law and procedure, 3rd ed. B, 1970. xxvi + 325p.

Water

MICHAEL, W. H. and WILL, J. S.
The law relating to water, 9th ed. by H. R. McDowell and C. F. Chamberlin. B, 1950. cvii + 785 + 82p.

Police

ALLEN, Sir C. K.
The Queen's peace. S, 1953. xi + 192p. (Hamlyn lectures, 5th series)

CRITCHLEY, T. A.
A history of police in England and Wales, 900-1966. Constable, 1967. xx + 347p.

GREAT BRITAIN. Royal Commission on the Police, 1960-62 (Chairman: Sir H. Willink)
Interim report. HMSO, 1960. v + 77p. (Cmnd 1222)
Minutes of evidence, days 1–27. HMSO, 1960-61. 1484p.
Final report. HMSO, 1962. vii + 197p. (Cmnd 1728)

HART, J. M. M.
The British police. Allen & Unwin, 1951. viii + 192p.

HOWARD, G.
Guardians of the Queen's peace. The development and work of Britain's police. Odhams, 1953. 256p.

MARSHALL, G.
Police and government. Methuen, 1965. 168p.

MORIARTY, C. C. H.
Police law, 20th ed. by Sir W. J. Williams. B, 1970. xx + 726p.

MORIARTY, C. C. H.
Police procedure and administration, 6th ed. by C. C. H. Moriarty and W. J. Williams. B, 1955. xvi + 368p.

Land drainage

COULSON, H. J. W. and FORBES, U. A.
Coulson and Forbes on the law of waters, sea, tidal and inland, and land drainage. SM, 1952. lx + 351p.

WISDOM, A. S.
The law of rivers and watercourses, 2nd ed. Shaw, 1970. lxv + 351p.

Libraries

HEWITT, A. R.
The law relating to public libraries, museums and art galleries, 2nd ed. Eyre & Spottiswoode, 1947. xiv + 160p.

HEWITT, A. R.
A summary of public library law in England and Wales, Scotland and Northern Ireland, 4th ed. Association of Assistant Librarians, 1965. 72p.

Local audit

BEDFORD, E.
Audits of local authorities, 2nd ed. B, 1948. lxxxi + 1011 + 57p.

HOBBS, C. R. H. H.
The law relating to district audit, 2nd ed. Knight, 1955. xxi + 329p.

(b) *Centralized Services*

The literature on these services is very scanty, largely because there is very little case-law. Thus there is no legal book on the Post Office. National Assistance appears largely because it represents the old Poor Law system, which was part of local government. For National Insurance CLARKE is a useful short compendium.

Factories and National Insurance are dealt with in the section dealing with Labour Law.

It must be noted that not all health administration is carried on under the National Health Service Act. The preventive health services which are in the hands of the local authorities are to some extent part of the National Health Service (e.g. maternal and child welfare services, ambulance services, etc.) but to some extent they are outside the National Health Service and carried on under the Public Health Acts (e.g., sanitary inspection). The local authorities employ for these services Medical Inspectors of Health. The medical inspection of school children is still part of the education service.

Select Bibliography

CLARKE, J. J.
Outlines of central government, including the judicial system of England, 14th ed. Pitman, 1965. x + 270p.

HALL, M. P.
Social services of England and Wales, 8th ed. by A. Forder. Routledge & Kegan Paul, 1971. xxv + 357p. (International library of sociology and social reconstruction)

MACKENZIE, W. J. M. and GROVE, J. W.
Central administration in Britain. Longmans, 1957. xvi + 487p.

ORMROD, R. F. G. and WALKER, H.
The National Health Service. Annotations to the National Health Service Acts, 1946 and 1949 by J. H. Ellison. B, 1950. 2 parts.

SPELLER, S. R.
The National Health Service Act, 1946. H. K. Lewis, 1948. xc + 497p. (Suppl.)

STEELE, R. D.
The National Assistance Act, 1948. B, 1949. vi + 156 + 32p.

(c) *Public Corporations*

The Public Corporation is now a general administrative device used in many different branches of administration, partly to operate public business enterprise, and partly to operate social services.

Thus the great nationalized industries are administered by Public Corporations, which had forerunners in the British Broadcasting Corporation, and in such more local bodies as London Transport and the Port of London Authority. The reader should approach them by way of the final chapter in GRIFFITH AND STREET. Thereafter he can do little more than consult the annotated editions of the great constituent Acts of Parliament, and the Annual Reports of the Public Corporations.

For the British Transport Commission and its Executives, and the Air Corporations, see the section dealing with Transport. For the National Coal Board see the section dealing with Mines and Minerals.

Select Bibliography

CHESTER, D. N.
The nationalized industries: a statutory analysis, 2nd revised ed. Allen & Unwin, for the Institute of Public Administration, 1951. 93p.

CHESTER, D. N.
"Organization of the nationalized industries", in *Political quarterly*, 21 (1950): pp. 122-134.

DALTON, Sir J.
The Electricity Act, 1947 . . . [With the text of the Act] B, 1948. vii + 278p. (Reprinted from Butterworths annotated legislation service)

FRIEDMANN, W. G.
"The new public corporations and the law", in *Modern law review*, 10 (1947): pp. 233-54 and 377-95.

FRIEDMANN, W. G., ed.
The public corporation: a comparative symposium. Toronto, Carswell, 1954. vi + 612p. (University of Toronto Law School. Comparative law series, vol. 1)

GRIFFITH, J. A. G. and STREET, H.
Principles of administrative law, 4th ed. Pitman, 1967. xlii + 338p. (Chapter VII: Public corporations)

ROBSON, W. A.
"The public corporation in Britain today", in *Harvard law review*, 63 (1950): pp. 1321–42.

ROBSON, W. A.
Nationalized industries and public ownership, 2nd ed. Allen & Unwin, 1962. xxxiii + 544p. (The lst edition was described as "a successor to *Problems of nationalized industry*, a symposium published (by Allen & Unwin) in 1952")

STEMP, L. F. and WING, R. A.
The Gas Act, 1948, with a general introduction and annotations . . . B, 1949. vi + 265p.

3. TAXATION

(a) *Direct Taxation*

The chief sources of revenue under this head are Income Tax including Surtax; Capital Gains Tax; Corporation Tax; Selective Employment Tax; Betterment Levy; Estate Duty and Stamp Duties.

General statutory provisions

BUTTERWORTHS TAX HANDBOOK 1970-71. B, 1970. lv + 909 + 68p. (Published annually)

SWEET & MAXWELL'S CONSOLIDATED INCOME TAX ACTS 1970. SM, 1970. 1100p.

These two publications comprise the text of the consolidated Income and Corporation Taxes Acts 1970 and the Taxes Management Act 1970 which are in operation from 6 April 1970. The Butterworths Tax Handbook is an annual publication containing the current amended tax statutes and the texts of the Finance Act 1970 and later years.

Income Tax and Surtax

Income tax is charged on all income arising in the United Kingdom and on all income arising abroad of individuals (including partnerships of individuals) resident in the United Kingdom. Exceptions include interest from certain United Kingdom government securities in the case of an individual not ordinarily resident there, and certain income arising abroad to the extent that it is not remitted to the United Kingdom in the case of individuals not domiciled there.

Personal reliefs and allowances are given to United Kingdom residents and to certain non-residents (on a basis proportionate to the ratio of their United Kingdom income to total income). These reliefs and allowances depend on individual circumstances and, since they are in effect deducted from the total income in arriving at the taxable income, the result is (in most cases) a reduction of the standard rate of tax. This is imposed annually as from April 6, and is currently (since the year of assessment 1971-72) 38·75 pence in the £. (Earned income of 2/9 relief up to £4,005, and thereafter of 15 per cent on an unlimited amount of earned income since 1971-72).

Income is not defined but is classified for assessment under a schedular system which had its origin in the Act of 1803, according to the nature of the source of the income. At present there are six main heads. Schedule A dealing with rents and other receipts from land; Schedule B—woodlands which, at the taxpayer's election, are not taxed as a commercial undertaking under Case I of Schedule D; Schedule C—interest on certain government securities; Schedule D, subdivided in seven Cases—profits of trades and businesses (Case I), and of professions (Case II), short-term capital gains (Case VII) (see below), and certain other income such as interest on loans (Case III) and foreign income (Cases IV and V); other profits and gains (Case VI); Schedule E—income from an office, employment or pension; Schedule F—dividend payments and other distributions by companies. Complementary to the schedular system is "taxation at source" which was first introduced in 1803 and continued in almost unaltered language until recent years; under this system the payer of an annuity or other payment chargeable under Schedule D, royalties, and distributions by companies chargeable under Schedule F, deducts the income tax and accounts for it to the Crown.

The incomes of husband and wife who are living together, and of minor children (under 18 years) who are unmarried and not regularly working, are aggregated and treated as one income in order to compute income tax and surtax, though a higher personal (married) allowance is given to the husband, and a working wife is treated as a single person insofar as her employment income is absorbed by her earned income allowances and reduced rate relief which are separate from and additional to the similar reliefs her husband may have. Provision for separate assessment of the several incomes of spouses results not in a lower taxable income but merely in an apportionment of the total of their joint incomes at the rate appropriate to that total income.

As from 1973-74, a progressive income tax provisionally based on a rate of 30 per cent is provided for in the Finance Act 1971. The standard rate will be abolished; higher rates will be fixed in the Finance Act 1973 for income above, as yet, undetermined levels; income tax and surtax will be unified and earned income relief abolished. Nevertheless, unearned income above a certain, as yet, unfixed level will be subject to a surcharge. The aggregation of minors' income with parents' is abolished from 1972-73. The rights of a working wife to separate taxation are provided for from 1973-74.

Since 1875 there has been a right of appeal to the Courts upon any question of law (including the question whether a finding of fact was so grossly unreasonable that no reasonable man could have so found). Since 1969, there is a provision, where an appeal to a higher court is hopeless, due to the doctrine of precedents, for an appeal by consent direct to the House of Lords who, furthermore, no longer regard themselves as invariably bound by their earlier decisions. In the course of many thousands of decisions collected in 46 volumes to date (many of which are also in the general series of law reports) the courts have interpreted the statutory provisions and greatly expanded their bare statements of principle. The present legislative trend, in order to counteract valid tax avoidance schemes which high rates of taxation have engendered, is to make detailed and sophisticated provisions which cover every foreseeable arrangement and combination of circumstances, and consequently it has become current legislative practice to reverse almost every court decision which reflects an interpretation of a statutory provision contrary to that of the Crown—in order to close the loopholes in the system of taxation.

Surtax is a deferred instalment of income tax chargeable in the case of an individual and his wife whose total income from all sources exceeds £2,000. In the case of earned income, various reliefs reduce the incidence of this tax considerably and exempt earnings up to £5,000. In certain circumstances the undistributed income of a *close company* may be charged to surtax. The circumstances of the abolition of surtax from 1973-74 have already been mentioned.

Statutory provisions

Income Tax Act, 1952 as amended by the annual Finance Acts to 1969.
Income Tax Management Act, 1964 as amended by the annual Finance Acts to 1969.
Capital Allowances Act, 1968 (see also, for investment grants, Industrial Development Act, 1966)
Income and Corporation Taxes Act, 1970 as amended by the annual Finance Acts from 1970.
Taxes Management Act, 1970 as amended by the annual Finance Acts from 1970.

Capital Gains Tax

The short-term tax, an income tax under Case VII of Schedule D, was (until the end of 1970-71) chargeable on individuals where there was a chargeable acquisition and disposal of chargeable assets (there are only a few exempt transactions or assets) within a twelve months' period. The long-term Capital Gains Tax alone now remains, and is chargeable on all individuals in respect of any chargeable disposal or deemed disposal of chargeable assets (again there are only a few exempt transactions or assets). Deemed disposals included, until the end of 1970-71, death, the termination of a life interest in settled property and the automatic elapse of fifteen-year periods in respect of settled property with no life interests. There is a general exemption for assets disposed of for £500 or less and an exempt level of £1,000 for movables.

There is no maximum time limit or geographical limit to the charge to which all resident individuals, traders within the United Kingdom and trusts deemed to be resident are liable; furthermore, remitted gains not otherwise chargeable are caught in the case of those resident taxpayers whose foreign domicile protects them on unremitted gains. All gains of a company are calculated on the 'long term' rules and are added to its income to arrive at profits chargeable to corporation tax.

There is a flat rate charge of 30 per cent (or less for individuals if a computation under the so-called "half-income rule" produces a lower figure). The charge on a disposal of business assets may be delayed by the "roll-over" relief given where the proceeds are re-invested. On retirement, there is an exemption of up to £10,000 on the disposal of a business or appropriate shares in a company.

Statutory provisions: short term income tax

Finance Act, 1962: ss. 10-16, 34 and Schedules 9, 10, as amended by the Finance Act, 1965 ss. 17, 18 and by annual Finance Acts to 1969.
Income and Corporation Taxes Acts, 1970 as amended by the annual Finance Acts from 1970, abolished by the Finance Act, 1971 from the end of 1970–71.

Statutory provisions: long-term flat rate tax (30 per cent of net gains)

Finance Act, 1965: ss. 19-46, 97 and Schedules 6-10, as amended by annual Finance Acts. (These provisions were not included in the consolidated statute of 1970, and continue as prior to 1970)

Taxation of Companies

Prior to the Finance Act, 1965, companies were liable for income tax at standard rate irrespective of the amount of their total income, as well as to profits tax. The tax on income distributed by way of interest or dividends was recoverable by the company at its option by deduction of tax at standard rate from such payments.

Corporation Tax

In general, as a result of the Finance Act, 1965, companies (as defined) are liable for corporation tax at a flat rate, 40 per cent for the financial year 1970, on their profits including their capital gains. In addition, companies are liable for income tax at standard rate on their dividends and distributions (a term widely defined) under a new Schedule F; also in certain circumstances, the undisturbed income of close companies (as defined) is charged to surtax. The reform of the system for taxing companies is under consideration at the present time.

The charge on a resident company for corporation tax relates to its world profits, that on a non-resident company trading in the United Kingdom is limited to the trading and related capital gains profits of a branch or agency in the United Kingdom.

The trading profits of a company are computed according to income tax principles (apart from certain special rules) and these are aggregated with the company's capital gains computed according to the rules of the latter long-term tax. Special reliefs relating to groups of companies enable set-off within the group of the profits and losses of member companies in any accounting period.

Statutory provisions

*Finance Act, 1938: s. 42 and Schedule 4.
*Income Tax Act, 1952, as amended (for income tax provisions applicable to companies)
*Finance Act, 1965: ss. 46-89, 97 and Schedules 10–22, as amended by annual Finance Acts to 1969.
*Income Tax Management Act, 1964, ss. 9.13
Capital Allowance Act, 1968 (For annotated text see STORZ, *Capital allowances and investment grants.* B, 1968. x + 240p; see also, for investment grants, Industrial Development Act, 1966)

---

* For the period ending 5 April 1969.

Income and Corporation and Corporation Taxes Acts, 1970, Part XI, as amended by the annual Finance Acts from 1970.
Taxes Management Act, 1970, as amended by the annual Finance Acts from 1970.

Estate Duty

This is basically a tax on the capital value of property which changes hands on death whether under a settlement or under the deceased person's will or intestacy. Certain transactions inter vivos are brought within the charge, such as gifts (or deemed gifts) made within 7 years of death, and the termination of a life-interest prior to its settled termination on the occasion of a specified death.

All property situated within the United Kingdom is within the charge, irrespective of the domicile of the deceased; foreign property is dutiable if the deceased had a United Kingdom domicile or if the title regulating the devolution of such property is governed by the law of Great Britain. The rate is calculated on the basis of capital values, the criterion being the open market value.

Since the Finance Act, 1971, the exempt band is £12,500 and above that the rate progresses in steps, on a specified slice of the principal value of the chargeable assets (and not on the aggregate value as a whole, as before that Act).

In the last few years stringent provisions have reduced the loop-holes in this so-called "voluntary duty" which could be avoided with sensible tax planning advice. In particular, the immunity of the discretionary trust has been severely curtailed.

Statutory provisions

Finance Act, 1894, as amended by the annual Finance Acts.
For annotated texts see:
HEWSON, G. D., ed.
Butterworths estate duty statutes, 2nd ed. B, 1971. xi + 223p.
(Operative for deaths after 30th March, 1971)
WHEATCROFT, G. S. A., ed.
Sweet & Maxwell's guide to the estate duty statutes. SM, 1968. xiv + 165p. (Suppl.)
This is a similar work with an introductory guide to the Finance Act, 1894, as amended by more than sixty later Finance Acts. It does not include amendments after 1969.

Selective Employment Tax

This tax, which is presently scheduled for early abolition, is on employers in the service, as opposed to the producing and manufacturing industries, and is intended to exert pressures in the direction of the economic use of labour. The classification of industries for the purposes of liability is based on the "Standard Industrial Classification", 1968 edition (previously the 1963 edition). In addition to the basic charges, a system of refunds and premium payments relates to exempt and favoured industries.

The tax, which was being refined in its application, originally too blunt, has been an important source of revenue in the United Kingdom.

Statutory provisions

Finance Act, 1966: s. 44 read with the Selective Employment Payments Act, 1966

(premium and refund payments to employers in specified industries) as amended by later Finance Acts.
Standard Industrial Classification, revised 1968. HMSO, 1968. 52p.

Betterment Levy

This was, from April 6, 1967, a flat charge of (most recently) 40 per cent on the development value, as opposed to the current use value of land, and was abolished as from July 23, 1970. The charge arose on the occurrence of any of the chargeable events specified in the six Cases A-F. The calculations were complicated and depended on the relevant Case. The levy interacted with capital gains taxation and with estate duty. Specific provisions are made, in terms of the Finance Act, 1971, for the capital gains treatment of land with development value, the base value being as at April 6, 1965.

Statutory provisions

Land Commission Act, 1967: Part III, s. 27 et seq., and Schedules 4-17, as amended by later Finance Acts.

Stamp Duties

These date from the eighteenth century, but the modern law is based on statutes of the nineteenth century.

Statutory provisions

Stamp Duties Management Act, 1891, and:
Stamp Act, 1891, as amended by later Revenue Acts and Finance Acts.

Extra-statutory Concessions

These were originally published as an appendix to the 103rd report of the Commissioners of Inland Revenue, 1960, several amendments and additions being made in subsequent reports. An up-to-date list is now contained in a booklet: I.R. 1 (1970) issued by the Board of Inland Revenue.

Select Bibliography*

General and introductory works

BEATTIE, C. N.

Elements of the law of income and capital gains taxation, 9th ed. S, 1970. xxxii + 326p.

A good and broad outline of the present tax system, covering income tax and surtax, capital gains taxation and corporation tax, particularly from a lawyer's angle.

JOHNSTON, Sir A.

The Inland Revenue, Allen & Unwin, 1965. 201p. (New Whitehall series, no. 13)

* An asterisk against an author's name indicates that the text of the relevant legislation is included. Unless otherwise indicated every book referred to has an adequate index.

PINSON, B.

Revenue law, comprising income tax, surtax, capital gains tax, corporation tax; estate duty tax; stamp duties; tax and estate planning, 5th ed. SM, 1971. lxvi + 641p.

A good and easily read outline with some detail, of all the present direct taxes—the only book of its kind written from the angle of a lawyer. Some elementary tax planning is discussed.

SPICER, E. E. and PEGLER, E. C.

Income tax and profits tax, 27th ed. by K. S. Carmichael. HFL, 1966. xlvi + 739p.

A companion volume to CARMICHAEL'S works on *Corporation tax* and *Capital gains tax* for accountancy practitioners and students, but useful for lawyers.

Historical works

DOWELL, S.

A history of taxation and taxes in England, 2nd ed. Longmans, Green, 1888. 4 vols (Reprinted by Cass, 1965, with a new introduction by A. R. Ilersic. Vols 5 and 6 in preparation)

FARNSWORTH, A.

Addington: author of the modern income tax. S, 1951. xii + 140p.

SABINE, B. E. V.

A history of income tax. Allen & Unwin, 1966. 288p.

ZIEGLER, P.

Addington: a life of Henry Addington, first Viscount Sidmouth. Collins, 1965. 478p.

Comparative law

DALE, A.

Tax harmonization in Europe. Taxation Publishing Co., 1963. 162p.

LAZAR, L.

"Taxation", in *Annual survey of Commonwealth law*, 1965- . B. (Annual article)

WHEATCROFT, G. S. A., ed.

Estate and gift taxation: a comparative study. SM, 1965. ix + 158p. (British tax review guides, no. 3)

Works primarily for accountants but useful for law students and practitioners

HUGHES, P. F. and COOPER, J. M.

Taxation manual, 11th ed. Taxation Publishing Co., 1969. xl + 712p.

An adequate manual with accounting examples.

*HUGHES, P. F. and GRAHAM, T. L. A., eds

Corporation tax. Taxation Publishing Co., 1966. xxiii + 861p. (Suppl.)

HUGHES, P. F. and TINGLEY, K. R.

Taxation of capital gains, 2nd ed. Taxation Publishing Co., 1969. xxxv + 823p. (Suppl.)

*HUGHES, P. F. and others

The betterment levy. Taxation Publishing Co., 1968. xxxiv + 862p. (Suppl.)

This work includes a detailed analysis of the effect of the betterment levy on the liability to income tax and surtax, corporation tax, capital gains tax and estate duty, and includes many examples.

Practitioners' textbooks: general works

*SIMON, J. A., Viscount Simon

Simon's taxes: income tax, corporation tax, capital gains tax, 3rd ed. B, 1970– . 9 vols (Loose-leaf)

A comprehensive work with a detailed up-to-date text, examples and full discussion of the case law and statutory provisions containing all treaties, statutory provisions, regulations and circulars relevant to income tax and surtax, profits tax, corporation tax and capital gains tax.

*WHEATCROFT, G. S. A., ed.

British tax encyclopedia. SM, 1962- . 8 vols (Set consists of 5 numbered loose-leaf volumes and 3 bound text-books, for details of which see "Income tax" and "Corporation tax", infra)

This is a comprehensive work on the income tax and surtax, profits tax, corporation tax and capital gains tax which includes the annotated text of the Income and Corporation Taxes Act 1970 (vol. 1); Acts prior to 1970 including double taxation provisions, and Capital Gains Tax Acts (vol. 2); Acts from 1970 (vol. 3); the tax circulars and regulations, profits tax legislation, regulations and circulars, and examples (vol. 4); double taxation treaties and regulations (vol. 5)

Practitioners' textbooks: specialized works

a. Administration of tax and tax planning

DE VOIL, P. W.

Tax appeals. B, 1969. xxiii + 139p.

GRUNDY, M.

Tax and the family business, 4th ed. SM, 1970. viii + 173p.

Useful within its limited scope.

MORCOM, J. B.

Estate duty saving and capital gains tax, 4th ed. B, 1969. lx + 460p.

A useful (though discursive) and comprehensive discussion on the workings of the tax system as a whole, including the incidence of income tax and surtax, stamp duty and corporation tax.

POTTER, D. C. and MONROE, H. H.

Tax planning with precedents, 6th ed. by D. A. Shirley and S. J. L. Oliver. SM, 1970. xxxix + 485p.

An excellent work which gives an overall picture of the tax system (including estate duty) in operation.

b. Income tax and capital gains tax (including short-term income tax)

CARMICHAEL, K. S.

Capital gains tax. HFL, 1968. xxiii + 436p.

An adequate outline for accountancy practitioners and students but useful for lawyers.

*SOPHIAN, T. J.

The taxation of capital gains, 2nd ed. B, 1967. xxviii + 738p. (Suppl.)

Detailed discussion of the law in useful form.

*WHEATCROFT, G. S. A.

Wheatcroft on capital gains taxes, by G. S. A. Wheatcroft, A. E. W. Park and P. G. Whiteman. SM, 1967. xxxviii + 633p. (Suppl.) (Now published as part of the *British tax encyclopedia*)

A comprehensive textbook with detailed discussion and numerous examples.

WHITEMAN, P. G. and WHEATCROFT, G. S. A.

Whiteman and Wheatcroft on income tax and surtax. SM, 1971. civ + 888p. (Suppl.) (Published as part of the *British tax encyclopedia*)

A comprehensive work on personal taxation.

c. Corporation tax

*BEATTIE, C. N.

Corporation tax, 2nd ed. B, 1966. xxxii + 768p. (Suppl.)

An excellent work on a comprehensive basis.

CARMICHAEL, K. S.

Corporation tax, 2nd ed. HFL, 1969. xvii + 320p.

Primarily for accountancy practitioners and students but adequate as an elementary text for lawyers.

*MUSTOE, N. E.

Close companies, 2nd ed. B, 1967. xxvii + 346p. (Suppl.)

*TALBOT, J. E. and WHEATCROFT, G. S. A.

Corporation tax and income tax upon company distributions. SM, 1968. xxviii + 401 + [22]p. (Suppl.) (Now published as part of the *British tax encyclopedia*)

A full discussion with examples.

d. Estate duty

BEATTIE, C. N.

Elements of estate duty, 7th ed. by J. Tiley. B, 1970. xxix + 211p.

A work written solely for the student but a useful introduction for the practitioner.

*DYMOND, R.

Death duties, 14th ed. by R. K. Johns. SLS, 1965. 2 vols. (Suppl.)

A most comprehensive work written in a discursive style; the separate volume of statutory provisions (vol. 2) is useful.

*GREEN, G. M.

Death duties, 7th ed. by D. J. Lawday and E. J. Mann. B, 1971. lxxx + 1216 + 41p.

A comprehensive work written in a succinct manner with the statutory provisions etc. in appendices.

e. Selective employment tax

BRITTENDEN, F. H.

A guide to the selective employment tax, 2nd ed. B, 1967. ix + 148p.

A useful guide but no more.

GREAT BRITAIN. Treasury

Selective employment tax. HMSO, 1966. 11p. (Cmnd 2986)

f. Betterment levy

*ENCYCLOPEDIA OF BETTERMENT LEVY AND LAND COMMISSION LAW AND PRACTICE. General editor: D. Heap. SM, 1967– . (Loose-leaf)

A comprehensive work containing the up-to-date statutory text and regulations with commentary.

*HARRIS, B. and NUTLEY, W. G.

Betterment levy and the Land Commission. B, 1967. xxi + 688 + 14p. (Loose-leaf service volume issued 1968)

This work is approved by the Royal Institution of Chartered Surveyors.

g. Stamp duties

MONROE, J. G.

The law of stamp duties, 4th ed. SM, 1964. xxxii + 313p.

Probably the best work on this topic.

*SERGEANT, E. G.

Sergeant on stamp duties, 5th ed. by B. J. Sims and others. B, 1968. lxiv + 487p. (Suppl.)

A completely adequate work on the subject for all purposes.

h. Government publications

GREAT BRITAIN. Board of Inland Revenue

Report . . . for the year ending March 31 . . . HMSO, 1857- . (Published annually)

GREAT BRITAIN. Board of Inland Revenue

Income Tax Act, 1952, and Finance Acts, etc. so far as they relate to Income Tax, Capital Gains Tax and Corporation Tax, with Statutory Regulations and Orders, cross references to former enactments, etc. HMSO, 1952-70. 2 vols (loose-leaf)

This work is superseded, *for the period beginning 6 April 1970*, by the following:

GREAT BRITAIN. Board of Inland Revenue

Taxes Acts, being the Taxes Management Act 1970, the Income and Corporation Taxes Act 1970, the Capital Allowances Act 1968, Part III of the Finance Act 1965, and other enactments relating to the Income Tax, Corporation Tax and Capital Gains Tax, as in force from April 6, 1970, with tables etc. HMSO, 1970- . 3 vols (To be published annually with amendments)

i. Periodical

BRITISH TAX REVIEW, 1956- . SM. (Six issues per year)

An academic journal of high quality.

j. Law reports and digests

ANNOTATED TAX CASES, vol. 1- , 1922- . Gee.

REPORTS OF TAX CASES, vol. 1- , 1875- . HMSO. (Index to vols 1–40 B, 1964. 400p.)

The official series. Individual reports are also printed separately as *Tax cases leaflets* and *Profits tax leaflets*.

TAXATION REPORTS, vol. 1- , 1939- . Taxation Publishing Co.

HARRISON, Sir E. R.

A digest and index of tax cases, 6th ed. by C. E. Garland. HMSO, 1949. lix + 1204p. (Suppl.)

GARLAND, C. E.

Case commentary on the Income Tax Acts. HMSO, 1953- . (Loose-leaf. Companion volume to the 6th edition of Harrison's *Digest and index*)

(b) *Indirect taxation*

The chief sources of revenue under this head are customs and excise duties, including the purchase tax. Lawyers appear to have little concern with these duties and no up-to-date text books are available. The purchase tax is to be abolished and a form of value-added tax (as yet undetermined) will be introduced, which will affect most transactions not exempted. The interest of lawyers is likely to be considerably increased.

Statutory provisions

Customs and Excise Act, 1952
Import Duties Act, 1958
Purchase Tax Act, 1963 (as amended by Order in Council)
The relevant Finance and other amending statutes.

Select Bibliography

GREAT BRITAIN. Commissioners of Customs and Excise
Report for the year ending March 31 . . . HMSO, 1857– . (Published annually)

GRIEVE, A. T.
Purchase tax. SM, 1958. x + 208p.

HALSBURY'S LAWS OF ENGLAND, 3rd ed. B, 1952–64. 43 vols (Suppl.) (Vol. 33: Revenue)

4. DEFENCE AND THE ARMED FORCES

(a) *Introduction*

1. English law in relation to national defence and the administration of the armed forces of the Crown have been modified considerably since 1964. The general theme has been one of centralization of organization: many aspects of law in relation to the separate branches of the armed forces have been integrated, and the process of integration of service law is likely to continue. The Armed Forces Act, 1971 is the latest of a series of Acts of Parliament concerning the modernization of service law.

2. One consequence of these changes in the law has been to reduce greatly the number of books on this subject. Whilst the traditional works on service law have considerable value from the point of view of the historical development of English law in relation to defence, it is essential to refer to official publications for statements of the present law. These official publications—especially those listed below—have tended to become much more comprehensive in recent years than was earlier the case, and many of them contain valuable historical surveys of aspects of the law in relation to the armed forces.

3. In order to understand thoroughly the fundamental principles of English law in relation to the three branches of the Armed Forces, a working knowledge must be acquired of English constitutional history and institutional law. The section in this work dealing with the latter should, therefore, be consulted in addition to the items cited below.

(b) *Defence Organization*

The Defence (Transfer of Functions) Act, 1964, an Act of Parliament, provided for a central organization not only covering defence policy and planning but also aiming at common service policies in relation to such matters as recruitment and weapon procurement. This organization took the form of an enlarged Ministry of Defence which embraced the former Service departments known as the Admiralty, the War Office and the Air Ministry. These are now in lesser form the Navy, Army and Air Force Departments of the Ministry of Defence. Adjustments and refinements in the new organization created by the Act have been brought about by executive action announced in the annual statements on the Defence Estimates, the most important of which are listed below.

Select Bibliography

GREAT BRITAIN. Ministry of Defence
Central organization for defence. HMSO, 1963. 14p. (Cmnd 2097)

GREAT BRITAIN. Ministry of Defence
Statement on the defence estimates, 1934/35- . HMSO. (Issued as Command papers) (Title varies. 1940-45 not published) (In some years a Supplementary statement is also issued)

(c) *Service law in general*

1. At present three separate bodies of law exist with regard to the three branches of the Armed Forces, although the legal framework of the Army and that of the Royal Air Force approximate closely to one another. The law relating to the Royal Navy differs considerably from that of the other two Services, especially in relation to discipline. It should be emphasised, however, that the trend towards integration of Service law is continuing, and has already seen expression in statutes such as the Armed Forces Act, 1966.

2. It should be emphasised that a large part of Service law is non-disciplinary and does not, therefore, fall to be considered by courts-martial, being of a purely non-penal and administrative nature. Discipline is, in fact, only one of many matters covered by Service law: extensive administrative regulations provide for such matters as enlistment, pay and conditions of service.

Select Bibliography

BORRIE, G. J.
"Courts-martial, civilians and civil liberties", in *Modern law review,* 32 (1969): pp. 35-52.

GREAT BRITAIN. Select Committee on the Armed Forces Bill
Special report. HMSO, 1966. 146p.

PHILLIPS, O. Hood
Constitutional and administrative law, 4th ed. SM, 1967. xxxix + 865p. (Part III, chapter 17)

STUART-SMITH, J.
"Military law; its history, administration and practice", in *Law quarterly review,* 85 (1969): pp. 478-504.

WADE, E. C. S. and PHILLIPS, G. G.
Constitutional law, 8th ed. by E. C. S. Wade and A. W. Bradley. Longmans, 1970. xxxvi + 767p. (Part I, chapters 27-29)

(d) *Naval Law*

1. Naval law may be defined as the law contained in:

(a) The Naval Discipline Act, 1957, the Defence (Transfer of Functions) Act, 1964, and the Armed Forces Acts, 1966 and 1971;

(b) Orders and regulations made under the Naval Discipline Act, among which are the Naval Court Martial Manual and the Naval Detention Quarters Rules;

(c) Naval case law, i.e. the decisions of the Defence Council, advised by the Judge Advocate of the Fleet, and of the Courts-Martial Appeal Court upon the construction of the Naval Discipline Act or of the orders and regulations made thereunder or upon the application of naval law and custom to particular facts.

2. The Naval Discipline Act includes a code of offences and punishments ("Articles of War"), provisions as to procedures for the trial and punishment of offences and miscellaneous and general provisions on the application of the Act.

3. Naval law, as distinct from maritime law in the international sense, is concerned almost entirely with discipline. The naval disciplinary system operates independently of the civil criminal law and, although the code of offences and punishments is essentially the same as that applying in the Army and Air Force, the procedures for applying it differ in a number of respects from those of the other Services.

4. The Defence Council is advised on matters of naval law by the Judge Advocate of the Fleet who is appointed by the Queen on the advice of the Lord Chancellor and who is normally a Queen's Counsel of standing. Unlike the Judge Advocate General, the Judge Advocate of the Fleet does not head a staff of barristers responsible for advising on legal and procedural questions arising in the course of trial. This task is the responsibility of the Chief Naval Judge Advocate, who is a senior officer of the Supply and Secretariat Branch and a barrister. He draws on the services of some twenty General List officers of the Supply and Secretariat specialization who are also barristers. These officers are distributed through the Fleet mostly in various staff appointments. They advise as necessary on disciplinary problems, officiate at courts-martial as judge advocate, and act as required as prosecutor or accused's friend.

5. The powers of summary punishment available to a naval commanding officer are more extensive than those available to an Army or RAF commanding officer. He can, for example, award a sentence of three months' imprisonment or detention, whereas his counterparts in the other Services have no power to award imprisonment and may not award more than twenty-eight days' detention. The naval arrangements reflect the needs of a Service largely made up of self-contained and highly mobile units. An award by a naval commanding officer of imprisonment, detention or disrating requires the approval of a Flag Officer.

6. The Royal Navy has two types of court, the naval court-martial and the disciplinary court. The latter is available only in time of war to try a limited range of offences by officers below the rank of commander. The naval court-martial is the equivalent of the general court-martial of the Army and Air Force.

7. All proceedings of naval courts-martial are reviewed by the Defence Council, without the necessity for an appeal. The Defence Council is advised by the Judge Advocate of the Fleet regarding the legality of the proceedings, has wide powers to quash or substitute findings and to annul, remit, commute or otherwise vary sentences.

8. An appeal against the finding of a naval court-martial may with the leave of the court be brought to the Courts-Martial Appeal Court. This Court has been

in operation since 1952 and has begun to build up a body of precedent, though comparatively few naval cases have come before it.

Select Bibliography

GREAT BRITAIN. Ministry of Defence. Navy Department
Naval court-martial manual, B.R. 11. HMSO, 1969- . Loose-leaf. (Suppl.)
GREAT BRITAIN. Ministry of Defence. Navy Department
Queen's regulations for the Royal Navy, B.R. 31, revised ed. HMSO, 1967- . Loose-leaf. (Suppl.)

(e) *Military Law*

1. In the narrow sense of the term, military law is that body of law applicable to the Army alone and covering both administrative and disciplinary matters. It is almost entirely statutory in its basis, other than insofar as the Crown retains any residual prerogative power. The main relevant statutes are the Army Act, 1955, the Army and Air Force Act, 1961, the Defence (Transfer of Functions) Act, 1964 and the Armed Forces Acts, 1966 and 1971; the Army Act, 1955, requires certain matters to be covered in Queen's Regulations and in other powers of Regulation authorised under the Act, not all of which are generally available. There is said to be a small area of military customary or common law and also "customs of the service and military usage".

2. Military law is in the main administered by the Army through the Directorate of Army Legal Services, and also by the Office of the Judge-Advocate General and the Treasury Solicitor's Department.

3. The penal aspects of military law are enforced through the medium of courts-martial, which have jurisdiction to try and punish persons subject to military law for military offences, in relation to which courts-martial have exclusive jurisdiction, and for "civil" offences (i.e. non-military criminal offences), in relation to which the jurisdictions of the ordinary courts and courts-martial are co-extensive in the United Kingdom. The decisions of courts-martial are not part of our system of judicial procedure. The Courts-Martial Appeal Court, established by statute in 1951 (and now regulated by the Courts-Martial (Appeals) Act, 1968) has, however, produced a small but valuable number of precedents.

4. It should be remembered that military law extends not only to members of the Armed Forces but also to employed civilians and followers accompanying the Regular Forces abroad at any time. Conversely the subjection of members of the Armed Forces (and of the civilian component) of other States to the jurisdiction of United Kingdom Courts whilst they are stationed in the United Kingdom, is regulated by statute in the shape of the Visiting Forces Act, 1952.

Select Bibliography

GREAT BRITAIN. Ministry of Defence. Army Department
Manual of military law. Part 1, 11th edition. HMSO, 1965- . Part 2, 9th edition. HMSO, 1965- . Part 3, 1st edition. HMSO, 1958- . 3 vols. Loose-leaf (Suppl.)

GREAT BRITAIN. Ministry of Defence. Army Department
Queen's regulations for the Army. HMSO, 1961- . Loose-leaf. (Suppl.)

(f) *Air Force Law*

1. When the Royal Air Force was constituted in 1917 in place of the Royal Flying Corps, the existing military law was applied to it with necessary slight modifications. This close similarity between the legal systems of the Army and the Royal Air Force has continued, and for general purposes reference may be made to (e) *Military Law*, above. The present statutory basis for Air Force Law is the Air Force Act, 1955, as amended by the Army and Air Force Act, 1961, the Defence (Transfer of Functions) Act, 1964, and the Armed Forces Acts, 1966 and 1971. As with the Army, certain matters are covered in Queen's Regulations and other Regulations under the Act.

2. Air Force Law is administered through the Directorate of Legal Services (Royal Air Force): once again, the Office of the Judge Advocate General and the Treasury Solicitor's Department share in this task. The enforcement of penal aspects of Air Force Law is virtually identical to that system described above in relation to the Army.

Select Bibliography

Air Force Law

GREAT BRITAIN. Ministry of Defence. Air Force Department
Manual of Air Force law, 4th ed. HMSO, 1964-1970. 2 vols. Loose-leaf. (Suppl.)

GREAT BRITAIN. Ministry of Defence. Air Force Department
The Queen's regulations for the Royal Air Force, 4th ed. HMSO, 1957- . Loose-leaf. (Suppl.) (Originally entitled *Queen's regulations and Air Council instructions for the Royal Air Force*)

XII: INTERNATIONAL LAW

1. PUBLIC INTERNATIONAL LAW

Introduction

As in the previous edition of this Guide, the bibliography is not intended to be comprehensive. It is designed for use by lawyers at home and abroad who are not professedly international lawyers. The aim is to provide a list of books which give a characteristic view of the English attitude to international law, together with a few of the older classics. The list has not been strictly limited to works written and published in the United Kingdom. It includes a few books by authors such as VERZIJL (Holland) and D. P. O'CONNELL (Australia) whose books seem to fall naturally into the British tradition.

In the present edition, a few works of marginal relevance have been omitted and several new works have been added. The list has also been somewhat rearranged and is presented under three main headings. These are "General Sources", "Particular Topics—Peace" and "Particular Topics—Armed Conflict, War and Neutrality". There is inevitably some overlap especially under the first and third of these headings. Accordingly, if the reader wishes to find material relating either to peace or to armed conflict, war and neutrality, he is advised to look not only under "Particular Topics" but also under "General Sources".

General Sources

While Hackworth's American *Digest of international law* has been continued by Miss Whiteman, a *British digest of international law* has been begun under the editorship of Professor PARRY, who has also produced eight volumes of *British international law cases*. However, the *British digest* has to make up for much lost time. Phase I, up to the outbreak of the First World War, is not yet complete and Phase II, when it begins to appear, will still be at the mercy of the Public Records Acts 1958 and 1967 which make confidential documents available for public use when they are thirty years old. With the continued publication of the *British year-book of international law*, the *International and comparative law quarterly* and E. LAUTERPACHT's contemporary survey of *British practice in international law* periodic information on current British attitudes and views is readily available.

As to cases, the International Law Reports cover the ground, but there has been room for an up-to-date book of selected cases and materials. This gap has been largely filled by the third edition of L. C. GREEN's *International law through the cases* which has been published recently.

General Textbooks

OPPENHEIM, once the standard treatise, is now out-of-date. Volume I *Peace* was last edited in 1955 and Volume II *Disputes, war and neutrality* as long ago as 1952. Since then it has been neither revised nor replaced. The well-known books by BRIERLY, SCHWARZENBERGER and STARKE have their own value, but would not generally be regarded as a substitute for Oppenheim. Useful new textbooks have also been written by Ian BROWNLIE and D. P. O'CONNELL and another introductory textbook, written by Michael AKEHURST of Manchester University, was published in 1970. Whether, having regard to the rapid growth of international law in the last twenty years, it is any longer feasible either to re-edit Oppenheim or to produce a comparable work within the covers of one or two volumes remains to be seen.

Select Bibliography

a. General sources

Treaties

AITCHISON, Sir C. U., comp.
A collection of treaties, engagements and sanads relating to India and neighbouring countries, 5th ed. Calcutta, Government of India Central Publications Branch, 1929-33. 14 vols. (Coverage dates range from mid-18th century onwards)

ANNUAL REGISTER, 1758- . Longmans.

CHALMERS, G.
A collection of treaties between Great Britain and other powers. Stockdale, 1790. 2 vols. Vol. 1, xvi + 564p. Vol. 2, viii + 538p.

GREAT BRITAIN. Foreign and Commonwealth Office
Treaty series. HMSO, 1892- .

GREAT BRITAIN. Foreign Office
Handbook of commercial treaties, 4th ed. HMSO, 1931. liii + 1171p.

HERTSLET, L., comp.
A complete collection of the treaties and conventions and reciprocal regulations at present subsisting between Great Britain and foreign powers . . . Vols 1-19, B; vols 20-31, HMSO, 1840-1925. 31 vols. (Spine title: Hertslet's commercial treaties. Coverage dates: 1354-1921)

JENKINSON, C., Earl of Liverpool
A collection of all the treaties of peace, alliance and commerce between Great Britain and other powers, from the treaty signed at Munster in 1648, to the treaties signed at Paris in 1783. Printed for Debrett, 1785, reprinted by Gregg, 1968. 3 vols.

PARRY, C., ed.
The consolidated treaty series, 1648/49-1918. New York, Oceana, 1969- . (Annotated. Publication still in progress; vols 1-35, 1648/49-1737/39 issued to date)

PARRY, C. and HOPKINS, C. A.
An index of British treaties, 1101-1968. HMSO, 1970. 3 vols. (Annotated)

Cases

BENTWICH, N. de M.
Students' leading cases and statutes on international law. SM, 1913. xix + 247p.

COBBETT, W. P.
Cases on international law, edited by W. L. Walker. Vol. 1: Peace, 6th ed. SM, 1947. xx + 416p. Vol. 2: War and neutrality, 5th ed. SM, 1937. xxxix + 398p.

GREEN, L. C.
International law through the cases, 3rd ed. S, 1970. xxiii + 855p. (Library of world affairs, no. 17)

HAMBRO, E. I., comp.
The case law of the International Court: a repertoire of the judgments, advisory opinions and orders of the International Court of Justice . . . Vols 1-5B. Leyden, Sijthoff, 1952-68. 9 vols. (Vol. 4C is the Bibliography on the International Court including the Permanent Court 1918-1964, prepared by J. Douma)

HUDSON, M. O., ed.
World court reports: a collection of the judgments, orders and opinions of the Permanent Court of International Justice. Washington, Carnegie Endowment for International Peace, 1934-43. 4 vols. (Coverage dates: 1922-42)

INTERNATIONAL LAW REPORTS, vol. 1- , 1919/22- . B, etc. (1919/22-1931/32, entitled *Annual digest of public international law cases;* 1933/34-1949, entitled *Annual digest and reports of public international law cases*). Ed. by Lauterpacht.

MOORE, J. B.
History and digest of the international arbitrations to which the United States has been a party. Washington, Government Printer, 1898. 6 vols.

MOORE, J. B., ed.
International adjudications, ancient and modern . . . Modern series, vols 1-6. New York, OUP, 1929-33. 6 vols. Ancient series, vol. 2, New York, OUP, 1936. xlii + 567p.

ORFIELD, L. B. and RE, E. D.
Cases and materials on international law, revised ed. Indianapolis, Bobbs-Merrill, 1965. xliv + 1102p.

PARRY, C., ed.
British international law cases: a collection of decisions of courts in the British Isles on points of international law. S, 1964-71. 8 vols. (British Institute studies in international and comparative law, no. 1)

UNITED NATIONS
Reports of international arbitral awards, vol. 1- , 1920- . Leyden, Sijthoff.

VERZIJL, J. H. W.
The jurisprudence of the world court: a case by case commentary. Vol. 1: The Permanent Court of International Justice (1922-40). Leyden, Sijthoff, 1965. 600p. Vol. 2: The International Court of Justice (1947-65). Leyden, Sijthoff, 1965. 604p.

Opinions of law officers of the Crown

Accessible in the Public Record Office down to 30 years before the current date, subject to exceptions made in accordance with the Public Records Acts 1958 and 1967.

MCNAIR, A. D., Baron McNair
International law opinions. CUP, 1956. 3 vols.

PARRY, C., ed.
Law officers' opinions to the Foreign Office, 1793-1860: a reproduction of the manuscript series with index and commentaries. Farnborough, Gregg, 1970- . (To be completed in 97 vols. 94 vols published by March 1972)

State papers and other documents

BROWNLIE, I., ed.
Basic documents in international law. Oxford, Clarendon Pr., 1967. viii + 243p.

GREAT BRITAIN. Foreign and Commonwealth Office
British and foreign state papers, vol. 1- , 1812/14- . HMSO. (Incorporating Hertslet's Commercial treaties since 1925)

ROYAL INSTITUTE OF INTERNATIONAL AFFAIRS
Documents on international affairs, 1928- . The Institute.

SMITH, H. A., ed.
Great Britain and the law of nations: a selection of documents illustrating the views of the government in the United Kingdom upon matters of international law. King, 1932-35. 2 vols. Vol. 1, xvi + 416p. Vol. 2, x + 422p. (London School of Economics legal studies, nos 1-2)

TEMPERLEY, H. W. W. and PENSON, L. M.
A century of diplomatic Blue Books, 1814-1914. CUP, 1938. xvi + 600p. Reprinted 1966 by Cass.

VOGEL, R.
A breviate of British diplomatic Blue Books, 1919-1939. Montreal, McGill UP, 1963. xxxv + 474p.

State practice

LAUTERPACHT, E., ed.
British practice in international law, 1963- . British Institute of International and Comparative Law. (Annual surveys. 1st vol. entitled *The contemporary practice of the United Kingdom in the field of international law—1962*)

PARRY, C., ed.
A British digest of international law, compiled principally from the archives of the Foreign Office. Consulting editor: Sir G. Fitzmaurice. S, 1965- . (To be completed in two phases: 1860-1914 (10 vols) and 1914-60, approximately 5 vols)

Periodicals

BRITISH YEARBOOK OF INTERNATIONAL LAW, vol. 1- , 1920/21- . OUP.

INTERNATIONAL AND COMPARATIVE LAW QUARTERLY, vol. 1- , 1952- . British Institute of International and Comparative Law, etc.

INTERNATIONAL LAW QUARTERLY, vols 1-4, 1947-51. S.

JOURNAL OF COMPARATIVE LEGISLATION AND INTERNATIONAL LAW, 1896-1951. Society of Comparative Legislation, etc. (1896-July 1917, entitled *Journal of the Society of Comparative Legislation*)

TRANSACTIONS OF THE GROTIUS SOCIETY, vols 1-44, 1915-59. British Institute of International and Comparative Law, etc. (Index to whole series published in 1969 by Oceana and Wildy)

also occasional articles in:

ANNUAIRE DE L'INSTITUT DE DROIT INTERNATIONAL, vol. 1- , 1874- . Basle, Editions Juridiques et Sociologiques.

CURRENT LEGAL PROBLEMS, vol. 1- , 1948- . S.

INTERNATIONAL AFFAIRS, vol. 1- , 1922- . Royal Institute of International Affairs. (Several title variations up to vol. 19, 1943)

INTERNATIONAL LAW ASSOCIATION
Report of the . . . annual conference, 1st- , 1873- . The Association.

RECUEIL DES COURS DE L'ACADÉMIE DELAHAYE, t.1- , 1925- . Leiden, Sijthoff, etc. (Index général des tomes 1-101, 1968)

UNITED NATIONS ASSOCIATION YEARBOOK, vols 1-4, 1946-1949/50. Hutchinson. (Vol. 1, 1946, entitled *United Nations yearbook*)
YEARBOOK OF WORLD AFFAIRS, 1947- . S.

Background

BENTWICH, N. de M. and others
Justice and equity in the international sphere. Constable, 1936. x + 59p.
BRIERLY, J. L.
The outlook for international law. Oxford, Clarendon Pr., 1944. 142p.
BUTLER, Sir G. G. and MACCOBY, S.
The development of international law. Longmans, 1928, xxxv + 566p.
EPPSTEIN, J.
The Catholic tradition of the law of nations. Burns, Oates & Washbourne, 1935. xxi + 525p.
FRIEDMANN, W. G.
The changing structure of international law. S, 1964. xvi + 410p.
FRIEDMANN, W. G.
An introduction to world politics, 5th ed. Macmillan, 1965. xii + 497p.
GATHORNE-HARDY, G. M.
A short history of international affairs, 1920-39, 4th ed. OUP, 1950. xi + 540p.
HEADLAM-MORLEY, Sir J. W.
Studies in diplomatic history. Methuen, 1930. vii + 312p.
HIGGINS, A. P.
Studies in international law and relations. CUP, 1928. viii + 314p.
JENKS, C. W.
Law in the world community. Longmans, 1967. xii + 164p.
JENKS, C. W.
A new world of law? A study of the creative imagination in international law. Longmans, 1969. xi + 341p. (Bibliography, pp. 301-26)
KEETON, G. W.
National sovereignty and international order. Peace Book Co., 1939. 191p.
KEETON, G. W. and SCHWARZENBERGER, G.
Making international law work, 2nd ed. S, 1946. x + 266p. (Library of world affairs, no. 1)
LAUTERPACHT, Sir H.
The function of law in the international community. Oxford, Clarendon Pr., 1933. xxiv + 469p.
LAUTERPACHT, Sir H.
Private law sources and analogies of international law, with a special reference to international arbitration. Longmans, 1927. xxiv + 326p. (Bibliography, pp. 307-12. Contributions to international law and diplomacy)
NIEMEYER, G.
Law without force: the function of politics in international law. OUP, 1941. xiv + 408p.
PARRY, C.
The sources and evidences of international law. Manchester UP, 1965. vii + 122p. (Melland Schill lectures, 1965)
SCHWARZENBERGER, G.
The frontiers of international law. S, 1962. xxii + 320p. (Library of world affairs, no. 59)

SCHWARZENBERGER, G.
The inductive approach to international law. S, 1965. xv + 209 + viip. (Library of world affairs, no. 67)

SCHWARZENBERGER, G.
Power politics: a study of world society, 3rd ed. S, 1964. xxi + 614p. (Bibliography, pp. 557-90. Library of world affairs, no. 18)

SMITH, H. A.
The crisis in the law of nations. S, 1947. 102p. (Library of world affairs, no. 4)

STONE, J.
Legal controls of international conflict: a treatise on the dynamics of disputes- and war-law. S, 1954. lv + 851p.

SURVEY OF INTERNATIONAL AFFAIRS, 1920/23- . Royal Institute of International Affairs.

TOYNBEE, A. J.
War and civilization. New York, OUP, 1950. xii + 165p. (Selected by A. V. Fowler from the author's *A study of history*)

WALKER, T. A.
A history of the law of nations. Vol. 1: From earliest times to the Peace of Westphalia, 1648. CUP, 1899. xxx + 361p.

WILLIAMS, Sir J. F.
International change and international peace. OUP, 1932. vi + 79p.

General textbooks

AKEHURST, M. B.
A modern introduction to international law. Allen & Unwin, 1970. 367p.

BRIERLY, J. L.
The law of nations: an introduction to the international law of peace, 6th ed. by Sir H. Waldock. Oxford, Clarendon Pr., 1963. xv + 442p.

BROWNLIE, I.
Principles of public international law. OUP, 1966. xxxi + 646p.

CAMBRIDGE ESSAYS IN INTERNATIONAL LAW: essays in honour of Lord McNair. S, 1965. [9] + 186p.

CHENG, B.
General principles of law as applied by international courts and tribunals. S, 1953. li + 490p. (Library of world affairs, no. 21)

GREIG, D. W.
International law. B, 1970. xx + 728p.

HALL, W. E.
A treatise on international law, 8th ed. by A. P. Higgins. Oxford, Clarendon Pr., 1924. xlvii + 952p.

HOLLAND, Sir T. E.
Lectures on international law, edited by T. A. Walker and W. L. Walker. SM, 1933. xlii + 576p.

HOLLAND, Sir T. E.
Studies in international law. Oxford, Clarendon Pr., 1898. viii + 314p.

LAUTERPACHT, Sir H.
The development of international law by the International Court, revised ed. S, 1958. xix + 408p. (Original edition entitled, *The development of international law by the Permanent Court of International Justice*)

LORIMER, J.
The institutes of the law of nations: a treatise of the jural relations of separate political communities. Edinburgh, Blackwood, 1883-84. 2 vols. Vol. 1, lxviii + 449p. Vol. 2, xxi + 620p.

O'CONNELL, D. P.
International law, 2nd ed. S, 1970. 2 vols. Vol. 1, xxxii + 595 + 35p. Vol. 2, xxiii + pp. 596-1309 + 35p. (Continuous pagination)

OPPENHEIM, L. F. L.
International law. Vol. 1: Peace, 8th ed. by H. Lauterpacht. Longmans, 1955. lvi + 1072p. Vol. 2: Disputes, war and neutrality, 7th ed. by H. Lauterpacht. Longmans, 1952. liii + 941p.

PHILLIMORE, Sir R. J.
Commentaries upon international law, 3rd ed. B, 1879-89. 4 vols.

ROSS, A. N. C.
A textbook of international law. General part. Longmans, 1947. 313p.

SCHWARZENBERGER, G.
International law as applied by international courts and tribunals, 3rd ed. Vol. 1. S, 1957. xlviii + 808p.

SCHWARZENBERGER, G.
A manual of international law, 5th ed. S, 1967. lix + 701p. (Bibliography, pp. 399-621. Library of world affairs, no. 3)

SMITH, H. A., ed.
Great Britain and the law of nations, a selection of documents illustrating the views of the government in the United Kingdom upon matters of international law. King, 1932-35. 2 vols. Vol. 1, xvi + 416p. Vol. 2, x + 422p.

SØRENSEN, M., ed.
Manual of public international law. Macmillan, 1968. lxv + 930p. (Bibliography, pp. 855-92)

STARKE, J. G.
An introduction to international law, 7th ed. B, 1972. xxvii + 631 + 44p.

VALLAT, Sir F.
International law and the practitioner. Manchester UP, 1966. vii + 159p. (Melland Schill lectures, 1964-65)

VERZIJL, J. H. W.
International law in historical perspective, vol. 1- . Leyden, Sijthoff, 1968- . (Scheduled to appear in a number of volumes which will cover 9 areas of subject matter. 4 volumes have been published to date)

WESTLAKE, J.
Chapters on the principles of international law. CUP, 1894. xix + 275p.

WESTLAKE, J.
The collected papers of John Westlake on public international law, edited by L. Oppenheim. CUP, 1914. xxix + 705p. (Bibliography, pp. 678-86)

WESTLAKE, J.
International law, 2nd ed. CUP, 1910-13. 2 vols. Vol. 1, xii + 372p. Vol. 2, xv + 343p.

WHEATON, H.
International law, ed. by A. B. Keith. Vol. 1: Peace, 6th English ed. S, 1929. lxxxvii + 620p. Vol. 2: War, 7th English ed. S, 1944. xxvii + 672p. (6th edition entitled, *Elements of international law*)

b. Particular topics

i. Peace

Territory

ARIAS, H.
The Panama Canal: a study in international law and diplomacy. King, 1911. xiv + 188p. (Studies in economics and political science, no. 25)

CURZON, G. N., Marquis Curzon of Kedleston
Frontiers. Oxford, Clarendon Pr., 1907. 58p. (The Romanes lecture 1907)

JENNINGS, R. Y.
The acquisition of territory in international law. Manchester UP, 1963. vii + 130p. (Melland Schill lectures, 1962)

KEETON, G. W.
The development of extraterritoriality in China. Longmans, 1928. 2 vols. Vol. 1, xvi + 405p. Vol. 2, viii + 422p.

LINDLEY, M. F.
The acquisition and government of backward territory in international law. Longmans, 1926. xx + 391p.

SMITH, H. A.
The economic uses of international rivers. King, 1931. ix + 224p. (Studies in economics and political science, no. 108)

VALI, F. A.
Servitudes of international law: a study of rights in foreign territory, 2nd ed. S, 1958. xvi + 349p.

High seas

BOWETT, D. W.
The law of the sea. Manchester UP, 1967. 7 + 117p. (Melland Schill lectures, 1967)

BRUEL, E.
International straits: a treatise on international law. SM, 1947. 2 vols. Vol. 1, 278p. Vol. 2, 426p.

COLOMBOS, C. J.
The international law of the sea, 6th revised ed. Longmans, 1967. xix + 886p.

JOHNSON, D. H. N. and SIMMONDS, K. R., eds
Developments in the law of the sea, 1958-1964. British Institute of International and Comparative Law, 1965. v + 208p. (Special publication no. 6)

SMITH, H. A.
The law and custom of the sea, 3rd ed. S, 1959. xiv + 291p. (Library of world affairs, no. 9)

Air and outer space

CHENG, B.
The law of international air transport. S, 1962. xlii + 726p. (Bibliography, pp. 635-69. Library of world affairs, no. 47)

CURRENT PROBLEMS IN SPACE LAW: a symposium. Report of a conference held by the British Institute of International and Comparative Law, May 4th 1965 . . . The Institute, 1966. viii + 168p. (Special publication no. 9)

FAWCETT, J. E. S.
International law and the uses of outer space. Manchester UP, 1968. vii + 92p. (Melland Schill lectures, 1968)

JENKS, C. W.
Space law. S, 1965. xviii + 476p. (Bibliography, pp. 463-9)

JOHNSON, D. H. N.
Rights in air space. Manchester UP, 1965. viii + 129p. (Melland Schill lectures, 1965)

MCNAIR, A. D., Baron McNair
The law of the air, 3rd ed. by M. R. E. Kerr and A. H. M. Evans. S, 1964. xxxviii + 588p.

SHAWCROSS, C. N. and BEAUMONT, K. M.
Shawcross and Beaumont on air law, 3rd ed. by P. B. Keenan, A. Lester and P. Martin. B, 1966. 2 vols. Vol. 1, xxix + 736p. Vol. 2, loose leaf in 2 binders

SPAIGHT, J. M.
Aircraft in peace and the law. Macmillan, 1919. viii + 233p. (Bibliography, pp. 217-27)

British Commonwealth

FAWCETT, J. E. S.
The British Commonwealth in international law. S, 1963. xvii + 243p. (Library of world affairs, no. 61)

HALL, H. D.
"British Commonwealth of Nations in war and peace", in *The British Commonwealth at war,* edited by W. Y. Elliott and H. D. Hall. (New York, Knopf, 1943), pp. 10-80.

NOEL-BAKER, P. J.
The present juridical status of the British Dominions in international law. Longmans, 1929. xii + 421p. (Contributions to international law and diplomacy)

STEWART, R. B.
Treaty relations of the British Commonwealth of Nations. New York, Macmillan, 1939. xxi + 503p.

Recognition

CHEN, T. C.
The international law of recognition; with special reference to practice in Great Britain and the United States, edited by L. C. Green. S, 1951. xxvii + 461p. (Bibliography, pp. 445-52. Library of world affairs, no. 16)

LAUTERPACHT, Sir H.
Recognition in international law. CUP, 1947. xix + 442p. (Cambridge studies in international and comparative law, no. 3)

Individuals

FRASER, C. F.
Control of aliens in the British Commonwealth of Nations. Hogarth Pr., 1940. 304p.

GEY VAN PITTIUS, E. F. W.
Nationality within the British Commonwealth of Nations. King, 1930. xvi + 238p.

JONES, J. M.

British nationality law, revised ed. Oxford, Clarendon Pr., 1956. xxvii + 306p.

MACARTNEY, C. A.

National states and national minorities. CUP, 1934. ix + 553p. (Royal Institute of International Affairs)

MACKENZIE, N. A. MACR., ed.

The legal status of aliens in Pacific countries. OUP, 1937. xii + 374p. (Institute of Pacific Relations, Honolulu, International research series)

PARRY, C.

British nationality, including citizenship of the United Kingdom and colonies and the status of aliens. S, 1951. xix + 216p.

PARRY, C.

Nationality and citizenship laws of the Commonwealth and of the Republic of Ireland. S, 1957-60. 2 vols. Vol. 1, liv + 1021p. Vol. 2, xxiv + pp. 1023-1285 (Continuous pagination)

PIGGOTT, Sir F. T.

Extradition: a treatise on the law relating to fugitive offenders. B, 1910. xiii + 349 + 15p.

Human rights

FAWCETT, J. E. S.

The application of the European Convention on Human Rights. Oxford, Clarendon Pr., 1969. xii + 368p.

LAUTERPACHT, Sir H.

An international bill of the rights of man. New York, Columbia UP, 1945. x + 230p.

LAUTERPACHT, Sir H.

International law and human rights. S, 1950. xvi + 475p.

MAIR, L. P.

The protection of minorities: the working and scope of the minorities treaties under the League of Nations. Christophers, 1928. xiv + 244p.

ROBERTSON, A. H.

Human rights in Europe. Manchester UP, 1963. ix + 280p.

ROBERTSON, A. H., ed.

Human rights in national and international law: the proceedings of the 2nd International Conference on the European Convention on Human Rights held in Vienna, 1965. Manchester UP, 1968. xvi + 396p.

STONE, J.

International guarantees of minority rights. OUP, 1932. xiii + 288p.

STONE, J.

Regional guarantees of minority rights. New York, Macmillan, 1933. xvi + 313p. (Harvard University, Bureau of International Research)

International transactions

a. Treaties

ARNOLD, R.

Treaty-making procedure: a comparative study of the methods obtaining in different states. OUP, 1933. vi + 69p.

HOLLOWAY, K.
Modern trends in treaty law: constitutional law, reservations and the three modes of legislation. S, 1967. xx + 737p.

JONES, J. M.
Full powers and ratification: a study in the development of treaty-making procedure. CUP, 1946. xv + 182p. (Cambridge studies in international and comparative law)

MCNAIR, A. D., Baron McNair
The law of treaties. Oxford, Clarendon Pr., 1961. xxi + 789p.

ROXBURGH, Sir R. F.
International conventions and third states. Longmans, 1917. xvi + 119p. (Contributions to international law and diplomacy)

STEWART, R. B.
Treaty relations of the British Commonwealth of Nations. New York, Macmillan, 1939. xxi + 503p.

WILCOX, F. O.
The ratification of international conventions: a study of the relationship of the ratification process to the development of international legislation. Allen & Unwin, 1935. 349p.

b. Diplomacy

BARCLAY, Sir T.
Problems of international practice and diplomacy. SM, 1907. xix + 383p.

DUNN, F. S.
The practice and procedure of international conferences. OUP, 1929. xiv + 229p. (Johns Hopkins University studies in historical and political science)

HARDY, M.
Modern diplomatic law. Manchester UP, 1968. ix + 150p. (Melland Schill lectures, 1968)

SATOW, Sir E. M.
A guide to diplomatic practice, 4th ed. by Sir N. Bland. Longmans, 1957. xviii + 510p.

SATOW, Sir E. M.
International congresses. HMSO, 1920. 168p. (United Kingdom Foreign Office, Historical Section, Handbooks, no. 151)

c. Other matters

FRIEDMAN, S.
Expropriation in international law, revised by the author and translated by I. C. Jackson. S, 1953. xv + 236p. (Library of world affairs, no. 20)

KOCH, F. E.
The double taxation conventions. Vol. 1: Taxation of income. S, 1947. xxiv + 441p. (Suppl. 1950. xv + 185p.)

LILLICH, R. B.
International claims: postwar British practice. Syracuse, New York, Syracuse UP, 1967. xvi + 192p. (The procedural aspects of international law, no. 6)

MANN, F. A. A.
The legal aspect of money; with special reference to comparative private and public international law, 3rd ed. Oxford, Clarendon Pr., 1971. l + 615p.

SCHWARZENBERGER, G.
Foreign investment and international law. S, 1969. xxiii + 237p. (Bibliography, pp. 201-26 by A. M. Sutton. Library of world affairs, no. 68)

WORTLEY, B. A.
Expropriation in public international law. CUP, 1959. xviii + 169p. (Cambridge studies in international and comparative law, vol. 6)

State succession

KEITH, A. B.
The theory of state succession: with special reference to English and colonial law. Waterlow, 1907. xii + 101p.

O'CONNELL, D. P.
The law of state succession. CUP, 1956. xl + 425p. (Cambridge studies in international and comparative law, vol. 5)

O'CONNELL, D. P.
State succession in municipal law and international law. CUP, 1967. 2 vols. Vol. 1: Internal relations. cxi + 592p. Vol. 2: International relations. cxi + 430p. (Cambridge studies in international and comparative law, vol. 7)

International institutions

AKEHURST, M. B.
The law governing employment in international organizations. CUP, 1967. xxvii + 294p. (Cambridge studies in international and comparative law, vol. 8)

ALEXANDROWICZ, C. H.
International economic organizations. S, 1952. xii + 263p. (Library of world affairs, no. 19)

ALEXANDROWICZ, C. H.
World economic agencies: law and practice. S, 1962. xvii + 310p.

BECKETT, Sir W. E.
The North Atlantic Treaty, the Brussels Treaty, and the Charter of the United Nations. S, 1950. viii + 75p. (Library of world affairs, no. 12)

BENTWICH, N. de M. and MARTIN, A.
A commentary on the Charter of the United Nations. Routledge & Kegan Paul, 1950. xxviii + 239p. (2nd impression, 1951, has an appendix on the development of the Charter up to March 1951)

BOWETT, D. W.
The law of international institutions, 2nd ed. S, 1970. xviii + 384p. (Library of world affairs, no. 60)

GREAT BRITAIN. Foreign Office
A commentary on the Charter of the United Nations, signed at San Francisco on 16th June 1945. HMSO, 1945. 84p. (Cmd 6666)

HIGGINS, R.
The development of international law through the political organs of the United Nations. OUP, 1963. xxi + 402p. (Bibliography, pp. 384-95)

JENKS, C. W.
The headquarters of international institutions. Royal Institute of International Affairs, 1945. 102p.

JENKS, C. W.
The proper law of international organisations. S, 1962. xliii + 282p.

JENKS, C. W.
The world beyond the Charter in historical perspective: a tentative synthesis of four stages of world organisation. Allen & Unwin, 1969. 199p.

KELSEN, H.
The law of the United Nations. S, 1950. xvii + 903p. (Suppl., 1951. pp. 905-94. Library of world affairs, no. 11)

ROBERTSON, A. H.
The Council of Europe: its structure, functions and achievements, 2nd ed. S, 1961. xv + 288p. (Library of world affairs, no. 32)

ROBERTSON, A. H.
European institutions: co-operation, integration, unification, 2nd ed. S, 1966. xxi + 427p. (Library of world affairs, no. 44)

ROBERTSON, A. H.
The law of international institutions in Europe: being an account of some recent developments in the field of international law. Manchester UP, 1961. ix + 140p. (Melland Schill lectures, 1961)

ROYAL INSTITUTE OF INTERNATIONAL AFFAIRS
United Nations documents, 1941-45. The Institute, 1946. 271p.

STONE, J.
The Atlantic charter: new worlds for old. Angus & Robertson, 1943. ix + 245p.

Pacific settlement of disputes

DAVID DAVIES MEMORIAL INSTITUTE OF INTERNATIONAL STUDIES
The peaceful settlement of international disputes: the legal aspects, revised ed. Europa Publications, 1971. 300p.

HIGGINS, A. P.
The Hague peace conferences and other international conferences concerning the laws and usages of war, texts of conventions, with commentaries. CUP, 1909. xiv + 632p.

JENKS, C. W.
The prospects of international adjudication. S, 1964. xl + 805p.

ROSENNE, S.
The law and practice of the International Court. Leyden, Sijthoff, 1965. 2 vols. Vol. 1, xxiii + 506p. Vol. 2, xi + pp. 507-998 (Continuous pagination)

SIMPSON, J. L. and FOX, H. M.
International arbitration, law and practice. S, 1959. xx + 330p.

WRIGHT, P. Q.
The role of international law in the elimination of war. Manchester UP, 1961. vii + 119p. (Melland Schill lectures, 1961)

ii. Armed conflict, war and neutrality

Background

HARRIS, Sir A. T.
Bomber offensive. Collins, 1947. 288p.

MAURICE, Sir F. B.
Lessons of Allied co-operation, naval, military and air, 1914-18. OUP, 1942. vii + 195p.

MEDLICOTT, W. N.
The economic blockade. HMSO, 1952-1959. 2 vols. (History of the Second World War: United Kingdom civil series)

RICHMOND, Sir H. W.
Sea power in the modern world. Bell, 1934. 266p.

ROYAL INSTITUTE OF INTERNATIONAL AFFAIRS
Sanctions: the character of international sanctions and their application, 2nd ed. The Institute, 1935. 72p.

SPAIGHT, J. M.
Air power and the cities. Longmans, 1930. ix + 244p.

SPAIGHT, J. M.
Aircraft and commerce in war. Longmans, 1926. viii + 111p.

SPAIGHT, J. M.
Aircraft in war. Macmillan, 1914. ix + 172p.

SPAIGHT, J. M.
The atomic problem. Barron, 1948. vii + 53p.

General

BOWETT, D. W.
Self defence in international law. Manchester UP, 1958. xv + 294p.

BOWETT, D. W.
United Nations forces: a legal study of United Nations practice. S, 1964. xxiv + 579p.

BROWNLIE, I.
International law and the use of force by states. OUP, 1963. xxviii + 532p.

DRAPER, G. I. A. D.
The Red Cross Conventions. S, 1958. ix + 228p.

GREAT BRITAIN. Ministry of Defence. Air Force Department
Manual of Air Force law, 4th ed. HMSO, 1964-70. 2 vols. Loose-leaf. (Suppl.)

GREAT BRITAIN. Ministry of Defence. Army Department
Manual of military law. Part 1, 11th edition. HMSO, 1965– . Part 2, 9th edition. HMSO, 1965– . Part 3, 1st edition. HMSO, 1958– . 3 vols. Loose-leaf. (Suppl.)

SCHWARZENBERGER, G.
International law as applied by international courts and tribunals. S, 1957-68. 2 vols. (Vol. 2: The law of armed conflict)

SCHWARZENBERGER, G.
The legality of nuclear weapons. S, 1958. 69p.

SINGH, N.
Nuclear weapons and international law. S, 1959. xix + 267p.

SPAIGHT, J. M.
Air power and war rights, 3rd ed. Longmans, 1947. viii + 523p.

Neutrality

BONJOUR, E.
Swiss neutrality: its history and meaning, translated by M. Hottinger. Allen & Unwin, 1946. 135p.

PARES, R.
Colonial blockade and neutral rights, 1739-63. OUP, 1938. vii + 323p.

PYKE, H. R.
The law of contraband of war. OUP, 1915. xl + 314p.

Legal effects

MCNAIR, A. D., Baron McNair and WATTS, A. D.
The legal effects of war, 4th ed. CUP, 1966. li + 469p.

WEBBER, G. J.
The effect of war on contracts, 2nd ed. SLS, 1946. lxviii + 754 + 48p.

WOLFF, E.
The problem of pre-war contracts in peace treaties. S, 1946. xii + 143p.

Prize law

COLOMBOS, C. J.
A treatise on the law of prize, 3rd ed. Longmans, 1949. 421p.

HURST, Sir C. J. B. and BRAY, F. E., eds
Russian and Japanese prize cases ... arising out of the Russo-Japanese war, 1904-05. Wyman, 1912-13. 2 vols.

LLOYD'S REPORTS OF PRIZE CASES, 1st series 1914-22. 10 vols. 2nd series, 1940-57. 1 vol. Lloyd's, 1915-58.

PRIZE CASES DECIDED IN THE PRIZE COURT DURING THE GREAT WAR ... and in the courts of the overseas dominions and on appeal to the Judicial Committee of the Privy Council, 1914-22, edited by E. C. M. Trahern and A. W. Grant. S, 1915-22. 3 vols.

PRIZE CASES DECIDED IN THE UNITED STATES SUPREME COURT, 1789-1918. OUP, 1923. 3 vols. (Published for the Carnegie Endowment for International Peace. Division of International Law)

REPORTS OF PRIZE CASES ... 1745-1859, edited by E. S. Roscoe. S, 1905. 2 vols.

ROSCOE, E. S.
A history of the English prize court. Lloyd's, 1924. viii + 115p.

End of war and occupation

FRAENKEL, E.
Military occupation and the rule of law: occupation government in the Rhineland, 1918-23, edited by E. Todd. OUP, 1944. xi + 267p.

FRIEDMANN, W. G.
The Allied military government of Germany. S, 1947. x + 362p.

MAURICE, Sir F. B.
The Armistices of 1918. OUP, 1943. vii + 104p. (Issued under the auspices of the Royal Institute of International Affairs)

PHILLIMORE, W. G. F., Baron Phillimore
Three centuries of treaties of peace and their teaching. Murray, 1917. xvi + 227p.

PHILLIPSON, C.
Termination of war and treaties of peace. T. F. Unwin, 1916. xix + 486p.

RENNELL, F. J., Baron Rennell
British military administration of occupied territories in Africa, 1941-47. HMSO, 1948. viii + 637p.

War crimes

FYFE, Sir D. Maxwell, ed.
War crimes trials. Hodge, 1948-52. 9 vols.

LACHS, M.
War crimes: an attempt to define the issues. S, 1945. viii + 108p.

MAUGHAM, F. H., Viscount Maugham
U.N.O. and war crimes. Murray, 1951. 143p.

MULLINS, C.
The Leipzig trials: an account of the war criminals' trials and a study of German mentality. Witherby, 1921. 238p.

UNITED NATIONS WAR CRIMES COMMISSION
History of the United Nations War Crimes Commission. HMSO, 1948. xx + 592p. (Bibliography, pp. 557-73)

UNITED NATIONS WAR CRIMES COMMISSION
Law reports of trials of war criminals, selected and prepared. HMSO, 1947-49. 15 vols.

2. PRIVATE INTERNATIONAL LAW

In the English legal system private international law and the conflict of laws are synonymous and equal in scope and contents, unlike the position in many civil law systems, in which the conflict of laws is only a part of private international law. The subject is in certain respects narrower than *droit international privé*; it excludes, for example, the general treatment of nationality and the condition of foreigners. On the other hand, it is wider than the corresponding subject in many foreign countries, in that it includes matters such as the jurisdiction of English courts in cases involving foreign elements and the recognition and enforcement of foreign judgments and other acts of state in England. For the most part this branch of law is judge-made. All the books listed below are used in common law countries by both students and practitioners, but DICEY is primarily a practitioner's book. For this subject reference to periodical literature is particularly necessary, in addition to the law reviews both here and in other common law countries, notably the *International and comparative law quarterly* and the *British yearbook of international law.* A valuable source of material on both the common law and other systems is the long series of *Recueil des cours de l'Académie de la Haye.* Reference is often useful to the published volumes of Acts and Documents of the Hague Conference of Private International Law. Attention must also be directed to the French journal *Clunet*, which is now printed in English as well as French and contains extensive references to English law.

Select Bibliography

ANTON, A. E.
Private international law; a treatise from the standpoint of Scots law. Edinburgh, Green, 1967. lx + 626p.

BLOM-COOPER, L. J.
Bankruptcy in private international law. Eastern Pr., 1954. xii + 159p.

BRESLAUER, W.
The private international law of succession in England, America and Germany. SM, 1937. xxviii + 339p.

CASTEL, J. G.
Conflict of laws; cases, notes and materials, 2nd ed. Toronto, B, 1968. xxvi + 1104p.

CHESHIRE, G. C. and NORTH, P. M.
Private international law, 8th ed. B, 1970. lxxi + 709p.

COOK, W. W.
The logical and legal bases of the conflict of laws. Cambridge, Mass., Harvard UP, 1942. xx + 473p.

DICEY, A. V. and MORRIS, J. H. C.
The conflict of laws, 8th ed. by J. H. C. Morris and others. S, 1967. cxxv + 1289p. (Suppl.)

FALCONBRIDGE, J. D.
Essays on the conflict of laws, 2nd ed. Toronto, Canada Law Book Co., 1954. xxxii + 862p.

FARNSWORTH, A.
The residence and domicil of corporations. B, 1939. xxxvii + 370p.

GRAVESON, R. H.
Cases on the conflict of laws. SM, 1949. xx + 659p.

GRAVESON, R. H.
The conflict of laws, 6th ed. SM, 1969. xxxix + 698p.

HANCOCK, M.
Torts in the conflict of laws. Ann Arbor, Univ. of Michigan Pr., 1942. lviii + 288p.

KUHN, A. K.
Comparative commentaries on private international law, or conflict of laws. New York, Macmillan, 1937. xii + 381p.

LALIVE, P. A.
The transfer of chattels in the conflict of laws. OUP, 1955. xix + 200p.

LORENZEN E. G.
Selected articles on the conflict of laws. New Haven, Yale UP, 1947. 542p.

MANN, F. A.
The legal aspect of money: with special reference to comparative private and public international law, 3rd ed. Oxford, Clarendon Pr., 1971. l + 615p.

MORRIS, J. H. C.
Cases on private international law, 4th ed. Oxford, Clarendon Pr., 1968. xxxii + 531p.

NYGH, P. E.
Conflict of laws in Australia. Sydney, B, 1968. 42 + 765p.

RABEL, E.
The conflict of laws: a comparative study. Ann Arbor, Univ. of Michigan Pr., 4 vols. (Vol. 1: 2nd ed. by U. Drobnig, 1958; Vol. 2: 2nd ed. by U. Drobnig, 1960; Vol. 3: 2nd ed. by H. Bernstein, 1964; Vol. 4: 1st ed. by E. Rabel, 1958)

READ, H. E.
Recognition and enforcement of foreign judgments in the common law units of the British Commonwealth. Cambridge, Mass., Harvard UP, 1938. xiv + 371p.

SCHMITTHOFF, C. M.
The English conflict of laws, 3rd ed. S, 1954. xliii + 514p.

STORY, J.
Commentaries on the conflict of laws, 8th ed. by M. M. Bigelow. Boston, Little, Brown, 1883. xxxix + 901p.

SUMMER INSTITUTE ON INTERNATIONAL AND COMPARATIVE LAW, University of Michigan Law School, August 5-20th, 1949.
Lectures on the conflict of laws and international contracts. Ann Arbor, University of Michigan Law School, 1951. xiv + 200p.

THOMAS, J. A. C.
Private international law. Hutchinson, 1955. 174p.
WEBB, P. R. H. and BROWN, D. J. L.
A casebook on the conflict of laws. B, 1960. l + 478p.
WOLFF, M.
Private international law, 2nd ed. OUP, 1950. xlvii + 631p.

Periodicals

BRITISH YEARBOOK OF INTERNATIONAL LAW, vol. 1- , 1920/21- . OUP. (Index to vols. 1-36 by J. G. Collier, 1963)
INTERNATIONAL AND COMPARATIVE LAW QUARTERLY, vol. 1- , 1952- . British Institute of International and Comparative Law, etc.
JOURNAL DU DROIT INTERNATIONAL, vol. 1- , 1874- . Paris, Editions Techniques. (1874-1945, entitled *Journal du droit international privé.* Known as *Clunet* after the name of the founder, Edouard Clunet)
RECUEIL DES COURS DE L'ACADÉMIE DE LA HAYE, t.1- , 1925- . Leiden, Sijthoff. (Index général des tomes 1-101, 1968)

XIII NORTHERN IRELAND

I. GENERAL SOURCES OF LAW

Northern Ireland is an integral part of the United Kingdom which, unlike Scotland and Wales, has enjoyed since 1920 a considerable measure of devolutionary self-government. It is a common law country in the traditional sense in that its general body of law is made up from primary sources, such as statute law and judicial decisions, and secondary sources, such as custom and convention. But a departure from the tradition exists in the partially written constitution contained in the Government of Ireland Act 1920, under which the Northern Ireland courts have power to determine the constitutionality of statutes passed by the Northern Ireland Parliament, appeals lying to the House of Lords.

Statutes of the following Parliaments are in force: (i) the Parliament of Ireland, from 1310 to 1800 (ended by the Act of Union 1801); (ii) the Parliaments of Great Britain, England and Ireland, from 1226 to 1800; (iii) the Parliament of the United Kingdom, from 1801 to the present day; (iv) the Parliament of Northern Ireland, from 1921 to the present day.

The Northern Ireland courts recognise the distinction between "law" and "equity" and adhere to the doctrine of precedent. Decisions of the House of Lords on appeal from Ireland are clearly binding, and other decisions of the House are generally followed. Decisions of lower English courts, and of pre-1920 Irish courts, are, at most, of persuasive authority.

There is a lack of modern encyclopediae, case digests, and text books devoted exclusively to Northern Ireland law. However, there is much periodical literature, to which there now exists a comprehensive reference work in O'HIGGINS' *Bibliography of periodical literature relating to Irish law* (1966). For this reason, few references in this chapter have been made to periodical literature. There are also a few legal periodicals covering Northern Ireland law. Very useful bibliographies covering Northern Ireland law will be found in DONALDSON's *Some comparative aspects of Irish law* (1957), volume 4 of SWEET AND MAXWELL's *Legal bibliography of the British Commonwealth of Nations* (1957) and DELANY's *Bibliographical introduction to legal history and ethnology of Ireland* (1963).

Select Bibliography

a. Legislation

HALSBURY'S STATUTES OF ENGLAND, 3rd ed. B, 1968- . (To be completed in 41 volumes)

NORTHERN IRELAND
Chronological table of the statutes affecting Northern Ireland, 13th ed. Belfast, HMSO, 1971. x + 785p. (Covers legislation to 31 December 1969)

NORTHERN IRELAND
Index to the statutes in force, Northern Ireland, 13th ed. Belfast, HMSO, 1971. cxvi + 1306p. (Covers legislation to 31 December 1969)

NORTHERN IRELAND
The Public General Acts, Northern Ireland, 1921- . Belfast, HMSO. (Published annually. Each Act also published separately)

NORTHERN IRELAND
The statutes revised, Northern Ireland, 1226-1950, as amended up to the end of 1954. Belfast, HMSO, 1956. 16 vols.

NORTHERN IRELAND
The statutory rules and orders of Northern Ireland, 1922- . Belfast, HMSO, 1925- . (Published annually)

NORTHERN IRELAND
Index to the statutory rules and orders of Northern Ireland, 11th ed. Belfast, HMSO, 1968. viii + 491p. (Covers rules and orders in force at 31 December 1967)

b. Law reports and digests

DIGEST OF CASES DECIDED BY THE SUPERIOR AND OTHER COURTS IN IRELAND AND NORTHERN IRELAND [The "*Irish Digest*"]
1867-93 edited by R. D. Murray and G. Y. Dixon. Dublin, Ponsonby, 1899.
1894-1918 edited by T. H. Maxwell. Dublin, Falconer, 1921.
1919-28 and 1929-38 edited by R. H. Ryland. Dublin, Falconer, 1930-40.
1939-48 edited by R. A. Harrison. Dublin, Falconer, 1952.
1949-58 edited by R. A. Harrison. Dublin, Incorporated Council of Law Reporting for Ireland, [1962]

NORTHERN IRELAND LAW REPORTS, 1925- . Belfast, Incorporated Council of Law Reporting for Northern Ireland. (Published quarterly) (*Consolidated table of cases reported and consolidated index summary 1925-53* published ca. 1954)

RYAN, E. F., comp.
Notes of Irish cases, 1959-1968. Cork UP, 1970. xv + 94p. (Published as an interim index before the appearance of the corresponding volume of the *Digest*, see supra)

A further guide will be found in:

SURRENCY, E. C.
"Research in the law of Northern Ireland", in *Northern Ireland legal quarterly*, 15 (1964): pp. 77-109.

c. Legal periodicals

GAZETTE OF THE INCORPORATED LAW SOCIETY OF NORTHERN IRELAND, 1964- . Belfast, Incorporated Law Society of Northern Ireland. (Published quarterly)

IRISH JURIST, vols 1-31, 1935-65; New series vol. 1- , 1966- . Dublin, Jurist Publishing Co. (Old series entitled *Irish jurist and reports*. New series published twice yearly)

IRISH LAW TIMES AND SOLICITORS' JOURNAL (including the *Irish law times reports*) 1867- . Dublin, Smurfit, etc., 1868- .

NORTHERN IRELAND. Stationery Office
List of publications [of the Northern Ireland Government] Belfast, HMSO. (Annual. Monthly catalogues also issued)

NORTHERN IRELAND LEGAL QUARTERLY, 1936- . Belfast, Northern Ireland Legal Quarterly, Inc. (Until 1961 published by the Incorporated Law Society of Northern Ireland. 1962-3, not published)

d. General works

DELANY, V. T. H.

"Ireland", in *Bibliographical introduction to legal history and ethnology*, edited by J. Gilissen (Brussels, Institut de Sociologie de l'Université Libre, 1963), section C/6.

DONALDSON, A. G.

Some comparative aspects of Irish law, Durham, N. C., Duke UP and CUP, 1957. xii + 293p. (Duke University Commonwealth Studies Center publications, no. 3)

HAND, G. J.

English law in Ireland, 1290-1324. CUP, 1967. xii + 280p. (Cambridge studies in English legal history)

NEWARK, F. H.

Notes on Irish legal history, 2nd ed. Belfast, Queen's University, 1964. 29p.

O'HIGGINS, P.

A bibliography of periodical literature relating to Irish law. Belfast, Northern Ireland Legal Quarterly Inc., 1966. xvi + 401p.

SHERIDAN, L. A.

"Northern Ireland", in *The United Kingdom: the development of its laws and constitutions, vol. 1: England and Wales, Northern Ireland, the Isle of Man*, edited by G. W. Keeton and D. Lloyd. (S, 1955), chapters 18-22.

SWEET & MAXWELL, LTD.

A legal bibliography of the British Commonwealth of Nations, 2nd ed. SM, 1955-64. 7 vols. (Vol. 4: Irish law to 1956, edited by L. F. and W. H. Maxwell)

ULSTER YEAR BOOK: official handbook of Northern Ireland. Belfast, HMSO, 1926- . (Published annually since 1969, previously triennially)

2. CONSTITUTIONAL LAW

(a) *The Constitution*

Under the Government of Ireland Act, 1920 and various amending Acts, the Northern Ireland Parliament was established at Stormont and given power to make laws for the "peace, order and good government" of the Province, subject to certain matters specifically excepted and reserved to the Westminster Parliament. Among these matters are the Crown, the Armed Forces, foreign affairs, external trade, coinage and legal tender, the Post Office and postal services, the Supreme Court, custom and excise duties, income tax and surtax. In addition, section 75 of the 1920 Act contains a general reservation of legislative authority on Northern Ireland affairs to Westminster, though by convention, and despite recent events, this power has rarely been used to intervene in matters on which Stormont has competence, and the Ireland Act, 1949 declared and affirmed that Northern Ireland would not in any event cease to be part of the United Kingdom without the consent of the Northern Ireland Parliament.

There is a Governor of Northern Ireland appointed by the Crown as its permanent representative, with the powers of the Royal Prerogative.

In addition to the general powers of the Northern Ireland courts to determine the constitutionality of statutes passed at Stormont in the light of the 1920 Act, that Act contains special provisions for referral of constitutional questions to the Judicial Committee of the Privy Council, whose decision is final, conclusive and binding upon all courts.

Because of the social and political disturbances of the past few years, there has been much talk of constitutional reform. One matter frequently mentioned has been direct rule from Westminster, which would radically alter the present nature of the devolutionary constitution in Northern Ireland. To be effective, Westminster would probably have to resume direct responsibility for many of the matters now the responsibility of the Northern Ireland Parliament, such as housing, the social services, the police force, education, transport and local government.

(b) *Legislature*

There is a bicameral Parliament, with a House of Commons of 52 members and a Senate of 24 members. The four Commons seats for the Queen's University of Belfast constituency were abolished in 1968 and replaced by four new territorial constituencies. Senators are elected by way of proportional representation by members of the House of Commons, except the two ex-officio senators, the Lord Mayor of Belfast and Mayor of Londonderry. Senators hold office for a term of eight years, but half their number is elected every four years. The Electoral Law Act (N.I.) 1968 provided for the establishment of a permanent boundary commission for review of the distribution of seats at Northern Ireland parliamentary elections.

Generally speaking the rules and conventions of parliamentary procedure at Westminster are followed at Stormont. An exception is that the Governor may convene a joint sitting of both Houses when a public Bill passed by the Commons has been rejected by the Senate in two successive sessions; a majority vote of the persons present at the joint sitting is sufficient to pass the Bill.

(c) *Executive*

The central Government is based upon the Westminster cabinet system, with government departments headed by Ministers. The seven main departments are the Ministries of Finance, Home Affairs, Health and Social Services, Education, Agriculture, Commerce and Development. A Ministry of Community Relations was established in 1970. The Civil Service is also organised along the lines of the Westminster model.

Local government is administered by some 73 local authorities, consisting of county councils, county borough councils, borough councils, urban district councils and rural district councils. Local authority functions are also given to bodies like new town commissions. However, the Government in 1969 set up a special independent body to review the subject of local government. This review body reported in June 1970, with recommendations that in future local government services should be divided between central government ministries responsible for regional (wide-area) services (health, education, housing, planning, etc.) and 26 district councils responsible for district (local) services (cleansing, drainage, sewerage, recreation, entertainment, etc.). These recommendations have been generally accepted by the Northern Ireland Government. The Local Government (Boundaries) Act (N.I.) 1971 provided for 26 local government districts, each district to be divided into wards, and for the setting up of an independent statutory commission to make recommendations as to the boundaries and names of the districts and wards and the number of wards in each district. The chairman of the Local Government Boundaries Commission (previously President of the Northern Ireland

Lands Tribunal) was appointed in April 1971. The Electoral Law Act (N.I.), 1969 amended the franchise for local government elections by assimilating the secondary qualifications of local government electors to those of electors at Northern Ireland parliamentary elections, thus abolishing the "property" qualification for local authority elections and the company vote.

(d) *Judiciary*

The Supreme Court of Judicature, consisting of the High Court and Court of Appeal, has a structure and procedure similar to that of England, and indeed remains under the jurisdiction of Westminster. A Court of Criminal Appeal was established in 1930. The High Court has two divisions: Queen's Bench, which has a Crown side and civil side (including probate, divorce and admiralty matters) and Chancery. The High Court Judges also hold Assize Courts. However, the Judicature (Ireland) Act, 1877 came under the review of a committee appointed by the Lord Chancellor in 1965, and, in its Report published in March 1970, it recommended *inter alia* abolition of divisions of the High Court and the establishment of a Court of Appeal with both civil and criminal jurisdiction. And as a result of that committee's recommendation, the Northern Ireland Government has set up another committee to review the county court and assize system.

The head of the judiciary is the Lord Chief Justice, whose jurisdiction includes that governing persons of unsound mind and minors, which used to be exercised by the Lord Chancellor of Ireland. There are two Lord Justices of Appeal and four puisne Justices, though it is common for the former to sit in the High Court and the latter in the Court of Appeal, when the occasion demands. There are, however, no masters and interlocutory proceedings are taken by a judge. Further, there is a general right to trial by jury (of seven) in all civil cases in the Queen's Bench.

The main inferior courts are the county courts and magistrates' courts, both of which have original criminal and civil jurisdiction. The county court judges, entitled Recorders in Belfast and Londonderry, are subject to civil jurisdictional limits of £300 in common law matters (though there is a £50 damages limit in libel and slander cases), £1000 in equity matters, £2000 in probate matters, but in all cases involving land an annual value of £75. Under the Criminal Injuries to Persons (Compensation) Act (N.I.) 1968, however, county court civil jurisdiction in Northern Ireland is unlimited. The general criminal jurisdiction of the county courts extends to cover most indictable offences. Appeals lie from the county courts in civil cases to the judge of assize and, in some circumstances, to the High Court, in criminal cases to the Court of Criminal Appeal and cases may be stated for the opinion of the Court of Appeal. There is no jury in civil cases in the county courts.

Magistrates' courts are generally conducted by a Resident Magistrate, who is a qualified lawyer, sitting alone. There are exceptions, for example, juvenile courts composed of one Resident Magistrate and two lay members, one of whom must be a woman. Appeals lie from magistrates' courts to the county court and cases may be stated for the opinion of the Court of Appeal.

Coroners' courts are held by medical practitioners appointed by the Ministry of Home Affairs, though since 1959 new appointees as coroners must be barristers or solicitors of not less than five years' standing. There are numerous special tribunals sitting in Northern Ireland, such as the Lands Tribunal of Northern Ireland which was established in 1964 to deal with questions relating to compensation for compulsory acquisition of land, appeals against rating valuation etc.

(e) *Revenue Matters*

Public revenue in Northern Ireland consists of "Reserved Revenue" controlled by Westminster, and "Transferred Revenue" controlled by Stormont. The former includes income tax and surtax, capital gains tax and corporation tax, customs duties and purchase tax. The latter includes estate duty, stamp duties, motor vehicles duties and selective employment tax. Generally the rates for estate duty are lower than in England, and the *inter vivos* gifts vulnerability period is four years only.

H.M. Treasury deducts and retains from "Reserved Revenue" the sum assessed to be Northern Ireland's contribution, known as the "Imperial Contribution", towards the cost of imperial services, such as the Inland Revenue Service. The balance, known as the "Residuary Share of Reserved Taxes", is paid into the Northern Ireland exchequer. Questions affecting financial relations between the governments at Westminster and Stormont may be referred to the Joint Exchequer Board, which is composed of a chairman appointed by the Crown and representatives of H.M. Treasury and the Northern Ireland Ministry of Finance.

Additional money is received from H.M. Treasury under agreements designed to equalise burdens on the Westminster and Stormont exchequers in respect of the cost of social services, such as old age pensions, family allowances, health services and supplementary benefits, and for the Northern Ireland agricultural industry. With Northern Ireland Supply Estimates for 1971-72 being some £40½ million higher than the original estimates for the previous year and the Northern Ireland Government's revenue being considerably reduced by the 1971 Westminster tax changes, a new Social Services Agreement was concluded in 1971 between the two Governments to replace existing arrangements with the British Treasury. Under this there will be a more generous calculation of the cost of the Health Service to be met by the Northern Ireland Government, in effect, 2% instead of 2.5% of United Kingdom expenditure with Northern Ireland receiving 90% instead of 80% of the excess. Further, under the new agreement family allowances and supplementary benefits will be treated in the same way as regional employment premiums, that is, H.M. Treasury may pay Northern Ireland up to the whole cost of the service. And also to come within the whole cost arrangement are the three new social services recently instituted by Westminster, namely, family income supplements, constant attendance allowances and pensions for the over-80s.

Only about one-third of local authority revenue in Northern Ireland comes from rates levied by the authorities. The residue comes mainly from central government grants and borrowing. There is a general grant, known as the "General Exchequer Contribution", designed to compensate for derating and to supplement the resources of the poorer authorities, and a Government Loans Fund exists for making loans to local authorities and other bodies for capital projects.

(f) *Public Order and Civil Rights*

Considerable changes have resulted from the recent political and social disturbances. The regular police force is still the Royal Ulster Constabulary, under the control of the Northern Ireland Ministry of Home Affairs. Until recently there was also a part-time security force, the Ulster Special Constabulary (known as "B Specials"), which generally was used for routine police matters such as guard duty, but which could be, and was sometimes, mobilised for full-time duty to assist the regular force.

"Specials" were abolished in 1970, many of their duties being taken over by the newly established Ulster Defence Regiment, which is under the control of the

Ministry of Defence. There is also being formed a police reserve force, and the Police Act (N.I.), 1970 provided for the establishment of a Police Authority, a Police Association and a Police Advisory Board for Northern Ireland, and for mutual assistance to be given between the police force in Northern Ireland and other United Kingdom police forces.

A considerable delegation to the Executive of power to interfere with traditional civil liberties exists in the Civil Authorities (Special Powers) Act (N.I.), 1922 (and regulations made under it), by which the Minister of Home Affairs has general powers "to take all such steps and issue all such orders as may be necessary for preserving the peace and maintaining order". However, under pressure from the recent civil rights campaign, the Government has undertaken to review these statutory powers and regulations and, if appropriate after review, to put some of them into "cold storage". That same pressure has resulted in the introduction of "one man—one vote" for local government elections and a "points system" for local authority housing allocation, plus the establishment of a central housing authority for Northern Ireland in 1971. A Parliamentary Commissioner for Northern Ireland ("ombudsman") was appointed in 1969, and a Commissioner for Complaints (local government "ombudsman") was appointed in 1970, thus going a step further than the rest of Britain. In addition to the establishment of a Ministry of Community Relations, a Community Relations Commission was set up in 1970 to aid in the task of improving community relations, and of reducing discrimination in fields such as employment and housing.

Considerable legislative control of public meetings and processions is provided by the Public Order Act (N.I.), 1951 and the Flags and Emblems Act (N.I.), 1954. Further control was introduced by the Public Order (Amendment) Act (N.I.), 1970, covering "counter-demonstrations", obstruction of public places, protection of public buildings and activities, prohibition of quasi-military organisations and carrying offensive weapons.

The Protection of the Person and Property Act (N.I.), 1969 penalises acts of intimidation and the making or possession or use of devices containing an inflammable liquid or substance. The Prevention of Incitement to Hatred Act (N.I.), 1970 lays down penalties for incitement to hatred on the grounds of religious belief, colour, race or ethnic or national origins, and for circulation of false statements or false reports.

Select Bibliography

BETH, L. P.

The development of judicial review in Ireland 1937-1966. Dublin, Institute of Public Administration, 1967. [iv] + 66 + [9]p.

CALVERT, H. G.

Constitutional law in Northern Ireland: a study in regional government. Belfast, Northern Ireland Legal Quarterly Inc., and S, 1968. xxi + 400p.

COMERTON, E. A.

A handbook on the Magistrates' Courts Act (N.I.) 1964. Belfast, Inn of Court and Incorporated Law Society of Northern Ireland, 1968. xliv + 458p.

HALSBURY'S STATUTES OF ENGLAND, 3rd ed. B, 1968- . (To be completed in 41 volumes) (Vol. 23: Northern Ireland)

MANSERGH, P. N. S.

The government of Northern Ireland: a study in devolution. Allen & Unwin, 1936. 335p.

MONTROSE, J. L.
"Legal aspects of taxation and grant under Northern Ireland system of devolution", in *Federalism*, edited by G. Sawer (Melbourne, Cheshire & Co., 1952), pp. 1-33.

NORTHERN IRELAND. Supreme Court of Judicature
Rules of the Supreme Court (Northern Ireland) 1936. HMSO, 1936. vi + 908p. (S.R. & O. 1936. No. 70, as amended)

QUEKETT, Sir A. S.
The constitution of Northern Ireland. Belfast, HMSO, 1928-46. 3 vols.

WYLIE, J. O.
The Judicature Acts (Ireland), and Rules of the Supreme Court (Ireland) 1905. Dublin, Sealy, Bryers & Walker, 1906. lxxxviii + 1709p.

3. PUBLIC LAW

(a) *Social Legislation*

Generally legislation governing national insurance, industrial injuries, family allowances and supplementary benefits follows the English pattern in accordance with the "step-by-step" policy consistently followed in this area by the Northern Ireland Government. The same is the position with respect to the general health service, mental health and welfare services.

An extensive system of primary, secondary and further education exists. Local education authorities manage "county" schools, which are financed entirely out of public funds, while "voluntary" schools, managed by statutory committees containing public representatives, receive substantial financial assistance. In addition to several technical and other colleges there are two universities, at Belfast and Coleraine, and a new Ulster College, comprising several constituent colleges with advanced legal courses, is being established.

(b) *Planning and Housing*

Planning control is still exercised through a system of interim development control under the Planning (Interim Development) Act (N.I.), 1944. Further it is not mandatory, but only permissive, for planning authorities to prepare statutory plans. No such plans have ever been made, but some are now being prepared and the Government has announced proposals for more modern legislation on planning. Building and development of new towns and cities is provided for under the New Towns Act (N.I.), 1965, extended to cover existing towns and cities in 1968, and some areas, including a new city, to be known as Craigavon, in Co. Armagh, have already been designated. The creation, management and control of national parks, nature areas, areas of outstanding beauty and of scientific interest was provided for by the Amenity Lands Act (N.I.), 1965, and the Land Development Values (Compensation) Act (N.I.), 1965 imposed strict control on the recovery of compensation as a result of planning decisions. There was, however, no equivalent in Northern Ireland to the Land Commission Act, 1967. The Planning and Land Compensation Bill (N.I.), 1971, if enacted, will introduce provisions for protection against planning blight and will make several detailed amendments in the law relating to planning permission and planning decisions.

Extensive housing legislation exists providing for central government grants and subsidies to private builders and local authorities for building new houses, for conversion, improvement and reconstruction of existing housing and for slum clearance and redevelopment schemes. Various detailed amendments to these schemes will be made by the Housing Bill (N.I.), 1971, if it is enacted. A special statutory body with the duty of providing housing accommodation, the Northern Ireland Housing Trust, which was under the general control of the Ministry of Development, was established in 1945. Under the Housing (Executive) Act (N.I.), 1971, a central housing authority for Northern Ireland (the "Housing Executive") was established. This body, along with an advisory housing council, will be responsible for all public housing programmes throughout the Province, thereby taking over the housing functions of the Housing Trust, new town commissions and local authorities. Compulsory acquisition of land in Northern Ireland is usually carried out through a "vesting order" by an appropriate Government Ministry, whereby the land is immediately vested in the acquiring authority, usually referred to as a statutory undertaker, and the claims of the various persons interested in the land are transferred to public funds. Under the Mineral Development Act (N.I.), 1969, most mines and minerals were vested in the Ministry of Commerce, which has wide powers of facilitating the discovery and working of minerals in Northern Ireland.

(c) *Administrative Law*

The law is generally the same as that in England. However, the Tribunals and Inquiries Act, 1958 only applies to a limited extent, for example, in respect of Tribunals listed in the Act which function in Northern Ireland within the sphere of excepted and reserved matters. There is no Northern Ireland version of the 1958 Act. But the Crown Proceedings Act, 1947 has been adapted to suit Northern Ireland. It has already been pointed out that a Parliamentary Commissioner for Northern Ireland was appointed in 1969, and a Commissioner for Complaints with jurisdiction over local government matters in 1970.

Under the Judgments (Enforcement) Act (N.I.), 1969 provision was made for the enforcement of most judgments through a central Enforcement of Judgments Office.

(d) *Labour Law*

The law is generally the same as that in England. However, the Trade Disputes and Trade Unions Act (N.I.), 1927 was only partially repealed in Northern Ireland in 1958, so as to preserve a "contracting-in" position as opposed to the "contracting-out" position with respect to contributions to political funds substituted in England in 1946. Further, there is no equivalent in Northern Ireland to the Trade Disputes Act, 1965 and in December 1970 the Northern Ireland Government issued a statement that it would not necessarily follow the English Industrial Relations Bill introduced by the Conservative Government, though it promised a comprehensive review of industrial relations. The Equal Pay Act (N.I.), 1970, was enacted to prevent discrimination as regards terms and conditions of employment on grounds of sex.

(e) *Criminal Law and Evidence*

The law is generally the same as that in England with respect to substance and procedure, but there are some differences worth noting. There is no equivalent to the Obscene Publications Act, 1959, or the Sexual Offences Act, 1967. The Criminal Justice Act (N.I.), 1966, deals extensively with the subject of mens rea, contains a definition of insanity and retains capital punishment for certain types of murder. In an effort to combat the recent disturbances, the Criminal Justice (Temporary Provisions) Act (N.I.), 1970, provided for the imposition of minimum sentences of imprisonment on persons convicted during the emergency period. An amending Act passed in late 1970 removed from the scope of the Minimum Sentences Act offences not connected with rioting and offences committed by persons under the age of 17 years.

Criminal law administration is also largely the same, with a system of prisons, borstals, training schools, remand homes and a probation service. Grand juries were only abolished in 1969. There is, as yet, no provision for majority jury verdicts, and the 1964 Judges' Rules have not been adopted. In April 1971, the Government published a report proposing establishment of a system of public prosecutors for most cases in courts of summary jurisdiction, so as to relieve police officers from this task.

Select Bibliography

KNIGHT, M.
Criminal appeals. Belfast, Northern Ireland Legal Quarterly Inc. and S, 1970. xxx + 243p.

LAWRENCE, R. J.
The government of Northern Ireland: public finance and public services. OUP, 1965. xiii + 198p.

NORTHERN IRELAND. Ministry of Health and Social Services
Supplementary benefits handbook. Belfast, HMSO, 1970. vi + 54p.

OSBOROUGH, W. N.
"Democratic principles and the administration of criminal justice in Northern Ireland", in *The accused: a comparative study*, edited by J. A. Coutts (S, 1966), chapter 8: pp. 127-37.

RHODES, E., ed.
Public administration in Northern Ireland. Londonderry, Magee University College, 1967. 124p.

4. PRIVATE LAW

(a) *Family Law*

The law is generally the same as that in England, but there are some differences. There is no equivalent to the following legislation: The Guardianship of Infants Act, 1925; Abortion Act, 1967; Matrimonial Homes Act, 1967; Divorce Reform Act, 1969; Family Law Reform Act, 1969, and Matrimonial Proceedings and Property Act, 1970. Several differences in detail exist in other legislation. For example, there is no power in Northern Ireland of enforcement of maintenance orders by attachment of wages; the court has no power, when awarding maintenance, to regulate the custody of, or access to, children, nor is there effective provision to preclude a husband's making dispositions to defeat a wife's claim to financial relief; under the Adoption Act (N.I.), 1968, the courts in Northern Ireland have wider powers of dispensing with consent of parents or guardians than courts in England.

A reduction in the age of majority to 18 years was introduced by the Age of Majority Act (N.I.), 1969.

(b) *Commercial Law*

The law relating to contract, quasi-contract, agency, hire-purchase, sale of goods, banking and companies is generally the same as that in England. However, by section 5 of the Law Reform (Husband and Wife) Act (N.I.), 1964, a contract for the benefit of a third person, being the wife, husband or child of one of the contracting parties, is enforceable by the third person in his or her own name as if he or she were a party to it. There is no equivalent to the Companies Act, 1967, though a Government committee on company law was set up in 1970.

(c) *Tort*

The law is generally the same as that in England, there being an equivalent to all the major English Acts.

(d) *Limitation of Actions*

The law is generally the same as that in England with the Statute of Limitations (N.I.), 1958, corresponding to the Limitation Act, 1939.

(e) *Property and Succession*

Land law is substantially different from English law, being largely in the pre-1925 position. There is no equivalent to the Law of Property Act, 1925 and the Settled Land Act, 1925. Nor is there any equivalent to the Land Charges Act, 1925, but there has been a universal registry of deeds system since 1707 and a statutory charges register has operated since 1951. There has been a registration of title system since 1891, under which most agricultural land has been compulsorily registrable for several decades, and the Land Registration Act (N.I.), 1970 envisages extension of compulsory registration to urban land, so as to cover the whole Province eventually and to replace the registry of deeds.

There are few agricultural tenancies in Northern Ireland due to the land purchase scheme, which was wound up in 1935. Under this, agricultural tenants were enabled to buy out the freehold, through a state loan secured by an annuity charged on the land, and the freehold title was then registered compulsorily in the Land Registry.

Partial consolidation of the law of landlord and tenant is contained in the Landlord and Tenant Law Amendment Act, *Ireland* 1860, section 3 of which provides that "the relation of landlord and tenant shall be deemed to be founded on the express or implied contract of the parties, and not upon tenure or service, and a reversion shall not be necessary to such relation." However it is doubtful whether this has had an extensive effect on the development of the law, though it does facilitate the creation of the full relationship of landlord and tenant between the grantor and grantee of a fee farm grant.

Much urban land is held under very complicated titles; it is common to have a "pyramid of interests" existing on land, consisting of fee farm grants and sub-grants, leases and sub-leases, each containing extensive exceptions, reservations, covenants and conditions. A Government survey on land law, under the auspices of the

Director of Law Reform, has recently been completed by four members of the Law Faculty of Queen's University of Belfast, and in their Report, published in January 1971, recommendations are made for extensive reform of the substantive land law of Northern Ireland.

Public control of the relationship of landlord and tenant is maintained through rent restriction legislation, which provides a system of "old" and "new" control similar to that which used to exist in England. There is no consolidation measure like the Rent Act, 1968. There is modern legislation relating to business tenancies, but no equivalent to the Agricultural Holdings Acts, though similar legislation was passed in the nineteenth century which became largely obsolete after the land purchase scheme. Leasehold enfranchisement at the option of tenants of long leases was introduced by the Leasehold (Enlargement and Extension) Act (N.I.), 1971.

The law relating to devolution was overhauled by the Administration of Estates Act (N.I.), 1955, which corresponds generally to the English 1925 Act.

(f) *Equity and Trusts*

The law is generally the same as that in England, there being an equivalent to all the major English Acts. There are, however, some differences. There is no Public Trustee in Northern Ireland (except for some limited matters connected with the land purchase scheme) nor any judicial, custodian or managing trustees. The Charities Act (N.I.), 1964, section 24, contains a provision dealing with imperfect trusts. There are no Charity Commissioners for Northern Ireland, the Ministry of Finance being the Charity Authority.

Select Bibliography

CARSWELL, R. D.

Trustee Acts (Northern Ireland): a handbook on the Trustee Acts (Northern Ireland) 1958 and 1962, and the Trustee Investments Act 1961. Belfast, Inn of Court and Incorporated Law Society of Northern Ireland, 1964. xxviii + 216p.

CHERRY, R. R.

The Irish Land Law and Land Purchase Acts, 1860-1901 ... with notes of cases, 3rd ed. Dublin, Falconer, 1903. xlvii + 1048p. (Suppl.)

DELANY, V. T. H.

The law relating to charities in Ireland, revised ed. Dublin, Thom, 1962. xxxi + 253p.

DE MOLEYNS, T.

The landowner's and agent's practical guide, 8th ed. by A. W. Quill and F. P. Hamilton. Dublin, Ponsonby, 1899. lxvi + 1290p.

DOWRICK, F. E.

Notes on the Irish law of contract. B, 1954. vi + 33p. (An Irish supplement to *Law of Contract*, by G. C. Cheshire and C. H. S. Fifoot, 3rd ed. 1952)

EDGE, J. H.

Forms of leases and other forms relating to land in Ireland, 2nd ed. Dublin, Ponsonby, 1884. xix + 429p.

FERGUSON, W. D. and VANCE, A.

The tenure and improvement of land in Ireland, considered with reference to the relation of landlord and tenant, and tenant right. Dublin, Milliken, 1851. xxi + 450p.

FURLONG, J. S.
The law of landlord and tenant as administered in Ireland, 2nd ed. Dublin, Ponsonby, 1869. 2 vols.

GLOVER, W. E.
A treatise on the registration of ownership of land in Ireland. Dublin, Falconer, 1933. xv + 489p.

HARRIS, L. G. E.
A treatise on the law and practice in lunacy in Ireland. Dublin. Corrigan & Wilson, 1930. xxxiii + 300p.

KEETON, G. W. and SHERIDAN, L. A.
Equity. Pitman and Northern Ireland Legal Quarterly Inc., 1969. lxxx + 585p.

KIELY, T. O'N.
Principles of equity as applied in Ireland. Dublin, Fodhla Printing Co., 1936. vi + 398p.

LEITCH, W. A.
A handbook on the Administration of Estates Act (*Northern Ireland*), *1955.* Belfast, Incorporated Law Society of Northern Ireland, 1956. xvii + 228p. (Reprinted with annotations from 1956 to 1967 by SLS, 1968)

MADDEN, D. H.
A practical treatise on the registration of deeds, conveyances and judgment mortgages, 2nd ed. Dublin, McGee, 1901. xxxviii + 440p.

MARRINAN, P. A. and TUGHAN, N.
The motoring laws of Northern Ireland. Belfast, Adams, 1928. viii + 152p.

NELSON, H. A.
Probate law and practice of the Registries of the High Courts in Northern Ireland and Irish Free State, supplementary ed. Belfast, Allen, 1937. xv + 414 + 114p.

NORTHERN IRELAND. Ministry of Finance
Survey of the land law of Northern Ireland. Belfast, HMSO, 1971. xxv + 425p.

PATTON, W. F.
Law relating to affiliation orders in Northern Ireland. Belfast, Carswell, 1925. viii + 90p.

SHERIDAN, L. A.
Irish supplement to Challis's law of real property, 3rd ed. (B, 1911) B, 1956. x + 33p.

STUBBS, W. C. and BAXTER, J. S.
Irish forms and precedents: being a supplementary volume to the "Encyclopaedia of forms and precedents". B, 1910. lviii + 741 + 82p.

5. MISCELLANEOUS

(a) *Legal Profession*

The legal profession in Northern Ireland is controlled and organised as it is in England, with the two distinct branches of barristers and solicitors. The Inn of Court of Northern Ireland was formed in 1926 and regulates admissions to, and the general conduct of, the Bar. The Inn, however, has no buildings and candidates for the Northern Ireland Bar have to keep terms in one of the Inns of London. Further, there is no chamber system. The Incorporated Law Society was established by Royal Charter in 1922; it supervises the education and training of apprentice solicitors and regulates the general conduct of solicitors.

(b) *Legal Education*

The Faculty of Law of the Queen's University of Belfast provides a comprehensive system of legal education, including a four year honours LL.B. undergraduate programme, and a postgraduate programme under which a Diploma in Laws and the degrees of LL.M., Ph.D. and LL.D. may be conferred. In addition, the Faculty provides facilities for bar students and solicitors' apprentices to take courses, without necessarily reading for a degree, so as to satisfy requirements of the Inn of Court and Incorporated Law Society. The Law Society also provides courses on its own.

(c) *Legal Aid*

A system of legal aid and advice in criminal and civil cases, under the general administration of the Northern Ireland Law Society in civil cases, was provided for under the Legal Aid and Advice Act (N.I.), 1965. Application may be made to the court in criminal cases. Legal aid may be made available to any person whose disposable income does not exceed £950 per annum or whose capital does not exceed £500, contributions having to be made by persons whose disposable income exceeds £300 or whose capital exceeds £125, but the scheme does not cover Tribunals. The provisions relating to legal advice in criminal and civil cases came into operation in late 1970. The legal aid scheme covers the Lands Tribunal.

(d) *Law Reform*

An office of the Director of Law Reform was established in 1965 within the Ministry of Finance, with terms of reference similar to those of the Law Commissions for England and Wales, and Scotland. The major difference is that the Northern Ireland body is part of the civil service and not an independent body.

Select Bibliography

BRETT, C. E. B.
"The Legal Aid and Advice Bill (Northern Ireland)", in *Northern Ireland legal quarterly*, 15 (1964): pp. 352-70.

INCORPORATED LAW SOCIETY OF NORTHERN IRELAND
Handbook. Belfast, Incorporated Law Society of Northern Ireland, 1959. xiii + 403p. (Revised periodically and currently under major revision)

INCORPORATED LAW SOCIETY OF NORTHERN IRELAND
Report . . . on legal aid in criminal proceedings, 1966/7- . Belfast, Incorporated Law Society of Northern Ireland. (Published annually)

INCORPORATED LAW SOCIETY OF NORTHERN IRELAND
Report on the legal aid scheme and the comments and recommendations made by the Advisory Committee, 1965/6- . Belfast, HMSO. (Published annually)

LAW REFORM AND THE FUTURE OF LEGAL EDUCATION IN NORTHERN IRELAND, in *Northern Ireland legal quarterly*, 16 (1965): pp. 459-63 and 463-66. (Editorials)

LINDSAY, J. R.
" A review of the Supreme Court of Northern Ireland", in *Northern Ireland legal quarterly*, 7 (1946): pp. 3-19. (Editorial)

MACDERMOTT, J. C., Baron MacDermott
"Law and practice in Northern Ireland", in *Northern Ireland legal quarterly*, 10 (1953): pp. 47-77.

MONTROSE, J. L.
"Legal education in Northern Ireland", in *Journal of legal education*, 5 (1952): pp. 18-25.

MURRAY, N. H.
The status, responsibility, professional conduct and remuneration of solicitors. Belfast, Incorporated Law Society of Northern Ireland, 1964. 69p.

RITCHIE, J.
"The Inn of Court of Northern Ireland", in *Northern Ireland legal quarterly*, 15 (1964): pp. 463-69.

XIV. SCOTS LAW

The present bibliography aims to set out the standard works used by the legal profession in Scotland. It does not aim to catalogue what a fully equipped library would contain. Volume 5 of SWEET & MAXWELL's *Legal bibliography of the British Commonwealth of Nations* (1957, 2nd ed.) contains over a hundred pages devoted to Scots law, much of the material being of historical interest only. Cumulative supplements to this publication are issued from time to time. The present bibliography is concerned with modern Scots law and not with Scottish legal history—as to which most of the relevant authorities are mentioned in the Legal Bibliography of SWEET & MAXWELL, in the first volume of the Stair Society Publications—*Sources and literature of the law of Scotland*, and in subsequent volumes of the same series.

1. LITERATURE AND WRITTEN SOURCES

Separate Scottish Legal System Guaranteed by British Fundamental Law

Scottish law and English law have had very different sources and histories, and the advocates of assimilation have not prevailed. The separate legal system and law courts of Scotland were guaranteed by the Treaty of 1707, whereby Scotland and England agreed upon certain conditions to merge their separate international status in the new corporate Union of Great Britain. The Treaty is supplemented by certain fundamental statutes passed in 1707, and this body of fundamental law includes conditions or articles which may be varied by Parliament when need arises; other conditions are stated to be applicable "in all time coming". No constitutional machinery has yet been provided for amending terms of the latter of these categories, but it is apparently the view of the Scottish courts that, constitutionally, the fundamental law cannot be varied at will in disregard of the Treaty by an ordinary session of the Parliament of Great Britain. The doctrine of "Parliamentary Sovereignty" is no part of the law of Scotland. It is true that from time to time Parliament has disregarded its constitutional limitations and, by what was, in effect, a usurpation of power, legislated contrary to the express provisions of the Treaty. Much of this legislation may, however, be regarded as ratified by the assent of the people of Scotland. Since there is no Constitutional Court to which such matters may be referred, breaches of the Constitution cannot be declared *ultra vires* judicially. The Treaty of Union is set out in the Act of Union passed by the Parliaments of Scotland and England. The associated legislation is to be found in collections of United Kingdom Statutes. (Note that in collections of revised statutes the full text is not given.)

The main sources of law in written form are statute law; case law; institutional treatises (which have special authority); and legal treatises which are of persuasive authority according to the reputation of their authors.

Statute Law

With regard to statute law, it may be observed that decisions of the Scottish Parliament (i.e. prior to 1707 when the Scottish and English Parliaments were abolished and the new Parliament of Great Britain established) may be repealed by proof of desuetude and contrary practice. This doctrine does not apply to the statute law of the Parliament of Great Britain since the Union—which is now, of course, the bulk of the statute law in actual operation. The Treaty of Union, however, expressly provides (Article XVII) that no alteration by the Parliament of Great Britain may be made in laws which concern "private right" except for evident utility of the subjects within Scotland. In matters which concern Scotland and England alike, e.g. taxation and commercial law, there has been promulgation of a considerable body of law which might be described as the law of Great Britain, rather than as Scottish or English law. Some fields of the law are more suitable for uniform legislation than others. All statutes may be lawfully repealed by the Parliament of Great Britain, except, it is submitted, where restrictions were imposed in the Treaty of Union 1707 and associated fundamental legislation.

Case Law

The Supreme Courts of Scotland are the Court of Session for civil causes and the High Court of Justiciary in matters of criminal jurisdiction. These courts exercise their functions both by benches of judges (usually to hear appeals) and by judges acting alone or with a jury.

Though no express provision was made in the Treaty of Union regarding appeals from the Supreme Courts of Scotland, the House of Lords as the judicial organ of the new Parliament of Great Britain claimed to succeed to the appellate jurisdiction formerly exercised in civil causes alone by the Three Estates of the Scottish Parliament prior to 1707. As no provision was made until 1876 for a Scottish judge to sit in the House of Lords, that body has had opportunity on occasion to influence the law of Scotland in the direction of English solutions to legal problems. Even today the Scottish judges are in a minority in the House of Lords. This, some have argued, gives the Scottish Lords of Appeal undue authority in relation to the Scottish Bench, and (depending on whether the matter of the appeal involves an obvious specialty of Scottish law or not) gives them too much or too little authority, in relation to the English law lords. Where the problem is not clearly peculiar to Scots law the opinions of the Supreme Appellate Court in civil causes (the House of Lords) not infrequently reflect the English legal training of the majority of the court. All the law lords, however, enjoy a very high judicial reputation and it is the general wish of the legal profession in Scotland to retain this appellate jurisdiction, though the majority of practising lawyers consider that on grounds of expense and convenience it should sit in the Scottish capital to hear Scottish appeals, and that the English law lords should avoid the language and concepts of English law in deciding Scottish appeals. The House of Lords is also regarded as a useful means of securing uniform interpretation of legislation applicable to Scotland and England. The fact that the House of Lords hears civil appeals from both Scotland and England has in some fields of law led to reliance in Scotland on English decisions as persuasive authority; the English courts likewise on occasion refer to Scottish decisions. No equivalent considerations arise in the field of criminal law, since no appeal lies to the House of Lords from the Scottish Supreme Criminal Court. The older view of Scots law excluded the doctrine of *stare decisis*, but now, largely through the influence of the House of Lords, a modified doctrine of *stare decisis* has been accepted in Scotland. Decisions of a Division (i.e., three or four judges) of the Court of Session are binding on judges sitting alone, and normally on another Division. Decisions are elaborately reported and are a very important source of law. There is, however, no absolute rule that a Division must follow a precedent of a mere quorum. The normal method of setting aside an obnoxious precedent is to convene a special sitting of seven judges or the Whole Court. Such special Sessions can set aside previous precedents, provided they are not of the House of Lords. The functions of law and equity have not been divided in the Scottish administration of justice (see more fully T. B. SMITH, *Doctrine of judicial precedent in Scots law*, Edinburgh, Green, 1952). In the High Court of Justiciary, the decision of a quorum of judges is normally followed unless a full bench is convened to review the law. Again, there is no absolute rule that a single precedent must be accepted by a court of equal authority to that which has already declared the law.

Institutional Treatises

The foundations of modern Scots law were established in the late seventeenth century. At that time the civil law of Scotland was virtually recast in harmony with the best contemporary Continental teaching of Roman law and natural law by Viscount STAIR, a President of the Court of Session and the most celebrated of the Scottish institutional writers. Feudal land law and customary law in such matters as succession were blended with a substantial reception of Roman law. The institutional writers such as STAIR and his successors—BANKTON, ERSKINE, HUME (all eighteenth century), and BELL (early nineteenth century)—are still powerful authority in the Scottish law, and their status may be compared with that of Domat and Pothier in France prior to the codification of the law in that country. Though the opinion of an institutional writer cannot prevail against a decision of the House of Lords, it will carry approximately equal weight to the decision of a quorum of the Court of Session.

Other Legal Treatises

Legal treatises which have not achieved institutional authority are persuasive and not authoritative sources of law. Works by authors who have been elevated to the judicial Bench have, however, special force, e.g. M'LAREN, *Wills and succession*. The *Corpus Juris* is still regarded as persuasive authority, and Scots law has always recognized the importance of comparative law (particularly considering the approach of Roman law and English law) in reaching solutions to novel problems. The law of South Africa has somewhat similar sources to Scots law, and it is regretted that more attention has not been paid to the contributions of Roman-Dutch law.

The fact that the date of publication of some of these works is not recent does not infer that they are not in general use, since the useful life of a standard book on Scots law is reasonably long. On the other hand, this factor adds to the importance of consulting articles in the learned journals which discuss recent developments of the law.

Select Bibliography

a. Statutes

EDINBURGH GAZETTE, no. 1- , 1793- . Edinburgh, printed by authority.

GREAT BRITAIN

The Statutes: third revised edition ... 1235-1948. HMSO, 1950. 33 vols. (Cover title: *Statutes revised*)

This is a United Kingdom revision comprising Scottish Statutes from 1707-1948.

SCOTLAND

The Acts of the Parliaments of Scotland, 1424-1707, 2nd revised ed. HMSO, 1966. lix + 191p.

A number of these statutes are still important in practice, but they were not revised, as were English pre-Union statutes in the third edition of *Statutes Revised.*

SCOTLAND

Public General Statutes affecting Scotland, 1707-1847. Edinburgh, Blackwood, 1876. 3 vols.

SCOTTISH CURRENT LAW STATUTES, 1949- . Edinburgh, Green.

b. Acts of Sederunt and Acts of Adjournal

Acts of Sederunt regulate adjective law in the Court of Session. Codified HMSO, 1913, and since superseded *quoad* Rules of Court by Rules enacted in the *Court of Session, Scotland, Act of Sederunt (Rules of Court, consolidation and amendment) 1965*. S.I. 1965 No. 321 (S. 16). These consolidated Rules of Court are published in the *Parliament House Book*, issued annually by Green, Edinburgh.

Acts of Adjournal exercise legislative control in procedural matters affecting the Criminal courts (including the Sheriff Courts) comparable to Acts of Sederunt in the Court of Session.

c. Case reports

Decisions by the Scottish Courts on Election cases, Income Tax, Pensions, Appeals, Development cases, etc. which are concerned with United Kingdom legislation will be found in the special series of reports dealing with these questions. Scottish appeals to the House of Lords which are deemed to be of general interest are published in the *Appeal cases* series, published by the Incorporated Council of Law Reporting in England, and often in the *All England law reports*, as well as the Scottish Reports. Not all Scottish Appeals to the House of Lords are, however, published in this series. An article upon the printed law reports, 1540-1935, with tabular statement of all the reports except MURRAY, J. *Reports of cases tried in the Jury Court from its institution in 1815*. Edinburgh, 1818-31, 5 vols., is contained in Volume 1 of the Stair Society publications at page 42.

i. Current reports

SCOTS LAW TIMES REPORTS, 1893- . Edinburgh, Green. Weekly.

These include House of Lords, Court of Session, Justiciary, Lands Valuation Appeal Court and Teind Court decisions in one series, and also Notes of recent decisions and Sheriff Court and Lyon Court reports, all of which are bound together. The method of citation is, e.g. 1949 S.L.T.8; S.L.T. (Notes) 12; 1949 S.L.T. (Sh.Ct.), 15; S.L.T. (Lyon Ct.)

SESSION CASES, 1821- . Edinburgh, Clark, for The Scottish Council of Law Reporting.

A volume of Session Cases comprises decisions of the Court of Session, the Lands Valuation Appeal Court, The Court of Justiciary and the House of Lords. Occasionally the Justiciary Reports are bound separately. Citation—S.C., J.C., S.C. (H.L.). Session Cases were in the hands of private reporters until 1907, and from 1907 the citation is e.g. 1907 S.C. 15. The earlier Session Cases consist of five series referred to by the initial letter of the editor's or reporter's name. These series are listed below.

First series: Shaw 16 vols. 1821-38

Second series: Dunlop 24 vols. 1838-62

Third series: Macpherson 11 vols. 1862-73
Fourth series: Rettie 25 vols. 1873-98
Fifth series: Fraser 8 vols. 1898-1906

SESSION NOTES, 1925-48. Edinburgh, Clark.
These were issued with Session Cases until publication was discontinued in 1948, the ground covered by this series being already adequately covered by Notes on Recent Decisions in the *Scots Law Times*.

ii. House of Lords reports

The reports of decisions of the House of Lords in Scottish cases from 1850 appear at the beginning of the Session Cases, and are cited thus: 10M. (H.L.) 4; 1907 S.C. (H.L.) 4. The older House of Lords cases are to be found in private reports. These are:

Robertson's Reports:	1 vol.	1707-27
Paton's Reports:	6 vols.	1726-1821
Dow's Reports:	6 vols.	1812-18
Bligh's Reports:	4 vols.	1819-21
Shaw's Reports:	2 vols.	1821-26
Wilson and Shaw's Reports:	7 vols.	1825-35
Shaw and M'Lean's Reports:	3 vols.	1835-38
M'Lean and Robinson's Reports:	1 vol.	1839
Robinson's Reports:	2 vols.	1840-41
Bell's Reports:	7 vols.	1842-50
Macqueen's Reports:	4 vols.	1851-65

iii. Criminal reports

Separate series of Criminal Reports appeared from 1819-1917, and the various series are referred to by the name of the reporter. From 1874 Justiciary Cases were also included in the volumes of Session Cases and since 1917 the series issued by individual reporters has gone into abeyance.
Earlier (Justiciary) Cases are reported in the Justiciary Reports, viz.—

Shaw:	1 vol.	1819-31
Syme:	1 vol.	1826-30
Swinton:	2 vols.	1835-41
Broun:	2 vols.	1842-45
Arkley:	1 vol.	1846-48
J. Shaw:	1 vol.	1848-52
Irvine:	5 vols.	1852-67
Couper:	5 vols.	1868-85
White:	3 vols.	1886-93
Adam:	7 vols.	1893-1916

iv. Older reports

ARNOT, H.
A collection and abridgement of celebrated criminal trials in Scotland from A.D. 1536 to 1784. Edinburgh, Smellie, 1785. xxiii + 400p.

BELL, R.
Cases decided by the Court of Session from November 1790 to July 1792. Edinburgh, Dickson, 1794. xxvi + 563p. (Known as *Bell's octavo cases*)

BELL, R.

Cases decided in the Court of Session (during summer session 1794, winter session 1794/5 and summer session 1795). Edinburgh, 1794-6. 2 parts. (Known as *Bell's folio cases*)

FACULTY OF ADVOCATES

Decisions of the Court of Session, 1752-1841

1752-1808, 14 vols.

1808-25, 7 vols.

1825-41, 21 vols.

(Cited by the date of the decision thus—10th January 1812 F.C.)

GRANT, P., Lord Elchies

Decisions of the Court of Session, from the year 1733 to the year 1754... Edinburgh, 1813. 2 vols. (Known as *Elchies decisions*)

HUME, D., Baron Hume

Decisions of the Court of Session 1781-1822. Edinburgh, Blackwood, 1839. xxxiii + 951p.

MCLAURIN, J., Lord Dreghorn

Arguments and decisions in remarkable cases, before the High Court of Justiciary and other supreme courts in Scotland. Edinburgh, 1774. (Covers 1670-1773)

MORISON, W. M.

The decisions of the Court of Session, from its institution until the separation of the Court into two divisions in the year 1808... Edinburgh, Constable, 1811. 42 volumes in 21. (The whole work is paginated consecutively. Citation, e.g. (1703)M. 1062. There are five supplementary volumes covering 1628-1794, known as *Brown's Supplement.*)

MURRAY, J.

Reports of cases tried in the Jury Court from its institution in 1815. Edinburgh, Constable, 1818-31. 5 vols.

PITCAIRN, R.

Criminal trials in Scotland from A.D. 1488-A.D. 1624... Edinburgh, Tait, 1833. 3 vols.

SCOTTISH JURIST, 1829-73. Edinburgh, Constable. 46 vols.

SCOTTISH LAW REPORTER, 1865-1924. Edinburgh, Baxter. 61 vols.

SCOTTISH LAW REVIEW AND SHERIFF COURT REPORTS, 1885-1963. Glasgow, Hodge. 79 vols.

Abbreviated S.L. Rev. this publication comprised reports of cases in the Sheriff Courts of Scotland and notes of English cases. The Scottish Law Review also published Sheriff Court decisions of the Scottish Land Court—the latter as a supplement. Sheriff Court cases in the S.L. Rev. are cited, e.g. (1934) Sh. Ct. Rep. 12; Land Court cases are cited S.L.C.R.

v. Digests

AN ANALYTICAL DIGEST OF CASES DECIDED IN THE SUPREME COURTS OF SCOTLAND...

[The "Faculty Digest"], 1868-1950. Glasgow, Hodge, for the Faculty of Advocates. 1924-65. 10 vols. (Supplemented by the *Annual Digest*)

SCOTS DIGEST, 1800-1947. Edinburgh, Green, 1908-48. 14 vols.

SCOTTISH CURRENT LAW YEARBOOK, 1951- . Edinburgh, Green.

This publication supersedes the twelve monthly issues of the Scottish edition of *Current Law*)

SHERIFF COURT DIGEST, 1885-1944. Glasgow, Hodge, 1906-48. 5 vols.

d. Institutional writers

BELL, G. J.
Commentaries on the law of Scotland and on the principles of mercantile jurisprudence, 7th ed. by J. M'Laren. Edinburgh, Clark, 1870. 2 vols.

BELL, G. J.
Principles of the law of Scotland, 10th ed. by W. Guthrie. Edinburgh, Clark, 1899. cvii + 903p.

CRAIG, Sir T.
The jus feudale, translated by J. A. Clyde. Edinburgh, Hodge, 1934. 2 vols.

DALRYMPLE, J., Viscount Stair
The institutions of the laws of Scotland, new ed. by J. S. More. Edinburgh, Bell & Bradfute, 1832. 2 vols.

ERSKINE, J.
An institute of the law of Scotland, new ed. by J. B. Nicolson. Edinburgh, Bell & Bradfute, 1871. 2 vols.

ERSKINE, J.
Principles of the law of Scotland, 21st ed. by John Rankine. Edinburgh, Green, 1911. xv + 906p.

HOME, H., Lord Kames
Principles of equity, new ed. Edinburgh, Bell & Bradfute, 1825. xvi + 525 + 20p.

MACDOWALL, A., Lord Bankton
An institute of the laws of Scotland in civil rights. Edinburgh, Fleming, 1751-3. 3 vols.

e. Encyclopaedias and dictionaries

BELL, W.
A dictionary and digest of the law of Scotland, 7th ed. by G. Watson. Edinburgh, Bell & Bradfute, 1890. vii + 1138p.

DALRYMPLE, A. W. and GIBB, A. D.
A dictionary of words and phrases judicially defined, and commented on by the Scottish Supreme Courts. Edinburgh, Green, 1946. viii + 382p.

ENCYCLOPAEDIA OF THE LAWS OF SCOTLAND, vols. 1-16. Edinburgh, Green, 1926-35. (Supplementary volume, 1949-51 in 2 parts with appendix, 1952)

GIBB, A. D.
Students' glossary of Scottish legal terms. Edinburgh, Green, 1946. 96p.

f. General textbooks

ANTON, A. E.
Private international law: a treatise from the standpoint of Scots law. Edinburgh, Green, 1967. lx + 626p.

BRODIE-INNES, J. W.
Comparative principles of the laws of England and Scotland. Edinburgh, Green, 1903. cx + 868p.

BURN-MURDOCH, H.
Notes on English law as differing from Scots law. Edinburgh, Green, 1924. xx + 126p.

GIBB, A. D.
A preface to Scots law, 4th ed. Edinburgh, Green, 1964. vii + 168p.

GIBB, A. D.
Select cases in the law of Scotland, 2nd ed. Edinburgh, Green, 1951. xvii + 194p.

GLOAG, W. M. and HENDERSON, R. C.
Introduction to the law of Scotland, 7th ed. by A. M. Johnston and J. A. D. Hope. Edinburgh, Green, 1968. cxix + 875p. (Suppl.)

SMITH, T. B.
The doctrines of judicial precedent in Scots law. Edinburgh, Green, 1952. xii + 115p.

SMITH, T. B.
A short commentary on the law of Scotland. Edinburgh, Green, 1962. xx + 980p.

STAIR SOCIETY
Publications, vol. 1- . Edinburgh, Maclehouse, etc., for the Society, 1936- .

SWEET & MAXWELL, LTD.
A legal bibliography of the British Commonwealth of Nations, 2nd ed. SM, 1955-64. 7 vols. (Vol. 5: Scottish law to 1956 . . .)

WALKER, D. M.
Principles of Scottish private law. Oxford, Clarendon Pr., 1970. 2 vols.

WALKER, D. M.
The Scottish legal system, 3rd ed. Edinburgh, Green, 1969. xl + 488p.

g. Constitutional and administrative law

COX, J. T., ed.
Practice and procedure in the Church of Scotland, 5th ed. by J. B. Longmuir. Edinburgh, Blackwood, 1964. 844p.

DICEY, A. V. and RAIT, R. S.
Thoughts on the union between England and Scotland. Macmillan, 1920. xxvi + 394p.

FRASER, W. I. R.
An outline of constitutional law, 2nd ed. Hodge, 1948. xvi + 346p.

HUTTON, W.
Local government (Scotland) Act, 1947. Edinburgh, Hodge, 1949. 644p.

MACKINNON, J.
The union of England and Scotland. Longmans, 1896. xviii + 524p.

MCLARTY, M. R. and PATON, G. C. H., eds
A source book and history of administrative law in Scotland. Hodge, 1956. vi + 267p.

MILLER, J. B.
An outline of administrative and local government law in Scotland. Edinburgh, Green, 1961. xxxii + 342p.

MITCHELL, J. D. B.
Constitutional law, 2nd ed. Edinburgh, Green, 1968. xxxix + 364p.

MURRAY, C. de B.
How Scotland is governed, revised ed. Glasgow, Art and Educational Publishers, 1947. 228p.

PRYDE, G. S., ed.
The treaty of union of Scotland and England, 1707. Nelson, 1950. viii + 120p.

2. CONTRACTS

The law of contracts in Scotland is largely based on the institutional works discussed above. The main points of difference from English law which must be stressed are as follows: Scots law will enforce any promise for a lawful purpose, and does not regard "consideration" as the badge of concluded agreement as does English law. The *jus quaesitum tertio* is recognized in Scots law, and a substantial contractual capacity is conceded to minors who have, however, a right to reduce certain bargains clearly to their prejudice within the *quadriennium utile* after achieving majority. There are various rules which are somewhat complicated with regard to the proving of agreements by written evidence after specified periods of time, and certain transactions, e.g. with regard to land, must be entered into in writing.

Select Bibliography

CLARK, F. W.
A treatise on the law of partnership and joint stock companies, according to the law of Scotland. Edinburgh, Clark, 1866. 2 vols.

FRASER, P., Lord Fraser
Treatise on master and servant, employer and workman, and master and apprentice, according to the law of Scotland, 3rd ed. by W. Campbell. Edinburgh, Clark, 1882. lix + 834p.

GLOAG, W. M.
The law of contract: a treatise on the principles of contract in the law of Scotland, 2nd ed. Edinburgh, Green, 1929. xcvi + 830p.

TROTTER, W. F.
The law of contract in Scotland. Edinburgh, Hodge, 1913. lxxvii + 410p.

UMPHERSTON, F. A.
The law of master and servant. Edinburgh, Green, 1904. xxxv + 331p.

3. COMMERCIAL LAW

Many of the standard works on the commercial law are authoritative both in Scotland and England, and will be found in the English section. It may be sufficient to mention here:

Select Bibliography

BENNETT, A. C. and BENNETT, R. A.
The Companies Act 1948, with reference to Scotland. Edinburgh, Green, 1950. xx + 204p.

CLARK, F. W.
A treatise on the law of partnership and joint stock companies, according to the law of Scotland. Edinburgh, Clark, 1866. 2 vols.

GOUDY, H.
A treatise on the law of bankruptcy in Scotland, 4th ed. by T. A. Fyfe. Edinburgh, Clark, 1914. lvi + 784p.

GOW, J. J.
The law of hire purchase in Scotland, 2nd ed. Edinburgh, Green, 1968. xxxviii + 259p.

GOW, J. J.
The mercantile and industrial law of Scotland. Edinburgh, Green, 1964. cix + 779p.

LEVIE, W. E.
Levie on the law of bankruptcy in Scotland, 4th ed. by A. Rankin. Edinburgh, Hodge, 1950. 160p.

LILLIE, J. A.
The mercantile law of Scotland, 6th ed. Edinburgh, Green, 1965. xxxvi + 411p.

MILLER, I. P.
Industrial law in Scotland. Edinburgh, Green, 1970. xlviii + 461p.

4. PROPERTY

The Scottish law of moveables is substantially Roman in derivation and its divisions should be familiar to Continental scholars. It is discussed in the various works already referred to, and in particular in the works of the institutional writers. The land law is still fundamentally feudal. Possibly the most lucid exposition is found in WOOD's *Lectures on conveyancing*, 1903 edition, which is not, however, completely up to date. The normal student's introduction to Scottish land law is BURNS's *Handbook of conveyancing*. The following works may be consulted:

Select Bibliography

BELL, A. M.
Lectures on conveyancing, 3rd ed. Edinburgh, Bell & Bradfute, 1882. 2 vols.

BURNS, J.
Conveyancing practice according to the law of Scotland, 4th ed. by F. MacRitchie. Edinburgh, Green, 1957. xlv + 969p.

BURNS, J.
Handbook of conveyancing, 5th ed. Edinburgh, Green, 1938. iv + 400p.

FARRAN, C. D'O.
The principles of Scots and English land law: a historical comparison. Edinburgh, Green, 1958. xxxi + 284p.

FRASER, D. G.
Rent and house-letting Acts in Scotland, 2nd ed. by R. A. Bennett. Edinburgh, Green, 1952. xxxiii + 326p.

GLOAG, W. M. and IRVINE, J. M.
Law of rights in security, heritable and moveable, including cautionary obligations. Edinburgh, Green, 1897. xxxiv + 1023p.

HALLIDAY, J. M.
The Conveyancing and Feudal Reform (Scotland) Act, 1970. Edinburgh, Green, 1970. xix + 246p.

HUNTER, R.
A treatise on the law of landlord and tenant, 4th ed. by W. Guthrie. Edinburgh, Bell & Bradfute, 1876. 2 vols.

MENZIES, A.
Conveyancing according to the law of Scotland, revised by J. S. Sturrock. Edinburgh, Bell & Bradfute, 1900. xxxvii + 1025p.

PATON, G. C. H. and CAMERON, J. G. S.
The law of landlord and tenant in Scotland. Edinburgh, Green, 1967. lvii + 673p. (Suppl.)

RANKINE, Sir J.
The law of land ownership in Scotland, 4th ed. Edinburgh, Green, 1909. lxvii + 1216p.

RANKINE, Sir J.
The law of leases in Scotland: a treatise, 3rd ed. Edinburgh, Green, 1916. xlvii + 1024p.

WOOD, J. P.
Lectures delivered to the class of conveyancing in the University of Edinburgh, 1892-1900. Edinburgh, Bell & Bradfute, 1903. xii + 913p.

5. TRUSTS

The Scottish law of trusts was evolved quite separate, so far as is known, from the English Chancery concepts, and was conceived of by Stair and Erskine as a combination of the contracts of mandate and deposit. Subsequently, however, English trust doctrines have had a substantial influence in Scotland. Mention may be made of "the radical right", a doctrine which infers that where a man has transferred his property to trustees for specific purposes, e.g. for the payment of his creditors, he himself retains a radical right of property which he may assert if, on fulfilment of the trust purposes, any property remains. The best introductory work is Mackenzie STUART's *The law of trusts*, 1932. The following practitioners' works are in general use:

Select Bibliography

IRONS, J. C.
The law and practice in Scotland relative to judicial factors. Edinburgh, Green, 1908. xl + 779p.

M'LAREN, J., Lord MacLaren
The law of wills and succession as administered in Scotland, 3rd ed. Edinburgh, Bell & Bradfute, 1894. 2 vols. (Suppl.)

MENZIES, A. J. P.
The law of Scotland affecting trustees, 2nd ed. Edinburgh, Green, 1913. xii + 1015p.

STUART, A. M.
The law of trusts. Edinburgh, Green, 1932. xxxii + 436p.

THOMS, G. H.
Treatise on judicial factors, curators bonis and managers of burghs, 2nd ed. by H. J. E. Fraser. Edinburgh, Bell & Bradfute, 1881. xxxii + 685p.

WARDHAUGH, J. B.
Trust law and accounts, 4th ed. Edinburgh, Green, 1951. xxiii + 226 + 130p.

6. WILLS, EXECUTORS, ADMINISTRATION, BONA VACANTIA, ETC.

The succession to heritage (land etc.) in Scotland was governed by the feudal rule of preference of the male and primogeniture. The Succession (Scotland) Act, 1964, has however, in the case of deaths on or after 10th September, 1964, made the law of succession to heritable and moveable property uniform. The surviving spouse and children have legal rights in the estate of the deceased. The surviving spouse is entitled to *jus relictae* (or *jus relicti*) in the moveables. The children, as a class, share in the legitim fund, which, if there is a surviving spouse, will amount to one-third of the moveables. So far as formalities of will are concerned a holograph will is valid in Scotland, i.e. a will in the handwriting of the testator and signed by him. Such a will need not be witnessed. A further development of this doctrine is that a man may "adopt as holograph" a will typed or written by another and signed by him, if in his own hand he specifies that he adopts the will as holograph. The more formal will is authenticated by the signatures of witnesses as well as of the testator. A good introductory work to wills is MURRAY's *The law of wills in Scotland.* The following works may be consulted:

Select Bibliography

CURRIE, J. G.
The confirmation of executors in Scotland, according to the practice in the Commissariot of Edinburgh, 6th ed. revised by A. E. McRae. Edinburgh, Green, 1965. xxxii + 410p.

DOBIE, W. J.
Manual of the law of liferent and fee in Scotland. Edinburgh, Green, 1941. xxvi + 335p.

HENDERSON, R. C.
The principles of vesting in the law of succession, 2nd ed. Edinburgh, Green, 1938. xl + 423p.

M'LAREN, J., Lord MacLaren
The law of wills and succession as administered in Scotland, 3rd ed. Edinburgh, Bell & Bradfute, 1894. 2 vols. (Suppl.)

MACMILLAN, A. R. G.
The law of bona vacantia in Scotland. Edinburgh, Green, 1936. xiv + 74p.

MESTON, M. C.
The Succession (Scotland) Act, 1964, 2nd ed. Edinburgh, Green, 1969. xvi + 158p.

MURRAY, C. de B.
The law of wills in Scotland. Edinburgh, Green, 1945. xv + 187p.

7. DELICT (Reparation)

The normal term used in Scotland for an action for damages on account of harm sustained from the wrongful act of another is an action for reparation. The expressions *delict* and *quasi-delict* are also used, but it may be well to stress that in Scotland *quasi-delict* infers negligent wrongdoing. Though English authorities on negligence are now freely cited in the Scottish Courts, it must be stressed that Scots law has never known an equivalent to the English law of Torts. A remedy is given wherever there has been damage to a lawful interest occasioned by the fault of another. In some cases, e.g. nuisance and liability for breach of statutory duty, the concept of *culpa* is construed freely to afford a remedy to the pursuer (as the party who complains is known in the Scottish procedure). The Scottish action for damages for negligence was developed from the *lex aquilia.* Until affected by English doctrines the Scottish law of liability for damage due to faulty premises did not accept the exclusive categories of invitees, licensees and trespassers. These have now been abolished by the Occupiers Liability (Scotland) Act, 1960. Possibly the best short expositions of the law prior to that Act are in articles in the *Encyclopaedia of the laws of Scotland* by Mr. Hector MCKECHNIE, Q.C., titles *Negligence* and *Reparation.* Scottish law prior to that Act does not make a division between libel and slander, as is done in England, nor will mere trespass on land ground an action for damages.

Select Bibliography

BROUN, J. C. C.

The law of nuisance in Scotland. Edinburgh, Green, 1891. xxxvi + 258p.

COOPER, F. T.

The law of defamation and verbal injury, 2nd ed. by D. O. Dykes. Edinburgh, Green, 1906. xli + 363p.

GLEGG, A. T.

The law of reparation in Scotland, 4th ed. by J. L. Duncan. Edinburgh, Green, 1955. xl + 518p.

MCKECHNIE, H.

"Negligence", in *Encyclopaedia of the laws of Scotland* (Edinburgh, Green, 1926-35), vol. 10, pp. 241-98.

MCKECHNIE, H.

"Reparation", in *Encyclopaedia of the laws of Scotland* (Edinburgh, Green, 1926-35), vol. 12, pp. 485-537.

SMITH, J. G.

The law of damages: a treatise on the reparation of injuries, administered in Scotland, 2nd ed. Edinburgh, Clark, 1889. lx + 488p.

WALKER, D. M.

The law of damages in Scotland. Edinburgh, Green, 1955. lxxii + 843p.

WALKER, D. M.

The law of delict in Scotland. Edinburgh, Green, 1966. 2 vols.

8. PERSONS

The law of husband and wife in Scotland has gone through substantial changes in the last thirty years so far as the formation of the marriage tie is concerned. Two forms of irregular marriage which had survived because Scotland adopted the Reformed religion prior to the Council of Trent, were abolished by statute shortly before Hitler's War. Possibly the most notable factor in the law of parent and child is that the common law of Scotland conceded considerable contractual capacity to minors, i.e. girls over twelve, boys over fourteen. For certain transactions they required the concurrence of their curator, if they had one, but a child who was forisfamiliated, i.e. who with the consent of his father had set himself up in the world independently, could act as a responsible contracting party, and even a child with curators could enter into a number of transactions which would be binding on him in the law. A minor may also make a valid will and may marry without parental consent. In recent years a great body of statute law applicable to both Scotland and England has complicated the law regarding custody and maintenance. In 1930 the law of Scotland first recognized adoption, though an informal method of adoption had existed with statutory recognition before that date. Scots law has always recognized legitimation of a child *per subsequens matrimonium*, and also will regard a child legitimate if born of a putative marriage though (contrary to the knowledge of at least one party) an impediment to the ostensible marriage existed. There have been many statutory changes in regard to divorce and the rights of adopted children and of illegitimate children. The following works may be consulted:

Select Bibliography

COWAN, M. G.
The Children and Young Persons (Scotland) Act, 1932: a manual. Edinburgh, Hodge, 1933. xxii + 428p.

FRASER, P., Lord Fraser
Treatise on husband and wife according to the law of Scotland, 2nd ed. Edinburgh, Clark, 1876-78. 2 vols.

FRASER, P., Lord Fraser
Treatise on master and servant, employer and workman, and master and apprentice, according to the law of Scotland, 3rd ed. by W. Campbell. Edinburgh, Clark, 1882. lix + 834p.

FRASER, P., Lord Fraser
A treatise on the law of Scotland relative to parent and child, and guardian and ward, 3rd ed. by J. Clark. Edinburgh, Green, 1906. xxiv + 959p.

TROTTER, T.
The law as to children and young persons . . . Glasgow, Hodge, 1938. xlix + 420p.

UMPHERSTON, F. A.
The law of master and servant. Edinburgh, Green, 1904. xxxv + 331p.

WALTON, F. P.
A handbook of husband and wife according to the law of Scotland, 3rd ed. by W. E. R. Hendry and A. M. Johnston. Edinburgh, Green, 1951. xxix + 443p.

9. CRIMINAL LAW

The Scottish criminal law so far as substantive law is concerned is uncodified, and is to be found in the judicial decisions and in the works of authoritative writers. The institutional work of HUME is still the most important practitioner's work. There is no good elementary treatise on criminal law in Scotland, though the article in the *Encyclopaedia* and the chapter in GLOAG AND HENDERSON'S *Introduction to the law of Scotland* are sufficient to acquire a general understanding. There are a considerable number of technical terms used in connection with the criminal law, and for these a dictionary of Scottish legal terminology should be consulted.

Scottish criminal procedure is mainly statutory. In addition to HUME, the following works are important, ALISON, BURNETT, GORDON and MACDONALD being indispensable.

Select Bibliography

ABERDEEN CITY POLICE
Road traffic law, new revised ed. Aberdeen, Avery, 1952. (Loose-leaf)

ABERDEEN CITY POLICE
Scottish criminal law, police duties and procedure. Aberdeen, Avery, 1953. (Loose-leaf)

ALISON, Sir A.
Practice of the criminal law of Scotland. Edinburgh, Blackwood, 1833. xliii + 729p.

ANDERSON, A. M., Lord Anderson
The criminal law of Scotland, 2nd ed. Edinburgh, Bell & Bradfute, 1904. xviii + 401p.

BURNETT, J.
A treatise on various branches of the criminal law of Scotland, edited by R. Craigie. Edinburgh, Constable, 1811. vii + 612 + lxviii + xvp.

GLOAG, W. M. and HENDERSON, R. C.
Introduction to the law of Scotland, 7th ed. by A. M. Johnston and J. A. D. Hope. Edinburgh, Green, 1968. cxix + 875p. (Chapter 49)

GORDON, G. H.
The criminal law of Scotland. Edinburgh, Green, 1967. lxxiii + 1104p.

HUME, D., Baron Hume
Commentaries on the law of Scotland, respecting crimes, 4th ed. by B. R. Bell. Edinburgh, Bell & Bradfute, 1844. 2 vols.

MACDONALD, J. H. A., Lord Kingsburgh
A practical treatise on the criminal law in Scotland, 5th ed. by J. Walker and D. J. Stevenson. Edinburgh, Green, 1948. lix + 398p.

MACKENZIE, Sir G.
The laws and customs of Scotland in matters criminal, 2nd ed. Edinburgh, printed for Mr. Andrew Symson, 1699. 435p.

MILL, J.
The Scottish police: an outline of their powers and duties. Edinburgh, Green, 1944. 208p.

RENTON, R. W. and BROWN, H. H.
Criminal procedure according to the law of Scotland, 3rd ed. by F. C. Watt and others. Edinburgh, Green, 1956. liii + 607p.

TROTTER, T.
Summary criminal jurisdiction according to the law of Scotland. Edinburgh, Hodge, 1936. xxiii + 617p.

10. EVIDENCE, PLEADING AND PROCEDURE INCLUDING JURISDICTION

The Rules of Court are contained in the *Parliament House Book* published annually by Messrs. Green and Sons, Ltd., Edinburgh. The best introductory work on procedure in the Court of Session is THOMSON AND MIDDLETON. The following works cover the field of adjective law in its various aspects:

Select Bibliography

BURN-MURDOCH, H.
Interdict in the law of Scotland with a chapter on specific performance. Edinburgh, Hodge, 1933. xliv + 548p.

DICKSON, W. G.
A treatise on the law of evidence in Scotland, 3rd revised ed. by P. J. H. Grierson. Edinburgh, Clark, 1887. 2 vols.

DOBIE, W. J.
Law and practice of the Sheriff Courts in Scotland. Edinburgh, Hodge, 1948. lvi + 794p.

DUNCAN, G. and DYKES, D. O.
The principles of civil jurisdiction as applied in the law of Scotland. Edinburgh, Green, 1911. xvi + 394p.

GUILD, D. A.
The law of arbitration in Scotland. Edinburgh, Green, 1936. xv + 148p.

LEWIS, W. J.
Manual of the law of evidence in Scotland. Edinburgh, Hodge, 1925. xv+462p.

LEWIS, W. J.
Sheriff Court practice, 8th ed. Edinburgh, Green, 1939. xlvi + 612p.

MACKAY, A. J. G.
Manual of practice in the Court of Session. Edinburgh, Green, 1893. xv+801p.

MACLAREN, J. A.
Court of Session practice. Edinburgh, Green, 1916. cxci + 1224p.

PARLIAMENT HOUSE BOOK, 1825/26- . Edinburgh, Green, etc. (Published annually)

RANKINE, Sir J.
Personal bar: a treatise on the law of personal bar in Scotland. Edinburgh, Green, 1921. xxxviii + 322p.

STEWART, J. G.
A treatise on the law of diligence. Edinburgh, Green, 1898. lviii + 893p.

THOMSON, G. R. and MIDDLETON, J. T.
Manual of Court of Session procedure. Edinburgh, Green, 1937. xxxi + 477p.

WALKER, A. G. and WALKER, N. M. L.
The law of evidence in Scotland. Edinburgh, Hodge, 1964. xl + 493p.

II. LEARNED JOURNALS, ETC.

JOURNAL OF THE LAW SOCIETY OF SCOTLAND, 1956- . Edinburgh, The Society.

JURIDICAL REVIEW. The law journal of the Scottish Universities, 1889- . Edinburgh, Green.

The above journal is concerned mainly with questions of Scottish and Comparative law.

SCOTS LAW TIMES, 1893- . Edinburgh, Green. (Weekly)

SCOTTISH JURIST, 1829-73. Edinburgh, Constable. 46 vols.

SCOTTISH LAW REVIEW AND SHERIFF COURT REPORTS, 1885-1963. Glasgow, Hodge. 79 vols.

Scottish contributions will also be found in journals published in England, such as:

INTERNATIONAL AND COMPARATIVE LAW QUARTERLY, vol. 1- , 1952- . British Institute of International and Comparative Law, etc.

LAW QUARTERLY REVIEW, vol. 1- , 1885- . S.

MODERN LAW REVIEW, vol. 1- , 1937- . S.

XV. THE CHANNEL ISLANDS

1. JERSEY

Consideration of the sources of the law of Jersey may be directed first to the common or customary law and, secondly, to the law derived from legislation.

The common or customary law of Jersey is based upon the "Ancienne Coutume de Normandie"—the common law of the ancient Duchy of Normandy, of which the Channel Islands originally formed part. This ancient Norman law remains the law of Jersey, except in so far as it has, in the course of time, been modified by local usage, judicial decision or legislative enactment.

The principal authority as to the ancient customary law of Normandy is "Le Grand Coutumier du Pays et Duché de Normandie", which was probably compiled during the thirteenth century. The edition ordinarily cited in the Royal Court of Jersey is that of 1539, which contains, besides the text and a gloss, a commentary by Guillaume LE ROUILLÉ first published in 1534. The text of the "ancienne coutume" was last published in 1881 in Jersey, by W. L. DE GRUCHY. The last commentator on the "ancienne coutume" was TERRIEN, whose posthumous work was first published in 1574.

Reference is also made both to the "Coutume Réformée de Normandie" which was compiled towards the end of the sixteenth century, and which represented the then existing law of Continental Normandy, and to the commentators thereon, notably D'AVIRON (1599), BÉRAULT (1614), GODEFROY (1626), BASNAGE (1678), PESNELLE (1704), ROUTIER (1742), FLAUST (1781) and HOUARD (1780-82).

The strongest authority as to the customary law is, however, to be found in decisions of the Privy Council, which is the ultimate Court of Appeal for the Island, and in decisions of the Royal Court of Jersey. The decisions of the Privy Council prior to 1868 are to be found in a series of six volumes published in Jersey between 1897 and 1906. A classified summary of the decisions of the Royal Court of Jersey has been published periodically since the year 1885.

There are very few text-books on the customary law of Jersey. The most authoritative are those of POINGDESTRE, Lieutenant-Bailiff from 1669 to 1676, LE GEYT, Lieutenant-Bailiff from 1676 to 1694 and LE GROS, Lieutenant-Bailiff from 1946 to 1947.

Valuable information as to the customary law is also contained in the Statements of HEMERY AND DUMARESQ and PIPON AND DURELL (1789) and in various reports made by Royal Commissioners appointed from time to time to enquire into the laws and customs in force in the Island. The most important of the Commissioners' Reports with regard to the criminal law is that published in the year 1846, and, with regard to the civil law, that published in 1861.

The legislative sources of the law of Jersey may be said to consist of Royal Charters, Orders of the Sovereign in Council, Acts of Parliament, Laws passed by the States and sanctioned by the Sovereign in Council, and local Regulations.

Legislation is normally effected at the present time by the States but an Act passed by the States requires confirmation by the Sovereign in Council before it can acquire the force of law. Such legislation is published in a series of "Recueils des Lois" commencing in 1771. An Act of the States confirmed by the Sovereign in Council may empower the States or a Committee of the States to make Orders or Regulations which have legislative effect without confirmation by the Sovereign in Council.

Regulations may also be passed by the States to have force of law for three years without requiring confirmation by Order of the Sovereign in Council. Such Regulations may either relate to matters which are purely municipal or administrative, or contain provisions of an experimental nature which, if found satisfactory, may later be made the subject of permanent legislation. Regulations relating to municipal matters may be renewed at the expiration of each period of three years. Such Regulations, together with the delegated legislation referred to in the preceding paragraph, are published in a series of "Regulations and Orders".

Acts of the United Kingdom Parliament dealing with matters which affect the Island incidentally, but which are not exclusively the domestic concern of the Island, may contain a provision that they shall extend to Jersey, or may empower the Sovereign to extend to the Island by Order in Council the whole or part of the Act, with such adaptations, exceptions and modifications as may be required. Such Acts are transmitted by Order in Council to the Royal Court for registration and, in the case of Acts extended by Order in Council, are now published in the "Recueils des Lois".

Select Bibliography

Legislation and law reports

JERSEY
Orders in Council, laws, etc., 1771- . Jersey, Bigwoods, etc. (Usually biennial. Known by spine title: *Recueil des lois.* 1771-1945 entitled *Lois et règlements passés par les États de Jersey.* Volumes for 1771-1936 are numbered 1-7, and were republished 1957-69 under title *Recueil des lois*, with amendments. Prior to 1968 title page and part of text in French)

JERSEY
Regulations and orders, vol. 1- , 1939- . Jersey, Bigwoods. (Annual)

JERSEY. Cour Royale
Judgments of the Royal Court of Jersey and of the Court of Appeal of Jersey, 1950-66. Jersey, Bigwoods, 1967. xli + 713p.

ORDRES DU CONSEIL ET PIÈCES ANALOGUES ENREGISTRÉS À JERSEY, edited by H. M. Godfray then by A. Messeroy, 1536-1867. Jersey, Labey & Blampied, 1897-1906. 6 vols. (Includes a number of Privy Council decisions on appeals from Jersey)

TABLE DES DÉCISIONS DE LA COUR ROYALE DE JERSEY, vols. 1-9. 1885-1958. Jersey, Bigwoods, 1896-1959. (The only form in which the decisions are available, as there are no printed reports up to 1950)

Reports and Royal Commissions

HEMERY, J. and DUMARESQ, J.
Statement of the mode of proceeding and of going to trial in the Royal Court of Jersey, prepared in consequence of an order from the lords of the Committee of Council, dated 21st July 1789. 1789. 59p.

PIPON, T. and DURELL, J. T.
Mode of proceeding in trials in Jersey. 1789.

GREAT BRITAIN. Commission appointed to enquire into the civil, municipal and ecclesiastical laws of the Island of Jersey

Report. HMSO, 1861. [6] + cxxv + 811p. (Issued as a Command paper: [2725])

GREAT BRITAIN. Commission appointed to enquire into the state of the criminal law in the Channel Islands

1st report: *Jersey*. HMSO, 1847. li + 288p. (Issued as a Command paper: [865])

Commentaries

a. L'Ancienne coutume

DE GRUCHY, W. L., ed.

L'Ancienne coutume de Normandie, réimpression avec des légères annotations. Jersey, Le Feuvre, 1881. xxv + 420p.

LE ROUILLÉ, G.

Le grand coustumier du pays et duché de Normandie . . . avec plusieurs additions . . . Rouen, Nicolas le Roux, 1539. Various pagings.

b. La Coutume reformée

BASNAGE, H.

La coutume réformée du paiïs et duché de Normandie. Rouen, Lucas, 1678-81. 2 vols.

BÉRAULT, J

La coustume réformée du pays et duché de Normandie, 2nd ed. Rouen, Du Petit-Val, 1614. 1064 + 6 + 36p.

FLAUST, J. B.

Explication de la coutume et de la jurisprudence de Normandie dans un ordre simple et facile. Rouen, l'auteur, 1781. 2 vols.

GODEFROY, J.

Commentaires sur la coustume réformée du pays et duché de Normandie, anciens ressorts et enclaues d'iceluy. Rouen, Du Petit-Val, 1626. 2 vols. in 1.

HOÜARD, D.

Dictionnaire analytique, historique, étymologique, critique et interprétatif de la coutume de Normandie . . . Rouen, Le Boucher le Jeune, 1780-82. 4 vols. (Suppl.)

PESNELLE, N.

Coutume de Normandie, expliquée par M. Pesnelle. Rouen, Maurry, 1704. viii + 576 + 48p.

ROUTIER, C.

Principes généraux du droit civil et coutumier de la province de Normandie. Rouen, Le Boucher, 1742. xvi + 644p.

Text books

LE GEYT, P.

Privilèges loix et coustumes de l'isle de Jersey avec un essay pour des reglemens politiques. Jersey, Bigwoods, 1953. viii + 150p.

LE GROS, C. S.

Traité du droit coutumier de l'île de Jersey. Jersey, Les Chroniques de Jersey, 1943. xii + 511p.

POINGDESTRE, J.
Les lois et coutumes de l'île de Jersey. Jersey, Bigwoods, 1928. 347p. (Société des Gens de Droit de Jersey, St. Hélier)

SHERIDAN, L. A.
"The Channel Islands", in *The United Kingdom: the development of its laws and constitutions,* edited by G. W. Keeton and D. Lloyd, part 2. (S, 1955. The British Commonwealth: the development of its laws and constitutions, vol. 1) pp. 1141-53.

2. GUERNSEY

The civil law of the Bailiwick of Guernsey, like that of so many other places, has grown up with the community, as it were, rather than developed spontaneously, from a statute or even a number of statutes.

It is not quite correct to say that it is the Coutume de Normandie, for the Islands in their early days applied only certain portions of the customary law—obviously only those which were necessary or those which conveniently responded to the then customs and habits of the Islanders.

The Law of Inheritance, passed in 1840, is much more declaratory of the custom than a statute propounding new principles of law. It was amended in 1954 so as to abolish (1) the "droit de préciput"; (2) the "droit de douaire"; (3) the "droit de franc veuvage", and (4) the "droit d'aînesse". In 1967 the Children and Young Persons Law was revised and brought up to date and again in 1971.

Cases which came to trial were decided by reference to those parts of the Coutume which were acknowledged to apply and to the prevailing custom of the country. In those days the principal authority was and, to some extent still is, the "*Commentaires du droit civil tant public que privé, observé au pays et Duché de Normandie*", published by TERRIEN in 1574. The other commentators such as BASNAGE and BÉRAULT are also still accepted in the courts.

Although Guernsey has developed socially and commercially to a remarkable degree, the main body of the civil law has changed very little. While so much of it, *i.e.* the law of contract and tort, has gone substantially unchanged in the course of the centuries, a considerable amount of legislation has gone during the past fifty years to the making of a body of statute law designed to respond to the modern needs of society. The most important instances are the Company Law of 1908, followed by a Bankruptcy Law in 1929. There was no Married Women's Separate Property Law until 1928. The Matrimonial Causes Law which introduced, for the first time, a law of divorce, was passed in 1939, but by reason of the enemy occupation of the Island, was not put into use until after the war.

What was quite new was the setting up in 1961 of a Court of Appeal. The effect was to provide access to an Appeal Court in Guernsey without the necessity of going to the Privy Council. But access to the Privy Council still remains.

In the field of social legislation the civil law of the Island had added to it between 1928 and 1951 provision for old age pensions, contributory and non-contributory pensions, old age and blindness pensions, workers' insurance, widows' and orphans' pensions, and family allowances.

In a short introduction such as this, it is not possible to cover the whole field of development of the civil law—still less to draw comparisons with other systems.

In addition to the written customary law, the Orders in Council and Ordinances which constitute our civil law, it should be noted that certain Acts of the Imperial Parliament such as the Army Act apply, expressly, to these Islands.

Select Bibliography

Legislation

GUERNSEY

Orders in Council, and other matters of general interest registered on the records of the Island of Guernsey, vol. 1- , 1803- . Guernsey, printed by Guernsey Herald Ltd. (Usually published biennially or triennially. Spine title: *Ordres en Conseil*)

GUERNSEY

Ordinances of the States, vol. 1- , 1533/1800- . Guernsey, printed by Guernsey Herald Ltd. (Published triennially. Spine title: *Recueil d'Ordonnances*)

Commentaries

a. L'Ancienne coutume

TERRIEN, G.

Commentaires du droit civil tant public que privé, observé au pays et duché de Normandie . . . Paris, Du Puys, 1574. 4 + 728 + 30p.

b. La Coutume reformée

BASNAGE, H.

La coutume réformée du païs et duché de Normandie. Rouen, Lucas, 1678-81. 2 vols.

BÉRAULT, J., and others

Commentaires sur la coutume de Normandie, par MM. Bérault, Godefroy et la paraphrase de M. d'Aviron, nouvelle édition. Rouen, l'Imprimiere privilégiée, 1776. 2 vols.

XVI. ISLE OF MAN

1. CONSTITUTIONAL STATUS AND BASIS OF LAW

The Isle of Man is a dependency under the British Crown with a considerable degree of autonomy. It is not part of the United Kingdom but is included in the British Islands. It is not a foreign dominion of the Crown so as to be exempt from the power of the English High Court to issue writs of habeas corpus.

The common law of England does not extend to the Isle of Man. The ancient breast law, i.e. the law existing in the breast of the judges, modified and developed by statutes passed by the insular legislature through the centuries, has produced the present system of jurisprudence. However, as a general rule the law of the Isle of Man in the more essential matters is the same as the law of England, and normally the principles of equity administered by the English courts are followed by the courts of the Isle of Man unless they conflict with well-established local precedents.

2. THE LEGISLATURE AND THE LEGISLATIVE PROCESS

The Isle of Man is governed by an ancient legislature known as Tynwald, a term derived from the period when the Island was under the suzerainty of the Kings of Norway. Tynwald has two branches, the Legislative Council and the House of Keys. The Legislative Council consists of the Lieutenant-Governor, the Bishop of Sodor and Man, the First Deemster, the Attorney-General and seven members elected by the House of Keys. The House of Keys consists of twenty-four members elected by full adult suffrage. The branches sit separately for legislative purposes: the Legislative Council has no power of veto over legislature passed by the Keys. The branches sit together for executive and financial purposes: when so assembled they are known as "Tynwald Court".

Bills after having been passed in the usual way by both branches or by the Keys alone, are signed by the members of both branches in Tynwald Court and are then sent for the Royal Assent. After receiving the Royal Assent, Bills only become law when the Royal Assent has been announced to Tynwald and a certificate to this effect signed by the Lieutenant-Governor and the Speaker of the House of Keys. The Act is also promulgated in English and in Manx on Tynwald Hill, in the centre of the Island, on 5th July each year.

The Manx legislature is empowered to enact statutes concerning matters not transcending the frontiers of the Island. Legislation in relation to certain matters falling outside this category is normally enacted by the Parliament at Westminster and extended to the Isle of Man. Acts of Parliament are only applicable to the Island when it is expressly named therein or included by necessary implication: extension is normally effected by Order in Council made pursuant to an application section in the Acts in question and after consultation with Tynwald. Acts of Parliament extending to the Isle of Man usually cover only such matters as patents, copyright, trademarks, wireless, telegraphy, civil aviation and aspects of merchant shipping.

3. JUDICATURE AND SUPERIOR COURTS

The High Court of Justice of the Isle of Man is staffed by the two Deemsters: it has Chancery and Common Law Divisions. The Staff of Government Division is the Court of Appeal and is composed of the Judge of Appeal (an English barrister appointed by the Crown) and a Deemster other than one whose judgment is appealed against. A further appeal (in both civil and criminal cases) lies to the Judicial Committee of the Privy Council.

The supreme criminal court is the Court of General Gaol Delivery, staffed by a Deemster sitting with a jury.

4. PROPERTY

(a) *Real Property*

The nature of the tenure of Manx real estate is customary fee simple and, with certain exceptions, mines, minerals and quarries of slate, flag and stone vest in the Government Property Trustees for the public service of the Isle of Man.

The customary tenant or owner is in general entitled to take, raise and dispose of stone and slates on his own lands so that they may be employed for his own use or for the use of his neighbour: he is not entitled to sell them commercially unless licensed. He is, however, compelled, if a quarry is on his lands, to allow other tenants to quarry for their own use upon payment of reasonable compensation for damage.

(b) *Registration of Deeds, etc.*

The original deeds are recorded in the General Registry and certified copies are available: alternatively, deeds can be enrolled in the General Registry and the original handed out.

A uniform system of registration of all deeds, conveyances, wills and other instruments affecting real property was first created by an Act of Tynwald of 1847 and is now governed by the Registration of Deeds Act, 1961. Registration of documents relating to real property is not compulsory, but the priority of rights derived from them is generally determined by dates of registration.

(c) *Leases*

The law, though generally similar to English law, varies in two respects. First, a demise for a term of not more than one year may be made by verbal agreement; for a longer period it must be in writing. Secondly, a lease for more than 21 years is valid, but should be recorded under the Registration of Deeds Acts.

(d) *Perpetuities and Accumulations*

The law is now governed by the Perpetuities and Accumulations Act, 1968, an Act of Tynwald which follows very closely the provisions of the relevant English legislation, i.e. the Perpetuities and Accumulations Act, 1964.

(e) *Bills of Sale*

There is no local equivalent of the English Bills of Sale Acts. By the common law of the Island, and by statute, a person in possession of goods with the reputation of being the owner thereof is presumed to be the owner: if he is in possession when the goods are seized by a person enforcing judgment, the goods are available for payment of debts. On the other hand, this rule is qualified by the general recognition of the practice of hiring of certain classes of goods, either with or without the right of ultimate purchase.

5. FAMILY LAW

(a) *Child Law*

By the common law of the Island, a child was legitimised on the marriage of the parents within a year or two after its birth. This law has been replaced by several Acts of Tynwald under which the legitimacy law of the Island accords with that of the United Kingdom. The law relating to legal adoption is in parity with that of the United Kingdom.

(b) *Matrimonial Law*

The law is based on, and similar to, the English law with appropriate modifications for local application. A foreign decree of divorce is recognised in the Isle of Man upon the same principles as those applied from time to time in the United Kingdom.

6. SUCCESSION

(a) *Wills*

The Wills Act, 1869, an Act of Tynwald, contains provisions similar to those of the corresponding Act of Parliament, Lord Kingsdown's Act, 1861. A will made by a domiciled Manxman is revoked on marriage unless expressed to have been made in contemplation of marriage. In general the law relating to the formalities of the execution of wills and their construction is the same as that in the United Kingdom.

The practice of resealing probates which exist in between the English courts and those of British Colonies has not been adopted in the Isle of Man. An exemplification of English probate or letters of administration has, however, always been accepted as *prima facie* proof of the matters stated therein, and the Manx courts have made grants in the Isle of Man to those persons who would receive them in England in similar circumstances in preference to any outsiders.

(b) *Intestacy*

By the terms of the Administration of Estates Act, 1960, if an intestate leaves a husband or wife but no issue, the residuary estate is held in trust for the surviving spouse absolutely. If an intestate leaves both a surviving spouse and issue (i) the surviving spouse takes the personal chattels absolutely; (ii) £2000 net and costs charged on the residuary estate is held for the benefit of the survivors together with 4% interest until this sum is paid or appropriated; (iii) the residuary estate is held as to half on trust for the survivor absolutely and as to the other half on statutory trusts for the issue of the intestate. If an intestate leaves issue but no husband or wife surviving, the residuary estate is held on statutory trusts for the issue of the intestate.

(c) *Real and Personal Estate*

Until 1960 the rule of primogeniture always prevailed in the Isle of Man and on intestacy real property devolved generally on the same principles as those which were applied in England prior to 1925. By the Administration of Estates Act 1960 this rule was abolished in respect of the real estate of any person dying after the commencement of the Act: by the Act all real and personal estate was henceforth to be assimilated and consequently devolves as one fund in a manner which closely follows the present English law. The old rule and the present method of ascertainment of heirs still operates, however, in respect of persons whose death occurred prior to 1960.

7. CONTRACT AND TORT

The law of the Isle of Man is in general similar to that of England in these respects. Torts actionable by the law of England are also actionable by that of the Isle of Man, subject to certain statutory differences. Manx law tends to follow English law in the creation of statutory provisions in the field of tort: recent changes in the law relating to occupier's liability in England have, for example, been adopted in the Isle of Man by court legislation.

With the exception of technical differences in relation to the sealing of deeds, the law of contract in the Isle of Man is similar to that of England. One statutory anomaly has recently been in effect eliminated: until 1968 the maximum rate of interest in the Isle of Man was 6%, loans made at higher rates of interest being irrecoverable. By two Acts of Tynwald, the Usury Acts of 1968 and 1970, the Lieutenant-Governor has now been empowered to fix interest rates at up to 10%, subject to the approval of Tynwald.

8. PRIVATE INTERNATIONAL LAW

As the Isle of Man is outside the territorial jurisdiction of the English courts as far as the meaning of Order 11, rule 1, of the Rules of the Supreme Court is concerned, there has been a tendency for local rules to develop with regard to such matters as choice of law and jurisdiction. Nevertheless, Manx courts have in general followed the practice of their English counterparts in relation to such matters as the incidents of domicile, the status of marriage and matrimonial causes.

The judgments of courts outside the Isle of Man are not enforceable *per se* in the Island, but form a ground of action and proceedings may be brought for the amount of the foreign judgment. That judgment is proof of the amount due and the subject-matter will not be re-opened in proceedings in the Isle of Man unless the defendant has merely appeared in the foreign proceedings under protest or to argue the question of jurisdiction.

The practice of Manx courts is flexible with regard to the proof of foreign law. Where proof of English law is concerned, the courts will usually determine the question themselves rather than requiring the production of expert evidence on the subject.

9. OTHER BRANCHES OF LAW

In those branches of public and private law not discussed separately Manx law and English law may be said to be in close correspondence, statutory provision in England being often re-enacted in appropriate form by Acts of Tynwald. This process can be clearly seen in relation to such matters as the law concerned with business associations, trusts and evidence. Whilst the exact provisions of Manx law can thus only be established by reference to the appropriate local legislation, English case authorities are often of avail in a particular Manx situation.

10. TEXT BOOKS

The close identity between English law and Manx law in most areas of law has reduced the need for specialist text-books on Manx law and they are, therefore, conspicuous by their absence. Even where, as in the case of real property, Manx law is unique, there are no up-to-date text-books and the classic works are all out of print.

In these circumstances resort must be had to official publications. All the official publications in print (including the bulk of the statutes) may be obtained from the Finance Department, Government Office, Douglas, Isle of Man.

Select Bibliography

1. Literature giving general accounts of the constitutional law and status and of the legal system of the Isle of Man

HALSBURY'S LAWS OF ENGLAND, 3rd ed. B, 1952–64. 43 vols. (Suppl.) (Vol. 5: Commonwealth and Dependencies—Part 3, section 10; Part 4, section 1 (4); Part 5, sections 1 (9) and 2 (2))

HOLLAND, D. C.
"The Isle of Man", in *The United Kingdom: the development of its laws and constitutions*, edited by G. W. Keeton and D. Lloyd, part 1. (S, 1955. The British Commonwealth; the development of its laws and constitutions, vol. 1) Chapter 21, pp. 485-93.

PHILLIPS, O. Hood
Constitutional and administrative law, 4th ed. SM, 1967. xxxix + 865p. (Part VII, Chapter 32, pp. 708–11)

ROBERTS-WRAY, Sir K.
Commonwealth and Colonial law. S, 1966. liv + 1008p. (Appendix I, pp. 675–77)

WADE, E. C. S. and PHILLIPS, G. G.
Constitutional law, 8th ed. by E. C. S. Wade and A. W. Bradley. Longmans, 1970. xxxvi + 767p. (Part I, chapter 30, pp. 420–21)

2. Literature dealing specifically with the Isle of Man

a. Constitutional law and history

GREAT BRITAIN. Commission on the Constitution
Isle of Man; joint evidence of the Home Office and Tynwald, 27th February 1970. Douglas, Island Development Co., 1970. 57p.

GREAT BRITAIN. Commissioners of Inquiry for the Isle of Man

Report, 1792. 1805. 150 + 654p. (Last section consists of appendices)

GREAT BRITAIN. Home Office. Departmental Committee on the Constitution, etc. of the Isle of Man (Chairman: Lord MacDonnell)

Report. HMSO, 1911–13. 2 vols. (Cd 5950 and Cd 6026)

GREAT BRITAIN. Home Office. Joint Working Party on the Constitutional Relationship between the Isle of Man and the United Kingdom (Chairman: Lord Stonham)

Report. HMSO, 1969. iv + 126p.

ISLE OF MAN. Commission on the Isle of Man Constitution (Chairman: Lord MacDermott)

Report. Douglas, printed by authority by Norris Modern Pr., 1959. 2 vols.

MOORE, A. W.

A history of the Isle of Man. Unwin, 1900. 2 vols. (See in particular volume 2, book VI)

PARR, J.

An abstract of the laws, customs and ordinances of the Isle of Man, vol. 1, edited with notes by Sir J. Gell. Douglas, Manx Society, 1867. xvi + 241p. (Publications of the Manx Society, vol. 12)

This volume does not in fact, contain any of the text of Parr's *Abstract* of c. 1690, but merely includes introductory material on the constitutional history of the Isle of Man.

SHERWOOD, R., ed.

The constitution of the Isle of Man, consisting of Part III of the Report of the Commissioners of Inquiry for the Isle of Man in 1792, with the appendix and other documents. Douglas, Manx Society, 1882. xii + 336p. (Publications of the Manx Society, vol. 31)

b. Legislation and the legislative process

ISLE OF MAN

Reports of Boards of Tynwald and of Committees of the Manx Legislature, 1933– . Douglas, Island Development Co. (Annual)

These volumes contain reports on many aspects of both public and private law, on constitutional development and on the consolidation of the existing law.

ISLE OF MAN

Standing orders of the House of Keys, adopted 14th January 1964. Douglas, Island Development Co., 1964. 75 + xvip.

ISLE OF MAN

Standing orders of the Legislative Council, adopted 5th April 1966. Douglas, Island Development Co., 1966. 22p.

ISLE OF MAN

Standing orders of Tynwald, adopted 9th January 1962. Douglas, Island Development Co., 1962. 80 + xvip.

ISLE OF MAN

Statutes of the Isle of Man, revised ed., vol. 1– . 1417/1824– . Douglas, Island Development Co., etc., 1883– .

This series is supplemented by annual volumes entitled *Acts of Tynwald*. Periodically these annual volumes are revised and incorporated in the series of Statutes.

ISLE OF MAN

Index to Statutes of the Isle of Man, in operation on the 6th July 1957. Douglas, Victoria Pr., 1959. ii + 475p.

ISLE OF MAN

The Times reports of debates in the Manx Legislature, vol. 1– , 1887– . Douglas, Island Development Co., etc.

Mostly annual volumes, each volume commencing with the autumn session of the legislature and ending in the following July. Debates in Tynwald Court, in the Legislative Council and in the House of Keys are fully reported: the reports are issued in parts and consolidated at the end of each legislative session. Volumes up to and including volume 49 (1931–32) have appendices containing *Reports of Boards of Tynwald and of Committees of the Manx Legislature*. These have subsequently been published separately (*see supra*).

c. Law reports

There are no current published Manx law reports. Fully indexed records of cases heard in the High Court of Justice of the Isle of Man, the Court of General Gaol Delivery and the High-Bailiff's Court are, however, preserved in the General Registry, Douglas. In addition, cases are reported in the Isle of Man newspapers. A number of important decisions on appeal from the Isle of Man to the Judicial Committee of the Privy Council have been reported in the various series of English law reports.

BLUETT, J. C.

The advocate's note book, being notes and minutes of cases heard and determined before the judicial tribunals of the Isle of Man. Douglas, Johnson, 1847. xiv + 564p.

FARRANT, R. D.

Digest of Manx cases heard and decided during the period 1925–47. Douglas, 1948. xiv + 136p.

d. Public law and the procedure of the courts

FARRANT, R. D.

Mann, its land tenure, constitution, lord's rent and deemsters. OUP, 1937. vii + 83p.

ISLE OF MAN. High Court of Justice

Rules of the High Court of Justice of the Isle of Man, 1952. Made under the Judicature Act, 1883. Douglas, 1952. iv + 137p.

JOHNSON, J.

A view of the jurisprudence of the Isle of Man, with the history of its ancient constitution, legislative government and extraordinary privileges; together with the practice of the courts. Edinburgh, printed by Ramsay, 1811. 234 + vip.

KNEALE, S. J.

Manx Coroners, revised ed. Douglas, printed by Victoria Pr., 1963. xiv + 70p.

e. Private law

MOORE, R. B.

The Isle of Man and international law. Douglas, Brown, 1926. ix + 54p.

SHERWOOD, R.

Manx law tenures; being a short treatise on the law relating to real estate in the Isle of Man, with notes by Sir J. Gell. Douglas, Robinson, 1899. viii + 152 + 13 + 11p.

XVII. THE COMMONWEALTH

Most of the works listed in the bibliography that follows are concerned in some measure with juridical aspects of the Commonwealth association, and with the status and inter-relationship of the countries of the Commonwealth, considered in terms of constitutional law. For this purpose, constitutional law includes Acts of the United Kingdom Parliament and of the legislatures of Commonwealth countries, statutory instruments made under the authority of statutes, instruments made by the Crown in virtue of its residuary prerogative powers, and decisions of the courts, and also the binding usages (or constitutional conventions) of Commonwealth relations and certain authoritative declarations that have been issued after Commonwealth conferences.

A preliminary warning is necessary. The legal order that the Commonwealth once embodied has partly disintegrated. Books written about the Commonwealth before 1931 are now only of historical interest. Books written a few years ago may already be largely out of date. But because the present constitutional structure of the Commonwealth is incomprehensible without some knowledge of its historical evolution from the British Empire, certain collections of authoritative documents and historical surveys have been included in the bibliography.

The Commonwealth, in mid-October 1972, consisted of the United Kingdom, 30 other full members (Canada, Australia, New Zealand, India, Bangladesh, Sri Lanka, Malaysia, Ghana, Nigeria, Cyprus, Sierra Leone, Tanzania, Jamaica, Trinidad and Tobago, Uganda, Kenya, Malawi, Malta, Zambia, The Gambia, Singapore, Guyana, Botswana, Lesotho, Barbados, Mauritius, Swaziland, Tonga, Western Samoa and Fiji); one "special member" (the independent Republic of Nauru); six internally self-governing states in association with the United Kingdom (Antigua, Dominica, Grenada, St. Christopher-Nevis-Anguilla, St. Lucia, and St. Vincent), and one (the Cook Islands) in association with New Zealand; and a dwindling number of colonies, protected states, protectorates and other dependent territories. The Channel Islands and the Isle of Man are also part of the Commonwealth.

The constitutional laws of colonies and other United Kingdom dependencies are to be found partly in Acts of the United Kingdom Parliament, partly in local legislation, but mainly in statutory and prerogative instruments made by the Queen in Council, which are published in the annual volumes of *Statutory Instruments* (HMSO).

The constitutional laws of the British associated states in the Caribbean are to be found in similar sources, and in particular the West Indies Act, 1967 and Orders in Council (published in *Statutory Instruments*) laying down their constitutions.

The constitutional laws of the full members of the Commonwealth (which are all sovereign states) are contained to a small extent in United Kingdom Acts, and for the rest, mainly in local legislation. Several of the independence constitutions, however, are still substantially those conferred immediately before the date of independence and published in *Statutory Instruments.*

No attempt will be made to present a full bibliography of books on the constitutional laws of individual countries, but a few selected works will be listed, together with bibliographical guidance.

Select Bibliography

Collections of Constitutions and other authoritative documents

DAWSON, R. MCG., ed.
The development of Dominion status, 1900–36. OUP, 1937, reprinted 1965 by Cass. xiv + 466p.

JENNINGS, Sir W. I.
Constitutional laws of the Commonwealth, 3rd ed. OUP, 1957. (Vol. 1: The Monarchies. A second volume, planned to cover countries other than monarchies, was never published. Previous edition, 1952, complete in one volume)

KEITH, A. B., ed.
Selected speeches and documents on British Colonial policy, 1763–1917. OUP, 1948, reprinted 1961. 2 vols in 1.

KEITH, A. B., ed.
Speeches and documents on the British Dominions, 1918–31. OUP, 1938, reprinted 1961. xlvii + 501p.

MADDEN, F., comp.
Imperial constitutional documents, 1765–1965: a supplement, 1st edition reprinted with additions. Oxford, Blackwell, 1966. viii + 119p. (A supplement to Keith's books)

MANSERGH, P. N. S., ed.
Documents and speeches on British Commonwealth affairs, 1931–52. OUP, 1953. 2 vols.

MANSERGH, P. N. S., ed.
Documents and speeches on Commonwealth affairs, 1952–62. OUP, 1963. xxi + 775p.

PEASLEE, A. J.
Constitutions of nations, 3rd ed. The Hague, Nijhoff, 1965–68. 4 vols.

Historical surveys

The following deal mainly with the dependent territories of the Commonwealth:

CAMBRIDGE HISTORY OF THE BRITISH EMPIRE. (General editor: J. H. Rose)
CUP, 1929–63. 8 vols in 9. (Vol. 1: The old Empire from the beginnings to 1783; vol. 2: The new Empire 1783–1870; vol. 3: The Empire-Commonwealth 1870–1919)

HANCOCK, Sir W. K.
Survey of British Commonwealth affairs. OUP, for the Royal Institute of International Affairs, 1937–42. 2 vols. in 3. (Vol. 1: Problems of nationality, 1918–36)

HOLDSWORTH, Sir W. S.
A history of English law. Methuen, 1903–66, reprinted 1966. (Various editions) (Vol. 2, pp. 35–139 and 229–79)

KEITH, A. B.
Constitutional history of the first British Empire. OUP, 1930. xi + 443p.

HALL, H. D.

Commonwealth: a history of the British Commonwealth of Nations. Van Nostrand Reinhold, 1971. xxxvi + 1015p.

KEITH, A. B.

Responsible government in the Dominions, 2nd ed. OUP, 1928. 2 vols.

MANSERGH, P. N. S.

The Commonwealth experience. Weidenfeld & Nicolson, 1969. xix + 471p.

MANSERGH, P. N. S.

Survey of British Commonwealth affairs: problems of external policy 1931–39. OUP, 1952. xx + 481p.

MANSERGH, P. N. S.

Survey of British Commonwealth affairs: problems of wartime co-operation and post-war change, 1939–52. OUP, 1958, reprinted 1968 by Cass. xvi + 469p.

The above two works were published as companion volumes to Hancock's *Survey* (see above)

WIGHT, M. J.

The development of the legislative council, 1606–1945. Faber & Faber, 1946. 187p.

For a good bibliographical guide, see:

WINKS, R. W., ed.

The historiography of the British Empire-Commonwealth. Durham, N. C., Duke UP, 1966. xiv + 596p.

YEARBOOK OF THE COMMONWEALTH, 1969– . HMSO.

(Successor to the *Commonwealth Office yearbook*, 1967–68, which itself replaced both the *Colonial Office list* and *Commonwealth Relations Office year book*, after the merging of the two Departments in August 1966)

Recent general works on Commonwealth relations

COWEN, Z.

The British Commonwealth of Nations in a changing world. Chicago, Northwestern UP, 1965. vii + 118p. (Julius Rosenthal lectures, 1964)

HAMILTON, W. B. and others, eds

A decade of the Commonwealth 1955–1964. Durham, N. C., Duke UP, 1966. xx + 567p. (Duke University Commonwealth Studies Center, Publications no. 25)

INGRAM, D.

The Commonwealth at work. Oxford, Pergamon Pr., 1969. viii + 151p.

MANSERGH, P. N. S.

The Commonwealth experience. Weidenfeld & Nicolson, 1969. xix + 471p.

MAZRUI, A. A.

The Anglo-African Commonwealth. Pergamon Pr., 1967. viii + 163p.

MILLER, J. D. B.

The Commonwealth in the world, 3rd ed. Duckworth, 1965. 304p.

WALKER, P. Gordon

The Commonwealth. Secker & Warburg, 1962. 408p.

Constitutional law of the Commonwealth

The most authoritative and comprehensive work on all legal aspects of Commonwealth affairs is:

ROBERTS-WRAY, Sir K. O.
Commonwealth and Colonial law. S, 1966. liv + 1008p.

Other general works, in the nature of monographs rather than encyclopaedic surveys

DE SMITH, S. A.
The vocabulary of Commonwealth relations. Athlone Pr., 1954. 27p.

FAWCETT, J. E. S.
The British Commonwealth in international law. S, 1963. xvii + 243p. (Library of world affairs, no. 61)

LATHAM, R. T. E.
The law and the Commonwealth. OUP, for the Royal Institute of International Affairs, 1949. (Reprinted from Hancock's *Survey of British Commonwealth affairs*, vol. 1: pp. 510–632)

The above, though dated, is a brilliant jurisprudential essay.

MARSHALL, G.
Parliamentary sovereignty and the Commonwealth. OUP, 1957. x + 277p.

PARRY, C.
Nationality and citizenship law of the Commonwealth and of the Republic of Ireland. S, 1957–60. 2 vols: Vol. 1, liv + 1021p. Vol. 2, xxiv + pp. 1023–1285 (Continuous pagination)

PHILLIPS, O. Hood
Constitutional and administrative law, 4th ed. SM, 1967. xxxix + 865p. (Part VII)

A succinct general review of the legal aspects of Commonwealth relations.

WHEARE, Sir K. C.
The constitutional structure of the Commonwealth. OUP, 1960. xiv + 201p.

WHEARE, Sir K. C.
The Statute of Westminster and Dominion status, 5th ed. OUP, 1953. xvi + 347p.

See also, on international law aspects of the Commonwealth association:

STEWART, R. B.
Treaty relations of the British Commonwealth of Nations. New York, Macmillan, 1939. xxi + 503p.

WILSON, R. R., ed.
International and comparative law of the Commonwealth. Durham, N.C., Duke UP, 1968. vii + 247p. (Duke University Commonwealth Studies Center, publication no. 33)

WILSON, R. R., ed.
The international law standard and Commonwealth developments. Durham, N.C., Duke UP, 1966. xii + 306p. (Duke University Commonwealth Studies Center, publication no. 27)

General legal works of reference

Apart from ROBERTS-WRAY, *ante*, two general works can be consulted:

ANNUAL SURVEY OF COMMONWEALTH LAW, 1965– . B.

An important new encyclopaedia.

HALSBURY'S LAWS OF ENGLAND, 3rd ed. B, 1952–64. 43 vols. (Suppl.) (Vol. 5: Commonwealth and Dependencies)

As volume 5 was published in 1953, it should only be used with the cumulative supplement.

Comparative works on the constitutional laws of individual Commonwealth countries

BURNS, Sir A., ed.
Parliament as an export. Allen & Unwin, 1966. 271p.

DE SMITH, S. A.
The new Commonwealth and its constitutions. S, 1964. xvi + 312p.

EVATT, H. V.
The King and his Dominion governors. 2nd ed. with a new introduction by Z. Cowen. Cass, 1967. xxxviii + 324p.

FORSEY, E. A.
The royal power of dissolution of parliament in the British Commonwealth. Toronto, OUP, 1943, reprinted with addenda and corrections, 1968. xxvii + 324p.

LEYS, C. and ROBSON, P., eds
Federation in East Africa. OUP, 1965. viii + 244p.

WATTS, R. L.
New federations: experiments in the Commonwealth. OUP, 1966. xii + 419p.

WISEMAN, H. V.
The Cabinet in the Commonwealth. S, 1958. xvi + 364p.

The following comparative works deal mainly but not exclusively with constitutional and legal questions in Commonwealth countries:

ANDERSON, J. N. D., ed.
Changing law in developing countries. Allen & Unwin, 1963. 292p. (Studies on modern Asia and Africa, no. 2)

FRANCK, T. M.
Comparative constitutional process: cases and materials. SM, 1968. xliii + 595p.

GROVES, H. E.
Comparative constitutional law: cases and materials. Dobbs Ferry, N.Y., Oceana, 1963. xxv + 628p.

MCKINNON, V. S.
Comparative federalism. The Hague, Nijhoff, 1964. xxvii + 188p.

SAWER, G.
Modern federalism. Watts, 1969. vii + 204p.

SHERIDAN, L. A.
Constitutional protection. Dobbs Ferry, N.Y., Oceana, 1963. li + 172p.

WHEARE, Sir K. C.
Federal government, 4th ed. OUP, 1963. 266p.

Constitutions and laws of dependent territories

The following well-known works are now mainly of historical interest:

HALL, W. E.
A treatise on the foreign powers and jurisdiction of the British Crown. OUP, 1894. xv + 304p.

JENKYNS, Sir H.
British rule and jurisdiction beyond the seas. OUP, 1902. xxiii + 300p.

WIGHT, M. J., ed.
British colonial constitutions, 1947. OUP, 1952. xxvi + 571p. (Bibliography, pp. xix + xx)
ROBERTS-WRAY, *ante*, is the leading modern work.

Bibliography

SWEET & MAXWELL, LTD.
A legal bibliography of the British Commonwealth of Nations, 2nd ed. SM, 1955–64. 7 vols. (Vol. 7: British Commonwealth excluding the United Kingdom, Australia, New Zealand, Canada, India and Pakistan)

Customary and modern law

ALLOTT, A. N.
Judicial and legal systems in Africa, 2nd ed. B, 1970. xi + 314p.
ALLOTT, A. N.
New essays in African law. B, 1970. xxxiv + 348p.
ELIAS, T. O.
British Colonial law. S, 1962. xxvi + 323p.
PARK, A. E. W.
The sources of Nigerian law. SM, 1963. xvii + 161p.
ROBERTS-WRAY, Sir K. O.
Commonwealth and Colonial law. S, 1966. liv + 1008p.

Transplantation of the Common Law and British legal education

DANIELS, W. C. E.
The Common Law in West Africa. B, 1964. lvi + 424p.
GOWER, L. C. B.
The independent Africa: the challenge to the legal profession. Cambridge, Mass., Harvard UP, 1967. viii + 154p. (Oliver Wendell Holmes lectures, 1966)
LASKIN, B.
The British tradition in Canadian law. S, 1969. xv + 138p. (Hamlyn lectures, 21st series)
SETALVAD, M. C.
The Common Law in India. S, 1960. viii + 227p. (Hamlyn lectures, 12th series)

Constitutional laws of individual Commonwealth countries

N.B.—Not every book cited is fully up-to-date. For developments since 1964, reference should be made to the *Annual Survey of Commonwealth Law*, q.v.

Australia

CAMPBELL, E.
Parliamentary privilege in Australia. CUP, 1966. vii + 218p.
COWEN, Z.
Federal jurisdiction in Australia. OUP, 1960. xv + 212p.
HOWARD, C.
Australian federal constitutional law. Sydney, Law Book Co. of Australasia, 1968. xlviii + 387p.

LANE, P. H.
Some principles and sources of Australian constitutional law. Sydney, Law Book Co. of Australasia, 1964. xxii + 303p.

LUMB, R. D.
The constitutions of the Australian states, 3rd ed. Brisbane, Univ. of Queensland Pr., 1968. xvii + 127p.

MITCHELL, R. Else
Essays on the Australian constitution, 2nd ed. Sydney, Law Book Co. of Australasia, 1961. xxxii + 380p.

SAWER, G.
Australian federalism in the courts. CUP, 1967. vii + 262p.

SAWER, G.
Cases on the constitution of the Commonwealth of Australia, 3rd ed. Sydney, Law Book Co. of Australasia, 1964. xxxii + 674p.

WYNES, W. A.
Legislative, executive and judicial powers in Australia, 3rd ed. Sydney, Law Book Co. of Australasia, 1962. lxviii + 775p.

Canada

LASKIN, B.
Canadian constitutional law, 3rd ed. revised. Toronto, Carswell, 1969. xxxii + 1104p.

LEDERMAN, W. R. ed.
The courts and the Canadian constitution. Toronto, McClelland & Stewart, 1964. 248p.

LYON, J. N. and ATKEY, R. G.
Canadian constitutional law in a modern perspective. Univ. of Toronto Pr., 1970. vi + 1351p.

SCHMEISER, D. A.
Civil liberties in Canada. OUP, 1964. xviii + 302p.

STRAYER, B. L.
Judicial review of legislation in Canada. Toronto, Univ. of Toronto Pr., 1968. xiv + 275p.

TARNOPOLSKY, W. S.
The Canadian Bill of Rights. Toronto, Carswell, 1966. xxix + 246p.

New Zealand

ROBSON, J. L., ed.
New Zealand: the development of its laws and constitution, 2nd ed. S, 1967. xx + 532p. (The British Commonwealth: the development of its laws and constitutions, vol. 4)

SCOTT, K. J.
The New Zealand constitution. OUP, 1962. 188p.

Ceylon

JENNINGS, Sir W. I.
The constitution of Ceylon, 3rd ed. OUP, 1953. xii + 294p.

JENNINGS, Sir W. I. and TAMB'-AIYA, H. V.
The dominion of Ceylon: the development of its laws and constitution. S, 1952. xvi + 319p. (The British Commonwealth: the development of its laws and constitutions, vol. 7)

These books deal with the constitution of Ceylon prior to the adoption of the republican constitution of Sri Lanka in 1971.

India

BASU, D. D.
Commentary on the constitution of India. Calcutta, Sarkar, 1965–71. 9 vols.

GLEDHILL, A.
Fundamental rights in India. S, 1955. xvi + 134p.

GLEDHILL, A.
The Republic of India: the development of its laws and constitution, 2nd ed. S, 1964. xi + 399p. (The British Commonwealth: the development of its laws and constitutions, vol. 6)

SEERVAI, H. M.
Constitutional law of India. Bombay, Tripathi, 1967. xlviii + 1119p. (Suppl.)

Malaysia

SHERIDAN, L. A., ed.
Malaya and Singapore, the Borneo territories: the development of their laws and constitutions. S, 1961. xxii + 510p. (The British Commonwealth: the development of its laws and constitutions, vol. 9)

SHERIDAN, L. A. and GROVES, H. E.
The constitution of Malaysia. Dobbs Ferry, N. Y., Oceana, 1967. xxxiv + 398p.

Ghana

ELIAS, T. O.
Ghana and Sierra Leone: the development of their laws and constitutions. S, 1962. xii + 334p. (The British Commonwealth: the development of its laws and constitutions, vol. 10)

GHANA
The constitution of the Republic of Ghana, 1969. Accra, Ghana Publishing Corporation, 1969. 156p.

Kenya

GHAI, Y. P. and MCAUSLAN, J. P. W. B.
Public law and political change in Kenya. OUP, 1970. xxviii + 536p.

Nigeria

ELIAS, T. O.
Nigeria: the development of its laws and constitution. S, 1967. xii + 491p. (The British Commonwealth: the development of its laws and constitutions, vol. 14)

This work covers the period up to the military coups d'état.

Sierra Leone

ELIAS, T. O.

Ghana and Sierra Leone: the development of their laws and constitutions. S, 1962. xii + 334p. (The British Commonwealth: the development of its laws and constitutions, vol. 10)

There have been constitutional changes since this book was published.

Southern Rhodesia

PALLEY, C.

The constitutional history and law of Southern Rhodesia, 1888–1965. OUP, 1966. xxv + 872p.

Tanzania

COLE, J. S. R. and DENISON, W. N.

Tanganyika: the development of its laws and constitution. S, 1964. xi + 339p. (The British Commonwealth: the development of its laws and constitutions, vol. 12)

This work only covers the period before the union with Zanzibar.

Uganda

MORRIS, H. F. and READ, J. S.

Uganda: the development of its laws and constitution. S, 1966. xvi + 448p. (The British Commonwealth: the development of its laws and constitutions, vol. 13)

This work is of current relevance except for its commentary on the now superseded constitution.

Periodicals

The following journals published in England include from time to time notes and articles on the constitutional laws of the Commonwealth.

ANNUAL SURVEY OF COMMONWEALTH LAW, 1965– . B.

INTERNATIONAL AND COMPARATIVE LAW QUARTERLY, vol. 1– , 1952– . British Institute of International and Comparative Law, etc.

JOURNAL OF AFRICAN LAW, vol. 1– , 1957– . B.

JOURNAL OF COMMONWEALTH POLITICAL STUDIES, vol. 1– , 1961– . Leicester UP.

MODERN LAW REVIEW, vol. 1– , 1937– . S.

PARLIAMENTARIAN, 1920– . The Commonwealth Parliamentary Association. (1920–1965, entitled *Journal of the Parliaments of the Empire/Commonwealth*)

PUBLIC LAW, 1956– . S.

ROUND TABLE: a quarterly review of the politics of the British Commonwealth, 1910– . Macmillan.

TABLE: being the Journal of the Society of Clerks-at-the-Table in Commonwealth Parliaments, vol. 1– , 1932– . (1932–52 entitled *Journal of the Society . . . in Empire Parliaments*)

XVIII. JURISPRUDENCE

In England the term Jurisprudence is generally used to cover what is commonly referred to as legal philosophy or general theory of law in Continental practice. It never corresponds to *jurisprudence* in the French sense, which should be translated *case law* or *judge-made law*.

Modern English jurisprudence goes back to Austin, who was mainly interested in the analysis of legal concepts, including the definition of law itself. Austin's jurisprudence was largely derived from BENTHAM, the great utilitarian, who developed his science of legislation on utilitarian principles. Bentham also developed a critical jurisprudence from which Austin derived his own analytical approach, and for a long time after Bentham and Austin jurisprudence in England was largely identified with the analytical school.

Apart from the analytical school, the main contribution to jurisprudence in this country during the nineteenth century was in the field of historical jurisprudence whose principal exponent was Sir Henry Maine. Sir Henry Maine was influenced by the German jurist Savigny, but developed historical jurisprudence in a distinctively English way emphasising its connection with anthropology.

In more recent time the most significant contributions to English jurisprudence have been made by Professor H. L. A. HART, who while strongly critical of many aspects of Austinian jurisprudence, has nevertheless extended the frontiers of the analytical approach and imparted to it many fresh insights. Since the days of Bentham and Austin the natural law school of jurisprudence has never played a very significant role on the English scene, but the relationship of law to morality has continued in recent years to excite juristic interest. The publication of the Wolfenden Committee Report on *Prostitution and Homosexuality* in 1957 gave fresh impetus to this issue, and has led to an important controversy in which Professor HART and Lord DEVLIN have been the main protagonists.

Although the most significant influence in recent English jurisprudence has probably been that of the American Roscoe POUND and his school of sociological jurisprudence, it cannot be said that English jurisprudence has itself made any very conspicuous contribution in this sphere, at any rate unless claim is made to some of the writings of Julius STONE and Wolfgang FRIEDMANN. Another important influence on English jurisprudence has been Hans KELSEN, whose *Pure theory of law*, while possessing considerable affinities with the Austinian approach, was not derived from it, and indeed differs from it in important respects.

For the sake of completeness, some writings are included in the Select Bibliography which are representative of certain important trends or influences in English jurisprudence at the present day, but which are not the work of English writers.

Select Bibliography

BENTHAM, J.

A fragment on government and *An introduction to the principles of morals and legislation*, edited by Wilfrid Harrison. Oxford, Blackwell, 1948. lxvii + 435p.

BENTHAM, J.
An introduction to the principles of morals and legislation, edited by J. H. Burns and H. L. A. Hart. Athlone Pr., 1970. xliii + 343p. (The Collected Works of Jeremy Bentham)

BENTHAM, J.
Of laws in general, edited by H. L. A. Hart. Athlone Pr., 1970. xliii + 342p. (The collected works of Jeremy Bentham, principles of legislation)

BUCKLAND, W. W.
Some reflections on jurisprudence. CUP, 1945. viii + 118p.

CROSS, A. R. N.
Precedent in English law, 2nd ed. OUP, 1968. ix + 233p.

DEVLIN, P. A., Baron Devlin
The enforcement of morals. OUP, 1965. xiv + 139p.

DIAS, R. W. M.
Jurisprudence, 3rd ed. B, 1970. lxviii + 606p.

DOWRICK, F. E.
Justice according to the English common lawyers. B, 1961. ix + 251p.

FRIEDMANN, W. G.
Law in a changing society, 2nd ed. B, 1972. 580p.

GINSBERG, M., ed.
Law and opinion in England in the twentieth century. S, 1959. viii + 407p.

GLUCKMAN, M., ed.
Ideas and procedures in African customary law: studies presented at the eighth International African Seminar at the Haile Sellassie I University, Addis Ababa, January, 1966. OUP, for the International African Institute, 1969. xiii + 361p.

GLUCKMAN, M.
The judicial process among the Barotse of Northern Rhodesia, 2nd ed. Manchester UP, for the Institute for Social Research, University of Zambia, 1967. xxv + 469p.

GREAT BRITAIN. Committee on homosexual offences and prostitution (Chairman: Sir John Wolfenden)
Report. HMSO, 1957. 155p. (Cmnd 247)

GUEST, A. G., ed.
Oxford essays in jurisprudence. OUP, 1961. xviii + 292p.

HART, H. L. A.
The concept of law. OUP, 1961. x + 263p.

HART, H. L. A.
Law, liberty and morality. OUP, 1963. 88p. (The Harry Camp lectures at Stanford University, 1962)

HART, H. L. A.
The morality of the criminal law. OUP, 1965. 52p. (Lionel Cohen lectures, 1964)

HART, H. L. A.
Punishment and responsibility: essays in the philosophy of law. Oxford, Clarendon Pr., 1968. ix + 271p.

JOLOWICZ, H. F.
Lectures on jurisprudence . . . edited by J. A. Jolowicz. Athlone Pr., 1963. xxi + 391p. (University of London legal series, no. 7)

KANTOROWICZ, H. U.
The definition of law, edited by A. H. Campbell. CUP, 1958. xxiii + 112p.

KELSEN, H.
Pure theory of law: translation from the 2nd (revised and enlarged) German edition by Max Knight. CUP, 1967. x + 356p. (2nd edition originally published as *Reine Rechtslehre*. Vienna, Deulicke, 1960)
LLOYD, D., Lord Lloyd of Hampstead
The idea of law. Penguin Books, 1964, revised 1972. 363p.
LLOYD, D., Lord Lloyd of Hampstead
Introduction to jurisprudence, 3rd ed. S, 1972. xxxix + 873p.
MAINE, Sir H. J. S.
Ancient law, its connection with the early history of society and its relation to modern ideas . . . with an introduction and notes by Sir Frederick Pollock, new ed. Murray, 1930. xxiv + 440p.
MITCHELL, B.
Law, morality and religion in a secular society. OUP, 1967. ix + 141p.
MONTROSE, J. L.
Precedent in English law, and other essays, edited by H. G. Hanbury. Dublin, Irish UP, 1968. v + 368p.
OLIVECRONA, K.
Law as fact, 2nd ed. S, 1971. viii + 320p.
PATON, Sir G. W.
A textbook of jurisprudence, 3rd ed. by D. P. Derham. OUP, 1964. xv + 600p. (New edition in preparation)
POLLOCK, Sir F.
Jurisprudence and legal essays . . . selected and introduced by A. L. Goodhart. Macmillan, 1961. xlviii + 243p.
POUND, R.
An introduction to the philosophy of law. SM, 1959. 201p.
RAZ, J.
The concept of a legal system: an introduction to the theory of legal system. Oxford, Clarendon Pr., 1970. ix + 212p.
ROSS, A. N. C.
On law and justice. S, 1958. xi + 383p.
SALMOND, Sir J. W.
Jurisprudence, 12th ed. by P. J. Fitzgerald. SM, 1966. xxiii + 481p.
SAWER, G.
Law in society. OUP, 1965. [7] + 215p.
STONE, J.
Human law and human justice. S, 1965. xxiii + 415p.
STONE, J.
Legal system and lawyers' reasoning. S, 1964. xxiv + 454p.
STONE, J.
Social dimensions of law and justice. S, 1966. xxxv + 933p.
SUMMERS, R. S., ed.
Essays in legal philosophy. Oxford, Blackwell, 1968. viii + 307p.
SUMMERS, R. S., ed.
More essays in legal philosophy: general assessments of legal philosophies. Oxford, Blackwell, 1971. viii + 161p.
WORTLEY, B. A.
Jurisprudence. Manchester UP, 1967. xxi + 473p.

XIX. ROMAN LAW

One consequence of the early centralisation of the Common law and of the development of the Inns of Court for its study is that Roman law has never enjoyed, in the development of English law and the training of the English lawyer, the eminence that it obtained on the continent. Only recently, in the last year or so, the elementary acquaintance with the Institutes of Justinian which was required in the professional examination for admission to the Bar, has been eliminated and, from 1971 no examination in Roman law will be set for this purpose; no knowledge of Roman law at all is or has ever been required of the prospective solicitor.

In the universities, the study of Roman law was fostered from early times, originally as a necessary complement to study of the Canon law and later somewhat as an element of a general classical education. In the last century or so, the universities have accepted Law as a suitable branch of academic study and a place was found in the Law curriculum for Roman law. But in most universities all that has been required of the student has been a one year course based on the Institutes of Justinian and—in some—of Gaius. Even that modest requirement has now been dispensed with or the Roman law course has been made optional in several universities. However, there is still a number of universities in which the indicated course of Roman law is still compulsory and some in which additional optional courses of further study of Roman law are available; these courses generally require the study of a title or selected titles of the Digest or of a particular topic in Roman law. It might however fairly be added that, while general study of Roman law by all university students is declining, there has, certainly since World War II, been a marked development in the specialist study of Roman law, as will be evident from the range of monographs.

The Cambridge Ancient and Mediaeval Histories contain brief but highly informative chapters for providing a background to the study of Roman law; but the principal work is JOLOWICZ's *Historical introduction*, with comprehensive references to current literature, though there is also now available KUNKEL's *Roman legal and constitutional history*, an excellent translation by KELLY of the leading German students history with comprehensive bibliography.

The principal texts used are the Institutes of Gaius and Justinian: of Gaius, the best edition is ZULUETA and of Justinian the standard edition is MOYLE. The nature of more specialised studies in England has resulted in the edition of individual titles of the Digest, specimens being ZULUETA's *Digest XLI. 1 & 2*, and JOLOWICZ's *Digest XLVII. 2*.

English general treatises on Roman law follow the general plan and order of the Institutes. The leading work is BUCKLAND's *Textbook* which appeared in a new edition in 1963; while the substance of the work was not appreciably altered, valuable bibliographical introductions take account of work since the previous edition in 1932. SCHULZ's *Classical Roman law* is a fully documented work by a distinguished scholar and its precursor by ROBY is still of interest. For the real beginner, NICHOLAS is an excellent introduction and other books for the elementary student are BUCKLAND's *Manual*, LEAGE and LEE, the last of which contains a translation of almost the whole of Justinian's Institutes. CROOK is an interesting new approach by an ancient historian who, though interested in the law, is not a lawyer. An introductory collection of material for people essentially with no classical background is LAWSON, *Roman law reader.*

Brief introductions to Roman law are to be found in GIBBON's famous chapter, praised by Jhering and still worth reading, and in ZULUETA's and BUCKLAND's chapters in the *Cambridge Ancient History* and ROBY's chapter in the *Cambridge Mediaeval History*. MAINE contains much Roman material, handled in a way not unlike JHERING's in his *Geist des römischen Rechts*; and though many of his opinions are no longer accepted, he must still be read by every serious student.

SCRUTTON is an old but comprehensive contribution to its topic, on which further reading may be found in VINOGRADOFF, and, above all, in POLLOCK AND MAITLAND, HOLDSWORTH and PLUCKNETT, all listed in Chapter III, "History of English law". A comprehensive treatment of some aspects of this topic is to be found in JOLOWICZ, *Roman foundations.*

Roman law and common law is an excellent introduction to a comparison of the two systems by a distinguished Romanist, BUCKLAND, and a distinguished common lawyer, MCNAIR. It should be supplemented by BUCKLAND's *Equity in Roman Law*. ZULUETA's *Roman law of sale* and LAWSON's *Negligence in the civil law* provide valuable guides to the comparative study of particular topics.

There is no periodical devoted to Roman law, but articles on Romanist topics appear in the ordinary legal periodicals, especially *Law quarterly review*, *Cambridge law journal* and *Juridical review*—and in classical reviews, more particularly *Journal of Roman studies*; it might be added that the new series of the *Irish Jurist* also carries articles on ancient, and particularly Roman, law.

Select Bibliography

a. Historical and introductory

BUCKLAND, W. W.
"Classical Roman law", in *Cambridge Ancient History*, vol. XI (CUP, 1936), pp. 806–53.

GIBBON, E.
The history of the decline and fall of the Roman Empire, 2nd ed. by J. B. Bury. Methuen, 1925. 7 vols. (Vol. IV: Chapter 44, p. 470)

JHERING, R. von
Geist des römischen Rechts auf den verschiedenen Stufen seiner Entwicklung, 6th ed. Leipzig, Breitkopf und Härtel, 1906–23. 3 vols.

JOLOWICZ, H. F.
Historical introduction to the study of Roman law, 2nd ed. CUP, 1952. xxv + 596p.

KUNKEL, W.
An introduction to Roman legal and constitutional history, translated from the 4th German edition by J. M. Kelly. Oxford, Clarendon Pr., 1966. x + 217p.

LAST, H. M.
"The principate and the administration", in *Cambridge Ancient History*, vol. XI (CUP, 1936), pp. 393–434.

LAST, H. M.
"Rome and the Empire", in *Cambridge Ancient History*, vol. XI (CUP, 1936), pp. 435–78.

MAINE, Sir H. J. S.

Ancient law, its connection with the early history of society and its relation to modern ideas . . . with an introduction and notes by Sir Frederick Pollock, new ed. Murray, 1930. xxiv + 440p.

REID, J. S.

"The reorganisation of the Empire", in *Cambridge Medieval History*, vol. I (CUP, 1911), pp. 24–54.

ROBY, H. J.

"Roman Law", in *Cambridge Medieval History*, vol. II (CUP, 1913), pp. 53–108.

ZULUETA, F. de

"The development of law under the Republic", in *Cambridge Ancient History*, vol. IX (CUP, 1932), pp. 842–81.

b. Texts and translations

JOLOWICZ, H. F., ed.

Digest XLVII 2. De furtis, . . . with introduction, translation and notes. CUP, 1940. xci + 137p.

LAWSON, F. H.

The Roman law reader. Dobbs Ferry, N.Y., Oceana, 1969. xi + 242p.

MONRO, C. H.

The Digest of Justinian. CUP, 1904–09. 2 vols. (Books I–XV, translation only)

MOYLE, J. B.

Imperatoris Iustiniani institutionum libri quattuor, with introductions, commentary and excursus, 5th ed. Oxford, Clarendon Pr., 1912. vi + 682p.

MOYLE, J. B.

The Institutes of Justinian, translated into English, 5th ed. OUP, 1913. viii + 220p.

ZULUETA, F. de

Digest XLI, 1 and 2, with a translation and commentary. Oxford, Clarendon Pr., 1950. 111p.

ZULUETA, F. de

The Institutes of Gaius. OUP, 1946–53. 2 vols. (Vol. 1: Text and translation, vol. 2: Commentary)

c. General treatises

BUCKLAND, W. W.

Elementary principles of the Roman private law. CUP, 1912. viii + 419p.

BUCKLAND, W. W.

The main institutions of Roman private law. CUP, 1931. ix + 410p.

BUCKLAND, W. W.

A manual of Roman private law. CUP, 1939. xxix + 434p.

BUCKLAND, W. W.

A textbook of Roman law from Augustus to Justinian, 3rd ed. revised by Peter Stein. CUP, 1963. xxx + 764p.

CROOK, J. A.

Law and life of Rome. Thames & Hudson, 1967. 349p.

LEAGE, R. W.

Roman private law founded on the Institutes of Gaius and Justinian, 3rd ed. by A. M. Prichard. Macmillan, 1961. xxv + 502p.

LEE, R. W.

The elements of Roman law: with a translation of the Institutes of Justinian. SM, 1956. xxviii + 499p.

NICHOLAS, J. K. B. M.

An introduction to Roman law. Oxford, Clarendon Pr., 1962. xv + 281p.

ROBY, H. J.

Roman private law in the times of Cicero and of the Antonines. CUP, 1902. 2 vols.

SCHULZ, F.

Classical Roman law. Oxford, Clarendon Pr., 1951. xii + 650p. (There are bibliographies at the end of each chapter)

d. Monographs on specialized topics

BONNER, S. F.

Roman declamation in the late Republic and early Empire. Liverpool UP, 1949. viii + 177p. (Bibliography, pp. 169–177)

BUCKLAND, W. W.

Equity in Roman law. Univ. of London Pr., 1911. vii + 136p.

BUCKLAND, W. W.

Roman law of slavery: the condition of the slave in private law from Augustus to Justinian. CUP, 1908, reprinted 1970. xiv + 735p.

BUCKLAND, W. W. and MCNAIR, Sir A. D.

Roman law and common law, 2nd ed. revised by F. H. Lawson. CUP, 1952, reprinted 1965. xx + 439p.

CORBETT, P. E.

The Roman law of marriage. OUP, 1930. xii + 254p. (Bibliography, pp. ix–xii)

DAUBE, D.

Roman law: linguistic, social and philosophical aspects. Edinburgh UP, 1969. [8] + 205p. (Gray lectures, 1966)

DAUBE, D., ed.

Studies in the Roman law of sale, dedicated to the memory of Francis de Zulueta. OUP, 1959. xi + 195p.

DUFF, P. W.

Personality in Roman private law. CUP, 1938. xiii + 241p. (Bibliography, pp. xi–xiii)

GREENIDGE, A. H. J.

Infamia: its place in Roman public and private law. OUP, 1894. xii + 219p.

GREENIDGE, A. H. J.

The legal procedure of Cicero's time. OUP, 1901. xiii + 599p.

HONORÉ, A. M.

Gaius. A biography. OUP, 1962. xviii + 183p.

JOLOWICZ, H. F.

Roman foundations of modern law. OUP, 1957. xx + 217p.

KANTOROWICZ, H. U. and BUCKLAND, W. W., eds

Studies in the glossators of the Roman law: newly discovered writings of the twelfth century. CUP, 1938. xvi + 323p.

KELLY, J. M.

Roman litigation. OUP, 1966. viii + 176p.

LAWSON, F. H.

A common lawyer looks at the civil law. Ann Arbor, University of Michigan Law School, 1955. 238p. (Thomas M. Cooley lectures, 5th series)

LAWSON, F. H., ed.
Negligence in the civil law: introduction and select texts. OUP, 1950. xiv + 341p.

NYS, E.
Pages d'histoire du droit en Angleterre: le droit romain, le droit des gens et le college des docteurs en droit civil. Bruxelles, Weissenbruch, 1910. 159p.

SCHULZ, F.
History of Roman legal science. OUP, 1946, reprinted with new addenda, 1953. xvi + 358p.

SCHULZ, F.
Principles of Roman law, translated from a text revised and enlarged by the author, by M. Wolff. OUP, 1936. xvi + 268p. (Original German edition, entitled *Prinzipien des römischen Rechts,* published 1934 by Duncker &Humblot)

SCRUTTON, Sir T. E.
The influence of the Roman law on the law of England. CUP, 1885. xvi + 199p. (Cambridge University Yorke Prize essay, 1884)

SHERWIN-WHITE, A. N.
Roman society and Roman law in the New Testament. OUP, 1963. xii + 204p. (Sarum lectures, 1960–61)

STEIN, P.
Fault in the formation of contract in Roman law and Scots law. Edinburgh, Oliver & Boyd, 1958. 216p. (Aberdeen University series, no. 140)

STEIN, P.
Regulae juris: from juristic rules to legal maxims. Edinburgh UP, 1966. x + 206p.

STRACHAN-DAVIDSON, J. L.
Problems of the Roman criminal law. OUP, 1912. 2 vols.

VINOGRADOFF, Sir P.
Roman law in medieval Europe, 2nd ed. with a preface by F. de Zulueta. OUP, 1929. 155p.

WATSON, A.
Contract of mandate in Roman law. OUP, 1961. (ix) + 223p.

WATSON, A.
The law of obligations in the later Roman Republic. OUP, 1965. xii + 295p.

WATSON, A.
The law of persons in the later Roman Republic. OUP, 1967. xii + 269p.

WATSON, A.
The law of property in the later Roman Republic. OUP, 1968. xii + 243p.

WATSON, A.
The law of succession in the later Roman Republic. OUP, 1970. xii + 209p.

ZULUETA, F. de
The Roman law of sale. OUP, 1945. xi + 265p.

e. Periodicals

CAMBRIDGE LAW JOURNAL, vol. 1– , 1921– , CUP.

IRISH JURIST, new series, vol. 1– , 1966– . Dublin, Jurist Publishing Co. Ltd. (Continues *Irish jurist and reports,* 1935–65)

JOURNAL OF ROMAN STUDIES, 1911– . Society for the Promotion of Roman Studies.

JURIDICAL REVIEW: the law journal of the Scottish Universities, 1889– . Edinburgh, Green.

LAW QUARTERLY REVIEW, vol. 1– , 1885– . S.

XX. CANON LAW (OR ECCLESIASTICAL LAW)

It is not possible wholly to differentiate canon law from ecclesiastical law and the terms are frequently treated as synonymous, though often canon law is used to denote the more fundamental concepts with theological significance, while ecclesiastical law is concerned with comparative minutiae affecting the constitution and governance of the Church of England and the rights and obligations of her members. In this sense ecclesiastical law may be regarded as a branch of English canon law. Both, however, it is important to remember, are part of the law of England, susceptible to modification by Act of Parliament and enforced in the courts, both secular and ecclesiastical, the ecclesiastical courts being as fully the Queen's courts as are the secular courts.

The Church of England having always been an established Church, there were even before the Reformation many legally recognized local variations from the main body of Church law, though that main body provided the basis of English Church law. Since the Reformation, that main body has continued to provide the basis of English Church law, though with many important modifications. In order, therefore, to discover English Church law, it is necessary to have regard, *inter alia*, to the general body of canon law in so far as it was accepted in England before the Reformation, as well as to Acts of Parliament and to decided cases as in any other branch of English law. In this connection, however, it should be borne in mind that, although English habits of thought have permeated English Church law, so that precedent is quoted in the ecclesiastical courts as well as in the secular courts, precedent is not applied as strictly in the ecclesiastical courts as it is in the secular courts. In particular, a new ecclesiastical custom can quickly grow and change the law; desuetude is accorded some recognition; and fresh discoveries as a result of historical research can affect the binding force of precedent. The student should, therefore, beware of too readily accepting any statement as to a point of Church law, whether contained in a textbook or given in a judgment.

A further consequence of the identification of Church law with secular law is that, for a complete ecclesiastical picture, recourse must often be had to secular books on law. Thus, the nature of the parson's freehold in the churchyard cannot be appreciated without reference to the law of real property; and the Church's law with regard to marriage cannot be adequately considered apart from the secular law concerning marriage, divorce and nullity.

Indeed, research into English Church law is beset with dangers and difficulties and cannot be undertaken without covering a very wide field. The list of books given here contains but a small selection intended to provide no more than a starting-ground. The authorities quoted in these works will provide fruitful avenues for further legal research. Even so, it must be remembered that for a full understanding recourse should often be had to theological and historical treatises rather than to legal text-books (for example, on the Thirty-Nine Articles) and that no reference is made here to such works. The beginner would probably do well to start with the Report on *The Canon Law of the Church of England* and then go on to the article in HALSBURY. After that he would be wise to take advice.

The turn of the century saw a considerable controversy on the question whether Roman canon law took effect *ipso iure* in mediaeval England or only through acceptance by the English provinces; in this the protagonists were the distinguished historian and bishop, STUBBS, and the great lawyer-historian, MAITLAND. Otherwise there is little to show outside the periodical literature, especially the *Journal of ecclesiastical history*.

The law as it affects denominations and religious bodies other than the Church of England is to be found scattered over a wide field in other branches of the law, though some specific reference is contained in HALSBURY. For the most part, however, no separate treatment is provided, because the internal rules of these bodies do not form part of the general law of England. Like the rules of any other private association or club, they are contractual in their nature and can best be considered, therefore, under the law of contract or under the law relating to clubs and partnership and common and joint ownership.

A short list of English books on Roman Catholic canon law is appended. A foreign lawyer will probably gain most conveniently an insight into the constitutions and legal position of the very important Protestant Nonconformist Churches, such as the Methodist, Presbyterian, Congregational and Baptist Churches, by consulting one of the year-books, such as the *Congregational Yearbook*.

GREEN gives a good view of the Church in Wales, which, though formerly a part of the Church of England and still in full communion with it, has been disestablished.

Select Bibliography

a. General

CHURCH ASSEMBLY

Opinions of the legal board, 4th ed. Church Assembly Press & Publications Board, 1939. 251p.

CHURCH ASSEMBLY

Recent opinions on Church law, 4th ed. Church Assembly Press & Publications Board, 1947. 45p.

CHURCH OF ENGLAND

The Book of Common Prayer. Eyre & Spottiswoode, 1936. viii + 575p.

CHURCH OF ENGLAND

The Canons of the Church of England: canons ecclesiastical promulgated by the Convocations of Canterbury and York in 1964 and 1969. Society for Promoting Christian Knowledge, 1969. xiii + 94p.

CHURCH OF ENGLAND

The revised Canons of the Church of England further considered. Society for Promoting Christian Knowledge, 1954. [4] + 189p.

CHURCH OF ENGLAND. Archbishops' Commission on Canon Law

The canon law of the Church of England. Report. Society for Promoting Christian Knowledge, 1947. xvi + 244p.

CHURCH OF ENGLAND. Commission on Ecclesiastical Courts

The ecclesiastical courts: principles of reconstruction, being the report of the Commission ... set up by the Archbishops of Canterbury and York in 1951. (Lloyd-Jacob report). Society for Promoting Christian Knowledge, 1954. xix + 98p.

CRIPPS, Sir H. W.

A practical treatise on the law relating to the Church and the clergy. SM, 1937. lxiii + 637p.

DALE, Sir W. L.
The law of the parish church, 4th ed. B, 1967. xxvi + 183p.

GREEN, C. A. H.
The setting of the constitution of the Church in Wales. SM, 1937. viii + 376p.

HALSBURY'S LAWS OF ENGLAND, 3rd ed. B, 1952–64. 43 vols. (Suppl.) (Vol. 13: Ecclesiastical law, pp. 1–539)

LACEY, T. A.
Marriage in church and state, revised ed. by R. C. Mortimer. Society for Promoting Christian Knowledge, 1947. xxi + 219p.

MACMORRAN, K. M.
A handbook for churchwardens and parochial church councillors, new ed. by K. M. Macmorran and K. J. T. Elphinstone. Oxford, Mowbrays, 1971. vii + 134p.

MAITLAND, F. W.
Roman canon law in the Church of England: six essays. Methuen, 1898. vii + 184p.

MOORE, E. G.
An introduction to English canon law. OUP, 1967. xv + 176p.

PHILLIMORE, Sir R. J.
The ecclesiastical law of the Church of England, 2nd ed. by Sir W. G. F. Phillimore. SM, 1895. 2 vols.

N.B.—The above is suggested for reference only.

b. The Roman Catholic Church

CRONIN, C. J.
The new matrimonial legislation: a commentary on the decree of the Sacred Congregation of the Council, Ne temere, published on the 2nd of August 1907 . . . on betrothal and marriage, 2nd ed. revised and corrected. London, Washbourne and New York, Benziger, 1909. iv + 320p.

GUY, R. E.
The synods in English being the text of the four synods of Westminster translated into English. Stratford-upon-Avon, St. Gregory's Pr., 1886. iv + 312 + ivp.

LATTEY, C., ed.
Church and state: papers from the Summer School of Catholic Studies held in Cambridge, 27th July–6th August 1935. Burns, Oates & Washbourne, 1935. xiv + 338p.

MAHONEY, E. J.
Marriage preliminaries: the instruction "Sacrosanctum", 29 June 1941, with a commentary. Burns, Oates & Washbourne, 1949. 93p.

ROCCA, F.
Manual of canon law, translated by A. Thatcher. St. Paul, Minn., Bruce, 1959. 623 + xxp.

WESTMINSTER. Province. Roman Catholic Synod
Decreta quattuor Conciliorum Provincialium Westmonasteriensium, 1852–73, 2nd ed. Burns & Oates, 1885. xii + 454 + xxiiip.

There is no periodical devoted to Canonist studies but articles on Canon law topics appear in the following:

CLERGY REVIEW: a magazine for the clergy, permissu superiorum, 1931– . Tablet Publishing Co.

CONCILIUM: theology in the age of renewal, 1965– . (Published in several languages. English edition available from P.O. Box 497, London S.W.7) Each year appears as ten 'volumes' (sections). Vol. 8 deals with Canon law.

DOWNSIDE REVIEW: a quarterly review of Catholic thought, 1880– . Downside Abbey, Bath.

JURIST, 1941– . Washington D.C., Catholic University of America School of Canon Law.

c. The Protestant Nonconformist Churches

CONGREGATIONAL YEARBOOK, 1846– . Published annually by the Congregational Church in England and Wales, 11 Cartaret Street, London S.W.1.

d. Historical

BURN, R.

Ecclesiastical law, 9th ed. with additions by R. Phillimore. Sweet, 1842. 4 vols.

CHURCH OF ENGLAND

The Constitutions and Canons Ecclesiastical (of 1603) *and the Thirty-nine Articles of the Church of England.* Society for Promoting Christian Knowledge. (1852?) 100p. (Issued with *Certain sermons or homilies, appointed to be read in churches in the time of Queen Elizabeth.* S.P.C.K., 1852. xiv + 626p.)

GIBSON, E.

Codex iuris ecclesiastici anglicani, 2nd ed. OUP, 1761. 2 vols.

JOHNSON, J.

A collection of the laws and canons of the Church of England, new ed. with notes . . . by J. Baron. Oxford, Parker, 1850–51. 2 vols. (Library of Anglo-Catholic theology)

KEMP, E. W.

An introduction to canon law in the Church of England, etc. Hodder & Stoughton, 1957. 87p. (Lichfield Cathedral divinity lectures, 1956)

LYNDWOOD (or LYNDEWODE), W.

Provinciale, seu Constitutiones Angliae . . . cui adjiciuntur Constitutiones legatinae D. Othonis et D. Othoboni, . . . cum . . . annotationibus Joannis de Athone (or *Acton*). Oxoniae, Hall, 1679. 2 parts. Reprinted 1968 by Gregg.

MAITLAND, F. W.

Roman canon law in the Church of England: six essays. Methuen, 1898. vii + 184p.

MORTIMER, R. C.

Western canon law. Black, 1953. 92p. (Bibliography, pp. 91–92)

STUBBS, W.

Seventeen lectures on the study of medieval and modern history, 3rd ed. OUP, 1900. xiv + 492p.

STUBBS, W.

"An account of the courts which have exercised ecclesiastical jurisdiction in England up to the year 1832", in GREAT BRITAIN. Royal Commission on the Constitution and Working of the Ecclesiastical Courts. *Report* (Eyre & Spottiswoode, 1883. Command papers C.3760 and C.3760-I), vol. 1, pp. 21–51.

JOURNAL OF ECCLESIASTICAL HISTORY, vol. 1– , 1950– . Faber.

XXI. THE COMMON MARKET

LAW OF THE EUROPEAN ECONOMIC COMMUNITY

The practical and theoretical importance of the law of the European Economic Community for English lawyers follows in the first instance from the accession of Great Britain to the Treaty of Rome. This step can benefit Britain only if a sufficient number of lawyers with training in the law of the Community is available, not only for the purpose of manning such posts in the civil service of the community as will have to be filled by British subjects, but also in order to advise government agencies and private parties in the U.K. on those points of community law which are now of immediate practical interest to them. Quite apart however, from the membership of the United Kingdom in the Common Market, the Community law is of considerable importance to English lawyers. The law of the Community on restrictive practices will be applied by courts in all the member countries of the community to all contracts between firms in the Common Market area and outside firms no matter what the proper law of the contract might be. European Community law furthermore affects directly the subsidiaries of British firms in the other eight countries and is thus of vast importance in connection with British investments in Europe. Last not least, no intelligent discussion of the consequences of Britain joining the Common Market is possible without a working knowledge of the legal structure of the European Community and the tendencies prevailing in its development.

English literature on Common Market law is naturally in a state of development. British writers had to battle with a variety of difficulties such as the fact that they lacked all possibility of joining in the *disputatio fori* before the Court of the European Community, that their immediate concern with practical problems was necessarily sporadic and confined to certain sets of problems only, that English was not one of the official languages of the Community, that the Common Market law uses civil law (not Common law) concepts and—last not least—that the library facilities on European Community law in this country are very restricted. This renders it often necessary to resort to European Continental literature, in particular if more specialised or more recent problems are under investigation. Continental literature on its part is vast and nearly always presupposes an acquaintance on the part of the reader with the civilian lawyer's approach to methods of interpretation and legal development.

Professor Mathijsen has written a textbook on the law of the European Communities and Dr. ROBERTSON'S *European Institutions* also contains a useful first introduction. This should be followed up by reading Mr. E. H. WALL'S two works listed below. Texts and leading cases are available in good translations, but even the best of these must be used with very great care: where a number of different official texts exist, all of which are legally of equal value, even the most expert translator cannot be expected to meet all the nuances of meaning expressed in the four versions.

Some of the gaps left by English literature can be filled by consulting American publications. There are also several translations into English of a few leading German books. These are listed hereunder.

Users of works on European Community law should not overlook that this law merely supplement the nine different legal systems of the member states. It should therefore be read and understood on the basis of this civil law background. European integration proceeds with particular emphasis in the fields of company, tax, labour and social insurance law, and the law on restrictive practices, unfair competition and commercial agencies. On all these aspects of the law of the original member countries short summaries are available in German and French. As these are particularly useful for first-hand information a few are included in the following Bibliography.

Another difficulty facing the student of European Community law is its comparatively rapid development. This renders it necessary to resort on principle to more recent publications and has been the principal cause for the growing number of loose-leaf publications. The German legal and economic monthly "Aussenwirtschaftsdienst des Betriebsberaters" (Heidelberg) although not devoted predominantly to Community law has often anticipated other periodicals by its speedy reporting of recent events in Community law.

Select Bibliography

a. Introductory

BOWETT, D. W.
The law of international institutions, 2nd ed. S, 1970. xviii + 384p. (Library of world affairs, no. 60)

CARTOU, L.
Organisations européennes, 2e éd. Paris, Dalloz, 1967. li + 476p.

CATALANO, N.
Manuel de droit des Communautés européennes, 2e éd. Paris, Dalloz, 1965. 664p.

MATHIJSEN, P. S. R. F.
A guide to European Community law. SM, 1972. xxiv + 204p.

ROBERTSON, A. H.
European institutions: co-operation: integration: unification, 2nd ed. S, 1966. xxi + 427p. (Library of world affairs, no. 44)

SEIDL-HOHENVELDERN, I.
Das Recht der internationalen Organisationen einschließlich der supranationalen Gemeinschaften, 2e Aufl. Cologne, Heymann, 1971. xxxviii + 361p.

STEIN, E. and HAY, P. H.
Law and institutions in the Atlantic area: readings, cases and problems, with a volume of documents. Indianapolis, Bobbs-Merrill, 1967. 2 vols. (Preliminary edition, 1963, entitled *Cases and materials on the law and institutions . . .*)

WALL, E. H.
Europe: unification and law. Penguin Books, 1969. 220p.

b. General works including commentaries on the Treaty of Rome

CAEMMERER, E. von, and others, eds
Probleme des europäischen Rechts. Festschrift für Walter Hallstein zu seinem 65 Geburtstag. Frankfurt am Main, Klostermann, 1966. xi + 580p.

CAMPBELL, A.
Common Market law, revised ed. Longmans, 1969. 2 vols. (Suppl.)

COMMERCE CLEARING HOUSE, INC.
Common Market reporter. New York, 1962– . 2 looseleaf vols, and bound vol. of court decisions with transfer binder. (Running title: *Common Market reports*. Includes text of EEC treaty, CCH explanations, regulations, recommendations etc., court decisions and latest developments. CCH also publish a weekly newsletter entitled *Euromarket news* and monographs on specific subjects under the above running title. Suppl.)

GANSHOF VAN DER MEERSCH, W. J.
Organisations européennes, vol. 1. Brussels, Bruylant, 1966. 580p. (Vol. 2 not yet published)

GIDE, P. and others
Dictionnaire du Marché commun. Paris, Dictionnaire André Joly, 1968. 2 vols. (Looseleaf)

KEETON, G. W. and SCHWARZENBERGER, G., eds
A symposium on English law and the Common Market. S, 1963. viii + 231p. (Current legal problems, vol. 16, 1963)

MÉGRET, J., and others
Le droit de la Communauté économique européenne. Brussels, Presses Universitaires, 1970. 3 vols.

c. Law on restrictive practices

DERINGER, A.
The competition law of the European Economic Community. Chicago, Commerce Clearing House, 1968. xvii + 418p.

GRAUPNER, R.
The rules of competition in the European Economic Community. The Hague, Nijhoff, 1965. xxxvi + 283p.

OBERDORFER, C. W., and others
Common Market cartel law, 2nd American ed. Chicago, Commerce Clearing House, 1971. xviii + 302p. (English edition by F. Honig and others published by Butterworths in 1963 under the title: *Cartel law of the European Economic Community*. The 2nd German edition by A. Gleiss and M. Hirsch was published by Recht und Wirtschaft, Heidelberg, in 1965 under the title: *EWG-Kartellrecht, Kommentar*. Other editions have also been published in French and Italian)

d. The Court of the European Economic Community: constitution and procedure

ANDRÉ, A.
Beweisführung und Beweislast im Verfahren vor dem Gerichtshof der Europäischen Gemeinschaften. Cologne, Heymann, 1966. xi + 252p. (Kölner Schriften zum Europarecht, Band 6)

BASSE, H.
Das Verhältnis zwischen der Gerichtsbarkeit des Gerichtshofes der Europäischen Gemeinschaften und der deutschen Zivilgerichtsbarkeit. Berlin, Duncker & Humblot, 1967. 464p. (Bibliography, pp. 437-64. Schriften zum Prozeßrecht, Band 10)

BEBR, G.
Judicial control of the European Communities. S, 1962. xxi + 268p. (Bibliography, pp. 244–62. Library of world affairs, no. 58)

BRINKHORST, L. J. and SCHERMERS, H. G.
Judicial remedies in the European Communities: a casebook. Deventer, Kluwer, 1969. xxii + 275p.

EHLE, D.
Klage- und Prozeßrecht des EWG-Vertrages. Berlin, Neue Wirtschafts-Briefe, 1966. (Looseleaf)

GREAT BRITAIN. Lord Chancellor's Department
Legal and constitutional implications of United Kingdom membership of the European Communities. HMSO, 1967. 15p. (Cmnd 3301)

GREEN, A. W.
Political integration by jurisprudence: the work of the Court of Justice of the European Communities in European political integration. Leyden, Sijthoff, 1969. xxviii + 847p.

VALENTINE, D. G.
The Court of Justice of the European Communities. Vol. 1: Jurisdiction and procedure. Vol. 2: Judgments and documents, 1954–60. S, 1965. 2 vols.

WALL, E. H.
The Court of Justice of the European Communities: jurisdiction and procedure. B, 1966. xxxi + 321p.

e. Investment and establishment in the countries of the E.E.C.

BALEKJIAN, W. H.
Legal aspects of foreign investment in the European Economic Community. Manchester UP, 1967. iv + 356p. (Bibliography, pp. 335–47)

EVERLING, U.
The right of establishment in the Common Market. Chicago, Commerce Clearing House, 1964. xv + 219p.

STEIN, E. and NICHOLSON, T. L., eds
American enterprise in the European Common Market: a legal profile. Ann Arbor, University of Michigan Law School, 1960. 2 vols.

f. Constitutional and administrative problems, and relationship to the law of the member states

BÖRNER, B.
Die Entscheidungen der Hohen Behörde. Eine Studie zum supranationalen Verwaltungsprozeß. Tübingen, Mohr, 1965. xv + 255p.

COLOMBO, E., and others
L'Association à la Communauté économique européenne, aspects juridiques. Brussels, Presses Universitaires, 1970. 384p. (Publication de la Bibliothèque de l'Institut d'Etudes Européennes de l'Université Libre de Bruxelles; thèses et travaux juridiques)

HAY, P. H.
Federalism and supranational organisations, patterns for new legal structures. Urbana, Illinois UP, 1966. 335p.

LANG, J. T.
The Common Market and common law: legal aspects of foreign investment and economic integration in the European Community. Chicago UP, for the American Bar Foundation, 1966. xxxvii + 573p. (Bibliography, pp. 521–55)

WAGNER, H.
Grundbegriffe des Beschlußrechts der Europäischen Gemeinschaften. Cologne, Heymann, 1965. xvi + 370p. (Kölner Schriften zum Europarecht, Band 5)

ZULEEG, M.
Das Recht der Europäischen Gemeinschaften im innerstaatlichen Bereich. Cologne, Heymann, 1969. xx + 448p. (Kölner Schriften zum Europarecht, Band 9)

g. Law reports and periodicals

AUSSENWIRTSCHAFTSDIENST DES BETRIEBSBERATERS: RECHT DER INTERNATIONALEN WIRTSCHAFT, 1954– . Heidelberg, Recht und Wirtschaft. (1954–57 entitled *Recht der internationalen Wirtschaft*)

COMMON MARKET LAW REPORTS, vol. 1– , 1962– . Edinburgh, Nelson. (Looseleaf suppl. of restrictive practices cases, 1966–)

COMMON MARKET LAW REVIEW, vol. 1– , 1963– . S. (Published in co-operation with the British Institute of International and Comparative Law and the Europa Instituut of the University of Leyden)

DÖLLE, H. and ZWEIGERT, K.
Rechtsprechungssammlung zum Europarecht. Tübingen, Mohr, 1966– . 2 vols. (Looseleaf)

EUROPARECHT, vol. 1– , 1966– . Munich, Beck.

JOURNAL OFFICIEL DES COMMUNAUTÉS EUROPÉENNES, vol. 1– , 1958– . Brussels, The European Communities. (Also published in German, Italian and Dutch)

RECUEIL DE LA JURISPRUDENCE DE LA COUR DE JUSTICE DES COMMUNAUTÉS EUROPÉENNES, 1954/55– . Luxembourg, The Court of Justice. (1954/55–58 entitled *Recueil de la Jurisprudence de la Cour de Justice de la Communauté Européenne du Charbon et de l'Acier.* (Also published in German, Italian and Dutch)

h. Comparative works on those parts of the law of the member states of particular importance to students of European Community law

DE HOGHTON, G., ed.
The company: law, structure and reform in eleven countries. Allen & Unwin for Political and Economic Planning, 1970. 394p.

INTERNATIONALE UNION DER HANDELSVERTRETER UND HANDELSMAKLER
Europäische Handelsvertretergesetze. Eine Gegenüberstellung d. gesetzl. Bestimmungen in 10 europ. Staaten, 2e neubearb. und erg. Aufl. Braunschweig, Limbach, 1966. 43p.

JURA EUROPAE: LE DROIT DES PAYS DE LA COMMUNAUTÉ ÉCONOMIQUE EUROPÉENNE
Droit des sociétés, tomes 1-2: Droit fiscal, tome 1: Droit du travail, tomes 1-2. Paris, Éditions Techniques Juris-Classeurs, 1964– . Looseleaf vols, still in progress. (Parallel texts in French and German)

KLAUE, S.
Die europäischen Gesetze gegen Wettbewerbsbeschränkungen. Berlin, Schmidt, 1969– . (Looseleaf)

ULMER, E.
Das Recht des unlauteren Wettbewerbs in den Mitgliedstaaten der Europäischen Wirtschaftsgemeinschaft. Munich, Beck, 1965–68. 5 vols. in 6.

WYNENDAELE, J. van, and WOUTERS, H.
Le droit des sociétés anonymes dans les pays de la Communauté économique européenne. Brussels, Bruylant, 1961. 383p.

INDEX OF AUTHORS AND EDITORS

Where there is no author, the name of the publication has been included

SUBJECT INDEX

BIBLIOGRAPHIES

Published at the instance of the International Association of Legal Science.

1. DAVID, R. *French bibliographical digest (law)*. New York, The Cultural Division of the French Embassy, 1952, 103p.
2. SOLÁ CAÑIZARES, F. de, and FERNANDEZ DE VILLAVICENCIO, D. *Bibliografía jurídica española*. Barcelona, Instituto de Derecho Comparado, 1954. 127p.
3. TUNC, A., and TUNC, S. "Bibliographie des principaux ouvrages doctrinaux", in *Le droit des Etats-Unis d'Amérique, sources et techniques*, (Paris, Dalloz, 1955), pp. 459–491.
4. CHLOROS, A. G., ed. *Bibliographical guide to the law of the United Kingdom, the Channel Islands and the Isle of Man*, 2nd ed. London, Institute of Advanced Legal Studies, 1973. 302p.
5. CZACHÓRSKI, W., ed. *Bibliographie juridique polonaise, 1944–1956*. Warszawa, Państwowe Wydawnictwo Naukowe, 1958. 137p.
6. ALEXANDROWICZ, C. H. *A bibliography of Indian Law*. London and Madras, OUP, 1958. ix, 69p.
7. NASSIF, A. *Bibliographie juridique libanaise*. Beirut, Annales de la faculté de droit et des sciences économiques, 1958. 57p.
8. BLAGOJEVIĆ, B. T. *Bibliographie juridique yougoslave*. Beograd, Institut de droit comparé, 1959. 262p.
9. KNAPP, V., ed. *Bibliography of Czechoslovak legal literature, 1945–1958*. Prague, Institute of Law of the Czechoslovak Academy of Sciences, Publishing House of the Czechoslovak Academy of Sciences, 1959. 263p.
10. USSR ACADEMY OF SCIENCE. Institute of State and Law. *Literature on Soviet law: index of bibliography*. Moscow, Publishing House of the USSR Academy of Science, 1960. 280p.
11. IUUL, S., MALMSTRÖM, Å. and SØNDERGAARD, J. *Scandinavian legal bibliography*. Stockholm-Göteborg-Uppsala, Almquist and Wiksell, 1961. 196p.
12. DAVID, R. *Bibliographie du droit français, 1945–1960*. The Hague-Paris, Mouton et Cie., 1964. 252p.
13. LIVNEH, E. *Israel legal bibliography in European languages*. Mif'al Hashichpul. The Hebrew University Students Press, Jerusalem, 1963. 86p. (Supplement 1965. Jerusalem, 1965. pp. 87–118).
14. BIBLIOGRAPHIE *des deutschen Rechts in englischer und deutscher Sprache; eine Auswahl;* herausgegeben von der Gesellschaft für Rechtsvergleichung mit einer Einführung in das deutsche Recht von F. Baur, übersetzt von C. H. Peterson; Stand 31. December 1963. Karlsruhe, Verlag C. F. Müller, 1964. lv, 584p. (Ergänzungsband 1964–1968; Stand 31. December 1968, 1969. liii, 221p)
15. ANDREWS, J. L., CHARPENTIER, A. A., MARKE, J. J. and STERN, W. B. *The law in the United States of America: a selective bibliographical guide*. New York, New York University Press, 1965, reprinted 1966. vii, 100p.
16. BOULT, R. *Bibliographie du droit canadien—a bibliography of Canadian law*. Montreal, Wilson et Lafleur, 1966. xii, 393p.
17. BIBLIOGRAPHY *of Hungarian legal literature 1945–1965*. Published by the Institute for Legal and Administrative Sciences of the Hungarian Academy of Sciences. Edited by L. Nagy. Budapest, Akademiai Kiado, 1966. 315p.
18. BIBLIOGRAPHIE *du droit luxembourgeois*. Association Internationale des Sciences Juridiques, Comité National Luxembourgeois. Luxembourg. Office des Imprimés de l'Etat, 1967. 240p.